Communications
in Computer and Information Science   **2266**

Series Editors

Gang Li⊕, *School of Information Technology, Deakin University, Burwood, VIC,*
Australia
Joaquim Filipe⊕, *Polytechnic Institute of Setúbal, Setúbal, Portugal*
Zhiwei Xu, *Chinese Academy of Sciences, Beijing, China*

Rationale

The CCIS series is devoted to the publication of proceedings of computer science conferences. Its aim is to efficiently disseminate original research results in informatics in printed and electronic form. While the focus is on publication of peer-reviewed full papers presenting mature work, inclusion of reviewed short papers reporting on work in progress is welcome, too. Besides globally relevant meetings with internationally representative program committees guaranteeing a strict peer-reviewing and paper selection process, conferences run by societies or of high regional or national relevance are also considered for publication.

Topics

The topical scope of CCIS spans the entire spectrum of informatics ranging from foundational topics in the theory of computing to information and communications science and technology and a broad variety of interdisciplinary application fields.

Information for Volume Editors and Authors

Publication in CCIS is free of charge. No royalties are paid, however, we offer registered conference participants temporary free access to the online version of the conference proceedings on SpringerLink (http://link.springer.com) by means of an http referrer from the conference website and/or a number of complimentary printed copies, as specified in the official acceptance email of the event.

CCIS proceedings can be published in time for distribution at conferences or as post-proceedings, and delivered in the form of printed books and/or electronically as USBs and/or e-content licenses for accessing proceedings at SpringerLink. Furthermore, CCIS proceedings are included in the CCIS electronic book series hosted in the SpringerLink digital library at http://link.springer.com/bookseries/7899. Conferences publishing in CCIS are allowed to use Online Conference Service (OCS) for managing the whole proceedings lifecycle (from submission and reviewing to preparing for publication) free of charge.

Publication process

The language of publication is exclusively English. Authors publishing in CCIS have to sign the Springer CCIS copyright transfer form, however, they are free to use their material published in CCIS for substantially changed, more elaborate subsequent publications elsewhere. For the preparation of the camera-ready papers/files, authors have to strictly adhere to the Springer CCIS Authors' Instructions and are strongly encouraged to use the CCIS LaTeX style files or templates.

Abstracting/Indexing

CCIS is abstracted/indexed in DBLP, Google Scholar, EI-Compendex, Mathematical Reviews, SCImago, Scopus. CCIS volumes are also submitted for the inclusion in ISI Proceedings.

How to start

To start the evaluation of your proposal for inclusion in the CCIS series, please send an e-mail to ccis@springer.com.

Wenjuan Li · Liqun Chen · Javier Lopez
Editors

Emerging Information Security and Applications

5th International Conference, EISA 2024
Changzhou, China, October 18–19, 2024
Proceedings

Springer

Editors
Wenjuan Li ⓘ
The Education University of Hong Kong
New Territories, Hong Kong

Liqun Chen ⓘ
University of Surrey
Guildford, Surrey, UK

Javier Lopez ⓘ
University of Malaga
Málaga, Spain

ISSN 1865-0929 ISSN 1865-0937 (electronic)
Communications in Computer and Information Science
ISBN 978-3-031-80418-2 ISBN 978-3-031-80419-9 (eBook)
https://doi.org/10.1007/978-3-031-80419-9

This Springer imprint is published by the registered company Springer Nature Switzerland AG
The registered company address is: Gewerbestrasse 11, 6330 Cham, Switzerland

If disposing of this product, please recycle the paper.

Preface

This volume contains the papers that were selected for presentation and publication at The Fifth International Conference on Emerging Information Security and Applications (EISA 2024), which was hosted by Jiangsu University of Technology, Changzhou, China on 18–19 October 2024.

With the recent evolution of adversarial techniques, intrusions that may threaten the security of various assets, including information and applications, have become more complex. In addition, coordinated intrusions like worm outbreaks will continue to be a major threat to information, system and network security in the near future. The popularity of the Internet generates a large volume of different types of sensitive information. Therefore, there is a need for emerging techniques, theories and applications to protect information and practical security. EISA aims to provide a platform for both researchers and practitioners across the world, from either academia or industry, to exchange their ideas. It seeks original submissions that discuss practical or theoretical solutions to enhance information and application security in practice.

This year's Program Committee (PC) consisted of 38 members with diverse backgrounds and broad research interests. A total of 52 papers were submitted to the conference under a single-blinded reviewing mode. Papers were selected based on their originality, significance, relevance and clarity of presentation as assessed by the reviewers. Most papers were reviewed by three or more PC members. Finally, 15 full papers were selected for presentation at the conference, resulting in an acceptance rate of 28.8%, with 3 short papers accepted to the final program.

For the success of EISA 2024, we would like to first thank the authors of all submissions and all the PC members for their great efforts in selecting the papers. We also thank all the external reviewers for assisting the reviewing process. For the conference organization, we would like to thank the general chairs, Zhengjun Jing, Weizhi Meng and Sokratis Katsikas; the publicity chairs, Quanyu Zhao, Youqian Zhang and Na Ruan; and the publication chair, Peizhong Shi. Finally, we thank everyone else, speakers and session chairs, for their contribution to the program of EISA 2024.

October 2024

Wenjuan Li
Liqun Chen
Javier Lopez

Organization

General Chairs

Zhengjun Jing   Jiangsu University of Technology, China
Weizhi Meng   Technical University of Denmark, Denmark
Sokratis Katsikas   Norwegian University of Science and Technology, Norway

Program Chairs

Wenjuan Li   Education University of Hong Kong, Hong Kong SAR, China
Liqun Chen   University of Surrey, UK
Javier Lopez   University of Málaga, Spain

Steering Committee

Jiageng Chen   Central China Normal University, China
Liqun Chen   University of Surrey, UK
Steven Furnell   University of Plymouth, UK
Sokratis K. Katsikas   Norwegian University of Science and Technology, Norway
Javier Lopez   University of Málaga, Spain
Weizhi Meng (Chair)   Technical University of Denmark, Denmark

Publicity Chairs

Quanyu Zhao   Jiangsu University of Technology, China
Youqian Zhang   Hong Kong Polytechnic University, China
Na Ruan   Shanghai Jiao Tong University, China

Publication Chair

Peizhong Shi   Jiangsu University of Technology, China

Web Chair

Wei-Yang Chiu   Technical University of Denmark, Denmark

External Reviewers

Xilu Wang

Program Committee

Wun-She Yap   Universiti Tunku Abdul Rahman, Malaysia
Shoichi Hirose   University of Fukui, Japan
Yicheng Zhang   University of California, Riverside, USA
Chingfang Hsu   Central China Normal University, China
Wenjuan Li   Hong Kong Polytechnic University, Hong Kong
                                 SAR, China
Mingjun Wang   Xidian University, China
Albert Levi   Sabancı University, Turkey
Weizhi Meng   Technical University of Denmark, Denmark
Jun Shao   Zhejiang Gongshang University, China
Xiong Li   Hunan University of Science and Technology,
                                 China
Beibei Li   Sichuan University, China
Muhammad Rizwan   University of Surrey, UK
Giovanni Livraga   University of Milan, Italy
Je Sen Teh   Universiti Sains Malaysia, Malaysia
Xingye Lu   Hong Kong Polytechnic University, Hong Kong
                                 SAR, China
Zhe Xia   Wuhan University of Technology, China
Haiyang Xue   Singapore Management University, Singapore
Xue Yang   Tsinghua University, China
Gao Liu   Chongqing University, China
Qianhong Wu   Beihang University, China
Xin Jin   Ohio State University, USA
Reza Malekian   Malmö University, Sweden
Steven Furnell   University of Nottingham, UK
Lei Wu   Shandong Normal University, China
Ahmed Sherif   University of Southern Mississippi, USA
Chunhua Su   University of Aizu, Japan
Debiao He   Wuhan University, China

Mahmoud Nabil Mahmoud   North Carolina A&T University, USA
Long Meng   University of Surrey, UK
Stefanos Gritzalis   University of Piraeus, Greece
Jiangang Shu   Peng Cheng Laboratory, China
Sokratis Katsikas   Norwegian University of Science and Technology,
                            Norway
Cheng Huang   University of Waterloo, Canada
Joonsang Baek   University of Wollongong, Australia
Alessandro Brighente   University of Padua, Italy
Quanyu Zhao   Jiangsu University of Technology, China
Marcela Tuler de Oliveira University of Amsterdam, The Netherlands
Yuanjian Zhou   Jiangsu University of Technology, China

Contents

High-Efficiency Phase-Index Correlation Delay Shift Keying Modulation 1
Junyi Duan, Hua Yang, Chenkai Tan, and Tianci Zhao

Federated Learning Poison Attack Detection Scheme Based on Gradient
Similarity 20
Quanyu Zhao, Yuan Zhang, Zhengjun Jing, Yuanjian Zhou, and Zexi Xin

A Privacy-Preserving and Fault-Tolerant Data Aggregation Scheme
in Smart Grids 37
*Yongkang Zhu, Yuanjian Zhou, Zhengjun Jing, Quanyu Zhao,
and Tianci Zhao*

Local Differential Privacy for Key-Value Data Collection and Analysis
Based on Privacy Preference and Adaptive Sampling 54
*Zhengyong Zhai, Peizhong Shi, Yan Zhang, Chunsheng Gu,
Zhengjun Jing, and Quanyu Zhao*

Comparative Study of Artificial Intelligent Approaches for Phishing
Website Detection 72
Bingbing Li, Ogbebisi Chukwuebuka Amandi, and Mingwu Zhang

Exploring Interpretability in Backdoor Attacks on Image Classification 86
Jiaxun Li, Hao Chen, Gaoyuan Zhou, Mingxin Xu, and Hanwei Qian

Attribute-Based Secret Key Signature Scheme 99
Chengtang Cao, Zongzheng Huang, and Shupei Mo

Digital Token Transaction Tracing Method 107
Ling-Ling Xia, Qun Wang, Zhuo Ma, and Bo Song

GPT-Based Wasm Instruction Analysis for Program Language Processing 118
Liangjun Deng, Qi Zhong, Hang Lei, Yao Qiu, and Jingxue Chen

Research on Key Technologies of Fair Deep Learning 137
Xiaoqian Liu and Weiyu Shi

Adaptive Differential Privacy Based Optimization Scheme for Federated
Learning 153
Qi Yuan, Ershuai Xu, Hao Yuan, and Shuo Zhao

Cascading Failures Model with Noise Interference in Supply Chain
Networks 165
    Bo Song, Yi Qin, Yu-Rong Song, and Xu Wang

DefMPA: Defending Model Poisoning Attacks in Federated Learning
via Model Update Prediction 178
    Mengya Guo, Bing Chen, Baolu Xue, and Jiewen Liu

SDDRM: An Optimization Algorithm for Localized Differential Privacy
Based on Data Sensitivity Differences 192
    Li Bingbing, Shi Peizhong, Gu Chunsheng, Zhang Yan, Jing Zhengjun,
    and Zhao Quanyu

Blockchain-Based Key Management Scheme in Internet of Things 208
    Zihan Wang, Jiqun Zhang, Jingcheng Song, Yongwei Tang,
    and Hongyuan Cheng

Privacy Optimization of Deep Recommendation Algorithm in Federated
Framework 219
    Xiaopeng Zhao, Xiao Bai, Guohao Sun, and Zhe Yan

Delegated Proof of Stake Consensus Mechanism Based on the Overall
Perspective of Voting 230
    Chengtang Cao, Shupei Mo, and Zongzheng Huang

A Distributed Privacy-Preserving Data Aggregation Scheme for MaaS
Data Sharing 240
    Lin Zhu, Zhengjun Jing, Yuanjian Zhou, and Quanyu Zhao

Author Index 255

High-Efficiency Phase-Index Correlation Delay Shift Keying Modulation

Junyi Duan[1], Hua Yang[2], Chenkai Tan[3(✉)], and Tianci Zhao[4]

[1] Key Laboratory of Dynamic Cognitive System of Electromagnetic Spectrum Space (Nanjing Univ. Aeronaut. Astronaut.), Ministry of Industry and Information Technology, Jiangsu, Nanjing, China
[2] Nanjing University of Posts and Telecommunications, Jiangsu, Nanjing, China
[3] School of Computing, Macquarie University, Sydney, Australia
chenkai.tan@gmail.com
[4] Jiangsu University of Technology, Jiangsu, Changzhou, China

Abstract. In Improved High-data-rate Phase-Orthogonality Correlation-Delay-Shift-Keying (I-HPO-CDSK) modulation scheme, 3-bits information can be transmitted in parallel in the same spectral band and will not cause an intra-signal interference component. However, the transmitting power of I-HPO-CDSK is treble that of conventional chaotic modulation schemes, such as Differential-Chaos-Shift-Key (DCSK) and CDSK. By virtue of index modulation technology in Phase-Index Correlation-Delay-Shift-Keying (PI-CDSK) modulation scheme, PI-CDSK can synchronously transmit one data bit and one index bit in the same spectral band. Although the spectral efficiency of PI-CDSK is lower than that of I-HPO-CDSK, its energy efficiency is equal to DCSK and CDSK. Based on I-HPO-CDSK and PI-CDSK, we propose High-Efficiency PI-CDSK (HE-PI-CDSK) in this paper. In our scheme, 3-bits (including two index bits and one information bit) are beared in one carrier. Results show that, due to no interference and 3-bits transmitting in parallel, HPI-CDSK can acquire higher spectral efficiency and the same bit error rate performance as that of PI-CDSK. Moreover, our transmitting power is just one third of the I-HPO-CDSK.

1 Introduction

Because of the advantage of wideband and random-likeproperty, chaotic signal happens to satisfy the research for spread-spectrum digital communications [1,2]. Although the coherent chaotic communication system which needs carrier restoration in the demodulation has simpler hardware system, the synchronization mechanism performs poorly may result the high bit-error rate (BER). Therefore, in recent 20 years, due to no need carrier restoration in the demodulation, noncoherent chaotic communication has gradually attracted lots of scholars.

In 1996, Differential-Chaos-Shift-Keying (DCSK) is proposed as a classic noncoherent chaotic modulation scheme by Kolumbán [3]. With the advantage of no Intrasignal interference (ISI), DCSK and its improved schemes were designed to

W. Li et al. (Eds.): EISA 2024, CCIS 2266, pp. 1–19, 2025.
https://doi.org/10.1007/978-3-031-80419-9_1

satisfy the demands of various scenarios. In DCSK, one frame includes two equal time slots, the chaotic reference signal is transmitted during the first timeslot, and the reference repeated signal which carries one information bit is transmitted during the second timeslot [3]. Because only one time slot is used to transmit information bit in DCSK, this scheme squander a half spectral efficiency.Because the energy which is used to transmit each bit can be kept as constant in Frequency-modulated DCSK (FM-DCSK), its BER is lower than that of DCSK. However, by reason of half frame is used to transmit information bit in FM-DCSK, its spectral efficiency is same as that of DCSK. To overcome the shortage in spectral efficiency, as the DCSK enhanced schemes, High-Efficiency DCSK (HE-DCSK) and Reference-Modulated DCSK (RM-DCSK) can parallel transmit 2-bits information and improve the spectral efficiency. However, owing to no strict orthogonality between the two parallel transmitting paths, the ISI component will be introduced into the demodulation when the information-bearing signal correlates to reference signal in HE-DCSK and RM-DCSK. In Multi-Carrier DCSK (MC-DCSK), different spectral subcarrier is used to transmit reference signal and information signal respectively, and do has no ISI component during demodulation. However, because the predefined subcarrier is just used to transmit reference signal, the spectral efficiency of MC-DCSK is lower than that of DCSK [4,5]. LDPC code is also introduced to improve chaotic communication reliability [6,7], but LDPC coding module may increase both the transmitter and receiver complexity.

As an another classic noncoherent chaotic communication scheme, Correlation-Delay-Shift-Keying (CDSK) is proposed by Sushchik in 2000 [6]. CDSK transmits reference signal and the information signal synchronously, compared with DCSK, its spectral efficiency is double. However, the ISI component will be produced by the correlation between reference signal and the information signal during the demodulation, and so the BER of CDSK is significantly lower than that of DCSK. To further elevate the BER performance of CDSK, there are two paths in CDSK enhanced schemes [7–13], namely adding the information component and reducing the interference component.

By virtue of adding the information component during the demodulation, Generalized CDSK (GCDSK) can significantly improve the BER performance. However, because the increment results from the additional time delay modules, its hardware complexity is also increased.

For the purpose of reducing the interference component, a series of improved schemes are proposed in [8–13]. In Reference-adaptive CDSK (RA-CDSK) [8], the *ISI* and noise interference is less than that of CDSK, and its spectral efficiency is twice as much as CDSK. Through the Walsh encoding mechanism, ISI components can be eliminated in CDSK (CDSK-NII) [9] and its multiple access versions [10] without signal interference. However, hardware has also increased. Phase-Orthogonality CDSK (PO-CDSK) [11] and its enhanced versions [12,13] not only eliminating ISI but also transmitting more information synchronously. Yet more bits need more transmitting energy.

The introduction of index modulation in chaotic communication can improve Spectral efficiency, such as carrier index DCSK (CI-DCSK) [14] and high data rate CI-DCSK (HDR-CI-DCSK) [14]. In these schemes, subcarrier index bit can be used to transmit additional data bits and thus saved the transmitting energy. However, multi-subcarriers resource will cause the spectral efficiency lower in CI-DCSK and HDR CI-DCSK. Phase-index CDSK (PI-CDSK) [15] can transmit additional information data by 1-bit phase index. Compared with CI-DCSK and HDR CI-DCSK in the same preconditions, PI-CDSK can acquire higher spectral efficiency.

Aim to further elevate the spectral efficiency and energy efficiency, High-Efficiency PI-CDSK (HE PI-CDSK) is proposed in this paper. By virtue of IM technology and Walsh code, 2-bits phase index and 1-bit information can be transmitted in HE PI-CDSK. Moreover, the ISI component also can be eliminated in de demodulation of HE PI-CDSK.

2 System Model

The multiframe construction of HE PI-CDSK is shown in Fig. 1. Here, each multiframe is divided into $(\beta+1)$ frames; each frame is divided into β timeslots, β is spreading factor.

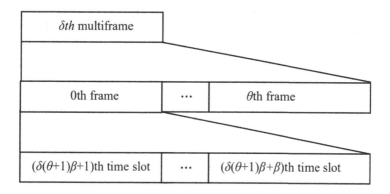

Fig. 1. The construction of multiframe

Figure 2 is the construction of HE PI-CDSK transmitter. During the kth time slot $(1 \leq k \leq \beta)$, the output of the repeated chaotic generator (RCG) module is given by

$$x(t) = x_k h_T(t), kT_C \leq t < (k+1)T_C, \qquad (1)$$

where x_k is the chaotic sample, T_C is the time slot length, $h_T(t)$ is the square-root-raised-cosine filter which has the unit energy

$$\int_{kT_C}^{(k+1)T_C} h_T^2(t - kT_C)dt = 1 \qquad (2)$$

In Fig. 2, l indicates the frame, two transmitting conditions are considered:

1) When $l = 0$, the switch T1 is connected to the bottom branch, and the switch T2 is connected to the first branch. The current chaotic signal $x(t)$ is delivered to the delay module and the transmitter antenna.
2) When $1 \leq l \leq \theta$, during the δth multiframe, the switch T1 is connected to the upward branch. When index bit $d_{index} = 00$, the switch T2 is connected to the second branch, the transmitting signal is the product of the output of time delay module and $d_{\delta,l}$ where $d_{\delta,l}$ is the current information bit. When index bit $d_{index} = 11$, the switch T2 is connected to the third branch, the transmitting signal is the product of the output of time delay module, $d_{\delta,l}$ and the Walsh code $\omega(t)$. When index bit $d_{index} = 01$, the switch T2 is connected to the fourth branch, the transmitting signal is the product of the output of time delay module, $d_{\delta,l}$ and cosine wave. When index bit $d_{index} = 10$, the switch T2 is connected to the fifth branch, the transmitting signal is the product of the output of time delay module, $d_{\delta,l}$ and sine wave.

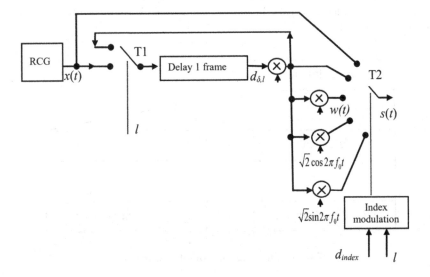

Fig. 2. The construction of HE PI-CDSK transmitter

Figure 3 is the construction of RCG module. During the first half of frame, the switch is connected to the top branch, and RCG directly outputs the chaotic signal which is generated by the chaotic generator. During the second half of frame, the switch T3 is connected to the bottom branch, and the output of RCG is identical to the sequence which is generated by the chaotic generator in the first half of frame.

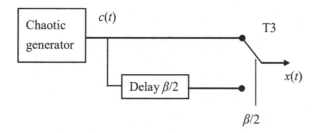

Fig. 3. RCG structure construction

During the lth frame, the transmitted signal is

$$
s(t) = \begin{cases}
x(t) & l = 0 \\
d_{\delta,l}(\prod_{i=0}^{l-1} d_{\delta,i})x(t - \beta l T_C) & 1 \le l \le \theta d_{index} = 00 \\
d_{\delta,l}(\prod_{i=0}^{l-1} d_{\delta,i})x(t - \beta l T_C)\omega(t) & 1 \le l \le \theta d_{index} = 11 \\
\sqrt{2}d_{\delta,l}(\prod_{i=0}^{l-1} d_{\delta,i})x(t - \beta l T_C)\cos(2\pi f_0 t) & 1 \le l \le \theta d_{index} = 01 \\
\sqrt{2}d_{\delta,l}(\prod_{i=0}^{l-1} d_{\delta,i})x(t - \beta l T_C)\sin(2\pi f_0 t) & 1 \le l \le \theta d_{index} = 10
\end{cases} , \quad (3)
$$

where f_0 is the carrier frequency which is set as the integer multiple of $1/T_C$. In Eq. (3)

$$
x(t) = \begin{cases}
c(t) & 1 \le k \le \beta/2 \\
c(t - \beta/2) & (\beta/2 + 1) < k \le \beta
\end{cases} , \quad (4)
$$

$$
\omega(t) = \begin{cases}
1 & 1 \le k \le \beta/2 \\
-1 & (\beta/2 + 1) < k \le \beta
\end{cases} . \quad (5)
$$

Figure 4 is the construction of HE PI-CDSK receiver. By comparing four paths energy, the receiver not only demodulates one information bit, but also detects two index bits.

Here, we assume the additive white Gaussian noise (AWGN) channel and the received signal is

$$
r(t) = s(t) + \xi(t), \quad (6)
$$

where $\xi(t)$ is additive white Gaussian noise, which mean is zero and power spectral density is $N_0/2$.

In the lth frame of the δth multiframe, the outputs of integral function are

$$
\alpha_{1,\delta,l,k} = \int_{(\delta(\theta+1)+l)\beta T_C+kT_C}^{(\delta(\theta+1)+l)\beta T_C+(k+1)T_C} [s(t) + \xi(t)]\, dt, \quad (7)
$$

$$
\alpha_{2,\delta,l,k} = \int_{(\delta(\theta+1)+l)\beta T_C+kT_C}^{(\delta(\theta+1)+l)\beta T_C+(k+1)T_C} [\omega(t)s(t) + \xi(t)]\, dt, \quad (8)
$$

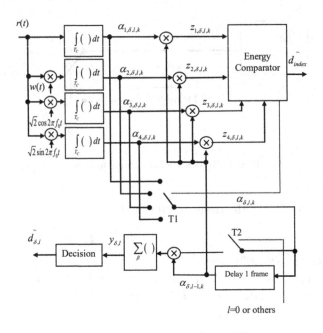

Fig. 4. The construction of HE PI-CDSK receiver

$$\alpha_{3,\delta,l,k} = \int\limits_{(\delta(\theta+1)+l)\beta T_C+kT_C}^{(\delta(\theta+1)+l)\beta T_C+(k+1)T_C} \left[\sqrt{2}\cos(2\pi f_0 t)s(t) + \xi(t)\right]dt, \qquad (9)$$

$$\alpha_{4,\delta,l,k} = \int\limits_{(\delta(\theta+1)+l)\beta T_C+kT_C}^{(\delta(\theta+1)+l)\beta T_C+(k+1)T_C} \left[\sqrt{2}\sin(2\pi f_0 t)s(t) + \xi(t)\right]dt. \qquad (10)$$

The transmitting energy of different path is compared by the Energy Comparator module. Then, $T1$ selects the maximum energy branch. For example, if the energy of cosine path is max, $T1$ connects to the third branch.

$$z_{x,\delta,l,k} = \alpha_{x,\delta,l,k}\alpha_{\delta,l-1,k}, \qquad (11)$$

where x indicates order number of path and $\alpha_{\delta,l-1,k}$ is the signal which is from the max energy path in the $(l-1)$th frame.

Then, based on energy comparison, the information signal will be correlated with the delay signal. The correlator output is

$$y_{\delta,l} = \sum_{k=1}^{\beta} \alpha_{\delta,l,k}\alpha_{\delta,l-1,k}. \qquad (12)$$

According to the result in Eq. (12), the estimated information bit is

$$\tilde{d}_{\delta,l} = \begin{cases} +1 & y_{\delta,l} \geq 0 \\ -1 & y_{\delta,L} < 0 \end{cases}. \tag{13}$$

3   Performance Analysis

3.1   AWGN Channel

BER for Index Bit. Because f_0 is a multiple of $1/T_C$ and $f_0 \gg (1/T_C)$, during the kth timeslot in lth frame of the δth multiframe,

$$\int_{(\delta(\theta+1)+l)\beta T_C+kT_C}^{(\delta(\theta+1)+l)\beta T_C+(k+1)T_C} \sin(2\pi f_0 t)\mathrm{d}t = 0, \tag{14}$$

$$\int_{(\delta(\theta+1)+l)\beta T_C+kT_C}^{(\delta(\theta+1)+l)\beta T_C+(k+1)T_C} \cos(2\pi f_0 t)\mathrm{d}t = 0, \tag{15}$$

$$\int_{(\delta(\theta+1)+l)\beta T_C+kT_C}^{(\delta(\theta+1)+l)\beta T_C+(k+1)T_C} \sin(2\pi f_0 t)\omega(t)\mathrm{d}t = 0, \tag{16}$$

$$\int_{(\delta(\theta+1)+l)\beta T_C+kT_C}^{(\delta(\theta+1)+l)\beta T_C+(k+1)T_C} \cos(2\pi f_0 t)\omega(t)\mathrm{d}t = 0, \tag{17}$$

$$\int_{(\delta(\theta+1)+l)\beta T_C+kT_C}^{(\delta(\theta+1)+l)\beta T_C+(k+1)T_C} \sin(2\pi f_0 t)\cos(2\pi f_0 t)\mathrm{d}t = 0. \tag{18}$$

To illustrate the work mechanism of HE PI-CDSK, we take $d_{index} = 00$ for example.

According to Eqs. (7,8,9,10), the outputs of four paths integral function can be expressed in Eqs. (18,19,20,21),

$$\begin{aligned} \alpha_{1,\delta,l,k} &= \int_{(\delta(\theta+1)+l)\beta T_C+kT_C}^{(\delta(\theta+1)+l)\beta T_C+(k+1)T_C} [s(t) + \xi(t)]\,\mathrm{d}t \\ &= \int_{(\delta(\theta+1)+l)\beta T_C+kT_C}^{(\delta(\theta+1)+l)\beta T_C+(k+1)T_C} d_{\delta,l}\left(\prod_{i=1}^{l-1} d_{\delta,i}\right)x(t - \beta l T_C)\mathrm{d}t \\ &\quad + \int_{(\delta(\theta+1)+l)\beta T_C+kT_C}^{(\delta(\theta+1)+l)\beta T_C+(k+1)T_C} \xi(t)\mathrm{d}t \\ &= d_{\delta,l}\left(\prod_{i=1}^{l-1} d_{\delta,i}\right)x_{\delta,0,k} + \xi_{\delta,l,k} \end{aligned} \tag{19}$$

$$\alpha_{2,\delta,l,k} = \int_{(\delta(\theta+1)+l)\beta T_C+kT_C}^{(\delta(\theta+1)+l)\beta T_C+(k+1)T_C} [s(t) + \xi(t)] \, dt$$

$$= \int_{(\delta(\theta+1)+l)\beta T_C+kT_C}^{(\delta(\theta+1)+l)\beta T_C+(k+1)T_C} d_{\delta,l}(\prod_{i=1}^{l-1} d_{\delta,i}) x(t - \beta l T_C) \omega(t) dt,$$

$$+ \int_{(\delta(\theta+1)+l)\beta T_C+kT_C}^{(\delta(\theta+1)+l)\beta T_C+(k+1)T_C} \xi(t) dt$$

$$= \xi_{\delta,l,k}$$

(20)

$$\alpha_{3,\delta,l,k} = \int_{(\delta(\theta+1)+l)\beta T_C+kT_C}^{(\delta(\theta+1)+l)\beta T_C+(k+1)T_C} [s(t) + \xi(t)] \, dt$$

$$= \int_{(\delta(\theta+1)+l)\beta T_C+kT_C}^{(\delta(\theta+1)+l)\beta T_C+(k+1)T_C} d_{\delta,l}(\prod_{i=1}^{l-1} d_{\delta,i}) x(t - \beta l T_C) \sqrt{2} \cos 2\pi f_0 t dt,$$

$$+ \int_{(\delta(\theta+1)+l)\beta T_C+kT_C}^{(\delta(\theta+1)+l)\beta T_C+(k+1)T_C} \xi(t) dt$$

$$= \xi_{\delta,l,k}$$

(21)

$$\alpha_{4,\delta,l,k} = \int_{(\delta(\theta+1)+l)\beta T_C+kT_C}^{(\delta(\theta+1)+l)\beta T_C+(k+1)T_C} [s(t) + \xi(t)] \, dt$$

$$= \int_{(\delta(\theta+1)+l)\beta T_C+kT_C}^{(\delta(\theta+1)+l)\beta T_C+(k+1)T_C} d_{\delta,l}(\prod_{i=1}^{l-1} d_{\delta,i}) x(t - \beta l T_C) \sqrt{2} \sin 2\pi f_0 t dt.$$

$$+ \int_{(\delta(\theta+1)+l)\beta T_C+kT_C}^{(\delta(\theta+1)+l)\beta T_C+(k+1)T_C} \xi(t) dt$$

$$= \xi_{\delta,l,k}$$

(22)

For the energy comparator, when $d_{index} = 00$, the four paths energy in one frame can be considered in Eqs. (23) and Eq. (24),

$$z_{1,\delta,l} = \sum_{k=1}^{\beta} \left[d_{\delta,l}(\prod_{i=0}^{l-1} d_{\delta,i}) x_{\delta,0,k} + \xi_{\delta,l,k} \right] \left[(\prod_{i=0}^{l-1} d_{\delta,i}) x_{\delta,0,k} + \xi_{\delta,l-1,k} \right]$$

$$= \sum_{k=1}^{\beta} d_{\delta,l}(\prod_{i=0}^{l-1} d_{\delta,i})^2 x_{\delta,0,k}^2 + \sum_{k=1}^{\beta} \left[d_{\delta,l}(\prod_{i=0}^{l-1} d_{\delta,i}) \right] \xi_{\delta,l-1,k}$$

(23)

$$+ \sum_{k=1}^{\beta} \left[(\prod_{i=0}^{l-1} d_{\delta,i}) \right] \xi_{\delta,l,k} + \sum_{k=1}^{\beta} \xi_{\delta,l,k} \xi_{\delta,l-1,k}$$

$$z_{2,\delta,l} = z_{3,\delta,l} = z_{4,\delta,l} = \sum_{k=1}^{\beta} [\xi_{\delta,l,k}] \left[\left(\prod_{i=0}^{l-1} d_{\delta,i} \right) x_{\delta,0,k} + \xi_{\delta,l-1,k} \right]$$

$$= \sum_{k=1}^{\beta} \left[\left(\prod_{i=0}^{l-1} d_{\delta,i} \right) x_{\delta,0,k} \xi_{\delta,l,k} + \xi_{\delta,l,k} \xi_{\delta,l-1,k} \right] \qquad (24)$$

As assumed that $\xi_{\delta,l,k}$ is the AWGN which has zero mean and power spectral density of $N_0/2$. Based on the chebyshev map, the means of four paths can be expressed in Eqs. (25,26),

$$E[z_{1,\delta,l}] = E \left[\sum_{k=1}^{\beta} d_{\delta,l} \left(\prod_{i=0}^{l-1} d_{\delta,i} \right)^2 x_{\delta,0,k}^2 + \sum_{k=1}^{\beta} \left(d_{\delta,l} \prod_{i=0}^{l-1} d_{\delta,i} \right) \xi_{\delta,l-1,k} \right]$$

$$+ E \left[\sum_{k=1}^{\beta} \left(\prod_{i=0}^{l-1} d_{\delta,i} \right) \xi_{\delta,l,k} + \sum_{k=1}^{\beta} \xi_{\delta,l,k} \xi_{\delta,l-1,k} \right] \qquad , \quad (25)$$

$$= E \left[\sum_{k=1}^{\beta} d_{\delta,l} \left(\prod_{i=0}^{l-1} d_{\delta,i} \right)^2 x_{\delta,0,k}^2 \right]$$

$$= d_{\delta,l} \beta E \left[x_{\delta,0,k}^2 \right]$$

$$E[Z_{2,\delta,l}] = E[Z_{3,\delta,l}]$$
$$= E[Z_{4,\delta,l}]$$
$$= E \left[\sum_{k=1}^{\beta} \left(\prod_{i=0}^{l-1} d_{\delta,i} \right) x_{\delta,0,k} \xi_{\delta,l,k} + \sum_{k=1}^{\beta} \xi_{\delta,l,k} \xi_{\delta,l-1,k} \right]. \qquad (26)$$
$$= 0$$

The variances of four paths can be seen in Eq. (27) and Eq. (28)

$$\text{Var}[z_{1,\delta,l}] = \text{Var} \left[\sum_{k=1}^{\beta} d_{\delta,l} \left(\prod_{i=0}^{l-1} d_{\delta,i} \right)^2 x_{\delta,0,k}^2 + \sum_{k=1}^{\beta} d_{\delta,l} \left(\prod_{i=0}^{l-1} d_{\delta,i} \right) x_{\delta,0,k} \xi_{\delta,l-1,k} \right]$$

$$+ \text{Var} \left[\sum_{k=1}^{\beta} \left(\prod_{i=0}^{l-1} d_{\delta,i} \right) x_{\delta,0,k} \xi_{\delta,l,k} + \sum_{k=1}^{\beta} \xi_{\delta,l,k} \xi_{\delta,l-1,k} \right] \qquad ,$$

$$= \beta \text{Var}[x_{\delta,0,k}] N_0 + \frac{\beta N_0^2}{4}$$

$$(27)$$

$$\begin{aligned}
\mathrm{Var}\,[z_{2,\delta,l}] &= \mathrm{Var}\,[z_{3,\delta,l}] \\
&= \mathrm{Var}\,[z_{4,\delta,l}] \\
&= \mathrm{Var}\left[\sum_{k=1}^{\beta}\left[\left(\prod_{i=0}^{l-1}d_{\delta,i}\right)\right]x_{\delta,0,k}\xi_{\delta,l,k} + \sum_{k=1}^{\beta}\xi_{\delta,l,k}\xi_{\delta,l-1,k}\right]. \\
&= \frac{\mathrm{Var}\,[x_{\delta,0,k}]\,N_0\beta}{2} + \frac{N_0^2\beta}{4}
\end{aligned} \tag{28}$$

The BER of index bit can be derived as

$$\begin{aligned}
BER_{index} &= Prob\left(|z_1| < |z_{others}|\right) \\
&= 1 - \int_0^{+\infty} F_{|others|}(r)\,f_{|z_1|}(r)\,dr
\end{aligned} \tag{29}$$

In Eq. (30),

$$F_{|z_{others}|}(r) = erf\left(\frac{r}{\sqrt{2\left(\mathrm{Var}\,[z_{others,\delta,l}]\right)}}\right), \tag{30}$$

$$f_{|z_1|}(r) = \frac{1}{\sqrt{2\pi\left(\mathrm{Var}\,[z_{1,\delta,l}]\right)}}\left(\exp\left(-\frac{(r - |E\,[z_{1,\delta,l}]\,|)^2}{2\left(\mathrm{Var}\,[z_{1,\delta,l}]\right)}\right) + \exp\left(-\frac{(r + |E\,[z_{1,\delta,l}]\,|)^2}{2\left(\mathrm{Var}\,[z_{1,\delta,l}]\right)}\right)\right), \tag{31}$$

where $erf(.)$ denotes the error function. Based on Eqs. (25,26,27,28,29,30,31), we can get the BER expression as

$$\begin{aligned}
BER_{index} = 1 - \frac{1}{\sqrt{2\pi\left(\gamma_b + \frac{\beta}{4}\right)}}\int_0^{+\infty}&\mathrm{erf}\left(\frac{r}{\sqrt{2\left(\frac{\gamma_b}{2} + \frac{\beta}{4}\right)}}\right) \\
\times\left(\exp\left(-\frac{(r - \gamma_b)^2}{2\left(\gamma_b + \frac{\beta}{4}\right)}\right)\right.&\left. + \exp\left(-\frac{(r + \gamma_b)^2}{2\left(\gamma_b + \frac{\beta}{4}\right)}\right)\right)dr
\end{aligned} \tag{32}$$

For chebyshev map, in Eq. (32),

$$E\left[x_{\delta,0,k}^2\right] = \mathrm{Var}\,[x_{\delta,0,k}] = 0.5, \tag{33}$$

$$E_b = \beta E\left[x_{\delta,0,k}^2\right], \tag{34}$$

$$\gamma_b = \frac{E_b}{N_0}. \tag{35}$$

When $d_{index} = 01 \setminus 10 \setminus 11$, we can get the same conclusion as Eq. (32).

BER for Information Bit. We assume that $d_{index} = 00$, according to Eq. (12),

$$
\begin{aligned}
y_{\delta,l} &= \sum_{k=1}^{\beta} \alpha_{\delta,l,k}\alpha_{\delta,l-1,k} \\
&= \sum_{k=1}^{\beta} \left[d_{\delta,l}\left(\prod_{i=0}^{l-1} d_{\delta,i}\right) x_{\delta,0,k} + \xi_{\delta,l,k}\right]\left[\left(\prod_{i=0}^{l-1} d_{\delta,i}\right) x_{\delta,0,k} + \xi_{\delta,l-1,k}\right] \\
&= \sum_{k=1}^{\beta}\left[d_{\delta,l}\left(\prod_{i=0}^{l-1} d_{\delta,i}\right)^2 x_{\delta,0,k}^2 \right.\\
&\quad + d_{\delta,l}\left(\prod_{i=0}^{l-1} d_{\delta,i}\right) x_{\delta,0,k}\xi_{\delta,l-1,k} \\
&\quad + \left(\prod_{i=0}^{l-1} d_{\delta,i}\right) x_{\delta,0,k}\xi_{\delta,l,k} \\
&\quad \left. + \xi_{\delta,l-1,k}\xi_{\delta,l,k}\right]
\end{aligned}
\tag{36}
$$

Based on the chebyshev map [16], we can get the mean and variance of $y_{\delta,l}$ as following:

$$
E\left[y_{\delta,l}\right] = \beta d_{\delta,l} E\left[x_{\delta,0,k}^2\right],
\tag{37}
$$

$$
\mathrm{Var}\left[y_{\delta,l}\right] = \beta\left(2\mathrm{Var}\left[x_{\delta,0,k}\right]\left(N_0/2\right) + N_0^2/4\right).
\tag{38}
$$

Under the AWGN, based on Gaussian approximation [17,18], the information bit BER expression is

$$
\begin{aligned}
BER_{information} &= \frac{1}{2}\mathrm{erfc}\left(\frac{E\left(y_{\delta,l}\right)}{\sqrt{2\mathrm{Var}\left(y_{\delta,l}\right)}}\right) \\
&= \frac{1}{2}\mathrm{erfc}\left(\left[\frac{2\beta\left(2E\left[x_{\delta,0,k}^2\right]\left(\frac{N_0}{2}\right) + \frac{N_0^2}{4}\right)}{\beta^2\mathrm{Var}^2\left[x_{\delta,0,k}\right]}\right]^{-\frac{1}{2}}\right) \\
&= \frac{1}{2}\mathrm{erfc}\left(\left[2\gamma_b^{-1} + \frac{\beta}{2}\gamma_b^{-2}\right]^{-\frac{1}{2}}\right)
\end{aligned}
\tag{39}
$$

When $d_{index} = 01 \setminus 10 \setminus 11$, we can get the same information BER as Eq. (39).

Based on (31) and (39), the BER of the PI-CDSK in AWGN channel can be calculated by

$$
BER_{HE\ PI-CDSK} = BER_{information}\left(1 - BER_{index}\right) + 0.5 BER_{information}.
\tag{40}
$$

Multipath Rayleigh Fading Channel. For multipath rayleigh fading channel, we assume $\lambda_i(t)$ is the i-th path coefficient is slow fading, the received signal can be written as

$$r(t) = \sum_{i=1}^{N} \lambda_i s(t - \tau_i) + \xi(t). \tag{41}$$

The i-th instantaneous signal-to-noise ratio (SNR) is

$$\gamma_i = (E_b/N_0)\,\lambda_i^2, \tag{42}$$

$$\bar{\gamma}_i = (E_b/N_0)\,E\left[\lambda_i^2\right]. \tag{43}$$

The instantaneous SNR per bit can be rewritten as

$$\gamma_b = (E_b/N_0)\sum_{i=1}^{N}\lambda_i^2. \tag{44}$$

In the two-path-channel model, the probability density function (PDF) of γ_b can be calculated as

$$f(\gamma_b) = \begin{cases} \frac{\gamma_b}{\bar{\gamma}_1^2}e^{-\frac{\gamma_b}{\bar{\gamma}_1}} & E\left[\lambda_1^2\right] = E\left[\lambda_2^2\right] \\ \frac{e^{-\frac{\gamma_b}{\bar{\gamma}_1}}-e^{-\frac{\gamma_b}{\bar{\gamma}_2}}}{\bar{\gamma}_1-\bar{\gamma}_2} & E\left[\lambda_1^2\right] \neq E\left[\lambda_2^2\right] \end{cases}. \tag{45}$$

For n-path-channel model ($n \geq 3$), we assume that all independent channels satisfy the same Rayleigh fading channel condition, the pdf of γ_b can be calculated as

$$f(\gamma_b) = \frac{\gamma_b^{n-1}}{\bar{\gamma}_i^{\,n}(n-1)!}\exp\left(-\frac{\gamma_b}{\bar{\gamma}_i}\right). \tag{46}$$

Based on Eq. (40), under Rayleigh multipath channel, the BER performance expression is

$$BER_{HE\ PI-CDSK\ Rayleigh} = \int_{0}^{+\infty} f(\gamma_b)\,BER_{HE\ PI-CDSK\ Rayleigh}\,(y_{\delta,l}|\gamma_b)\,d\gamma_b. \tag{47}$$

Spectral and Energy Efficiencies Analysis. We can compare the spectral efficiency and energy efficiency between several chaotic communication schemes in Table 1:

1) In one multi-frame, assuming HE PI-CDSK occupies $(\theta+1)$ frames to transmit 3θ bits (including 2θ index bits and θ information bits), the energy efficiency is $3\theta/(\theta+1)\beta$;

2) In one frame, since 3 bits (including index bit and information bit) are transmitted in one frequency band, the spectral efficiency is $3\theta/(\theta+1)$;

3) With the increase of multiplier and integral module, our hardware complexity is higher than that of DCSK and CDSK. However, compared with HPO-CDSK, I-HPO-CDSK and CI-CDSK, due to no frequency modulation module and less time delay module, the hardware complexity of HE PI-CDSK is lower.

Table 1. Spectral and energy efficiencies of DCSK, CDSK, HDR CI-DCSK, HPO-CDSK, I-HPO-CDSK, PI-CDSK, and HE PI-CDSK.

System	Spectral Efficiency	Energy Efficiency
CDSK	$1/\beta$	$1/2$
DCSK	$1/2\beta$	$1/2$
HDR CI-DCSK	$(P+1)\left(2^{P}+1\right)\beta$	$(P+1)/2$
HPO-CDSK	$2\theta/(\theta+1)\beta$	$2\theta/(2\theta+1)$
I-HPO-CDSK	$3\theta/(\theta+1)\beta$	$\theta/(\theta+1)$
PI-CDSK	$2\theta/(\theta+1)\beta$	$2\theta/(\theta+1)$
HE PI-CDSK	$3\theta/(\theta+1)\beta$	$3\theta/(\theta+1)$

Clearly, the overall efficiency performance of HE PI-CDSK (including Spectral Efficiency and Energy Efficiency) is the best in Table 1. Although its energy efficiency is inferior to that of HDR CI-DCSK when its index bit $P \geq 5$, the energy gain of HDR CI-DCSK mainly relies on its expense on spectral efficiency.

4   Simulation Results

In Section IV, we plot the comparison curves between HE PI-CDSK and various systems. Chebyshev map is adopted here where its generation function is $x_{k+1} = 4x_{k}^{3} - 3x_{k}$, the initial value $x_{0} = 0.1$. In the following figures, simulation result is marked as (S), the theory result is marked as (T).

Figure 5 evaluates the effect of AWGN channel on BER performance when the E_{b}/N_{0} level spans from $0dB$ to $16dB$, the spreading factor $\beta = 100,\ 200\ and\ 300$. Because no ISI component in the correlator output, simulation results excellent agree with the BER expression given in Eq. (40).Moreover, because more noise is caused by bigger spreading factor during the correlation detection in the receiver, the BER when $\beta = 100$ is lower than that of when $\beta = 300$.

Under Rayleigh multipath channel, the effect of BER performance is evaluated in Fig. 6 and Fig. 7. Model I is considered in Fig. 6, two fading paths have the same power gain, $E\left[\lambda_{1}^{2}\right]=E\left[\lambda_{2}^{2}\right]=0.5$. Model II is considered in Fig. 7, two fading paths have the different power gain, $E\left[\lambda_{1}^{2}\right] = 0.8$ and $E\left[\lambda_{2}^{2}\right] = 0.2$. The multipath delay is set as $\tau_{1} = 0$ and $\tau_{2} = 2$. Because the multipath delay is much smaller than the spreading factor, the multipath interference can be ignored in

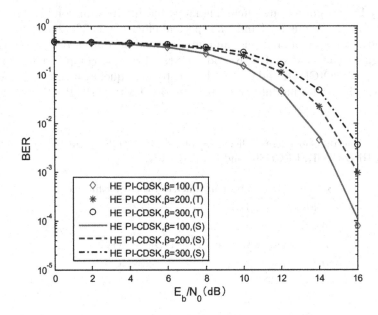

Fig. 5. Simulationand BER expression, for $\beta = 100, 200, 300$, under an AWGN channel.

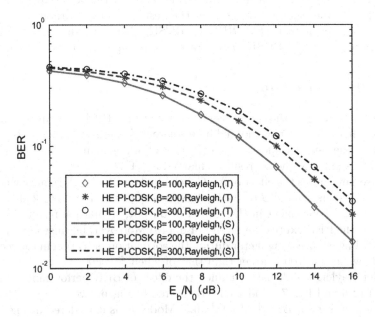

Fig. 6. Simulation and BER expression. for $\beta = 100, 200, 300$, under Rayleigh multi-path fading channel on model I.

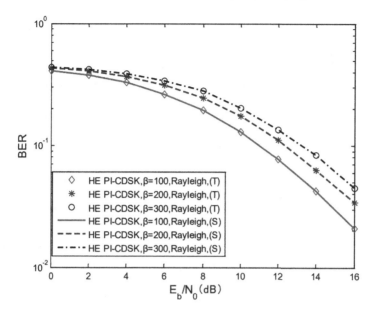

Fig. 7. Simulation and BER expression. for $\beta = 100, 200, 300$, under Rayleigh multipath fading channel on model II.

Fig. 6 and Fig. 7, the simulation curves excellent agree with the analytical results which are computed by Eq. (47).

In Figs. 8, 9, 10, 11, AWGN channel and Rayleigh multipath fading channel are considered, the BER comparison between HE PI-CDSK, DCSK, CDSK, HPO-CDSK, I-HPO-CDSK, HDR CI-DCSK and PI-CDSK are presented. Because HE PI-CDSK can thoroughly eliminate the ISI component during the demodulation, compared with CDSK, it has better BER performance. Due to needless of half frame to transmit the reference signal, compared with DCSK, the spectral efficiency and energy efficiency of HE PI-CDSK has been raised 6 times. Owing to transmit additional bits without energy consumption, the energy efficiency of HE PI-CDSK is treble than that of HPO-CDSK and I-HPO-CDSK. As a result, with the same transmitting energy, the BER performance of HE PI-CDSK is superior to that of DCSK, HPO-CDSK and I-HPO-CDSK. We can also find that, although the BER performance of HE PI-CDSK is equal to that of HDR CI-DCSK and PI-CDSK in Figs. 10 and Fig. 11, HE PI-CDSK performs best both in spectral efficiency and energy efficiency in Table 1.

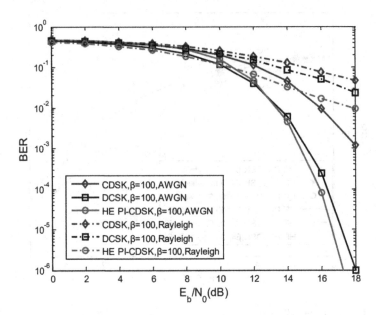

Fig. 8. BER comparison between HE PI-CDSK, DCSK, CDSK over AWGN channel and Rayleigh multipath fading channel on model I.

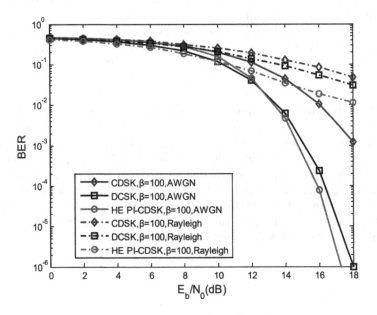

Fig. 9. BER comparison between HE PI-CDSK, DCSK, CDSK over AWGN channel and Rayleigh multipath fading channel on model II.

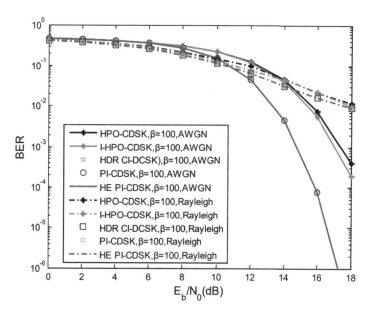

Fig. 10. BER comparison between HE PI-CDSK, PI-CDSK, CI-DCSK, HPO-CDSK, I-HPO-CDSK over AWGN channel and Rayleigh multipath fading channel on model I.

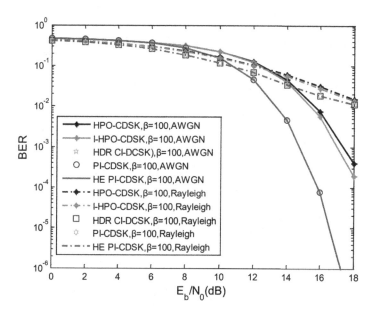

Fig. 11. BER comparison between HE PI-CDSK, PI-CDSK, CI-DCSK, HPO-CDSK, I-HPO-CDSK over AWGN channel and Rayleigh multipath fading channel on model II.

5   Conclusion

Based on the mechanism of Index modulation, in this paper, we have proposed High-Efficiency PI-CDSK (HE PI-CDSK) to further elevate the spectral efficiency and energy efficiency. Under AWGN and Rayleigh multipath fading channel, the theoretical BER expression of the proposed system is analytically studied and the simulations are performed.

Theoretical analysis and simulations show that, by transmitting 3-bits in parallel and without ISI component, HE PI-CDSK has better BER performance and efficiency performance (including spectral efficiency and energy efficiency) than those of previous chaotic communication schemes, such as DCSK, CDSK, HPO-CDSK, I-HPO-CDSK, HDR CI-DCSK and PI-CDSK.

Acknowledgments. This work is sponsored by the National Natural Science Foundation of China under grants [No. 61971240], by Key Laboratory of Dynamic Cognitive System of Electromagnetic Spectrum Space (Nanjing Univ. Aeronaut. Astronaut.), Ministry of Industry and Information Technology under grants [No. KF20181905], by Qing Lan Project and by Jiangsu Province 333 project [BRA2020322].

References

1. Ogorzalek, M.J.: Taming chaos. i. synchronization. IEEE Trans. Circ. Syst. I: Fundam. Theory Appl. **40**(10), 693–699 (1993)
2. Qihui, W., et al.: Cognitive internet of things: a new paradigm beyond connection. IEEE Internet Things J. **1**(2), 129–143 (2014)
3. Kolumbán, G., Vizvári, B., Schwarz, W., Abel, A.: Differential chaos shift keying: a robust coding for chaos communication. In: Proceedings of the NDES, vol. 96, pp. 87–92 (1996)
4. Yang, H., Jiang, G.-P.: High-efficiency differential-chaos-shift-keying scheme for chaos-based noncoherent communication. IEEE Trans. Circ. Syst. II Express Briefs **59**(5), 312–316 (2012)
5. Yang, H., Jiang, G.-P.: Reference-modulated DCSK: a novel chaotic communication scheme. IEEE Trans. Circ. Syst. II Express Briefs **60**(4), 232–236 (2013)
6. Sushchik, M., Tsimring, L.S., Volkovskii, A.R.: Performance analysis of correlation-based communication schemes utilizing chaos. IEEE Trans. Circ. Systems I: Fundam. Theory Appl. **47**(12), 1684–1691 (2000)
7. Tam, W.M., Lau, F.C.M., Tse, C.K.: Generalized correlation-delay-shift-keying scheme for noncoherent chaos-based communication systems. IEEE Trans. Circ. Syst. I: Regular Papers **53**(3), 712–721 (2006)
8. Duan, J., Jiang, G., Yang, H.: Reference-adaptive CDSK: an enhanced version of correlation delay shift keying. IEEE Trans. Circ. Syst. II Express Briefs **62**(1), 90–94 (2014)
9. Duan, J., Jiang, G., Yang, H.: Correlation delay shift keying chaotic communication scheme with no intrasignal interference. **38** (3), 681–687 (2016)
10. Duan, J.Y., Jiang, G.-P., Yang, H.: A novel multiple-access correlation-delay-shift-keying. Int. J. Bifurcat. Chaos **27**(02), 1750025 (2017)
11. Duan, J.-Y., Yang, H.: Phase-orthogonality CDSK: a reliable and effective chaotic communication scheme. IET Commun. **12**(9), 1116–1122 (2018)

12. Duan, J.-Y., Yang, H.: High-data-rate PO-CDSK: a high effective chaotic communication scheme. IET Commun. **14**(1), 21–27 (2020)
13. Duan, J.-Y., Yang, H.: I-HPO-CDSK: an improved chaotic communication scheme for high reliability and effectivity. IET Commun. **15**(3), 476–486 (2021)
14. Yang, H., Si-Yuan, X., Jiang, G.-P.: A high data rate solution for differential chaos shift keying based on carrier index modulation. IEEE Trans. Circ. Syst. II Express Briefs **68**(4), 1487–1491 (2020)
15. Duan, J.-Y., Yang, H.: Phase-index correlation delay shift keying modulation. IET Commun. **16**(4), 326–334 (2022)
16. Geisel, T., Fairen, V.: Statistical properties of chaos in Chebyshev maps. Phys. Lett. A **105**(6), 263–266 (1984)
17. Chernov, N.I.: Limit theorems and Markov approximations for chaotic dynamical systems. Probability Theory Related Fields **101**, 321–362 (1995)
18. Jiang, G.P., Yang, H., Duan, J.Y.: Chaotic Digital Modulation Scheme and Its Performance Analysis. Science Press, Beijing, 1st edn. IEEE Press (2015)

Federated Learning Poison Attack Detection Scheme Based on Gradient Similarity

Quanyu Zhao[1], Yuan Zhang[2], Zhengjun Jing[1(✉)], Yuanjian Zhou[1(✉)], and Zexi Xin[2]

[1] School of Computer Engineering, Jiangsu University of Technology, Changzhou, China
{jzjing,zhouyuanjian}@jsut.edu.cn
[2] Department of Computer Science and Technology, Nanjing University, Nanjing, China

Abstract. Selfish federated learning model trainers may launch data poisoning attacks by introducing specific factors into the data or tampering the sample data, either to obtain a model suitable for themselves or to make the model fail to converge. Detecting participant data poisoning attacks is an essential process in federated learning model training. This paper proposes a gradient similarity-based federated learning data poisoning attack detection scheme. In this scheme, the central server calculates the similarity of the uploaded gradient, and detects anomalies in the uploaded gradients based on historical gradient data, thereby determining whether a user has engaged in data poisoning during the training process. Unlike previous approaches, our method leverages gradient similarity to detect poisoning attacks not only in horizontal federated learning but also in vertical federated learning. In the experiments, we use cosine similarity and Manhattan distance to calculate the similarity of gradient differences uploaded by participants. We consider the participants acting as attacker and analyse the security of this scheme, The experimental results show that the similarity of gradient differences uploaded by honest participants continues to increase as the iterative training progresses, and when the model finally converges, the similarity of gradient differences stabilizes within a small range. When participants engage in local data poisoning, the similarity of gradient differences in uploaded data keeps fluctuating, and the model either fails to converge or the similarity of gradient differences fluctuates within a large range.

Keywords: Federated Learning · Poisoning Attacks · Gradient · Similarity

1 Introduction

With the successive introduction of privacy protection laws, various industries are increasingly demanding privacy protection for training data when deploying predictive or classification models. Machine learning models that perform better in training [1,2] require diverse, high-quality, and highly accurate massive data. However, high-quality and highly accurate massive data inevitably contain users' sensitive and private data, which contradicts the growing demand for privacy. Many devices, due to limited data resources, cannot independently complete the machine learning models training. Therefore, these devices choose federated learning to complete model training.

Federated learning [3–6] is a distributed machine learning approach with privacy protection capabilities. The central server does not collect participants' data, allowing user data to remain local, and users have control and usage rights over their data [7]. In federated learning, a central server gathers participants to jointly a model training. Initially, the central server creates an initialized global model and distributes it to participants. Participants deploy local models and train the models using their local data. After one iteration of training, participants send the model gradient to the central server. The central server aggregates all the gradient parameters, updates the global model, and distributes it again. Participants continue iterating the training until the global model training is completed. Federated learning ensures that participants collaborate to train the global model using their local data without the need for any participant to share their original data. This method not only protects the privacy of participants, but also maximizes the use of participant data to train models that are equally applicable to all participants.

With the research on federated learning, researchers have found that retaining participant data locally, uploading training gradients to a central server, does not guarantee the privacy and security of participant data. Firstly, the central server, in order to obtain a more accurate model, may require participants to use real original data for local training. The central server could be malicious or semi-honest. Although only gradient of participants are exchanged, the central server can still perform inversion attacks [8–11] on the gradients uploaded by participants, obtain participant's local training samples or specific sample data, compromise the privacy of participant data. In federated learning, some participants may be malicious, and they may inject toxic or erroneous sample data [12,13] during local training. Without central server validation of sample data, these toxic or erroneous sample data could poison the global model. There may also be malicious participants in federated learning who carry out data poisoning attacks on local sample data, causing the federated learning training model to fail to converge or incorrectly classify input samples.

Federated learning attackers do not aim to destroy the federated learning framework, but to disrupt the model training of federated learning. Based on different poisoning attack methods, we classify poisoning attacks into targeted poisoning attacks [14–16] and untargeted poisoning attacks [17,18]. Targeted poisoning attacks [14–16] refer to attackers causing the federated learning model to misclassify data with specific labels or incorrectly label specific data, without affecting other data. Untargeted poisoning attacks [17,18] refer to attackers causing the federated learning training model to fail to converge or misclassify all input data through poisoning.

Poisoning attacks [14–18] are among the most threatening attack methods in federated learning, it causes the model to misclassify or hindering it from converging. Malicious participants use random data samples or fake sample data, have no contributions during training and steal the training progress of other participants. Existing research [14–16] has found that poisoning attacks are one of the most threatening attacks in federated learning.

Existing robust aggregation schemes [20,33,34] randomly select a small subset of members for gradient aggregation and update the global model to mitigate model poisoning attacks. This strategy, which relies on selecting model aggregation members, can result in the waste of the training achievements and computing resources of other participants. Additionally, the globally trained model in collaborative training may be biased towards the selected members, undermining the fairness of other participants.

Based on observations of the federated learning model training process, we have reached two conclusions: 1 Malicious participants who carry out data poisoning attacks on training samples will inevitably lead to significant deviations in the uploaded gradients. After multiple rounds of local training and central server aggregation to update the global model, the impact of such deviations on the model will diminish. It is difficult for malicious participants to achieve their desired target training model through a single poisoning attack. 2 After the global model is subjected to data poisoning attacks, the convergence speed of the model will decrease, requiring more training rounds. Based on these two observations, this paper proposes a federated learning data poisoning detection scheme based on gradient similarity. The central server determines whether a participant has carried out a poisoning attack based on the similarity between the gradients from two rounds of participants. The central server aggregates gradients uploaded by honest participants, updates the global model, and shares the updated gradients with participants. Participants perform local model updates and iterate the training until the model training is completed.

The main contributions of the federated learning data poisoning detection scheme based on gradient similarity can be summarized as follows:

• First, we propose a federated learning data poisoning attack detection scheme based on gradient similarity, which can detect poisoning attacks. Unlike previous approaches, our method leverages gradient similarity to detect poisoning attacks not only in horizontal federated learning but also in vertical federated learning.

• We conduct experiments on two different datasets, using cosine similarity and Manhattan distance to calculate the similarity. The experiments demonstrate that our scheme can detect malicious poisoning attackers.

• The federated learning data poisoning attack detection scheme based on gradient similarity is robust, and it prevents disruptions to the global model's training due to participant disconnections or crashes. We proof the correctness, demonstrating that the central server can utilize the gradient to calculate gradient similarity and perform poisoning attack detection, while also aggregating the gradients of honest participants to update the global model.

• We analyse the security of this scheme, showing that it can resist poisoning attacks by malicious participants, thereby protecting the privacy and security of participants' local data and gradients.

The rests of our paper are listed as follow: Sect. 2 introduces the preliminary including related works and federated learning. Section 3 proposes federated learning data poisoning attack detection scheme based on gradient similarity, and Sect. 4 analyses the security of this scheme, designs and analyses the experiments. Section 5 concludes the paper.

2 Preliminary

2.1 Related Works

The most influential form of attack in federated learning is poisoning attacks, which can be categorized into model poisoning [18–20] and data poisoning [12,21,22]. Model poisoning attacks refer to malicious participants manipulating or tampering with local training data, resulting in biases, misclassification, and decreased performance of the global model. Model poisoning is primarily accomplished through techniques such as data injection [23], label flipping [24,25], gradient manipulation [26], data redistribution [27], and collaborative attacks among participants. Data poisoning [28,29] involves participants manipulating their local data by injecting harmful, incorrect, or misleading data samples into their local dataset, thereby disrupting the performance of the global model or producing misleading results.

To address model poisoning attacks, many research efforts [20,21,30–32] have proposed various solutions. Robust model aggregation methods [20,33,34] resist model poisoning attacks by selecting a subset of participants to upload gradient parameters for global model updates. While this approach can mitigate model poisoning to some extent, it does not completely eliminate the threat and wastes the resources of the remaining participants.

The main aggregation methods in federated learning include: robust federated learning aggregation scheme (RFLAC) [20,33,34], differential privacy-based federated learning aggregation scheme (DPFLAC) [5,6,36,37], gradient clipping-based federated learning schemes (GCFLC) [33], and local sensitive hash-based federated learning schemes (LSHFLC) [39,40].

RFLAC primarily uses technologies such as homomorphic encryption [43] and secure multi-party computation [33,35] to protect the privacy and security. Dong et al. [33] propose a robust gradient descent federated learning security aggregation scheme. This scheme first analyzes two robust distributed gradient descent algorithms based on median and trimmed mean operations and proves the error rate of the loss function. Zhu et al. [35] constructe a weighted federated learning security aggregation scheme. This scheme protects participants' data privacy and demonstrates its security against semi-honest participants.

DPFLAC [5,6,36,37] employ differential privacy techniques to add noise and protect the security and privacy. Wei et al. [5] demonstrate that different levels of privacy protection requirements can be satisfied. It also establishes a theoretical convergence constraint on the loss function of federated learning models, achieves a better balance between convergence and privacy protection. Truex et al. [36] propose a hybrid federated learning privacy protection scheme. This scheme reduces the added noise as the number of participants increases without compromising data privacy. Hu et al. [37] consider the diversity among different users and the differential privacy of different user data, propose a personalized federated learning scheme based on differential privacy.

GCFLC [33,38] involves participants calculating gradients and clipping them to ensure they fall within a specific threshold. This method prevents attackers from inferring sensitive information about participants by analyzing the magnitude of gradient changing. GCFLC always comes with some accuracy loss, so these approaches need to analyze loss functions and error rates. Guo et al. [38] use a dynamic method of adding Gaussian noise. This scheme employs adaptive threshold clipping to control sensitivity, allows participants' privacy budgets to be fully exploited.

LSHFLC [39,40] enables participants to transform locally computed gradients into hash codes using local sensitive hash functions and share only these hash codes rather than the original gradients. Seif et al. [40] proposes a wireless channel-based federated learning gradient aggregation privacy protection scheme. Li et al. [39] introduce a similarity federated learning scheme based on location-sensitive hash, improve training efficiency in federated learning.

In the masking-based federated learning schemes [41,42], the lack of verification of participants' training samples and the potential for malicious participants to tamper with model training gradients or participant crashes can lead to significant errors in federated learning gradient aggregation. Tenison et al. [42] propose a masking-based federated learning scheme based on a heterogeneous environment. This scheme allows trainers to use the updated standard averaging method as a replacement for the original method, offering better adaptability.

A federated learning scheme based on robustness not only fails to completely address model poisoning attacks but also results in a total waste of resources. A federated learning scheme based on differential privacy adds noise to the gradients. Balancing the amount of noise with gradient privacy remains a significant challenge. Federated learning schemes based on gradient clipping may cause some loss of precision in model parameters, affecting the model's utility. Federated learning schemes based on masking techniques, malicious participants tampering with training gradients will lead to significant errors in gradient aggregation, thereby impacting the model's utility.

2.2   Federated Learning

The entities involved in a federated learning model include a central server and participating edge devices. The central server first constructs the foundational federated learning training framework and initializes the model, distributing the initialized model to all participants. Participants deploy the initialized model locally and perform local model training using the stochastic gradient descent algorithm. The central server aggregates the participants' model training parameters, performs global model updates and distributes the updated model parameters to all participants, iterating the training process until the model training is complete. Participants may be different devices, organizations, or individuals, each with their private datasets for local model training.

Table 1. Symbols and Their Meanings Used in the Federated Learning Model

Symbol	Meaning
S	Central server
P_i	Participant i $(i = 1, 2, \ldots, n)$
n	Number of participants
M_0	Initialized global model
D_i	Local dataset of participant P_i
$\bar{\theta}_0$	Initialized global model parameters
$\bar{\theta}_t$	Global model parameters at iteration t
θ_t^i	Local model parameters of participant P_i at iteration t
T	Maximum number of iterations
t	Number of local training rounds
τ	Period after which local gradients are uploaded
η	Learning rate

Let's provide a detailed explanation of the symbols used in the federated learning model, as shown in Table 1. We assume that a central server S convenes n participants P_i, $(i = 1, 2, \cdots, n)$ for model training on the some tasks, such as image classification. Each participant P_i possesses its local dataset D_i. All participants share the federated learning training framework and the updating parameters of the global model. Participants locally train multiple times within one cycle and upload the training gradients to the central server. The central server aggregates all the gradients, updates the global model, and distributes the global model parameters once per round. Iterative training continues until the model training is completed.

Federated learning model training is generally divided into three phases: 1). Setup Phase: The central server summons participants to conduct federated learning model training and shares global model parameters. 2). Local Training Phase: Participants use their local datasets for local training and upload the local model training gradients to the central server. 3). Global Model Update Phase: The central server updates the global model and distributes the updated global model gradients. Algorithm 1 shows the federated learning gradient updating algorithm. Next, we will introduce each phase of federated learning in detail.

Algorithm 1. Federated Learning Gradient Updating Algorithm

1: **Input:** M_0, P_i $(i = 1, 2, \ldots, n)$, D_i $(i = 1, 2, \ldots, n)$, η, T, τ, t, $\overline{\theta}_0$
2: **Output:** Global model M
3: The central server S shares θ_0 and M_0 with all participants P_i
4: **for** $i = 1$ to n **do**
5:     **for** $t = 1$ to T **do**
6:         $\theta_i^t \leftarrow \theta_i^{t-1} - \eta \theta_i^{t-1}$
7:         **if** τ divides t **then**
8:             P_i uploads θ_i^t
9:             P_i downloads the updated global model M's gradient $\overline{\theta}_t$
10:            P_i updates the local model using $\overline{\theta}_t$
11:        **end if**
12:    **end for**
13: **end for**
14: **for** $t = 1$ to T **do**
15:    **if** τ divides t **then**
16:        **for** $i = 1$ to n **do**
17:            The central server S computes $\overline{\theta}_t \leftarrow \frac{1}{n} \sum_{i=1}^{n} \theta_i^t$
18:        **end for**
19:    **end if**
20: **end for**

Setup Phase: S shares the initialized global model M_0 among P_i ($i = 1, 2, \ldots, n$) and shares the public parameters $\{\overline{\theta}_0, T, t, \tau, \eta\}$. $\overline{\theta}_0$ represents the initialized global model parameters, T represents the maximum number of iterations for each participant, and t represents the number of local training rounds for participants. The period τ indicates that participants upload their local training gradients θ_t^i to S once every local training rounds. The learning rate η determines the step size of the model parameters in the gradient direction during each local training session. The model determines the direction and magnitude of parameter updates by computing the gradient of the loss function.

Local Training Phase: P_i deploys M_0 locally and uses the local dataset D_i to train the local model. After obtaining the model training gradients, the local model is updated and iterated τ times. P_i uploads θ_t^i to S and downloads θ_t from S. This iteration is repeated until T.

Global Model Update Phase: S aggregates θ_t^i uploaded by P_i ($i = 1, 2, \ldots, n$) and calculates the average $\overline{\theta}_t$, updates M based on $\overline{\theta}_t$, and distributes θ_t of M to participants.

Researchers have demonstrated that participants can affect the model's convergence or cause incorrect classification by poisoning the training data. The effectiveness of data poisoning is time-sensitive; with a single poisoning event, the effect of the poison decreases over time as training progresses, and after multiple iterations, the poison effect approaches zero. Poisoning in the later stages of training has a much greater impact on the model than in the early stages. To cause model non-convergence or specific target misclassification, poisoning must be repeated multiple times to continually activate the poison effect. Multiple participants jointly poisoning will greatly increase the damage to model training and more easily achieve the desired poisoning effect, makes the poisoning methods harder to hide.

Intuitively, untargeted poisoning attacks solve an optimization problem by finding the direction opposite to model convergence [17,18] and amplifying this direction to cause model divergence.

Targeted attacks by an attacker C_{target} are interested only in data with specific labels, aiming to make the model misclassify data with specific labels or assign incorrect labels to specific data. We assume that all data samples are in a set $D = \{D_1, D_2, \ldots, D_n\}$, and each data has its corresponding label $L = \{l_1, l_2, \ldots, l_n\}$. The attacker hopes to misclassify the label l_i of D_i to l_i' where $l_i' \neq l_i$ and minimize the loss function caused by the poisoning attack.

Although the starting points of targeted and untargeted attacks are different, both have certain effects on the local training gradients. After poisoning attacks by malicious participants, the trends of the uploaded local training gradients will show some fluctuations.

3   Federated Learning Poisoning Attack Detection Scheme Based on Gradient Similarity

3.1   Security Model

We consider a central server S gathers n participants P_i $(i = 1, 2, \ldots, n)$ to jointly train the same task model. The data set D_i $(i = 1, 2, \ldots, n)$ owned by each participant is non-ID and distributed differently. During the federated learning process, both the central server and the participants can be potential attackers. They may use their computing, storage, and communication resources to steal data or use gradient inversion attacks to obtain participants' private data. Malicious participants may also perform data poisoning during federated learning to hinder model convergence or obtain their desired model.

First, we make security assumptions about the central server and the participants. Based on these security assumptions, we construct a federated learning poisoning detection scheme. This scheme is not only suitable for participants but also resistant to data poisoning attacks by participants.

Central Server: the central server is honest and assists participants in completing model training. The central server only performs simple gradient aggregation, updates the global model and distributes the updated model parameters. They do not steal participants' data or initiate active attacks.

Participants: participants are semi-honest. They execute federated learning training tasks and upload local model training gradients. Participants execute the protocol correctly but are interested in other participants' data. They may attempt to steal data from other participants through federated learning or hinder global model convergence or cause misclassification of specific label data through poisoning attacks.

We assume that there are secure communication channels among participants and the central server. The central server is allowed to authenticate incoming messages to prevent man-in-the-middle attacks. During the joint training process, the communication channel will not be disrupted by other malicious attackers. All participants receive the shared federated learning framework and distributed keys. The central server receives the gradient parameters uploaded by participants. In this process, the only entities involved are the central server and the participants, then only the participants act as attackers. This scheme also resists malicious participants from obtaining other participants' private or sensitive data.

3.2 Federated Learning Poisoning Attack Detection Scheme Based on Gradient Similarity

During the federated learning process, the gradients of the local models trained by participants will continuously converge. In the early stages of local model training, the convergence direction is consistent, and the speed is fast, with significant differences between the gradients of adjacent rounds. In the later stages of local model training, the convergence speed slows down, the convergence direction changes, and the differences between the gradients of adjacent rounds become smaller. When participants perform data poisoning attacks during local model training, significant fluctuations occur in the differences between the gradients of adjacent rounds.

Based on two experimental observations, after participants poison sample data, the uploaded gradients will significantly differ from the historical gradient data, and the convergence speed of the global model will decrease. Based on the historical similarity data of the gradients uploaded by participant P_i after local model training, the central server determines whether there is a poisoning attacker in the local model training. To address data poisoning attacks, based on the gradient variation pattern of participants' local model training, we propose a federated learning poisoning detection scheme based on gradient similarity.

Assuming that malicious participants only perform poisoning attacks in the first two local model training sessions, the effects of the participants' poisoning attacks will approach zero after multiple rounds of iterative training. Additionally, in the early stages of federated learning, participants' local model training converges quickly, and the gradient similarity is low, making it meaningless to calculate gradient similarity. Therefore, we assume that the central server detects data poisoning attacks from the third round of gradient.

In the gradient similarity-based federated learning poisoning attack detection scheme, participants calculate the similarity between the differences of adjacent gradient uploads. The gradient differences and their similarity are uploaded to the central server. The central server checks the similarity to determine if there is a data poisoning attacker firstly, then aggregates the model gradients and updates the global model. Participants iteratively train until obtaining the final task model. Algorithm 2 shows the federated learning poisoning attack detection scheme based on gradient similarity. This scheme includes three phases: the setup

---

Algorithm 2 : Federated Learning Poisoning Attack Detection Algorithm Based
on Gradient Similarity

1: **Input:** M_0, P_i $(i = 1, 2, \ldots, n)$, D_i $(i = 1, 2, \ldots, n)$, η, T, τ, t, global model
 gradients $\bar{\theta}_t$, θ_t, m (the number of participants selected by the central server)
2: **Output:** Global model M
3: The central server shares $\bar{\theta}_0$ and M_0 with participants P_i
4: **for** $i = 1$ to n **do**
5:     **for** $t = 1$ to T **do**
6:         $\theta_t^i \leftarrow \theta_{t-1}^i - \eta\theta_{t-1}^i$
7:         **if** τ divides t **then**
8:             P_i uploads θ_t^i
9:             P_i downloads the global model gradients $\bar{\theta}_t$ and updates the local model
10:             **if** $t > 3$ **then**
11:                 P_i computes gradient similarity $Sim_t^i = Simfun(\theta_t^i - \theta_{t-1}^i, \theta_{t-1}^i - \theta_{t-2}^i)$
12:                 P_i uploads sim_t^i
13:             **end if**
14:         **end if**
15:     **end for**
16: **end for**
17: **for** $t = 1$ to T **do**
18:     **if** τ divides t **then**
19:         **for** $i = 1$ to n **do**
20:             The central server S checks sim_t^i uploaded by P_i
21:             Computes $\bar{\theta}_t \leftarrow \frac{1}{m}\sum_{i=1}^m \theta_m^i$
22:         **end for**
23:     **end if**
24:     The central server uses the aggregated gradient $\bar{\theta}_t$ to update the global model M
25: **end for**

---

phase, the local training phase of participants, and the central server's gradient
aggregating phase.

Setup Phase
S sets up the initialization framework and the main parameters. S shares M_0
and public parameters $\{\bar{\theta}_0, T, \tau, \eta\}$ among P_i $(i = 1, 2, \ldots, n)$.

The Local Training Phase of Participants
Participants P_i deploy the global model M_0 locally and train it using the local
dataset D_i firstly.

$$\theta_t^i \leftarrow \theta_{t-1}^i - \eta\theta_{t-1}^i \tag{1}$$

Iteratively update and train the local model τ times. Participants P_i upload
θ_t^i to S. From the third gradient uploading, participants calculate the similarity
Sim_t^i of the gradient between the differences of adjacent gradient,

$$Sim_t^i = Simfun(\theta_t^i - \theta_{t-1}^i, \theta_{t-1}^i - \theta_{t-2}^i) \tag{2}$$

and upload Sim_i^t and θ_i^i to S. S aggregates the gradients and updates the global model. Participants download the gradient $\overline{\theta}_t$, update the local model, and iteratively train until T or the model training task is completed.

Central Server's Gradient Aggregating Phase
The central server determines whether there is a data poisoning attacker within participants based on Sim_i^t. The similarity is computing by the equation

$$\text{Sim}_t^i > \xi \tag{3}$$

ξ is the similarity threshold of the gradient differences of participants during normal training for the same federated learning task. The central server selects participants with gradient difference similarity satisfying the equation $\text{Sim}_t^i \leq \xi$. These participants do not perform data poisoning attacks in local model training.

$$\overline{\theta}_t \leftarrow \frac{1}{m} \sum_{i=1}^{m} \theta_i^m \tag{4}$$

The central server uses $\overline{\theta}_t$ to update M and shares the updated global model with P_i ($i = 1, 2, \ldots, n$). Participants use the global model gradient to complete the local model updating, iterating until the model training task is completed.

4   Analysis

4.1   Security Analysis

In the gradient similarity-based federated learning poisoning attack detection scheme, S is honest and the gradients uploaded by participants are plaintext. Based on the security assumptions, this scheme only considers malicious participants as attackers, do not consider scenarios where the central server acts as an attacker or colludes with participants in attacks.

Participant P_i conducts local model training and uploads θ_t^i to S after each cycle. S aggregates the gradients to complete the global model updating. Participants download $\overline{\theta}_t$ of the updated global model M and update their local model M_i. In this process, P_i and S have exchanged data completely. Participant P_i has no direct contact or data exchange with other participants P_j ($j = 1, 2, \ldots, n, j \neq i$), so participant P_i can only obtain θ_t^j of other participants P_j from the downloaded global model gradient $\overline{\theta}_t$.

$\overline{\theta}_t$ is downloaded by P_i from S which is obtained by θ_t^i ($i = 1, 2, \ldots, n$) from those honest participants. When there are many participants P_i ($i = 1, 2, \ldots, n$) and their local datasets D_i ($i = 1, 2, \ldots, n$) are distributed similarly, the influence of each θ_t^i on M will significantly decrease. The probability of obtaining θ_t^i or local data from $\overline{\theta}_t$ will be reduced greatly. We consider the success probability of this attack to be negligible.

If D_i ($i = 1, 2, \ldots, n$) of P_i are distributed similarly, P_i can still obtain gradients θ_t^j of other participants P_j or local data from the gradient $\overline{\theta}_t$ of the global model M. Therefore, no federated learning algorithm can guarantee the privacy and security of participant data in such scenarios, this attack method is not within our scope of consideration. We only consider participants poisoning their local data to execute attacks.

Based on two experimental observations, we find that after participants poison their local datasets, the gradients uploaded by participants show significant fluctuations. Participants exhibit large differences in uploaded gradients in the early stages of normal local training, and smaller differences in the later stages, without significant fluctuations. Therefore, it is reasonable to use the similarity of gradients to detect poisoning attacks during local training in the gradient similarity-based federated learning poisoning attack detection scheme. If participants engage in poisoning attacks, they cannot control the gradient changes after local training. Therefore, detecting the similarity of gradients can resist poisoning attacks by participants in federated learning.

4.2 Experimental Analysis

In this scheme, we use cosine similarity and Manhattan distance to compute the similarity between gradient differences. We calculate the difference in adjacent two rounds between gradients uploaded by participants and compute the similarity between these differences in consecutive rounds as the similarity of uploaded gradient differences by participants.

To evaluate the accuracy of this scheme, we assume a central server gathers 10 participants for federated learning joint training, ultimately completes the task training to obtain a suitable federated learning model. We assume participants have independently and identically distributed datasets, and we conduct experiments by using two datasets: CIFAR-10 [44] and MNIST [45]. We set the maximum number of iterations for local training by participants to 100.

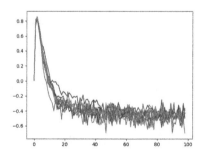 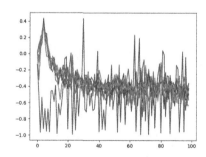

Fig. 1. Federated learning poisoning attack detection based on gradient cosine similarity (a) Honest Participants; (b) Participants with Poisoning Attacks

We record the gradients of local training models uploaded by participants in experiments and compute the cosine values and Manhattan distances between gradient differences. Using these cosine values and Manhattan distances, we respectively plot Fig. 1 based on gradient cosine similarity and Fig. 2 based on

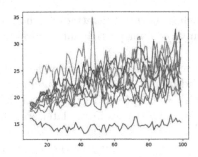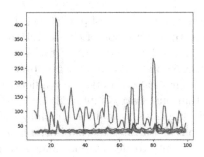

Fig. 2. Federated Learning Poisoning Attack Detection Scheme Based on Gradient Manhattan Distance Similarity; (a) Honest Participants; (b) Participants with Poisoning Attacks

gradient Manhattan distance similarity. The left subplot of Fig. 1, denoted as Fig. 1-(a), shows the cosine similarity between uploaded gradient differences when no poisoning attackers exist among participants. The right subplot of Fig. 1, denoted as Fig. 1-(b), shows the cosine similarity when one poisoning attackers exist among participants. The left subplot of Fig. 2, denoted as Fig. 2-(a), shows the Manhattan distance similarity when no poisoning attacker exist among participants. The right subplot of Fig. 2, denoted as Fig. 2-(b), shows the Manhattan distance when one poisoning attacker exist among participants.

Figure 1 and Fig. 2 intuitively demonstrate that when there are no poisoning attackers among 10 participants, the trends in similarity of uploaded gradient differences by participants are consistent, and the gradient differences uploaded during iterative training gradually decrease and stabilize within a small range. When there exist poisoning attackers among 10 participants, the similarity of gradient differences uploaded by attackers and honest participants differs significantly. The gradients uploaded by attackers exhibit larger fluctuations after data poisoning attacks, leading to larger gradient differences and reduced similarity between gradient differences.

In Fig. 1, we use the cosine function to calculate the similarity. With participants' local iterative training, the gradient differences uploaded by participants become smaller. The similarity between gradient differences in consecutive rounds becomes smaller, and the similarity will stabilize within a small range eventually.

Figure 1-(a) demonstrates that when no poisoning attackers exist within participants, With participants' local iterative training, the gradient differences will become smaller. In the initial stages of local training, the gradient differences are larger, and the direction of gradient changing is consistent, leading to similarity becomes higher and higher. In the later stages of participants' local training, the gradient differences become smaller, and the direction of gradient changing varies, resulting in fluctuating similarity within a certain range. Therefore, the cosine calculated from the gradient differences do not completely equal 0.

In Fig. 1-(b), we calculate the cosine similarity between gradient differences. In the initial stages of local training, the cosine similarity uploaded by attackers and honest participants also changes differently. The similarity uploaded by honest participants initially increases and then stabilizes. From the initial stage to the final convergence stage, in the local model training by attackers, the cosine similarity exhibits significant fluctuations. Figure 1 demonstrates the differential changes in cosine similarity between honest participants and attackers, allowing us to judge whether participants are engaging in data poisoning attacks or not.

We use Manhattan distance to calculate the similarity. With participants' local iterative training, the gradient differences and the similarity in consecutive rounds become smaller, and the similarity will eventually stabilize within a small range. Since the Manhattan distance in the initial stages of local training is larger, to obtain a more aesthetic graph, we select gradient differences from the 10th round onward to calculate Manhattan distances and obtain Fig. 2.

Figure 2-(a) demonstrates that when no poisoning attackers exist within participants, with participants' local iterative training, the gradient differences uploaded by participants will become smaller. In the initial stages of local training, the Manhattan distance of gradient differences is relatively large. In the later stages of participants' local training, the gradient differences become smaller, and the Manhattan distance of gradient differences also decreases, eventually fluctuating within a small range.

Figure 2-(b) demonstrates that when one poisoning attacker exists within participants, the Manhattan distance of gradient differences is initially large. As local iterative training continues, the Manhattan distance will becomes smaller, fluctuating within a certain range. From the initial stage to the final convergence stage of local model training by attackers, the Manhattan distance has always been large, fluctuating within a large range. Figure 2 demonstrates the differential changes in Manhattan distance by honest participants and attackers, allowing us to judge whether participants are engaging in data poisoning attacks or not.

Whether using cosine functions or Manhattan distance to calculate the similarity, with participants' local iterative training, the similarity increases and eventually fluctuates within a small range. The similarity has always been large and fluctuates within a large range throughout the local model training process by attackers. We believe that using other similarity calculation methods would lead to the same conclusions. Therefore, we can judge whether participants are engaging in data poisoning attacks by calculating the similarity. The experiments demonstrates that we could judge whether participants are engaging in data poisoning attacks by calculating the similarity.

5   Conclusion

We propose a federated learning poisoning attack detection scheme based on gradient similarity, in which a honest central server detect poisoning attacks by assessing the similarity of gradients. This process iteratively continues until obtaining the model training. We analyze the security and design experiments for federated learning poisoning attack detection based on gradient difference similarity, using cosine function and Manhattan distance to calculate the similarity between the gradient differences. The experimental results show that the similarity uploaded by honest participants will continuously increase with iterative training, and it will stably fluctuate within a smaller range when the model converges. When participants poison the local data, the similarity will continuously fluctuate, the model will not converge, or the similarity will fluctuate within a larger range when the model converges. The experiment demonstrates that federated learning based on gradient difference similarity could detect whether participants are performing data poisoning attacks or not.

Acknowledgment. This work was supported by the grant from the National Natural Science Foundation of China (grant numbers 61672270, 61602216); and the Natural Science Foundation of the Jiangsu Higher Education Institutions of China (grant numbers 24KJB520008, 21KJB120001).

References

1. Song, L., Shokri, R., Mittal, P.: Privacy risks of securing machine learning models against adversarial examples. In: Proceedings of the. ACM SIGSAC Conference on Computer and Communications Security, vol. 2019, pp. 241–257 (2019)
2. Nasr, M., Shokri, R., Houmansadr, A.: Comprehensive privacy analysis of deep learning: passive and active white-box inference attacks against centralized and federated learning. In: 2019 IEEE Symposium on Security and Privacy (SP), pp. 739–753. IEEE (2019)
3. Li, Q., Wen, Z., Wu, Z., et al.: A survey on federated learning systems: vision, hype and reality for data privacy and protection. IEEE Trans. Knowl. Data Eng. **35**, 3347–3366 (2021)
4. Hao, M., Li, H., Luo, X., et al.: Efficient and privacy-enhanced federated learning for industrial artificial intelligence. IEEE Trans. Industr. Inf. **16**(10), 6532–6542 (2019)
5. Wei, K., Li, J., Ding, M., et al.: Federated learning with differential privacy: algorithms and performance analysis. IEEE Trans. Inf. Forensics Secur. **15**, 3454–3469 (2020)
6. Stevens, T., Skalka, C., Vincent, C., et al.: Efficient differentially private secure aggregation for federated learning via hardness of learning with errors. In: 31st USENIX Security Symposium (USENIX Security 22), pp. 1379–1395 (2022)
7. Truong, N., Sun, K., Wang, S., et al.: Privacy preservation in federated learning: an insightful survey from the GDPR perspective. Comput. Secur. **110**, 102402 (2021)
8. Ovi, P.R, Dey, E., Roy, N., et al.: Mixed quantization enabled federated learning to tackle gradient inversion attacks. In: Proceedings of the IEEE/CVF Conference on Computer Vision and Pattern Recognition, pp. 5045–5053 (2023)
9. Huang, Y., Gupta, S., Song, Z., et al.: Evaluating gradient inversion attacks and defenses in federated learning. Adv. Neural. Inf. Process. Syst. **34**, 7232–7241 (2021)
10. Li, J., Rakin, A.S, Chen, X., et al.: ResSFL: a resistance transfer framework for defending model inversion attack in split federated learning. In: Proceedings of the IEEE/CVF Conference on Computer Vision and Pattern Recognition, pp. 10194–10202 (2022)
11. Hatamizadeh, A., Yin, H., Molchanov, P., et al.: Do gradient inversion attacks make federated learning unsafe? IEEE Trans. Med. Imaging **42**, 2044–2056 (2023)

12. Tolpegin, V., Truex, S., Gursoy, M.E., Liu, L.: Data poisoning attacks against federated learning systems. In: Chen, L., Li, N., Liang, K., Schneider, S. (eds.) ESORICS 2020. LNCS, vol. 12308, pp. 480–501. Springer, Cham (2020). https://doi.org/10.1007/978-3-030-58951-6_24
13. Shejwalkar, V., Houmansadr, A., Kairouz, P., et al.: Back to the drawing board: a critical evaluation of poisoning attacks on production federated learning. In: 2022 IEEE Symposium on Security and Privacy (SP), pp. 1354–1371. IEEE (2022)
14. Bagdasaryan, E., Veit, A., Hua, Y., et al.: How to backdoor federated learning. In: International Conference on Artificial Intelligence and Statistics, pp. 2938–2948. PMLR (2020)
15. Bhagoji, A.N., Chakraborty, S., Mittal, P., et al.: Analyzing federated learning through an adversarial lens. In: International Conference on Machine Learning, pp. 634–643. PMLR (2019)
16. Suciu, O., Marginean, R., Kaya, Y., et al.: When does machine learning FAIL? Generalized transferability for evasion and poisoning attacks. In: 27th USENIX Security Symposium (USENIX Security 18), pp. 1299–1316 (2018)
17. Mao, Y., Yuan, X., Zhao, X.: ROMOA: robust model aggregation for the resistance of federated learning to model poisoning attacks. In: Computer Security-ESORICS, et al.: 26th European Symposium on Research in Computer Security, Darmstadt, Germany, 4–8 October 2021, Proceedings, Part I 26, pp. 476–496. Springer International Publishing 2021 (2021). https://doi.org/10.1007/978-3-030-88418-5_23
18. Fang, M., Cao, X., Jia, J., et al.: Local model poisoning attacks to Byzantine-Robust federated learning. In: 29th USENIX security symposium (USENIX Security 20), pp. 1605–1622 (2020)
19. Wang, N., Xiao, Y., Chen, Y., et al.: FLARE: defending federated learning against model poisoning attacks via latent space representations. In: Proceedings of the ACM on Asia Conference on Computer and Communications Security, vol. 2022, pp. 946–958 (2022)
20. Shejwalkar, V., Houmansadr, A.: Manipulating the byzantine: optimizing model poisoning attacks and defenses for federated learning. In: NDSS (2021)
21. Chen, J., Zhang, X., Zhang, R., et al.: De-Pois: an attack-agnostic defense against data poisoning attacks. IEEE Trans. Inf. Forensics Secur. **16**, 3412–3425 (2021)
22. Jia, J., Cao, X., Gong, N.Z.: Intrinsic certified robustness of bagging against data poisoning attacks. In: Proceedings of the AAAI Conference on Artificial Intelligence, vol. 35, no. 9, pp. 7961–7969 (2021)
23. Wei, X., Li, Y., Li, Y., et al.: Detection of false data injection attacks in smart grid: a secure federated deep learning approach. IEEE Trans. Smart Grid **13**(6), 4862–4872 (2022)
24. Jiang, Y., Zhang, W., Chen, Y.: Data quality detection mechanism against label flipping attacks in federated learning. IEEE Trans. Inf. Forensics Secur. **18**, 1625–1637 (2023)
25. Awan, S., Luo, B., Li, F.: CONTRA: defending against poisoning attacks in federated learning. In: Bertino, E., Shulman, H., Waidner, M. (eds.) ESORICS 2021. LNCS, vol. 12972, pp. 455–475. Springer, Cham (2021). https://doi.org/10.1007/978-3-030-88418-5_22
26. Geiping, J., Bauermeister, H., Dröge H, et al.: Inverting gradients-how easy is it to break privacy in federated learning?. In: Advances in Neural Information Processing Systems, vol. 33, pp. 16937–16947 (2020)
27. Duan, M., Liu, D., Chen, X., et al.: Self-balancing federated learning with global imbalanced data in mobile systems. IEEE Trans. Parallel Distrib. Syst. **32**(1), 59–71 (2020)

28. Gupta, P., Yadav, K., Gupta, B.B., et al.: A novel data poisoning attack in federated learning based on inverted loss function. Comput. Secur. **130**, 103270 (2023)
29. Xiao, X., Tang, Z., Li, C., et al.: SCA: sybil-based collusion attacks of IIoT data poisoning in federated learning. IEEE Trans. Industr. Inf. **19**(3), 2608–2618 (2022)
30. Steinhardt, J., Koh, P.W.W., Liang, P.S.: Certified defenses for data poisoning attacks. In: Advances in Neural Information Processing Systems, vol. 30 (2017)
31. Shen, S., Tople, S., Saxena, P.: AUROR: defending against poisoning attacks in collaborative deep learning systems. in: Proceedings of the 32nd Annual Conference on Computer Security Applications, pp. 508–519 (2016)
32. Jagielski, M., Oprea, A., Biggio, B., et al.: Manipulating machine learning: poisoning attacks and countermeasures for regression learning. In: 2018 IEEE Symposium on Security and Privacy (SP), pp. 19–35. IEEE (2018)
33. Yin, D., Chen, Y., Kannan, R., et al.: Byzantine-robust distributed learning: towards optimal statistical rates. In: International Conference on Machine Learning, pp. 5650–5659. PMLR (2018)
34. Xie, C., Koyejo, O., Gupta, I.: Generalized byzantine-tolerant SGD. arXiv preprint arXiv:1802.10116 (2018)
35. Zhu, H., Li, Z., Cheah, M., et al.: Privacy-preserving weighted federated learning within oracle-aided MPC framework. arXiv preprint arXiv:2003.07630 (2020)
36. Truex, S., Baracaldo, N., Anwar, A., et al.: A hybrid approach to privacy-preserving federated learning. In: Proceedings of the 12th ACM Workshop on Artificial Intelligence and Security, pp. 1–11 (2019)
37. Hu, R., Guo, Y., Li, H., et al.: Personalized federated learning with differential privacy. IEEE Internet Things J. **7**(10), 9530–9539 (2020)
38. Guo, S., Wang, X., Long, S., et al.: A federated learning scheme meets dynamic differential privacy. CAAI Trans. Intell. Technol. **8**, 1087–1100 (2023)
39. Li, Q., Wen, Z., He, B.: Practical federated gradient boosting decision trees. In: Proceedings of the AAAI Conference on Artificial Intelligence, vol. 34, no. 04, pp. 4642–4649 (2020)
40. Seif, M., Tandon, R., Li, M.: Wireless federated learning with local differential privacy. In: 2020 IEEE International Symposium on Information Theory (ISIT), pp. 2604–2609. IEEE (2020)
41. Yang, L., Zhang, J., Chai, D., et al.: Practical and secure federated recommendation with personalized mask. In: International Workshop on Trustworthy Federated Learning, pp. 33–45. Springer International Publishing, Cham (2022). https://doi. org/10.1007/978-3-031-28996-5_3
42. Tenison, I., Sreeramadas, S.A., Mugunthan, V., et al.: Gradient masked averaging for federated learning. arXiv preprint arXiv:2201.11986, 2022
43. Mukherjee, P., Wichs, D.: Two round multiparty computation via multikey FHE. In: Advances in Cryptology-Eurocrypt 2016: 35th Annual International Conference on the Theory and Applications of Cryptographic Techniques, Vienna, Austria, 8-12 May 2016, pp. 735–763 (2016)
44. Krizhevsky, A., Hinton, G.: Learning multiple layers of features from tiny images (2009)
45. LeCun, Y., Bottou, L., Bengio, Y., et al.: Gradient-based learning applied to document recognition. Proc. IEEE **86**(11), 2278–2324 (1998)

A Privacy-Preserving and Fault-Tolerant Data Aggregation Scheme in Smart Grids

Yongkang Zhu, Yuanjian Zhou$^{(\boxtimes)}$, Zhengjun Jing, Quanyu Zhao, and Tianci Zhao

Jiangsu University of Technology, Changzhou, Jiangsu, China
zhouyuanjian2017@gmail.com, jzjing@jsut.edu.cn

Abstract. In the smart grids, the power supplier achieves power distribution and price regulation by the real-time data aggregation of meters' readings in each region. However, electricity readings of users usually contain sensitive information, such as living habits and lifestyles, which can leak of identity privacy of users. To address this problem, a privacy-preserving data aggregation scheme based on the additive homomorphism of shamir secret sharing was proposed which users only need to send the shares of secret data to the aggregator to complete the data aggregation operation. Meanwhile, our scheme can effectively resist collusion and man-in-the-middle attacks from external adversaries by adding random numbers to the data and binding with users' hash signatures. The whole process does not require the participation of a trusted authority. In addition, our scheme is fault-tolerant to a certain extent and dynamic: the aggregation operation can still be completed robustly in the case of network or part of aggregators failure, and the meters can free to leave or join the system. The security analysis demonstrates that the proposed scheme satisfies the security requirements of smart grids. Performance experiments indicate superior computational and communication efficiency compared to existing schemes.

Keywords: Data aggregation · Smart grids · Privacy · Fault-tolerant · Secret sharing

1 Introduction

The traditional power systems workflow generally includes generation, transmission, distribution to power users. Electricity supplied by power plants is usually of ultra-high voltage, which is converted from high voltage to low voltage through a low voltage distribution equipment before it can be supplied to power users. However, the lack of information flow between the various parts of the traditional power system results in high deployment costs of power equipment. Once equipment fails, extensive troubleshooting is required, which increases the maintenance cost. Therefore, in the past decade, many countries are increasing their efforts to develop the next generation of power grids, known as smart grids.

W. Li et al. (Eds.): EISA 2024, CCIS 2266, pp. 37–53, 2025.
https://doi.org/10.1007/978-3-031-80419-9_3

Smart grids, as a new generation grids, provides technical support for information interaction among users and power companies. Users record electricity consumption data in real time through smart meters and send it to power supplier. This power supplier adjusts the distribution strategy and electricity price according to the user's electricity consumption. However, the large-scale deployment of smart meters generates a huge amount of electricity consumption data, which not only brings a huge computational cost and storage burden to the smart grids. Meanwhile, it also brings security problems [1] to the information interaction among users and power supplier, such as the leakage of user privacy, loss or tampering of power consumption data.

Data aggregation is a good choice to solve the privacy leakage of smart grids [2–5]. In [2,3], they use the homomorphic encryption techniques to encrypt users' data so that the semi-trust aggregator (e.g., the GW) can aggregate all users' data without decryption. However, these schemes only consider the protection of users privacy data on GW side, and ignore the protection of power control center(CC). CC is responsible for maintaining the normal operation of the power grid and the management of users, and has high authority. Attacker may attacks CC to obtain user electricity consumption data. To prevent CC from leaking user private data, [4,5] use a clever key management approach, where the sum of all keys is zero, to decentralize the permissions of CC and enhance the security of the data aggregation scheme. However, these works are not fault-tolerant ability, meaning that once a user fails to report, the entire data aggregation system won't function fully. Meanwhile, the SM is a consumable device, which is easily worn out in an unprotected environment. Therefore, data aggregation schemes in smart grids need to be fault-tolerant.

Therefore, fault tolerance is an important requirement for data aggregation. If SM fails, the data cannot be uploaded, but the correct aggregation results can be obtained. To achieve the fault tolerance, Chen et al. [6] proposed a key establishment scheme based on dynamic member groups, if there is a damaged meter in a group, only this group is affected and other groups are normal. This scheme reduces the impact of faulty meters on aggregated data, but some data from working meters cannot be collected. In [1], a fault-tolerant multisubset aggregation scheme is proposed that that does not rely on a trusted authority (TA) and enables the retrieval of user counts and total electricity consumption per region. In [7], the shamir threshold secret sharing algorithm is employed to implement fault tolerance from the SM to the corresponding fog node. By increasing the random masking value, it ensures that the content of any single report remains unintelligible to potential attackers. However, if an SM fails, all meters except the faulty one must re-upload the ciphertext, leading to significant computation and communication costs.

In addition, privacy-preserving data aggregation that use traditional encryption technologies usually require the assistance of TA. However, in the real world, it is difficult for us to find an institution that can truly maintain trusted long time. Therefore, the industry urgently needs a data aggregation scheme that does not require a credible third party to participate in the entire process. Hence, there have been attempts to design schemes without relying on any TA. In [8], an efficient data aggregation scheme with local differential privacy is proposed. However, it cannot resolve the fault tolerance issues. In [9], He et al. proposed a privacy-preserving multifunction data aggregation scheme. This scheme does not rely on TA and uses shamir threshold secret sharing algorithm to allow SM to negotiate aggregation parameters. In 2019, for example, Xue et al. [10] proposed a privacy-preserving service outsourcing (PPSO) scheme for real-time pricing demand response in the smart grids. PPSO is designed to achieve fault tolerance and facilitate flexible customers' enrollment and revocation. However, it cannot resist attacks from the power supplier (i.e., insider attacks). Such attacks can have serious consequences for the scheme and is more difficult to detect than those external attacks. Therefore, we believe the important of designing aggregation schemes to resist internal attacks.

In summary, a novel privacy-preserving and fault-tolerant data aggregation scheme in smart grids is proposed. The contributions of this work are summarized as follows.

1. Our scheme obtains and publishes aggregate data through random number and shamir threshold secret sharing algorithm, while protecting the privacy and integrity of individual users.
2. Our use a threshold algorithm to ensure the accuracy of the aggregation results even if any number of SM fail to upload data.
3. The security and efficacy of our scheme are proved through the probability of data aggregation, failure in the system, as well as the communication overhead and computational complexity.

The rest of this paper is organized as follows: Section 2 introduces related works. Section 3 is a preliminary section. The system and adversary model, and security goals are described in Sect. 4. Section 5 presents the proposed scheme. Section 6 provides security analysis. In Sect. 7, we calculate the communication overhead and computational complexity of the scheme and performance comparisons. Finally, a conclusion be given in Sect. 8.

2   Related Works

Data aggregation is a process of information mining. Lots of valuable results may be obtained by manually or digitally analyzing the collected data. In recent years, many data aggregation schemes have been proposed and have been applied in many fields (e.g. smart grids systems [2, 11–24], wireless sensor networks and vanets). In the smart grids scenario, some schemes ensure user privacy in the aggregation process by encrypting data using traditional encryption algorithms. For example, scheme [12] uses elliptic curve based elgamal cryptosystem (ECC) to resist internal attackers. Scheme [13] proposes an aggregation framework based on elliptic encryption to protect the user's meter data from sophisticated attacks. Scheme [14] combines the Chinese Remainder theorem (CRT) with modified homomorphic encryption, which not only protects the privacy of sensitive data, but also provides usable statistical information for the power provider. These schemes require the participation of trusted authorities (TA) in the aggregation process. However, it is not easy to find a trusted authority in the real world.

With the help of multi-party secure computing (MPC), we realize that there is no need for a trusted third party to participate in the process of data aggregation. On the other hand, there are many schemes [15–17,25] for applying homomorphic encryption (HE) algorithms to data aggregation in smart grids, but the high computational complexity of homomorphic encryption is always a difficult problem to solve. The secret sharing (SS) is also a way to achieve the above goals [19–21]. Due to its own characteristics, it can also bring a certain degree of fault tolerance, but at the same time it needs to pay high communication overhead. In addition to protecting the user data itself, we can also protect user's privacy by masking the real identity. In [22], K. Alharbi and X. Lin used authentication to ensure that only legitimate users can access the data. The control of user access authority can also be achieved by adding an access control [15] or tree-structured [23] to the system.

Besides privacy protection, the fault tolerance and dynamics of the scheme in smart grids are also our considerations. Currently, many fault-tolerant schemes are implemented through secret sharing. For example, A. Hmk et al. in [17] are realized it by using buffers to store the metering data before aggregation. Z. Guan et al. [20] let TA contact to check the status of failed SM if there are failed meters. In addition to dealing with the failure of SM, we also need to consider the absence of meters or the addition of new ones during the aggregation process. For such problems, F. Li et al. [16] present a distributed incremental data aggregation approach, in which the aggregation is performed in a distributed manner in accordance to the aggregation tree.

3 Preliminaries

In this section, we will introduce the preliminary about secret sharing.

3.1 Shamir Threshold Secret Sharing Scheme

The secret sharing scheme was first proposed by Shamir [26] and Blakley [27] respectively in 1979. In simple terms. Secret sharing is to enable the shared secrets to be reasonably distributed in a user group, so as to achieve the purpose of all members in charge of the secrets. In shamir solution, only a specified number of secret shard holders can recover the original secret through calculations.

Suppose n is the number of sharers, t is the threshold value, and p is a large prime number. $p > n$ is required and p is greater than the maximum possible value of the secret s; secret space and share space are the same, they are both Galois field $GF(p)$.

Allocation Algorithm. Secret distributor D allocates shares to n sharers $P_i(1 \leq i \leq n)$ as follows:

- D randomly selects a $(t-1)$-order polynomial

$$f_t(s, x) = s + a_1 x + a_2 x^2 + ... + a_{t-1} x^{t-1} \in Z_p[x] \tag{1}$$

on $GF(p)$, making $f_t(s, 0) = s$ is the secret to be shared among the sharers. D keeps $f_t(s, x)$ secret;
- D selects n non-zero and distinct elements $x_1, x_2, ..., x_n$ in Z_p and calculates

$$y_i = f_t(s, x_i), 1 \leq i \leq n ; \tag{2}$$

- D distributes $(x_i, y_i)(1 \leq i \leq n)$ to the sharer P_i, the value x_i is known publicly, and y_i is the secret share of P_i.

Since t number pairs can uniquely determine $(t-1)$-order polynomial $f_t(s, x)$, s can be reconstructed from t shares. However, $f_t(s, x)$ cannot be determined from $t'(t' < t)$ shares, so s cannot be obtained.

Recovery Algorithm. Given any t points $(x_1, y_1), (x_2, y_2), ..., (x_t, y_t)$, $f_t(s, x)$ can be reconstructed by lagrange interpolation:

$$f_t(s, x) = \sum_{i=1}^{t} (y_i \cdot \prod_{j=1, j \neq i}^{t} \frac{x - x_j}{x_i - x_j}) \, (mod \; p), \tag{3}$$

which is calculated on Z_p. Once $f_t(s, x)$ is obtained, the secret s can be easily carried out by $s = f_t(s, 0)$.

The shamir threshold scheme has the following characteristics: (i) a new sharer can be added while the original sharers' secret shares remain unchanged; (ii) it has additive homomorphism: the share of the sum of two secrets $s_i + s_j$ is equal to the sum of their shares; (iii) it is unconditionally secure, i.e., their security does not depend on the computational complexity of a hard problem: rather, their security is [28] guaranteed by information theory.

3.2 Notations

The parameters and notations are described in Table 1.

Table 1. Notations

Symbols	Definition
CC	Control Center
TA	Trusted Authority
PS	Power supplier
BS	Base station
TPA	Third-party aggregator
HAN	Home area network
SM	Smart meter
d_i	SM$_i$'s electricity reading
rd	Number of rounds of aggregation
RO	Random oracle
ID_{SM_i}	Identity of smart meter SM$_i$
H, h	Hash function, such as SHA-1

4   System And Adversary Model And Security Goals

4.1   System Model

The system model of the smart grids considered in the paper is a three-tier architecture, as shown in Fig. 1, which includes six entities: a power supplier (PS), a list of base stations (BS), several sets of smart meters (SM), some third-party aggregators (TPA), a Control Center (CC), and a Trusted Authority (TA).

PS: The PS will transmit electricity to the BS within its scope of responsibility through high-voltage wires.

BS: Then, each BS will distribute electricity to groups of numerous home area network (HAN) in a geographical region after the transformation.

SM: Within the coverage of a HAN, a SM and a series of household appliances are connected. In order to obtain the sum of the SM readings of all HAN in the jurisdiction, each BS will employ TPA for data aggregation. The SM sends its periodic electricity readings to the TPA through an in-building network (e.g. WiFi) [29].

TPA: The TPA communicate with the BS through the public Internet.

CC: The PS and BS are managed and regulated by CC to maintain correct operation of the system and reasonable distribution of electricity.

TA: In addition to the above entities in the system, in order to achieve secure data aggregation, the participation of TA is also required. Its role is to generate random numbers used in the aggregation process.

4.2   Adversary Model

In our adversarial model, the TA and CC are honest and reliable, PS is also considered credible, in fact it is usually completely owned and controlled by government agencies. On the other hand, TPA is leased by BS from private companies for data collection, they are interested in exploring the electricity readings of each HAN and selling them to other companies. BS is usually managed by local state-owned enterprises, their internal employees may try to illegally obtain the aggregation results of local HAN data, so there is also the risk of leaking user privacy. Similar to the BS and TPA, SM is also honest-but-curious parties in our adversary model. They will strictly enforce the protocol, but they are not completely trustworthy: they may try to access other SM readings for their own purposes. In addition, we also consider the sudden offline or damage of the SM and TPA, which is a manifestation of their unreliability. Besides, we assume that HAN is not a secure channel, so there may be external attackers in HAN, who may impersonate a legitimate SM to send false data. Moreover, they may intercept the electricity consumption data sent by a SM and even try to modify and then re-transmit it, eventually leading to incorrect aggregation results.

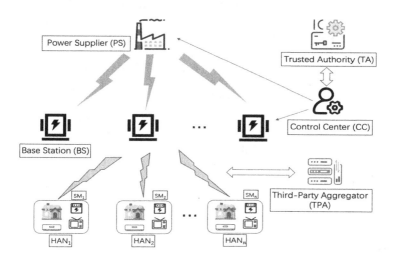

Fig. 1. The System Frame

4.3   Security Goals

For the above adversary model, this paper will achieve the following security goals in the schemes.

- **Confidentiality**
  In the whole process of transmission and aggregation, the user's data should be in a certain ciphertext state, so that other SM, TPA, BS and external attackers cannot get its any plaintext information, thus protecting the user's privacy.
- **Integrity**
  In the process of end-to-end communication, the receiver should verify the

consistency of the received data, and confirm that the received data is not forged or modified halfway. Similarly, in the data aggregation process of the TPA, it should be able to detect whether the information has been changed.

- **Fault-tolerant**
  Once an SM goes offline or fails, it cannot provide its own electricity reading data to TPA or other SM. In this case, the scheme of fault-tolerant data aggregation can still be implemented, the aggregation result of other SM data is still available, and even the SM that do not send data can be located by TPA for subsequent retransmission.

5   DATA Aggregation Schemes Based on SS

This section introduces a data aggregation scheme with fault tolerant. This execution process consists of four phases: system initialization, data distribution, data aggregation, data update. In this protocol scheme, we propose to employ shamir technique and take advantage of its additive homomorphic property separately in each BS [28]. This scheme consists of three phases: during the first phase, named Initialization Phase (IP), the random numbers are distributed to all SM by TA; during the second phase, called Distribution Phase (DP), the data shares of all SM managed by a BS are sent to the TPA; during the third phase, named Aggregation Phase (AP), TPA calculates the sum of all secret fragments, CC finally recover the sum of all data through shamir threshold secret sharing scheme without privacy leakage; in the last phase, Update Phase (UP), every SM will update its random number.

Without losing generality, we assume that there is a PS responsible for supplying electricity to z BS, in which there are n SM (or HAN) in the jurisdiction of the th base station BS_t. These BS are responsible for providing power to a total of N SM and the BS_t employs m TPA for data aggregation.

5.1   System Initialization

Firstly, All SM within each BS jurisdiction will register information in all TPA. In other words, TA will send $(i, h(ID_{SM_i}))$, which is the hash value of SM_i's real-world identity to the corresponding TPA.

Then, CC will choose a secret number R_{CC} and TA will generates z random numbers R_i, which satisfy

$$R_{CC} = \sum_{i=1}^{z} R_i \,, \tag{4}$$

And each R will be further divided into n random numbers, n is the number of SM managed by each BS. For example, R_t will be split as follows:

$$R_t = \sum_{i=1}^{n} r_{ti} \,, t = 1, 2, ..., z \,. \tag{5}$$

After that, TA will distribute each r to CC and to the corresponding SM. After TA completes the distribution of random numbers, it will be offline, and it is not required to participate in the subsequent process.

5.2   Distribution Phase

Next, each SM controlled by the BS will send the secret share generated by the sum of its own electricity reading d and random number to the corresponding TPA employed by the BS. SM will attach with the hash value of their own identity information and round number when sending shares, so that TPA can verify to avoid the data is forged or tampered. Specifically, for the SM_i within the jurisdiction of BS_t, detail the operations it performs in the following:

- SM_i makes m shares of its secret data $s_i = d_i + r_{ti}$ following shamir (k, m)-threshold scheme, using the indexs of the TPA employed by BS_t, i.e., $j = 1, 2, ..., m$, as seeds;
- it sends share $[i, rd, sh_j(s_i), H(h(ID_{SM_i})\|i\|rd\|sh_j(s_i))]$ to TPA_j, where $sh_j(s_i) = f_k(s_i, j) \bmod q$, $\forall j, j = 1, 2, ..., m$, and rd is the current number of rounds.
- after TPA_j receives the data, it will use the local rd, $h(ID_{SM_i})$ corresponding to SM_i's identity and H functions to authenticate $sh_j(s_i)$. If the result is correct, the share will be saved, otherwise it will be discarded.

It is worth noting that the maximum power number of the polynomial of the threshold scheme used by each SM is the same, which is $k - 1$, but their coefficients are all different and are kept secret from other SM. And for the sake of safety, the function should be changed for different aggregation rounds. For other BS, their managed SM send their data shares to the corresponding TPA in the same way. The whole procedure is graphically summarized in Fig. 2.

5.3   Aggregation Phase

After the DP completes, the AP begins. At this point, When TPA receive the secret share message, it will verify the hash signature information in the message. If the verification is passed, the TPA will keep the message, otherwise it will be discarded. If everything goes well, each TPA employed by the BS_t gets a data set composed of the received shares. Among them, TPA_j has: $\{sh_j(s_1), sh_j(s_2), ..., sh_j(s_i), ..., sh_j(s_n)\}$. Once TPA_j has received n shares from SM within its jurisdiction, it sums them up.

$$Sh_j = \sum_{i=1}^{n} sh_j(s_i) , \tag{6}$$

Owing to the homomorphic property, is a share of the sum of the SM data and R_t. Similarly, every TPA employed by the BS_t begins to aggregate the received data and determines a different share.

After a TPA, such as TPA_j, employed by the BS_t have completed the summation of the shares it received, it sends its contribution, (j, Sh_j), to the CC, and so do other aggregators. This phase goes on until k shares of sum are collected. In this process, if a TPA does not get the sum value due to it has not

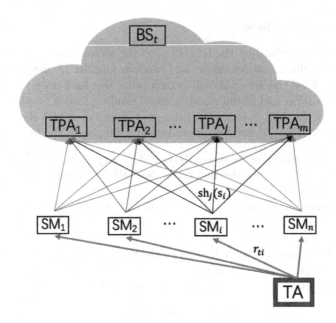

Fig. 2. The DP of our scheme

received all the shares or some received data is wrong, it will not send the sum. When CC collect k shares, through lagrange interpolation, it can recover

$$Sum_{BS_t} = R_t + \sum_{i=1}^{n} d_i \, , \tag{7}$$

which is the sum of R_t and the readings of SM within the BS_t's jurisdiction by interpolation according to (k, m)-threshold scheme. Other BS and their respective TPA perform similar aggregation operations, and eventually CC will get z sums. Then CC will add these sums up, and the secret number will be eliminated by subtracting R_{CC} in the process. Finally, PS will get the sum of electricity readings of all the SM in its jurisdiction.

$$Sum = \sum_{i=1}^{z} Sum_{BS_i} - R_{CC} = \sum_{i=1}^{N} d_i \, , \tag{8}$$

The whole process of this phase is shown in Fig. 3.

5.4   Update Phase

After a round of data aggregation, each meter increases the round number rd by one. To prevent the differential cryptanalysis attacks, we need to update the random number after each round of aggregation. For each SM, it iteratively

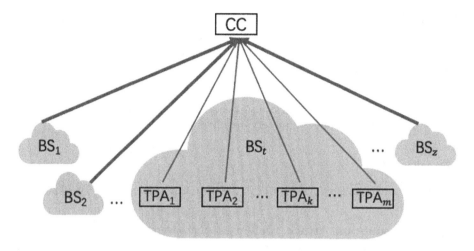

Fig. 3. The AP of our scheme

updates its own random number r to $RO(r)$. Correspondingly, CC will also renew its secret number:

$$R_{CC} = \sum_{j=1}^{z}(\sum_{i=1}^{n'} RO(r_{ji}))\,, \tag{9}$$

where n' represents the total number of smart meters per BS.

6   Security Analysis

In this section, we will theoretically analyze the privacy of the scheme. Considering the instability of network and (or) SM, we also evaluate the robustness and fault tolerance of the scheme.

6.1   Confidentiality

The confidentiality of our scheme is based on the privacy preserving property of Secret Sharing and random number. In the whole process of data aggregation, except PS, all parties in the system will not get any information about the electricity reading of users.

SM. In the DP, each SM is responsible for distributing the shares the sum of its own data and received random numbers to the corresponding TPA through the threshold scheme. Because the random number of SM is private, even if other SM or external adversaries obtain k shares, they cannot recover the electricity reading through the threshold scheme.

TPA. In the AP, after the summation, each TPA gets the sum of the electricity readings of all meters in the region and a random number. If there are more than k TPA launching conspiracy attacks, they still cannot get the sum of readings due to the existence of the random number.

BS. The data transmitted by BS also contains random numbers, so BS can't get any information about the meters' readings too.

6.2 Integrity

The integrity of data is realized by TPA verifying the hash value of SM identities.

Anti Impersonation Attack. Only when the adversary obtains the identity information ID_{SM} of the SM that it intends to disguise, the round number rd, the hash functions h and H can make the data sent by he pass the verification of the TPA. The adversary also needs to know the threshold scheme function's maximum power number used by the SM for data sharing, otherwise the recovery process cannot be performed correctly in the AP, so as to avoid the aggregation result using the adversary's disguised data. Therefore, it is very difficult for the adversary to successfully disguise as a legal SM and apply illegal data into the final result.

Anti Man-in-the-Middle Attack. When the adversary intercepts a share of data sent by a SM, if he modifies the share, he must generate the corresponding hash value for it, otherwise it cannot pass the verification of TPA. In addition, he needs to know exactly what function is used by the SM to generate this share, otherwise the CC cannot recover the data properly. In fact, even if the adversary has the ability to generate the correct hash value for the modified share and pass the verification of TPA, if the share is selected as one of the k thresholds parameters in the AP, it will lead to incorrect recovery and avoid the generation of error results; if the fragment is not used for data recovery, it will not have any impact on carrying out the correct results.

6.3 Anti Collusion Attack

The shamir secret sharing scheme itself cannot resist the collusion attacks initiated by more than k participants. Our scheme realizes the resistance to collusion attacks by adding random numbers.

6.4 Fault-Tolerant

Thanks to the characteristics of the threshold scheme, we can still recover the data in the absence of partial data segmentation. As a matter of fact, during the scheme execution, it might happen that the contribution of a SM's share cannot be received by TPA because: (i) TPA or SM may be offline for network reasons or down due hardware fails; (ii) the communication between SM and TPA is faulty due to network reasons.

Next, we will analyze the probability that BS cannot aggregate data successfully. Let us indicate by $P_{fail-DP}$ the probability that the DP fails and similarly by $P_{fail-AP}$ the probability that the AP fails. Assuming that the two stages are independent of each other, the probability of BS aggregation failure can be expressed as [28]:

$$P_{fail-BS} = P_{fail-DP} + (1 - P_{fail-DP}) \cdot P_{fail-AP} . \tag{10}$$

Obviously, the meaning of $P_{fail-DP}$ is as follows:

$$P_{fail-DP} = 1 - Pr(\text{at least } k \text{ TPA employed by the} \atop \text{BS receive the shares from all SM}) . \tag{11}$$

For BS_t, it can be further expressed as:

$$P_{fail-DP} = 1 - \sum_{i=k}^{m} \binom{m}{i}(1 - p_1)^{n \cdot i}(1 - (1 - p_1)^n)^{m-i} , \tag{12}$$

where p_1 is the probability that SM does not send share normally. Whereas for the AP, $P_{fail-AP}$ is provided by

$$P_{fail-AP} = \sum_{i=m-(k-1)}^{m} \binom{m}{i}p_2^i(1 - p_2)^{m-i} , \tag{13}$$

where p_2 is the probability that the collection of shares of a TPA employed by the BS_t does not succeed.

6.5 Dynamism of the Scheme

Our scheme can keep the availability and security of the system without reallocating random numbers for other SM when one or several SM leaves or new SM joins. We achieve this by updating the secret number R_{CC} in CC.

When a certain SM leaves, such as SM_i in the BS_t's jurisdiction, TA will go online and update R_{CC} to $R_{CC} - r_{ti}$. After the operation process at the end of AP through $Sum = Sum - R_{CC}$, the correct result can be obtained. When a new SM is added to the system, TA will register its identity information at the corresponding TPA and generate a random number r_{add} and for it and the update R_{CC} to $R_{CC} + r_{add}$.

7 Communication Cost and Complexity

In this section, communication cost and computational complexity of our scheme will be theoretically analyzed. For the sake of clarity, we assume that each of the z BS in the system is responsible for supplying power to n SM, and each BS employs m TPA for data aggregation.

7.1   Communication Cost

We measure the Communication cost by the number of connections required for all parties in the system in the DP and AP. Regarding the communication cost of the (k, m)-threshold scheme, the DP needs nm connections to distribute the shares to TPA. During the AP, if all goes well, it will take at least $k - 1$ connections to collect the shares of the sum among TPA. The communication cost of our scheme, C is therefore

$$C = z(nm + k) . \tag{14}$$

In addition, it is easy to know that in the initialization phase, the number of communications required is $zn + 1$, i.e. $N + 1$. Figure 4 shows the communication overhead of our scheme and different schemes in [28] with $z = 10$, $m = 20$ and $n = 50$ under different threshold k. The comparison results confirm that our scheme has lower communication overhead.

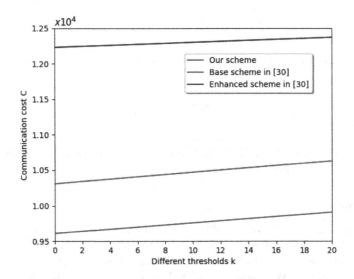

Fig. 4. Communication cost

7.2   Computational Complexity

As regards computational complexity of the system, during the DP, each SM adds its own reading and the random number up, and then obtains m secret shares through the threshold scheme. These operations are briefly recalled below, along with their contribution to complexity:

- the complexity of the summation of reading and the random number is $O(1)$;
- evaluate a $(k-1)$-order polynomial for an integer value, so as to generate one share of the secret. The complexity is $O(k-1)$;
- repeat the previous operation m times;

Table 2. Aggregation Cost

Scheme	Number of SM	Aggregation Time(ms)
[25]	100	3080
	300	9863
	600	18970
[20]	100	256
	300	795
	600	1402
Our Scheme	100	37
	300	76
	600	151

Therefore, for each SM, the computational complexity can be estimated as $O(mk)$, so that the complexity of the entire DP within the BS_t is $O(nmk)$. During the following AP, TPA will sum the received shares up, the computational complexity of this step is constant. Then, CC will recover the sum by computing one polynomial over $k-1$ points, whose complexity is $O(k)$, which is negligible with the complexity of SM in the DP. Since the above operations have to be repeated for each BS in the system, the overall computational complexity of our scheme becomes $O(znmk)$, that is $O(Nmk)$. Table 2 shows the variation in the aggregation time for different numbers of SM in the [20, 25] and our scheme. As can be seen from the table, the aggregation time of our scheme is lower when the number of SM is the same.

8   Conclusion

In this article, we proposed a privacy-protected and fault-tolerant data aggregation scheme in the smart grids scenario which can carry out the data aggregation without leaking the original readings of smart meters. Because the scheme is based on a threshold scheme, it has high robustness, that is, it can still complete the aggregation under some power equipment is broken down. The theoretical analysis shows that our scheme has high security and the efficiency of our scheme is greatly improved.

Acknowledgment. This work was supported by the Natural Science Foundation of the Jiangsu Higher Education Institutions of China(Grant No. 21KJB120001, 24KJB520008). Yuanjian Zhou, Zhengjun Jing and Quanyu Zhao are the corresponding authors.

References

1. Wang, X., Liu, Y., Choo, K.-K.R.: Fault-tolerant multisubset aggregation scheme for smart grid. IEEE Trans. Industr. Inf. **17**(6), 4065–4072 (2020)
2. Chen, L., Lu, R., Cao, Z.: PDAFT: a privacy-preserving data aggregation scheme with fault tolerance for smart grid communications. Peer-to-Peer Netw. Appl. **8**, 1122–1132 (2015)
3. Jia, W., Zhu, H., Cao, Z., et al.: Human-factor-aware privacy-preserving aggregation in smart grid. IEEE Syst. J. **8**(2), 598–607 (2013)
4. Garcia, F.D., Jacobs, B.: Privacy-friendly energy-metering via homomorphic encryption. In: Cuellar, J., Lopez, J., Barthe, G., Pretschner, A. (eds.) STM 2010. LNCS, vol. 6710, pp. 226–238. Springer, Heidelberg (2011). https://doi.org/10.1007/978-3-642-22444-7_15
5. Shi, E., Chan, H.T.H., Rieffel, E., et al.: Privacy-preserving aggregation of time-series data. In: Annual Network & Distributed System Security Symposium (NDSS), Internet Society (2011)
6. Chen, Y., et al.: A dynamic membership group-based multiple-data aggregation scheme for smart grid. IEEE Internet Things J. **8**(15), 12360–12374 (2021)
7. Zhang, X., et al.: Lightweight multidimensional encrypted data aggregation scheme with fault tolerance for fog-assisted smart grids. IEEE Syst. J. **16**(4), 6647–6657 (2022)
8. Gai, N., et al.: An efficient data aggregation scheme with local differential privacy in smart grid. Digital Commun. Netw. **8**(3), 333–342 (2022)
9. He, D., et al.: Efficient and privacy-preserving data aggregation scheme for smart grid against internal adversaries. IEEE Trans. Smart Grid **8**(5), 2411–2419 (2017)
10. Xue, K., et al.: PPSO: a privacy-preserving service outsourcing scheme for real-time pricing demand response in smart grid. IEEE Internet Things J. **6**(2), 2486–2496 (2018)
11. Okay, F.Y., Ozdemir, S.: A secure data aggregation protocol for fog computing based smart grids. In: 2018 IEEE 12th International Conference on Compatibility, Power Electronics and Power Engineering (CPE-POWERENG) (2018)
12. Vahedi, E., BaYat, M., Pakravan, M.R., Aref, M.R.: A secure ECC-based privacy preserving data aggregation scheme for smart grids. Comput. Netw. **129**(dec.24), 28–36 (2017)
13. Dong, X., Zhou, J., Alharbi, K., Lin, X., Cao, Z.: An ELGamal-based efficient and privacy-preserving data aggregation scheme for smart grid. In: IEEE, pp. 4720–4725 (2014)
14. Erkin, Z.: Private data aggregation with groups for smart grids in a dynamic setting using CRT. In: IEEE International Workshop on Information Forensics & Security (2016)
15. Ruj, S., Nayak, A., Stojmenovic, I.: A security architecture for data aggregation and access control in smart grids. IEEE Trans. Smart Grid **4**(1), 196–205 (2013)
16. Li, F., Bo, L., Peng, L.: Secure information aggregation for smart grids using homomorphic encryption. In: Smart Grid Communications (SmartGridComm), 2010 First IEEE International Conference on 2020 (2010)
17. Khan, H.M., Khan, A., Jabeen, F., Rahman, A.U.: Privacy preserving data aggregation with fault tolerance in fog-enabled smart grid. Sustain. Cities Soc. **64**, 102522 (2020)
18. Kamil, I., Moyinoluwa, S.O.: EPDAS: efficient privacy-preserving data analysis scheme for smart grid network. J. King Saud Univ. Comput. Inf. Sci. (2018)

19. Xue, K., Zhu, B., Yang, Q., Wei, D., Guizani, M.: An efficient and robust data aggregation scheme without a trusted authority for smart grid. IEEE Internet Things J. 99, 1 (2019)
20. Guan, Z., Si, G., Du, X., Peng, L., Zhou, Z.: Protecting user privacy based on secret sharing with fault tolerance for big data in smart grid. In: 2017 IEEE International Conference on Communications (ICC) (2017)
21. Guan, Z., Si, G., Du, X., Peng, L.: A data aggregation scheme based on secret sharing with error tolerance in smart grid
22. Alharbi, K., Lin, X.: LPDA: a lightweight privacy-preserving data aggregation scheme for smart grid. In: International Conference on Wireless Communications & Signal Processing (2013)
23. Lu, Z., Wen, Y.: Distributed algorithm for tree-structured data aggregation service placement in smart grid. IEEE Syst. J. 8(2), 553–561 (2014)
24. Lu, R., Liang, X., Xu, L., Lin, X., Shen, X.: EPPA: an efficient and privacy-preserving aggregation scheme for secure smart grid communications. IEEE Trans. Parallel Distrib. Syst. 23(9), 1621–1631 (2012)
25. Jo, H.J., Kim, I.S., Lee, D.H.: Efficient and privacy-preserving metering protocols for smart grid systems. IEEE Trans. Smart Grid 7, 11 (2016)
26. Shamir, A.: How to share a secret. Commun. ACM 22(11), 612–613 (1979)
27. Blakley, G.R.: Safeguarding cryptographic keys. In: AFIPS (1979)
28. Merani, M.L., Croce, D., Tinnirello, I.: Rings for privacy: an architecture for large scale privacy-preserving data mining. IEEE Trans. Parallel Distrib. Syst. 32(6), 1340–1352 (2021)
29. Gope, P., Sikdar, B.: Lightweight and privacy-friendly spatial data aggregation for secure power supply and demand management in smart grids. IEEE Trans. Inf. Forensics Secur. 14(6), 1554–1566 (2019)

Local Differential Privacy for Key-Value Data Collection and Analysis Based on Privacy Preference and Adaptive Sampling

Zhengyong Zhai, Peizhong Shi[✉], Yan Zhang, Chunsheng Gu, Zhengjun Jing,
and Quanyu Zhao

Jiangsu University of Technology, Changzhou 213001, Jiangsu, China
`spz0812@jsut.edu.cn`

Abstract. As a heterogeneous type of data becomes an extremely popular NoSQL data model, more and more researchers have focused on the collection and statistical analysis of key-value data with local differential privacy (LDP). However, it is difficult to achieve a good balance between privacy and utility, because the key-value data has strong correlation between keys and values. In this paper, we study the problem of frequency and mean estimation on key-value data by proposing a user-centric key-value data collection scheme called UEKV-GRR. To address the privacy preferences of different users, a Privacy Budget-based Sampling (PBS) algorithm and Privacy Budget-based Sampling for Encoding Perturbation (PBS-E) algorithm are designed to provide personalized privacy protection based on different users' privacy preferences. By theoretically analyzing the estimation error of different sampling methods, we select sampling method adaptively. Thus, the accuracy and usability of frequency estimation and mean estimation can be improved on the server side. Experimental results show that our proposed scheme UEKV-GRR is superior to existing schemes in accuracy.

Keywords: Local Differential Privacy · Privacy Preserving · Privacy Preference · Adaptive Sampling · Key-value Data · Frequency Estimation · Mean Estimation

1 Introduction

Differential privacy is a significant privacy preservation technology proposed by Dwork et al. [1] in 2006. Generally, there are two different types of differential privacy: centralized differential privacy and local differential privacy (LDP). In the application scenario of centralized differential privacy, there is a trusted server that possesses the real data of all users. However, in practice, it is difficult to find a trusted server. As for LDP, there typically exists a group of users and an untrusted server. Therefore, in the LDP model, each user perturbs his own data locally and sends the perturbed data to the untrusted server. Currently, LDP has been widely adopted in many fields such as data mining, recommendation systems, and crowdsourced sensing systems.

In the research community of LDP, previous work focused on basic statistical analysis, such as frequency estimation for categorical data [2–5] and mean estimation for numerical data [6–8]. Later, with the development and widespread application of big data technology, research on LDP has shifted towards statistical analysis of more complex data types [9–16]. Key-value data, as the primary data type for collection and analysis in non-relational databases, has been widely used in practice due to its flexible scalability and strong association between keys and values. However, there is relatively few studies on privacy-preserving of key-value data collection and analysis based on LDP. Existing research mainly includes: (1) the methods proposed in [17] combining Harmony [18] and Duchi methods [19] called PrivKV (Private Key-Value Data Collection) and PrivKVM (Iterative PrivKV). The PrivKV and PrivKVM have deficiencies in sampling methods, leading to lower accuracy in the final frequency and mean estimation results. (2) A method proposed in [20] combines padding and sampling method [12] with the GRR (Generalized Random Response) framework [3] and Unary Encoding (UE) mechanism [5] called PCKV (Locally Differentially Private Correlated Key-Value Data Collection with Optimized Utility). However, this method does not provide clear restrictions or explanations on the padding length for user datasets. Thus, the PCKV does not adapt well to privacy protection of key-value data in various scenarios. (3) Addressing the shortcomings of the PrivKVM method, a method called KVOH (Key-Value Data Collection with One-Hot) was proposed in [21] based on the GRR framework and one-hot encoding. However, the KVOH does not consider the impact of the entire value domain of key-value data. When the domain of keys is large, the KVOH is less accurate in frequency and mean estimation. (4) A method called SKV-GRR was proposed in [22], which combines the Duchi method and the GRR framework. Compared to previously proposed methods, it has been theoretically proven and experimentally verified to have higher accuracy in frequency and mean estimation. The SKV-GRR does not consider the privacy preferences of different users [23, 31]. And sampling method of SKV-GRR is susceptible to the size of the key-value data set, leading to significant estimation errors.

Based on the synthesis of literature [17, 20–22], the following problems exist in the collection and analysis of key-value data. Firstly, when sampling key-value data from the user, it is necessary to consider the privacy preferences of different users and the influence of the key and value domain on the sampling method. Otherwise, ignoring the privacy preferences of different users may result in lower accuracy. Secondly, due to the strong correlation between keys and values, perturbation algorithms need to ensure the correlation between keys and values while perturbing key-value data, or it will reduce data availability.

In conclusion, there is currently no effective solution that simultaneously addresses the issues of user privacy preferences and sampling method errors. Therefore, we propose a scheme for collecting and analyzing key-value data based on LDP. The main contributions of this paper are as follows:

Firstly, we propose the PBS (Privacy Budget-based Sampling) and PBS-E algorithm based on users' privacy preferences. Considering the privacy preferences of different users, we propose the sampling method that compares the users' privacy preferences with the privacy budget provided by the data collector.

Secondly, we propose the UEKV-GRR (User-centric Key-Value Data Collection) based on the PBS and PBS-E. For selecting the sampling method with smaller estimation error, we analyze the errors of perturbation algorithms under different sampling mechanisms. So, in UEKV-GRR, we choose to select appropriate sampling mechanism adaptively through error comparison.

2 Related Work

In LDP protection model, users' private data will not flow out of their local devices. Therefore, LDP protection models are widely applied in various privacy protection scenarios, such as frequency and mean estimation [2, 7, 8, 23], frequent item-set mining [12, 24] and range queries [10, 25]. In addition, there are also some works focusing on complex statistical analysis, such as key-value data collection [17, 20–22], high-dimensional data publishing [26, 27] and graph publishing [28, 29], etc. The RAPPOR method embedded in the Google Chrome browser [3], combined with the W-RR method proposed by Warner [30], achieves local protection of user browsing data. However, the basic RAPPOR method is susceptible to the influence of the domain size, where a larger domain of keys and values can cause significant estimation errors and communication costs. The improved RAPPOR method [3] compresses the domain size using Bloom filter technology to enhance estimation accuracy. Meanwhile, the SHist method [10] reduces communication costs to logarithmic levels by using hash function and matrix projection techniques. Additionally, the OUE (Optimized Unary Encoding) method [5] and the OLH (Optimized Local Hashing) method [5] respectively utilize unary encoding and local hashing technique to improve estimation accuracy and avoid the influence of domain size on estimation errors. The Duchi's scheme [19] combines the W-RR method with discretization operations to achieve mean estimation under the value v ($v \in [-1, 1]$). The results of the Duchi's scheme are fixed discrete values, but the estimation results deviate from $[-1, 1]$. Addressing the shortcomings of the Duchi's scheme, some researchers proposed PM (Piecewise Mechanism) method [7]. Through this method, a value within $[-1, 1]$ will be perturbed to a continuous interval $[-C, C]$.

While numerous frequency and mean estimation methods are currently available, there is a scarcity of research focused on the collection and analysis of key-value data. In [17], they proposed the PrivKV (Private Key-Value Data Collection) and PrivKVM (Iterative PrivKV) methods, combining Harmony [18] and Duchi [19] methods. However, due to flaws in their sampling methods, the precision of the frequency and mean estimation results is low. And in [20], they proposed the PCKV (Locally Differentially Private Correlated Key-Value Data Collection with Optimized Utility) method. They combined padding and sampling methods [12], the GRR [3] and unary encoding (UE) mechanism [5]. But, this method does not provide a clear limitation or explanation for the padding length of user data sets during the padding and sampling process. Thus, the PCKV does not adapt well to privacy protection for key-value data in various scenarios. In [21], considering the shortcomings of the PrivKVM method, they proposed the KVOH (Key-Value Data Collection with One-Hot) method based on the GRR and one-hot encoding. However, they do not consider the influence of the entire value domain of key-value data, resulting in lower precision of frequency and mean estimation results when the domain of keys is large. In [22], they proposed the SKV-GRR method, combining the Duchi's method and the GRR framework. Although, they theoretically prove and experimentally verify that the SKV-GRR shows higher accuracy in frequency and mean estimation compared to previously proposed methods. But they ignore the issue of user cooperation caused by user privacy preferences. Therefore, addressing the shortcomings of the above methods, we propose a key-value data collection method based on personalized adaptive sampling mechanism. In our method, we not only consider the privacy preference needs of users, but also achieve higher accuracy in frequency and mean estimation.

3 Preliminaries

3.1 Local Differential Privacy

The protection model under the LDP fully considers the possibility of data collectors stealing or leaking users' privacy during the data collection process. In this model, each user first performs privacy processing on the data before sending the processed data to the data collector. Then, the data collector performs statistics on the collected data to obtain effective analysis results. In other words, while performing statistical analysis on the data, the privacy information of individuals is protected from being leaked. The formal definition of LDP is as follows:

Definition 1. *(Local Differential Privacy, LDP). Given n users, where each user corresponds to one record, and a privacy algorithm M with its domain Dom(M) and range Ran(M). If the algorithm M satisfies the following inequality when obtaining the same output result $t*$ $(t* \subseteq Ran(M))$ on any two records t and $t'\left(t, t' \in Dom(M)\right)$, then the algorithm M satisfies ε-LDP (ε-Local Differential Privacy).*

$$\Pr[M(t) = t*] \le e^{\varepsilon} \times \Pr[M(t') = t*] \tag{1}$$

Theorem 1. *(The sequential composition property of LDP). Given any input $v \in D$ and multiple independent random algorithms $M_1(\cdot), M_2(\cdot), ..., M_n(\cdot)$, where $M_i(\cdot)(1 \le i \le n)$ satisfies ε_i-LDP. Then, the sequential composition of the random algorithms $M_1(v), M_2(v), ..., M_n(v)$ satisfies $\left(\sum_{i=1}^{n} \varepsilon_i\right)$-LDP.*

3.2 Perturbation Mechanisms

The implementation of ε-LDP algorithm relies on the randomized response proposed by Warner [30]. In the following sections, we will outline two perturbation mechanisms relevant to our work.

Randomized Response. Randomized Response (RR) technique was initially introduced for surveys addressing sensitive questions to respondents, aiming to protect the privacy of respondents through plausible deniability. Specifically, for users with true values x, this mechanism answers the true result with a higher probability $p = e^{\varepsilon}/(e^{\varepsilon} + 1)$

58   Z. Zhai et al.

or the opposite result with a lower probability $q = 1/(e^\varepsilon + 1)$. Thus, the probability that algorithm M outputs a result y is:

$$\Pr(M(x) = y) = \begin{cases} p, & y = x \\ q, & y = 1 - x \end{cases},$$ (2)

where $x, y \in \{0, 1\}$, and the perturbed value y is submitted to the data collector. However, this mechanism can only provide ε-LDP for binary data.

Generalized Randomized Response. Generalized Randomized Response (GRR) is an extension of Randomized Response (RR) technique. We assume that the user has a true value x ($x \in D$). And GRR outputs the true value with a higher probability $p = e^\varepsilon/(e^\varepsilon + d - 1)$ or any other value from the domain D except the x with a lower probability $q = 1/(e^\varepsilon + d - 1)$. Specifically, the probability that the algorithm M outputs a result y is:

$$\Pr(M(x) = y) = \begin{cases} p, & y = x \\ q, & y \in D \backslash x \end{cases},$$ (3)

where $y \in D$, $|D| = d$, and when $p/q = e^\varepsilon$, the GRR satisfies ε-LDP. Especially, when $d = 2$, GRR is equivalent to RR.

3.3 Problem Definition

Users' Privacy Preferences: Privacy preference denotes the extent to which users value their private information, which can be articulated as the inclination of users to safeguard the privacy data they provide based on their subjective intentions. For instance, in response to a specific investigative question, different users exhibit varying privacy preferences. Without loss of generality, we denote ε_{u_i} as representing the privacy-preserving preferences of user u_i and assume that user u_i will only engage with the data collector when the offered level of privacy preservation exceeds their expectations ($\varepsilon \le \varepsilon_{u_i}$). Conversely, if the provided level does not meet these expectations ($\varepsilon > \varepsilon_{u_i}$), user u_i is more likely to submit a false answer that could compromise the accuracy of estimation results [31].

In our system model, there is a data collector and several users. We define a set $U = \{u_1, u_2, ..., u_n\}$ containing n users, the domain of keys $K = \{k_1, k_2, ..., k_d\}$, the range of values $V \in [-1, 1]$, each user u_i owns multiple key-value pairs. The users' set of key-value data can be represented as $S_u = \{(k_j, v_j)|1 \le j \le l_u, k_j \in K, v_j \in V\}$, with a size of $|S_u| = l_u$. The main notations in this paper are given in Table 1.

Then the untrusted data collector is required to estimate various statistics of the key-value data provided by users. The system model assumed in this paper is shown in Fig. 1.

As shown in Fig. 1, the data collector collects key-value data from users, and usually conducts two basic statistical analysis, such as frequency estimation and mean estimation. We suppose the key computed by the server is k ($k \in K$), the frequency estimation result is $\hat{f}_k$, and the mean estimation result is $\hat{m}_k$, their calculation formulas are as follows:

Table 1. Notations.

Symbol	Description
U	the set of users
n	the number of users, $n = |U|$
K	the domain of keys
d	the number of keys, $d = |K|$
S_u	the set of key-value data owned by users
l_u	the number of key-value data in S_u, $l_u = |S_u|$
ε_{u_i}	the privacy preference of user u_i
f_k	the frequency of key k
m_k	the mean of values with key k

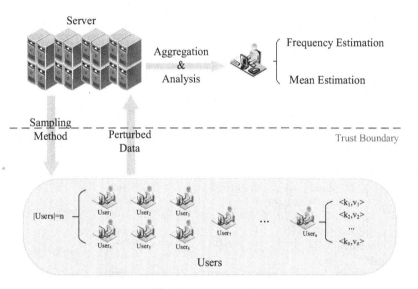

Fig. 1. System model.

Frequency Estimation:

$$\hat{f}_k = \frac{1}{n} |\{u_i | \exists < k, v > \in S_u\}|, \tag{4}$$

where $\left|\{u_i | \exists < k, v > \in S_{u_i}, u_i \in U\}\right|$ represents the number of users with the key k in the user set U.

Mean Estimation:

$$\hat{m}_k = \frac{1}{n \cdot \hat{f}_k} \sum\nolimits_{u \in U, <k,v> \in S_u} v, \tag{5}$$

where $\sum_{u \in U, <k,v> \in S_u} v$ represents the sum of corresponding values for k.

4 Key-Value Data Collection Scheme for User Privacy Preferences

4.1 UEKV-GRR Scheme

In the UEKV-GRR scheme, we select the sampling method adaptively by using estimation error as the selection criterion. The steps of the UEKV-GRR are shown as follows:

Algorithm 1: UEKV-GRR: User-centric key-value data collection

---

Input: The set of key-value pairs S, the set of key-value pairs owned
    by the user S_u, user's privacy preference ϵ_u, privacy budget ϵ
Output: The perturbed key-value pairs $\langle k', v', l_u \rangle$ $(l_u = |S_u|)$

1 **begin**
2   **if** $\frac{e^{\epsilon k}+d-2}{n(e^{\epsilon k}-1)^2} \leq \frac{2e^{\epsilon}}{n(e^{\epsilon}-1)^2}$ **then**
3   Randomly sample $\langle k,v \rangle \in S_u$
4      $\langle k,v,s \rangle$ =PBS($\langle k,v \rangle, \epsilon_u, \epsilon$)
5      $\langle k',v',l_u \rangle$ =KVP($\langle k,v,s \rangle, \epsilon$)
6   Return $\langle k',v' \rangle, l_u$
7   **else**
8   Randomly sample the j-th pair $\langle k,v \rangle \in S_u$ from S
9      $\langle k,v \rangle$ =PBS-E($\langle k,v \rangle, \epsilon_u, \epsilon$)
10      $\langle k',v' \rangle$ =KVEP($\langle k,v \rangle, \epsilon$)
11   Return $\langle k',v' \rangle$
12   **end if**
13 **end**

As shown in Algorithm 1, we first make a judgment about estimation error, which can be calculated by the formula (Line 2). The details of the formula will be shown in Sect. 4.2. Then we choose the sample method with smaller estimation error (line 3-4, line 8-9). After sampling the key-value data, the sampled data will be perturbed by the perturbation mechanism (line 5, line 10). Finally, the perturbed data will be sent to the data collector for statistical analysis.

1. **Key-value Data Perturbation.**

(1) **Sampling Method:** We design the sampling method PBS that samples the key-value data from S_u. And at the same time, considering the user's privacy preference, we also compare the user's privacy preference ε_u with the level of privacy protection ε

that provided by the data collector. The PBS can be expressed as:

$$PBS(< k, v >, \varepsilon_u, \varepsilon) = \begin{cases} < k, v >, & \varepsilon_u > \varepsilon \\ < k', 0 >, k' \in K \backslash k, & \varepsilon_u \leq \varepsilon \end{cases}. \tag{6}$$

When the user's privacy preference ε_u exceeds the level of privacy protection ε offered by the data collector, the non-dummy key-value data will be sampled. Otherwise, the key will be sampled randomly in the $K(|K| = d)$. The details of the algorithm are shown in Algorithm 2.

Algorithm 2: PBS: Privacy budget based sampling

Input: The set of key-value pairs owned by the user S_u, the user's privacy preference ϵ_u, privacy budget ϵ

Output: The sampled key-value pair $\langle k, v, s \rangle$ ($k \in K$, sampling statement $s \in \{0, 1\}$)

1 **begin**
2   Randomly Sample $\langle k, v \rangle \in S_u$
3   **if** $\epsilon_u > \epsilon$ **then**
4 | Return $\langle k, v, 1 \rangle$
5   **else**
6 | Randomly Sample $k' \in K \backslash k$
7 | Return $\langle k', 0, 0 \rangle$
8   **end if**
9 **end**

---

(2) **Perturbation Mechanism:** After the sampling process, the sampled key-value data is perturbed by the KVP (Key-Value Data Perturbation), which divides the ε into ε_k(the privacy budget assigned to the keys) and ε_v(the privacy budget assigned to the values), and perturbs the key and value respectively. The details of KVP are shown in Algorithm 3. The selected key k is perturbed by the GRR mechanism (line 2-3). Then, by evaluating the existence of k' within S_u and assessing whether the sampling statement s equals 0, the KVP algorithm realizes the correlation between key and value (line 4-7). Subsequently, in the discretization process, we discretize the continuous data into binary data (line 8-9). Then the RR mechanism is used to perturb the discretized data (line 10-11). Finally, the $\langle k', v' \rangle$ and l_u are submitted to the data collector.

Algorithm 3: KVP: Key-value data perturbation

Input: The sampled key-value pair $\langle k, v, s \rangle$ ($k \in K$, sampling
statements $\in \{0, 1\}$), privacy budget $\epsilon = \epsilon_k + \epsilon_v$
Output: Perturbed key-value pairs $\langle k', v', l_u \rangle$
$(k' \in K, v' \in \{-1, 1\}, l_u = |S_u|)$

1 begin
2     $k \to k'$:
3

$$k' = \begin{cases} k & \text{w.p. } \frac{e^{\epsilon_k}}{e^{\epsilon_k}+l_u-1} \\ x \in K \setminus k & \text{w.p. } \frac{1}{e^{\epsilon_k}+l_u-1} \end{cases}$$

   if $k' \in S_u, s \neq 0$ then
4       $v = \{v|\langle k', v \rangle \in S_u\}$
5   else
6       $v = 0$
7   end if
8     $v \to v_D$:
9

$$v_D = \begin{cases} 1 & \text{w.p. } \frac{v+1}{2} \\ -1 & \text{w.p. } \frac{v-1}{2} \end{cases}$$

10    $v_D \to v'$:
11

$$v' = \begin{cases} v_D & \text{w.p. } \frac{e^{\epsilon_v}}{e^{\epsilon_v}+1} \\ -v_D & \text{w.p. } \frac{1}{e^{\epsilon_v}+1} \end{cases}$$

12   return $\langle k', v', l_u \rangle$
13 end

---

(3) **Data Collection and Analysis:** After receiving the key-value data submitted by the
user, the data collector needs to calculate the frequency and mean. In the submitted
data, we assume that $l_u = j$, the number of 1's and -1's supporting k are donated as
$n_{1,k,j}$ and $n_{-1,k,j}$ respectively. Therefore, the number of users who satisfy the privacy
preference with $l_u = j$ is $n_j = \sum_{k \in K} (n_{1,k,j} + n_{-1,k,j})$.

Frequency Estimation: For frequency estimation of k under the condition $l_u = j$, since
the probability of sampling is $1/j$, it is necessary to multiply the frequency estimation
by j. The formula for frequency estimation under the condition $l_u = j$ and k is as follows:

$$\hat{f}_{k,j} = \frac{n_{1,k,j} + n_{-1,k,j} - n_j \cdot \frac{1}{e^{\epsilon_k}+d-1}}{n \cdot \left(\frac{e^{\epsilon_k}}{e^{\epsilon_k}+d-1} - \frac{1}{e^{\epsilon_k}+d-1} \right)} \cdot j. \tag{7}$$

Therefore, the frequency estimation of k is given by:

$$\hat{f}_k = \sum_{j=1}^{l_u} \hat{f}_{k,j}. \tag{8}$$

Mean Estimation: For the mean estimation of v under the condition $l_u = j$, the unbiased
sum is $(n_{1,k,j} - n_{-1,k,j}) / (2p - 1)$, where $p = e^{\epsilon_v} / (e^{\epsilon_v} + 1)$. When a user submits the

fake key that is not in S_u, the corresponding v is 0, which is assigned to 1 or -1 with a probability of 0.5 in discretization process. Then the formula for the mean value estimation under the condition $l_u = j$ and k is as follows:

$$\hat{m}_{k,j} = \frac{\left(n_{1,k,j} - n_{-1,k,j}\right) / (2p - 1)}{n \cdot \hat{f}_{k,j} \cdot \left(\frac{1}{s} \cdot \frac{e^{\varepsilon_k}}{e^{\varepsilon_k} + d - 1} + \left(1 - \frac{1}{s}\right) \cdot \frac{1}{e^{\varepsilon_k} + d - 1}\right)}. \tag{9}$$

Therefore, the mean estimation of k is given by:

$$\hat{m}_k = \frac{1}{n} \cdot \sum_{j=1}^{l_u} \left(\hat{m}_{k,j} \cdot n_j\right). \tag{10}$$

2. **Key-value Data Encoding and Perturbation.**

(1) **Sampling Method:** In this method, compared to the unequally spaced sampling mechanism, the PBS-E adopts the full-padding sampling mechanism that randomly samples the key-value data after user' s set has been completely padded. And, same as the PBS, the PBS-E also takes the user's privacy preference into account by comparing the user's privacy preference ε_u with the level of privacy protection ε provided by the data collector. The PBS-E can be expressed as:

$$\text{PBS} - \text{E}(< k, v >, \varepsilon_u, \varepsilon) = \begin{cases} < k, v >, \varepsilon_u > \varepsilon \\ < k, 0 >, \varepsilon_u \leq \varepsilon \end{cases}. \tag{11}$$

When the user's privacy preference ε_u is greater than ε, then the non-dummy key-value data will be sampled. Otherwise, the v will be set to 0. The details of the PBS-E are shown in Algorithm 4.

Algorithm 4: PBS-E: Privacy budget based sampling for KVEP

Input: The set of key-value pairs S, the user's privacy preference ϵ_u,
        privacy budget ϵ
Output: The sampled key-value pair $\langle k, v \rangle$

1 **begin**
2 | Randomly sample the j-th pair $\langle k, v \rangle \in S$
3 | **if** $\epsilon_u > \epsilon$ **then**
4 | | Return $\langle k, v \rangle$
5 | **else**
6 | | $v = 0$
7 | | Return $\langle k, v \rangle$
8 | **end if**
9 **end**

---

(2) **Perturbation Mechanisms:** After the sampling process, the sampled key-value data will be discretized as $v \in \{-1, 1\}$, and the discretized key-value data can be classified into three cases ($< 1, 1 >, < 1, -1 >, < 0, 0 >$). Then the discretized key-value data will be perturbed by the KVEP (Key-Value Data Encoding and Perturbation) algorithm based on the GRR mechanism. According to KVEP, the user perturbs the

key-value data without splitting the privacy budget ε. In this way, the KVEP will reduce the reduction of data availability caused by splitting the privacy budget. The details of the KVEP are shown in Algorithm 5.

Algorithm 5: KVEP: Key-value data encoding and perturbation

Input: The sampled key-value pair $\langle k, v \rangle$, privacy budget ϵ
Output: Perturbed key-value pairs $\langle k', v' \rangle$

1 **begin**
2   IF the j-th pair $\langle k, v \rangle$ IS $\langle 0, 0 \rangle$ THEN
3   Perturb the $\langle k, v \rangle$ as:
4

$$\langle k', v' \rangle = \begin{cases} \langle 0, 0 \rangle & \text{w.p. } \frac{e^\epsilon}{e^\epsilon + 2} \\ \langle 1, 1 \rangle & \text{w.p. } \frac{1}{e^\epsilon + 2} \\ \langle 1, -1 \rangle & \text{w.p. } \frac{1}{e^\epsilon + 2} \end{cases}$$

5   ELSE IF the j-th pair $\langle k, v \rangle$ IS NOT $\langle 0, 0 \rangle$ THEN
6   Discretize the v to v':
7

$$v' = \begin{cases} 1 & \text{w.p. } \frac{v+1}{2} \\ -1 & \text{w.p. } \frac{v-1}{2} \end{cases}$$

8   Perturb the $\langle k, v' \rangle$ as:
9

$$\langle k', v' \rangle = \begin{cases} \langle 1, 1 \rangle & \text{w.p. } \frac{e^\epsilon}{e^\epsilon + 2} \\ \langle 0, 0 \rangle & \text{w.p. } \frac{1}{e^\epsilon + 2} \\ \langle 1, -1 \rangle & \text{w.p. } \frac{1}{e^\epsilon + 2} \end{cases}$$

     return $\langle k', v' \rangle$
10 **end**

According to the algorithm 5, we first judge the sampled key-value data. If the $\langle k, v \rangle = \langle 0, 0 \rangle$, we perturb the $\langle k, v \rangle$ into $\langle k', v' \rangle$ with probability $e^\varepsilon / (e^\varepsilon + 2)$ or $1 / (e^\varepsilon + 2)$ (line 2-4). Otherwise, the continuous value v will be discretized into $\{-1, 1\}$ (line 6-7). Then, the $\langle k, v' \rangle$ will be perturbed into $\langle k', v' \rangle$ by GRR mechanism (line 8-9). Finally, the $\langle k', v' \rangle$ is submitted to the data collector.

(3) **Data Collection and Analysis:** After receiving the key-value pairs submitted by the user, the data collector needs to calculate the frequency of k_j and the mean of v_j. Now, we assume that the count of all key-value pairs received by the server is n, the count of the $< 1, 1 >$ received by the server is n_1, the count of the $< 1, -1 >$ received by the server is n_{-1}, the count of the $< 0, 0 >$ received by the server is n_0, and the probability of perturbation is $p = e^\varepsilon / (e^\varepsilon + 2)$.

Frequency Estimation: For the frequency estimation, the $\hat{f}_{k_j}$ with the perturbation probability $p = e^\varepsilon / (e^\varepsilon + 2)$ is calculated as follows:

$$\hat{f}_{k_j} = \frac{2 \cdot \left[n_1 + n_{-1} - n \cdot (1 - p) \right]}{(3p - 1) \cdot n}. \tag{12}$$

Mean Estimation: For the mean estimation of v_j, the $\hat{m}_{k_j}$ with the perturbation probability $p = e^{\varepsilon} / (e^{\varepsilon} + 2)$ is calculated as follows:

$$\hat{m}_{k_j} = \frac{n_1 - n_{-1}}{n_1 + n_{-1} - n \cdot (1-p)}. \tag{13}$$

4.2 Theoretical Analysis of UEKV-GRR

In this section, we deal with optimal budget allocation of KVP and estimation error analysis of the UEKV-GRR.

Optimized Budget Allocation of KVP

Theorem 2. *For the KVP, the optimal budget allocation scheme to divide the privacy budget ε into key and value for perturbation is:* $\varepsilon_k = \ln\{[l_u(e^{\varepsilon} + e^{\varepsilon - \varepsilon_k} - 2) + 2]/2\}, \varepsilon_v (0 \le \varepsilon_v \le \varepsilon)$.

Estimation Error Analysis of UEKV-GRR

Theorem 3. *For the KVP method, we assume that the set of users containing $k \in K$ is $U_k, |S_u| = l_u = s$ and $|K| = l$. When $\varepsilon_k = \ln\{[s(e^{\varepsilon} - 1) + 2]/2\}$ and $\varepsilon_v = \varepsilon$, the frequency estimation $\hat{f}_k$ and the mean estimation $\hat{m}_k$ are unbiased, that $E\left(\hat{f}_k\right) = f_k$ and $E\left(\hat{m}_k\right) \approx m_k$. At the same time, the variance of $\hat{f}_k$ and $\hat{m}_k$ satisfies the following equation:*

$$Var\left(\hat{f}_k\right) = \sum_{s=1}^{l}\left[\frac{(s - a_s + b_s - 2b_s s)f_{k,s}}{n(a_s - b_s)} + \frac{s^2 n_s b_s(1 - b_s)}{n^2(a_s - b_s)^2}\right], \tag{14}$$

$$Var\left[\hat{m}_k\right] = \sum_{s=1}^{l}\frac{n_s^2(a_s - b_s)^2 Var\left(\frac{n_{1,k,s} - n_{-1,k,s}}{n_{1,k,s} + n_{-1,k,s} - n_s b_s}\right)}{n^2(2p_s - 1)^2(a_s - b_s + b_s s)^2} \approx A + B, \tag{15}$$

$$A = \sum_{s=1}^{l}\frac{n_s^2\left((s - a_s + b_s - 2b_s s)(a_s - b_s)f_{k,s}n + s^2 b_s(1 - b_s)n_s\right)}{n^4(2p_s - 1)^2(a_s - b_s + b_s s)^2 f_{k,s}^2}, \tag{16}$$

$$B = \sum_{s=1}^{l}\frac{n_s^2\left((a_s - b_s - s)(a_s - b_s)f_{k,s}n + s^2 b_s(1 - b_s)n_s\right)}{(a_s - b_s+)^2 n^6 f_{k,s}^4}\left(\sum_{u \in U_{k,s}} v_u\right)^2, \tag{17}$$

where $f_{k,s}$ denotes the true frequency where the key is k and $l_u = s$, $a_s = \frac{e^{\varepsilon_k}}{e^{\varepsilon_k} + d - 1}$, $b_s = \frac{1}{e^{\varepsilon_k} + d - 1}$, $p_s = \frac{e^{\varepsilon_v}}{e^{\varepsilon_v} + 1}$.

From the variance of frequency estimation and mean estimation in Theorem 2, it can be found that the estimation error of KVP is related to $|S_u|$. And as the $|S_u|$ increases, the estimation error also increases.

Because when we calculate the mean of values, we are supposed to calculate the frequency of the key firstly. Therefore, the estimation error of mean estimation is also affected by the frequency estimation error. According to the Theorem 2, the error formula of frequency estimation is as follows:

$$Var\left(\hat{f_k}\right) = \sum_{s=1}^{l}\left[\frac{(s(e^{\varepsilon_k}+d-3)-e^{\varepsilon_k}+1)f_{k,s}}{n(e^{\varepsilon_k}-1)} + \frac{s^2 n_s(e^{\varepsilon_k}+d-2)}{n^2(e^{\varepsilon_k}-1)^2}\right]. \qquad (18)$$

When the $f_{k,s}$ is very small, the error formula for frequency estimation can be approximated as:

$$Var\left(\hat{f_k}\right) \approx \sum_{s=1}^{l}\left[\frac{s^2 n_s(e^{\varepsilon_k}+d-2)}{n^2(e^{\varepsilon_k}-1)^2}\right]. \qquad (19)$$

Therefore, when $l_u = l$, the error of the frequency estimation takes the maximum: $Var\left(\hat{f_k}\right)_{MAX} = \frac{l^2(e^{\varepsilon_k}+d-2)}{n(e^{\varepsilon_k}-1)^2}$. In contrast, if $l_u = 1$, the error of the frequency estimation takes the minimum:

$$Var\left(\hat{f_k}\right)_{MIN} = \frac{e^{\varepsilon_k}+d-2}{n(e^{\varepsilon_k}-1)^2}. \qquad (20)$$

Theorem 4. *For the KVEP method, we assume that n represents the number of users, the size of key domain is $|K| = d$, $\hat{n_k}$ represents the estimated number of key k, n_k represents the real number of key k, $\hat{f_k}$ represents the estimated frequency of key k and f_k represents the real frequency of key k. In the server-side, c_k represents the number of $k = 1$, v_k is the real value, v_k^* represents the v_k after perturbation, and the perturbation probability set as $p = \frac{e^{\varepsilon}}{e^{\varepsilon}+2}$, $q = \frac{1}{e^{\varepsilon}+2}$, then the $\hat{f_k}$ is unbiased, i.e. $E\left(\hat{f_k}\right) = f_k$, and the variance of $\hat{f_k}$ satisfies the following equation:*

$$Var\left(\hat{f_k}\right) = \frac{1}{n} \cdot \frac{2e^{\varepsilon}}{(e^{\varepsilon}-1)^2} - \frac{1}{n} \cdot \frac{f_k}{e^{\varepsilon}-1}. \qquad (21)$$

It can be found that when $f_k = 0$, the variance of $\hat{f_k}$ obtains the maximum value, $Var\left(\hat{f_k}\right)_{MAX} = \frac{1}{n} \cdot \frac{2e^{\varepsilon}}{(e^{\varepsilon}-1)^2}$. At this time, the error is maximum.

By comparing with the errors in frequency estimation of the KVP method and the KVEP method, when $\frac{e^{\varepsilon_k}+d-2}{n(e^{\varepsilon_k}-1)^2} > \frac{1}{n} \cdot \frac{2e^{\varepsilon}}{(e^{\varepsilon}-1)^2}$, the availability of KVEP is higher than that of KVP.

5   Experimental Evaluation

The experimental platform is 16-core Intel Corei7-14650HX with 16G RAM and Win10 system. All algorithms are implemented in python, and the experiments use three datasets: synthetic dataset, MovieLen dataset and JData dataset, as shown in Table 2. For the synthetic dataset, we set the amount of user to 100,000, the key domain to [1, ..., 100], the value domain to [−1, 1]. Each user owns at least one and up to two key-value pairs, where the key obeys the Bernoulli distribution and value obeys the normal distribution. The MovieLens dataset contains ratings of 27,000 movies by 138,000 users, and each user contains at least 20 valid ratings. We extract the top 10 movies with the highest number of ratings as the set of keys. Meanwhile, the ratings of each movie are represented by key-value data, where the key denotes the movie id, and the value denotes the movie rating mapped to the interval. The JData dataset comes from JD.com, which contains 50.6 million sales records in 2016. This dataset records 50.6 million purchases of 442 brands by 105,180 users during 2016.For this experiment, we extract the top 10 brands with the highest number of purchases as the set of keys. At the same time, we add the user's privacy preference in the three datasets. The user's privacy preference ε_u obeys the Bernoulli distribution. If the user's privacy preference is not satisfied, then the value v is randomly selected in the range of [−1, 1].

Table 2. Datasets.

Name	Distribution	Users	Keys
Synthetic dataset	normal	100000	100
MovieLens	–	138000	27000
JData	–	105180	442

Evaluation Metric: Experiments are conducted for the above three datasets. The mean square error (MSE) is used to measure the frequency and mean computation accuracy of PrivKV, PCKV-GRR, SKV-GRR and our proposed UEKV-GRR scheme. The MSE corresponding to the key and value can be expressed as:

$$MSE_{FREQ} = \frac{1}{|K|} \sum_{k \in K} \left(\hat{f_k} - f_k \right)^2, \tag{22}$$

$$MSE_{MEAN} = \frac{1}{|K|} \sum_{k \in K} \left(\hat{m_k} - m_k \right)^2, \tag{23}$$

where $\hat{f_k}$ and f_k are the estimated and true frequency of the key, and $\hat{m_k}$ and m_k are the estimated and true mean of the values corresponding to the key.

Compared to UEKV-GRR, PrivKV, PCKV-GRR, and SKV-GRR, we conduct simulation experiments on synthetic dataset, MovieLens dataset and JData dataset. We set the privacy budget ε as $\varepsilon = \{0.1, 1, 2, 3, 4, 5, 6\}$ for comparative analysis.

5.1 Experiments with Synthetic Dataset

For the synthetic dataset, we compare the performance of PrivKV, PCKV-GRR, SKV-GRR, and UEKV-GRR. The MSEs of frequency and mean estimation of the four schemes are shown in Fig. 2. It can be found that the MSE of frequency estimation and mean estimation of the four schemes show a decreasing trend when ε changes from 0.1 to 6. For frequency estimation, due to the use of different sampling mechanisms, we observe that when ε is small, the MSE of UEKV-GRR is far less than the MSEs of other schemes. For mean estimation, because of the influence of frequency estimation accuracy and perturbation algorithm, the MSE of UEKV-GRR scheme is the smallest for small privacy budget. This also means that when the level of privacy-preservation is high, our scheme has higher data availability compared to the other three schemes in terms of mean estimation and frequency estimation.

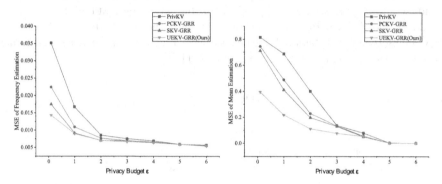

Fig. 2. Frequency estimation and mean estimation on the synthetic dataset.

5.2   Experiments with Real Datasets

We present the results of the four schemes on two real-world datasets in Fig. 3 and Fig. 4, where the MSE is calculated on the top 10 frequent keys. Figure 3 and Fig. 4 show the MSEs of frequency and mean estimation on MovieLens and JData datasets for PrivKV, PCKV-GRR, SKV-GRR, and UEKV-GRR as the privacy budget increases from 0.1 to 6. From the experimental results in Fig. 3 and Fig. 4, it is evident that as the privacy budget increases (the level of privacy protection decreases), the MSEs associated with the four methods exhibit a downward trend. At the same time, it can be found that the UEKV-GRR performs best among the four schemes for frequency estimation, especially when the privacy budget is small. For mean estimation, we observe that the MSE of UEKV-GRR scheme is much smaller than the other schemes.

By observing the results of the three sets of experiments based on different datasets, the estimation errors of the different methods are significantly reduced as the privacy budget ε varies from 0.1 to 6. Due to the adaptive sampling mechanism based on the user's privacy preference, it is evident that the accuracy of UEKV-GRR in frequency and mean estimation surpasses that of PrivKV, PCKV-GRR, and SKV-GRR at lower privacy budget. Therefore, in a more complex scenario where different users have different requirements for privacy-preservation levels, UEKV-GRR improves the availability of data while providing ε-LDP for key-value data.

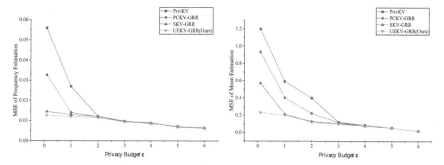

Fig. 3. Frequency estimation and mean estimation on the MovieLens dataset.

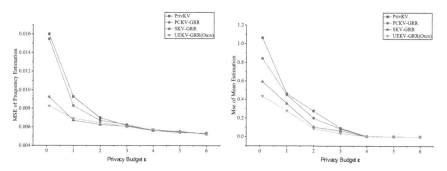

Fig. 4. Frequency estimation and mean estimation on the JData dataset.

6   Conclusion

In this paper, we propose a key-value data collection scheme UEKV-GRR based on ε-LDP. The UEKV-GRR combines the ε-LDP protection mechanism with the adaptive sampling scheme selection mechanism oriented to the user's privacy preference. And we also fully consider the impact of the user's privacy preference on the usability of the collected key-value data. According to our UEKV-GRR scheme, each user protects own key-value data by utilizing discretization and GRR technique. So, we can not only maintain the correlation between keys and values, but also reduce the estimation error from the sampling stage. Through our PBS and PBS-E algorithm, we can avoid the user fitness problem caused by the level of privacy protection, which is provided by the data collector not reaching the user's privacy preference. The data collector combines the results of key-value data perturbation to estimate the frequency of each key and the mean of the value. At the same time, we theoretically analyze the comparison of the estimation errors in detail. Experimental results show that the estimation accuracy of UEKV-GRR is higher than those of PrivKV, PCKV-GRR and SKV-GRR.

In view of the current threat posed by data poisoning attacks against LDP, in the future work, we will focus on exploring LDP-preserving schemes for key-value data to resist data poisoning attacks.

Acknowledgments. This study was supported in part by the National Natural Science Foundation of China (grant number 61602216 and 61672270), in part by the Jiangsu Province 'Qinglan Project' Outstanding Young Backbone Teachers Training object (grant number KYQ22003), in part by the Natural Science Foundation of the Jiangsu Higher Education Institutions of China (grant number 24KJB520007 and 24KJB520008).

References

1. Dwork, C.: Differential privacy. In: Bugliesi, M., Preneel, B., Sassone, V., Wegener, I. (eds.) Automata, Languages and Programming. ICALP 2006. Lecture Notes in Computer Science, vol. 4052, pp. 1–12. Springer, Berlin, Heidelberg (2006). https://doi.org/10.1007/11787006_1
2. Kairouz, P., Oh, S., Viswanath, P.: Extremal mechanisms for local differential privacy. In: Neural Information Processing Systems (NIPS), pp. 2879–2887. NIPS Endowment, Montreal Canada (2014)
3. Erlingsson, L., Pihur, V., Korolova, A.: RAPPOR: randomized aggregatable privacy-preserving ordinal response. In: ACM Conference on Computer and Communications Security (CCS), pp. 1054–1067. ACM, Scottsdale USA (2014)
4. Bassily, R., Smith, A.: Local, private, efficient protocols for succinct histograms. In: Symposium on Theory of Computing (STOC), pp. 127–135. ACM, Portland USA (2015)
5. Wang, T., Blocki, J., Jha, S.K.: Locally differentially private protocols for frequency estimation. In: Proceedings of the 26th USENIX Conference on Security Symposium, pp. 729–745. USENIX Association, Vancouver BC Canada (2017)
6. Dwork, C., Mcsherry, F., Nissim, K., et al.: Calibrating noise to sensitivity in private data analysis. J. Privacy Confidentiality **7**(3), 17–51 (2017)
7. Wang, N., Xiao, X., Yang, Y., et al.: Collecting and analyzing multidimensional data with local differential privacy. In: IEEE International Conference on Data Engineering (ICDE), pp. 1–12. IEEE Macao China (2019)
8. Li, Z., Wang, T., Lopuha-Zwakenberg, M., et al.: Estimating numerical distributions under local differential privacy. In: SIGMOD '20: Proceedings of the 2020 ACM SIGMOD International Conference on Management of Data, pp. 621–635. Association for Computing Machinery, Portland USA (2020)
9. Kulkarni, T.: Answering range queries under local differential privacy. In: SIGMOD '19: Proceedings of the 2019 International Conference on Management of Data, pp. 1832–1834. Association for Computing Machinery, Amsterdam Netherlands (2019)
10. Yang, J., Wang, T., Li, N., et al.: Answering multi-dimensional range queries under local differential privacy. In: Very Large Data Base (VLDB), pp. 378–390. VLDB Endowment, Tokyo Japan (2020)
11. Du, R., Ye, Q., Fu, Y., et al.: Collecting high-dimensional and correlation-constrained data with local differential privacy. In: 18th Annual IEEE International Conference on Sensing. Communication, and Networking (SECON), pp. 1–9. IEEE, Rome Italy (2021)
12. Wang, T., Li, N., Jha, S.: Locally differentially private frequent itemset mining. In: 2018 IEEE Symposium on Security and Privacy (S&P), pp. 127–143. IEEE, San Francisco USA (2018)
13. Wang, N., Xiao, X., Yang, Y., et al.: PrivTrie: effective frequent term discovery under local differential privacy. In: 2018 IEEE 34th International Conference on Data Engineering (ICDE), pp. 821–832. IEEE, Paris France (2018)
14. Wang, T., Li, N., Jha, S.: Locally differentially private heavy hitter identification. IEEE Trans. Dependable Secure Comput. **18**(2), 982–993 (2021)
15. Sun, P., Wang, Z., Wu, L., et al.: Towards personalized privacy-preserving incentive for truth discovery in mobile crowdsensing systems. IEEE Trans. Mob. Comput. **21**(1), 352–365 (2022)

16. Zhang, P., Cheng, X., Su, S., et al.: Effective truth discovery under local differential privacy by leveraging noise-aware probabilistic estimation and fusion. Knowl.-Based Syst. **261**, 1–15 (2023)

17. Ye, Q., Hu, H., Meng, X., et al.: PrivKV: key-value data collection with local differential privacy. In: 2019 IEEE Symposium on Security and Privacy (S&P), pp. 317–337. IEEE, San Francisco USA (2019)

18. Nguyên, T.T., Xiao, X., Yang, Y., et al.: Collecting and Analyzing Data from Smart Device Users with Local Differential Privacy. arXiv preprint, arXiv: 1606.05053 (2016)

19. Duchi, J.C., Jordan, M.I., Wainwright, M.J.: Minimax optimal procedures for locally private estimation. J. Am. Stat. Assoc. **113**(521), 182–201 (2018)

20. Gu, X., Li, M., Cheng, Y., et al.: PCKV: locally differentially private correlated key-value data collection with optimized utility. In: Proceedings of the 29th USENIX Conference on Security Symposium,pp. 967–984. USENIX Association, Boston USA (2020)

21. Sun, L., Zhao, J., Ye, X., et al.: Conditional Analysis for Key-Value Data with Local Differential Privacy. arXiv preprint, arXiv:1907.05014 (2019)

22. Zhu, H., Tang, X., Yang, L.T., et al.: Key-value data collection and statistical analysis with local differential privacy. Inf. Sci. **640**, 1–18 (2023)

23. Shen, Z., Xia, Z., Yu, P.: PLDP: personalized local differential privacy for multidimensional data aggregation. Secur. Commun. Netw. **2021**, 1–13 (2021)

24. Huang, Z., Qiu, Y., Yi, K., et al.: Frequency estimation under multiparty differential privacy: one-shot and streaming. Proc. VLDB Endowment **15**(10), 2058–2070 (2021)

25. Liang, W., Hong, et al.: An effective scheme for top-k frequent itemset mining under differential privacy conditions. Sci. China (Inf. Sci.) **63**(05), 200–202 (2020)

26. Mckenna, R., Maity, R.K., Mazumdar, A., et al.: A workload-adaptive mechanism for linear queries under local differential privacy. In: Very Large Data Base (VLDB), pp. 1905–1918. VLDB Endowment, Tokyo Japan (2020)

27. Chen, X., Wang, C., Yang, Q., et al.: Locally differentially private high-dimensional data synthesis. Sci. China (Inf. Sci.) **66**(1), 18 (2023)

28. Ren, X., Yu, C.M., Yu, W., et al.: LoPub: high-dimensional crowdsourced data publication with local differential privacy. IEEE Trans. Inf. Forensics Secur. **13**(9), 2151–2166 (2018)

29. Ye, Q., Hu, H., Au, M.H., et al.: LF-GDPR: a framework for estimating graph metrics with local differential privacy. IEEE Trans. Knowl. Data Eng. **34**(10), 4905–4920 (2020)

30. Warner, S.L.: Randomized response: a survey technique for eliminating evasive answer bias. J. Am. Stat. Assoc. **60**(309), 63–69 (1965)

31. Sun, L., Ye, X., Zhao, J., Lu, C., Yang, M.: BiSample: bidirectional sampling for handling missing data with local differential privacy. In: Nah, Y., Cui, B., Lee, SW., Yu, J.X., Moon, YS., Whang, S.E. (eds.) Database Systems for Advanced Applications. DASFAA 2020. Lecture Notes in Computer Science(), vol. 12112, pp. 88–104. Springer, Cham. https://doi.org/10.1007/978-3-030-59410-7_6

Comparative Study of Artificial Intelligent Approaches for Phishing Website Detection

Bingbing Li[✉], Ogbebisi Chukwuebuka Amandi, and Mingwu Zhang[✉]

Hubei University of Technology, Wuhan Hubei 430068, China
bbli@hbut.edu.cn

Abstract. Phishing attack has always been a latent threat to the privacy and security of Internet users. With the thriving development in the past decade, machine learning techniques have great potential to reduce this risk via efficiently classifying URLs as either legitimate or malicious. In this paper, extensive experiments are carried out to detect phishing websites based on variable machine learning models. After collecting and preprocessing data of both legitimate and malicious URLs, the mutual information method is adopted to select the most relevant features to achieve higher prediction accuracy. Then the model training and testing are implemented via variable machine learning and deep learning models, including Logistic Regression, Decision Tree, Random Forest, Gradient Boosting, SVM, MLP, Adaboost, GaussianNB, XGB, Light GBM and CatBoost. The results have revealed that Decision Tree Classifier can achieve the highest accuracy of 98.80% and along with good precision, recall, and F1 score. These results show that decision tree models are efficient in detecting phishing URLs and proves its potential for enhancing users security and privacy.

Keywords: Phishing Detection · Decision Tree Classifiers · Artificial Intelligent · Cybersecurity

1 Introduction

In the digital age, phishing attacks have emerged as a significant risk to the security and privacy of consumers. Phishing websites may be used as bait to trick Internet users into divulging sensitive information. Moreover, various online tools make it simpler to fabricate websites without comprehensive knowledge nowadays. It is difficult for average users to tell the phishing websites from the authentic and legitimate ones. To protect the privacy and digital assets of individuals, the fraudulent websites need to be identified as soon as possible. [9].

Traditional security measures, such as firewalls and antivirus software, alone are frequently unable to identify and prevent these assaults effectively as phishing attempts continue to improve and become more sophisticated. As a result, there is an increasing demand for advanced detection techniques that can adjust to the changing strategies used by phishers. As a promising candidate, artificial intelligence tools has been considered to be able to evaluate large volumes of data and provide well-informed forecasts. This characteristic makes them very efficient for the detection and classification of phishing websites. There have been several publications related to artificial intelligent methods to classify phishing websites. The aim of the comparative experiment in this study is to find out how well artificial intelligent methods can detect malicious URLs and the evaluation and comparison among the most popular models and algorithms.

In order to reach this goal, we choose well-known models such as Gradient Boosting Classifier, Logistic Regression, Random Forest Classifier, and Support Vector Machine (SVM), and decision trees. Meanwhile, a carefully selected collection of 10,000 described URLs will be used. The dataset has information related to URLs, IP addresses, domain reputation, SSL encryption, and JavaScript usage that is linked to attributes. These characteristics are chosen based on how well they facilitate phishing attacks and how well they can provide unique information for the purpose of categorization. To achieve better performance, the dataset will be pre-processed before training, including handling missing values and encoding categorical variables. In order to discover the most useful qualities for detecting fraudulent websites, feature selection approaches will be adopted as well. Moreover, we employ the mutual information classification method to ascertain the level of correlation between features and the objective variable, thereby identifying the most impactful features for selection. Then a comprehensive study and the experimental results are presented, focusing on the efficiency in detecting phishing websites. The reliability and effectiveness will be further compared with that of other papers in the field of phishing website detection.

The results of this study will enhance the existing knowledge on the identification of phishing attacks by utilising machine learning methods, with a specific emphasis on decision tree classifiers. The knowledge acquired from the experiment can be used to improve the creation of more sophisticated and precise phishing detection systems, therefore boosting the security of both individuals and organisations. Further, the work will outline the strengths and weaknesses of decision tree classifiers in the domain of phishing detection and offer recommendations for future research and practical applications. Thus, addressing the urgent problem of phishing attacks, this research paper investigates the application of decision tree classifiers to identify phishing websites. By use of a well chosen dataset and several assessment metrics, the research aims to measure the performance of decision tree classification. This work attempts to improve the development of more robust and efficient phishing detection systems, thereby increasing security measures, by using machine learning techniques.

2   Related Work

With the rapid rise in phishing attacks, there has been a major concern in recent years, prompting a lot of study into the invention of practical detection methods. Many approaches, both conventional and cutting-edge ones, have been carefully studied. This section will summarise the recently published work on phishing attack identification.

Basit et al. proposed a novel ensemble machine learning method for detecting phishing attacks [3]. Their research highlights how crucial it is to combine several classifiers in order to improve overall detection accuracy. This method provides a thorough plan for dealing with the dynamic nature of phishing attacks. A lightweight URL-based phishing detection system employing natural language processing (NLP) transformers tailored for mobile devices was introduced by Haynes et al. [8]. The focus on lightweight solutions is crucial for resource-constrained platforms, and the integration of NLP transformers indicates a shift towards advanced techniques in phishing detection. Chawla carried out research on phishing website analysis and detection using machine learning [4]. The study explores the nuances of phishing websites and uses machine learning to find recurring themes. This kind of thorough investigation advances our knowledge of the characteristics that set reputable websites apart from fraudulent ones.

Das Guptta et al. proposed a hybrid feature-based approach for detecting phishing websites using machine learning techniques [5]. This model combines multiple features, showcasing the effectiveness of integrating diverse characteristics for accurate phishing detection. Ojewumi et al. conducted a performance evaluation of various machine learning tools for detecting phishing attacks on web pages [14]. The study provides insights into the comparative effectiveness of different machine learning algorithms in the context of phishing detection. Ahammad et al. explored phishing URL detection using machine learning methods [1]. Their research focuses on the specific challenge of identifying phishing in URLs, employing machine learning techniques to enhance accuracy in differentiating between legitimate and malicious URLs.

Kolla et al. conducted a comparative study of machine learning techniques for phishing detection [10]. The research systematically compares the performance of various machine learning algorithms, providing valuable insights for selecting appropriate methods based on specific requirements. Gandotra and Gupta proposed an efficient approach for phishing detection using machine learning [7]. Their research likely contributes novel techniques or optimizations to improve the efficiency of phishing detection systems. Mohammada et al. presented an integrated machine learning model for URL phishing detection [13]. The integration of machine learning models is explored to enhance the overall detection capability, demonstrating a holistic approach to combating phishing threats. Alam et al. focused on phishing attacks detection using a machine learning approach [2]. Their study contributes to the broader understanding of how machine learning techniques can be effectively applied to identify and mitigate phishing threats. Deshpande et al. conducted research on the detection of phishing websites using machine learning [6]. The work delves into specific features or patterns characteristic of phishing websites, contributing to the broader understanding of phishing detection. Mithra Raj and Jothi explored website phishing detection using machine learning classification algorithms [12]. The research delves into the comparative analysis of different classification algorithms for detecting phishing websites.

Phishing detection research and background cover a broad range of techniques, from lightweight mobile device solutions to ensemble machine learning systems. Comparative research and analysis provide valuable information about the benefits and drawbacks of various methods, allowing for the development of more reliable and efficient phishing detection systems.

3 Methodology

The systematic overview on the workflow of artificial intelligence based scheme to detect phishing URLs is illustrated by Fig. 1. Generally, the scheme includes the following components: data collection and preprocessing, feature analysis and selection, model training, model testing, and prediction. The detailed description will be given in following sections.

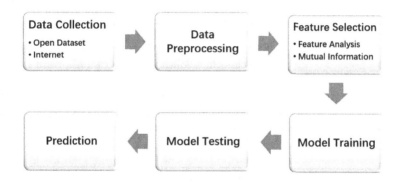

Fig. 1. Workflow overview of artificial intelligence based phishing URL detection.

3.1 Dataset and Preprocessing

The dataset utilized in this experiment has 10,000 observations, each of which represents a unique URL and its label, indicating whether the URL is benign or dangerous. This dataset was meticulously collected to guarantee that it contains a wide and representative sample of URLs from various sources, including legitimate and phishing websites. One of the initial tasks in preparing the dataset is to deal with missing values. Missing values can occur for a variety of reasons, including data collection errors or inadequate data entry. Missing values must be handled correctly in order to avoid bias and maintain the integrity of the analysis. This experiment removes all observations with missing values from the dataset. This strategy is used because removing such observations is preferable to entering missing values, which may introduce errors or biases into the data.

Categorical variables in dataset are non-numerical characteristics that distinguish different categories or groups. In our dataset, category variables store information on the specific attributes found in URLs, such as "has ip address", "has ssl", and "has javascript". It is necessary to convert categorical components into numerical representations before sending them into training models. To accomplish this, the categorical columns are encoded with labels. Label encoding is a technique for assigning distinct integer values to each category in a categorical variable. In this experiment, the categorical labels "has ip address", "has ssl", and "has javascript" are encoded into numerical numbers 0 and 1. The target variable, which represents the class labels of the URLs (benign or malicious), is also converted into binary values. The benign URLs are represented by 0 and malicious URLs by 1. By transforming the target variable into binary format, the model can effectively learn the patterns and characteristics associated with URLs, enabling it to distinguish between the two classes accurately during the training process.

3.2 Feature Analysis and Selection

Choosing the right features is very important when adopting artificial intelligent models to detect phishing websites. In this part of the model, we use mutual information classification to find the most useful features from the dataset. The goal is to choose the characteristics that contain the most important and distinguishing information for differentiating between harmless and harmful URLs. When we concentrate on these high-performing features, we can train the classifiers to focus on the most important characteristics. This will result in better predictive performance and more accurate detection of phishing attempts.

Mutual Information was used to perform feature selection. The top k features with the highest mutual information scores with the target variable ('label') are selected. The 'Mutual_info_classif' was used as the scoring function, which calculates the mutual information between each feature and the target variable. The general formula for calculating mutual information is based on Shannon's entropy shown as follows.

$$I(X;Y) = H(X) - H(X \mid Y) \tag{1}$$

where $H(X)$ is the entropy of X, the average level of information inherent to the variable's possible outcomes, and $H(X \mid Y)$ is the conditional entropy. This means that if X and Y are dependent, knowing one of the variables gives us information about the other one. In other words, the information of Y reduces the uncertainty of X. The mutual information between two random variable X and Y is expressed as follows:

$$I(X;Y) = \sum_{x \in X} \sum_{y \in Y} p(x,y) \log \left(\frac{p(x,y)}{p(x)p(y)} \right) \tag{2}$$

where: $I(X;Y)$ is the mutual information between variable X and Y. $p(x,y)$ is the joint probability distribution of X and Y. $p(x)$ and $p(y)$ are the marginal probability distributions of X and Y respectively.

Mutual information calculation returns an array containing the mutual information score for each feature. Higher score indicate higher mutual information and thus greater relevance to the target variable. This ensures that the classifiers are trained on the most valuable information, leading to improved performance in accurately differentiating between legitimate and malicious URLs. By leveraging mutual information classification, the model can pinpoint the features that are most informative and contribute significantly to predictive accuracy of the classifiers. Features selected include domain reputation, IP address, SSL encryption, URL properties, and JavaScript usage.

URL Characteristics. Phishers frequently create URLs that mimic legitimate websites but have subtle differences. These differences may include variations in URL length, the presence of some special characters, or the use of subdomains. Analyzing URL characteristics helps capture these slight variations and enables the classifier to identify suspicious URLs that resemble legitimate ones.

Address Presence. Legitimate websites usually have valid IP addresses associated with their domains. In contrast, phishing websites may lack valid IP addresses or use IP addresses that are associated with known malicious activities. Detecting the presence or absence of an IP address can be indicative of potential phishing attempts.

SSL Encryption. SSL encryption is employed by legitimate websites to secure data transmission between a user's browser and the website's server. Phishing websites may lack SSL certificates or use expired ones, leading to an insecure connection. Analyzing the presence of SSL encryption helps flag suspicious websites that might be attempting to deceive users.

JavaScript Usage. Phishing websites may use JavaScript to execute malicious scripts or redirect users to fraudulent pages. Analyzing the usage of JavaScript can help identify websites that exhibit suspicious behavior, indicating a potential phishing attempt.

Domain Reputation. is an essential factor in phishing detection. Fake websites are often short-lived and also have suspicious registration information. By considering factors like the age of the domain, its previous history, and registration details, the model can assign a reputation score to the domain. Lower reputation scores can be indicative of potential phishing websites.

3.3 Machine Learning and Deep Learning Models

In recent years, Artificial intelligence has shown encouraging results in real-time categorization tasks. The main benefit is its capacity to build adaptable models for particular applications, such as phishing detection. The following outlines the machine learning and deep learning techniques we employed in this paper:

Logistic Regression. A simple yet effective linear model used for binary classification tasks. Logistic regression is a supervised learning algorithm used for classification problems, utilizing regression techniques like logit and *sigmoid* for data processing. It uses regression type techniques in the background process [11]. It is well-suited for problems with a linear decision boundary. The logistic *sigmoid* function is used by logistic regression to convert its output and deliver a probability value that can be linked to a minimum of two distinct groups. Regression using logic functions best when there is a nearly linear connection in the data even if there could be intricate nonlinear interactions between factors, its performance is subpar [16].

Decision Tree Classifier. A tree-based model that makes decisions based on the values of features. Decision trees can capture complex relationships between features and the target variable, making them interpretable and easy to understand. This procedure applied recursively to build the whole tree. There is a threshold for splitting the tree [11].

Random Forest Classifier. An ensemble learning method that combines multiple decision trees to improve performance and reduce overfitting. The random forest algorithm is utilized for both classification and regression-related problems. It is a collection of decision trees, with the output being an average of the decision trees for regression problems and the most common result derived from all the decision trees for classification problems [1].

Gradient Boosting Classifier. Another ensemble learning technique that builds multiple weak learners (usually decision trees) sequentially, with each new learner focusing on the errors of the previous one. It's powerful and robust against overfitting. Gradient Boosting is a method used to train models incrementally and sequentially, identifying weak learners' shortcomings. It differs from Ada-Boost, which uses high-weight data points to identify shortcomings, and Gradient Boosting uses gradients in the loss function to measure the model's coefficients' fit to the underlying data. Understanding the loss function depends on the optimization goal [16].

Support Vector Machine (SVM): SVM is a supervised machine learning method used for classification and regression, gaining popularity due to its strong foundation in statistical learning theory and positive results in various data mining challenges. SVM is effective in nonlinear classification applications involving big datasets and problems, making it a new approach in data mining [1]. A powerful and versatile model used for both classification and regression tasks. SVM seeks to find the optimal hyperplane that best separates the data points of different classes.

AdaBoost Classifier: In certain ways, AdaBoost and Random Forest are similar in that they both combine weak classification models to create powerful classifiers. One model could classify items incorrectly. However, it might be beneficial for the overall classification if we combine many classifiers by choosing a group of samples in each iteration and give the final vote adequate weight. After each prediction round, trees are successively constructed as weak learners that correct erroneously predicted samples by giving them a higher weight. The model is picking up on past mistakes. The weighted majority vote-or, in the event of regression issues, the weighted median-is the ultimate forecast. The Ada-Boost algorithm is repeated by selecting the training set based on the accuracy of the previous training, with the weight of each classifier in each iteration varying [16].

Multilayer Perceptron (MLP): MLP is frequently referred to as vanilla feedforward neural network. It is possible to use multilayer perceptron for regression as well as classification issues. A multilayer perceptron is a directed graph neural network that connects many layers. As a result, the signal flow via each node is unique. All nodes have a nonlinear activation function, with the exception of the input nodes. Backpropagation is a supervised learning method used by MLP. MLP can be seen of as generalizations of linear models that process information via several steps before making a choice [10].

K-Nearest Neighbor Classifier (KNN): It is a simle and intuitive classification algorithm that makes predictions based on the majority class of its K nearest neighbors in the features space. it does not assume any underlying distribution of the data and can capture complex decision boundaries. KNN is suitable for both binary and multi-class classification tasks, especially when the data exhibits local patterns or clusters. The underlying data distribution in KNN does not require any assumptions. The KNN algorithm predicts the values of new datapoints using feature similarity, which implies that the value of a new datapoint is determined by how closely it resembles the points in the training set. There are numerous methods for determining how similar two recordings are to one another. Once the neighbors have been identified, the most frequent result or the average can be used to make the summary prediction.KNN is therefore applicable to situations involving regression or classification. Other than possessing the complete training dataset, there is no model to discuss [16].

Gaussian Naive Bayes: It is a probabilistic classifier that uses Bayes' theorem and the premise that features are independent. It calculates the conditional probability of each class based on the input features and forecasts the class with the highest likelihood. GaussianNB is efficient, especially for high-dimensional datasets, and it performs well under the independence assumption.

XGBoost Classifier (XGBoost): it is an efficient gradient boosting implementation that minimizes the loss function via a gradient descent approach. It is highly scalable and popular in machine learning contests and real-world applications. XGBoost is noted for its speed, accuracy, and capacity to handle big datasets, making it ideal for a variety of classification problems in this research experiment. The XGBoost algorithm outperforms popular methods on a single machine and can handle billions of instances in distributed or memory-limited scenarios. XGBoost's scalability is achieved by many algorithmic enhancements. Our inventions include a new tree learning approach for sparse data and a theoretically supported weighted quantile sketch procedure for handling instance weights in approximate tree learning. Parallel and distributed computers accelerate learning, allowing for rapid model exploration. XGBoost leverages out-of-core processing, allowing data scientists to process millions of instances on a desktop. Combining these strategies creates an end-to-end solution that can scale to larger data sets while using minimal cluster resources [16].

Light GBM Classifier (LGBM): LGBM is a gradient boosting system that uses a histogram-based technique to divide data into bins, resulting in shorter training times and less memory utilization. It is widely recognized for its effectiveness, ability to handle large amounts of data, and capability to process datasets with millions of samples and attributes. The LGBM is well-suited for research experiments that necessitate rapid and efficient performance.

CatBoost Classifier (CatBoost): it is a gradient-boosting package designed only for categorical data. It can manage categorical feature automatically, saving human preprocessing. CatBoost accelerates and improves training accuracy by fusing novel methods with symmetric decision trees. It can handle large datasets effectively and is suitable for classification operations involving categorical features.

4   Performance Evaluation

The experimental setup is an important step in the development and evaluation of the phishing detection model. The dataset is divided into training and testing sets. In addition, 12 well-known artificial intelligent models are used for training and evaluation: Logistic Regression, Decision Tree, Random Forest, Gradient Boosting, SVM, MLP, Adaboost, GaussianNB, XGB, Light GBM and CatBoost.. These models offer a variety of approaches, allowing for a thorough evaluation of their performance in detecting phishing websites.

The dataset is split into two sets, training set and testing sets. In this work, 90% of the data is used for training ('X_train', 'y_train'), and 10% is used for testing ('X_test','y_test'). X_train is a variable that contains the attributes of the samples in the training set, where each row corresponds to a sample and each column corresponds to a features while y_train is the variable that contains the corresponding labels (a column head in the dataset) which is the target value of the samples in the training set. X_test and y_test are similar to X_train and y_train, but they contain variable of the testing set.

4.1   Performance Metrics

After training of the models, prediction is made on test set. Evaluation metrics such as accuracy, prediction, recall and F1 score are calculated. The formulas used for calculating are as follows:

Accuracy is a commonly used metric to evaluate the performance of a classification model. It measures the overall correctness of the model's prediction across all classes.This measures the proportion of correctly classified samples out of the total numbers of samples.

$$\text{Accuracy} = \frac{\text{Number of Correct Prediction}}{\text{Total Number of Prediction}} \tag{3}$$

Since the experiment uses binary classification, accuracy is calculated as follows:

$$\text{Accuracy} = \frac{\text{TP} + \text{TN}}{\text{TP} + \text{TN} + \text{FP} + \text{FN}} \tag{4}$$

where TP represents True Positives, the number of correctly predicited positive instances. TN standing for True Negatives, shows the number of negative samples classified correctly. FP meaning False Positives, counts the number of negative instance incorrectly predicted as positive by the model. FN, False Negatives, denotes the number of positive instance incorrectly predicted as negative by the model.

Precision is a metric used to evaluate the performance of a classification model, particularly in scenarios where minimizing false positives is important. This measures the proportion of true positive predictions out of all positive predictions made by the models.

$$\text{Precision} = \frac{\text{TP}}{\text{TP} + \text{FP}} \tag{5}$$

Recall is also known as sensitive or true positive rate, which measures the proportion of true positive predictions out of all actual positive samples in the dataset.

$$\text{Recall} = \frac{\text{TP}}{\text{TP} + \text{FN}} \tag{6}$$

F1 Score is the combination of precision and recall into a single value. It is a metric used to evaluate the performance of a classification model in scenarios where correctly identifying positive instance is crucial. F1 score is the harmonic mean of precision and recall providing a balance between the two metrics.

$$\text{F1 Score} = 2 \times \frac{\text{Precision} \times \text{Recall}}{\text{Precision} + \text{Recall}} \tag{7}$$

The aforementioned metrics are widely used in the field of machine learning technology and enable a thorough assessment of the selected models.

4.2 Results and Analysis

The experimental results are presented and analyzed in this section. The metrics mentioned above are used to evaluate the performance of each model. Table 1 displays the results of each model in terms of the considered metrics. It is observed that the Decision Tree Classifier achieves the highest accuracy of 98.80% among twelve models, showing that it can distinguish between malicious and safe URLs most accurately. The effectiveness of decision tree classifier is further confirmed by the precision, recall, and F1 score metrics. The results of recall and precision indicate that it can effectively minimize false negatives and false positives, respectively. The F1 score reflects its ability to accurately identify phishing websites with balanced performance.

Table 1. Performance comparison among different classifiers

Tested Model	Accuracy	Precision	Recall	F1 Score
Logistic regression	0.751	0.8727	0.5746	0.6930
Decision Tree	**0.988**	**1.0000**	**0.9755**	**0.9876**
Random Forest	0.987	0.9979	0.9755	0.9866
Gradient Boosting	0.854	0.9673	0.7260	0.8294
SVM	0.551	0.5415	0.5337	0.5376
MLPs	0.652	0.9732	0.2965	0.4545
AdaBoost	0.809	0.9116	0.6748	0.7756
KNeighbors	0.95	0.9782	0.9182	0.9473
GaussianNB	0.748	0.9575	0.5072	0.6631
XGB	0.92	0.9417	0.8916	0.9160
Light GBM	0.918	0.9473	0.8814	0.9131
CatBoost	0.92	0.9555	0.8773	0.9147

Figure 2 presents a grouped bar chart that compares the efficacy among different classifiers for phishing website detection in a more intuitive way. It can be observed that the Decision Tree Classifier outperforms the other models in every metric. It has an impressive accuracy of 98.80% and an F1 score of 98.76%. Moreover, Random Forest obtained the second best results which are quite close to Decision Tree. The Logistic Regression classifier has a high precision but a low recall, indicating that it may incorrectly classify some positive instances as negative (false negatives). The Random Forest and Gradient Boosting classifiers perform similarly, with high accuracy and F1 scores. However, SVM performs poorly across all metrics, indicating that it has limitations in accurately detecting phishing websites in this situation.

The visualization demonstrates how well the Decision Tree Classifier distinguishes between legitimate and phishing URLs. The results are extremely

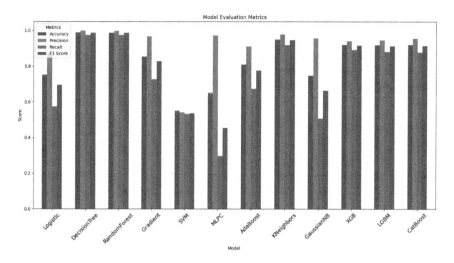

Fig. 2. Performance comparison of twelve different AI models.

valuable, making it ideal for the systems with the target of detecting phishing attempts. They provide valuable insights and lay the groundwork for future research and the development of effective phishing detection solutions.

4.3   Comparison with Other Research Papers

In this research, we conducted a comprehensive evaluation of the proposed decision tree model by employing a dataset comprising URLs associated with fraudulent websites. The decision tree classifier functioned admirably, with an impressive accuracy of 98.80 %. In addition, we conducted a comparative analysis with the data reported in other relevant research articles that studied machine learning models for phishing website identification in order to gain a better context and knowledge of the efficacy of our proposed technique. The result comparison with other research is summarized in the Table 2 below.

Table 2. Comparison of accuracy.

Research	Machine Learning Model	Accuracy
Our scheme	Decision Tree	**98.80%**
Ref. [15]	Artificial Neural Network	94.5%
Ref. [6]	Random Forest	97.3%
Ref. [12]	XGboost	96.71%

It is clear from the comparison that our recommended decision tree model performs better than the other models listed in the literature. It is important to point out that the models' balanced performance, considering both precision and recall, is represented by the F1 ratings displayed in the table. Our suggested approach has shown an improved F1 score, suggesting that it can effectively identify phishing websites (true positives) while also reducing false positives and false negatives.

5 Conclusion

This paper conducted extensive and comparative experiment on AI models for phishing website detection. The experimental results and analysis demonstrated how well the Decision Tree Classifier outperforms in detecting phishing websites based on the carefully seleted dataset. The high accuracy, precision, recall, and F1 score demonstrate its ability to distinguish between benign and malicious URLs. Furthermore, the comparative analysis with other research papers underscores the superiority of the Decision Tree Classifier in terms of accuracy, making it a valuable and promising model for enhancing cybersecurity in the digital age.

Acknowledgments. This work is supported in part by he Major Research Plan of Hubei Provience under Gran No. 2023BAA027, the National Natural Science Foundation of China under grants 62072134 and 62472150, and the Key Research and Development Program of Hubei Province under Grant 2021BEA163.

References

1. Ahammad, S.K.H., et al. Phishing URL detection using machine learning methods. Adv. Eng. Softw. **173**, 103288 (2022)
2. Alam, M.N., et al.: Phishing attacks detection using machine learning approach. In: 2020 Third International Conference on Smart Systems and Inventive Technology (ICSSIT), pp. 1173–1179. IEEE, 2020
3. Basit, A., Zafar, M., Javed, A.R., Jalil, Z.: A novel ensemble machine learning method to detect phishing attack. In: 2020 IEEE 23rd International Multitopic Conference (INMIC), pp. 1–5. IEEE, 2020
4. Chawla, A.: Phishing website analysis and detection using machine learning. Int. J. Intell. Syst. Appl. Eng. **10**(1), 10–16 (2022)
5. Das Guptta, S., Shahriar, K.T., Alqahtani, H., Alsalman, D., Sarker, I.H.: Modeling hybrid feature-based phishing websites detection using machine learning techniques. Ann. Data Sci. pp. 1–26 (2022)
6. Deshpande, A., Pedamkar, O., Chaudhary, N., Borde, S.: Detection of phishing websites using machine learning. Int. J. Eng. Res. Technol. (IJERT) **10**(05) (2021)
7. Gandotra, E., Gupta, D.: An efficient approach for phishing detection using machine learning. Multimedia Secur. Algorithm Dev. Anal. Appl. pp. 239–253 (2021)
8. Haynes, K., Shirazi, H., Ray, I.: Lightweight URL-based phishing detection using natural language processing transformers for mobile devices. Procedia Comput. Sci. **191**, 127–134 (2021)
9. Kalaharsha, P., Mehtre, B.M.: Detecting phishing sites–an overview. *arXiv preprint*arXiv:2103.12739 (2021)

10. Kolla, J., Praneeth, S., Baig, M.S., Reddy Karri, G.: A comparison study of machine learning techniques for phishing detection. J. Bus. Inf. Syst. (e-ISSN: 2685-2543), **4**(1), 21–33 (2022)
11. Lakshmanarao, A., Rao, P.S.P., Krishna, M.M.B.: Phishing website detection using novel machine learning fusion approach. In: 2021 International Conference on Artificial Intelligence and Smart Systems (ICAIS), pp. 1164–1169. IEEE, 2021
12. Mithra Raj, M., Arul Jothi, J.A.: Website phishing detection using machine learning classification algorithms. In: International Conference on Applied Informatics, pp. 219–233. Springer (2022)
13. Mohammada, G.B., Shitharthb, S., Kumarc, P.R.: Integrated machine learning model for an URL phishing detection. Int. J. Grid Distrib. Comput. **14**(1), 513–529 (2020)
14. Ojewumi, T.O., Ogunleye, G.O., Oguntunde, B.O., Folorunsho, O., Fashoto, S.G., Ogbu, N.: Performance evaluation of machine learning tools for detection of phishing attacks on web pages. Sci. Afr. **16**, e01165 (2022)
15. Salahdine, F., Mrabet, Z. EI., Kaabouch, N.: Phishing attacks detection a machine learning-based approach. In: 2021 IEEE 12th Annual Ubiquitous Computing, Electronics & Mobile Communication Conference (UEMCON), pp. 0250–0255. IEEE (2021)
16. Shahrivari, V., Darabi, M.M., Izadi, M.: Phishing detection using machine learning techniques. *arXiv preprint* arXiv:2009.11116 (2020)

Exploring Interpretability in Backdoor Attacks on Image Classification

Jiaxun Li[1,2], Hao Chen[1], Gaoyuan Zhou[1], Mingxin Xu[1], and Hanwei Qian[1(✉)]

[1] Jiangsu Police Institute, Nanjing City 210000, Jiangsu, China
303560601@qq.com
[2] Soochow University , Suzhou City 215123, Jiangsu, China

Abstract. This study delves into the issue of backdoor attacks on deep learning models in image recognition, proposing defense strategies based on interpretability techniques. Through experiments and analysis, we verify the impacts of different types of backdoor attacks on deep neural networks, and explore the application effectiveness of gradient-based activation mapping techniques in enhancing model interpretability. This paper not only provides a deep theoretical foundation for understanding and detecting backdoor attacks but also offers practical defense approaches and methods for developing more robust and secure deep learning models. Future research can further explore complex attack scenarios and defense mechanisms to address evolving security challenges.

Keywords: Deep Learning · Backdoor Attack · Neural Network

1 Introduction

In the current age of rapid advancements in information technology, continuous updates in computer hardware and software have significantly bolstered the capabilities of deep learning. This evolution has been facilitated by powerful computational abilities and the accessibility provided by various cloud computing platforms. These factors have democratized deep learning research, fostering explosive growth since 2012 when Hinton's team introduced Alex-Net, a pioneering deep convolutional neural network (CNN) that marked a significant leap in image recognition. Subsequent years witnessed continued innovation in network architectures and training methods, supported by advancements in GPU technology.

As societal demands for more sophisticated applications grow, so does the complexity of deep learning models. These models, typically structured with input, hidden, and output layers, employ hierarchical processing to extract and classify features. However, their complexity often renders them as "black box" systems, where understanding the internal mechanisms and learning patterns becomes challenging. This opacity poses security risks, particularly concerning adversarial examples and other vulnerabilities in critical applications [1–5].

The paper is structured as follows. Section 1 introduces the concept of backdoor attacks in deep learning and emphasizes the significance of interpretability-driven

W. Li et al. (Eds.): EISA 2024, CCIS 2266, pp. 86–98, 2025.
https://doi.org/10.1007/978-3-031-80419-9_6

defense strategies, alongside a review of current global and domestic research. It also outlines the overall thesis structure. Section 2 delves into fundamental neural network principles, backdoor attack methodologies, and interpretability techniques. Section 3 presents experimental analyses on backdoor attacks, interpreting their implications, and includes experiments using gradient-based activation mapping techniques for defense, with detailed result analyses. Section 4 concludes by summarizing defense strategies against deep learning image backdoor attacks and outlines future research directions aimed at enhancing model interpretability and security.

We make the following contributions:

- In the field of deep learning, this paper concludes that different models can exhibit variations in recognizing the same image. Models trained on different data sets may exhibit changes in their attention to image recognition tasks.
- Regarding backdoor detection, this paper finds that backdoor attacks can affect the data processed by the model, which in turn leads to shifts in the model's attention during decision-making. Enhancing the interpretability of this process can help in detecting backdoor attacks.

2 Background

2.1 Neural Networks

A neural network is a computational model inspired by biology, simulating the human brain's structure and functions. It consists of interconnected nodes acting as "neurons," where each node represents an output function. Connections between nodes, or weights, dictate signal importance. These weights adjust automatically during training, enabling tasks like pattern recognition and data classification [6]. Neural networks vary by connection type and parameters, categorized into feedforward, recurrent, etc. Feedforward networks, notably versatile, employ an input layer for data, hidden layers for processing, and an output layer for results, enhancing data processing and pattern recognition. Training uses example data to decode complex inputs through layered feature extraction, akin to human brain operations. Post-training, neural networks excel in tasks such as speech or image recognition. Adaptive and mimetic, they're integral to artificial intelligence.

Neural network evolution spans distinct phases—Perceptron, marked by McCulloch-Pitts' model, peaked with the perceptron, marred by Minsky's critique; Backpropagation, dominated by the algorithm's advent; and Deep Learning, soaring post-ImageNet's success [7].

Deep learning and neural networks have a close and inseparable relationship. Specifically, machine learning encompasses a broad range of methods and models, with neural networks being a significant model within this field. Neural networks simulate the way neurons in the human brain connect to automatically learn and recognize data. When we refer to deep neural networks, we are talking about neural networks with multiple layers and more complex structures. Deep learning is based on these deep neural networks, leveraging powerful data-driven and automatic learning mechanisms to achieve precise recognition and prediction of complex patterns. It is a key technology driving the advancement of artificial intelligence and is an important branch of machine learning. The relationship is roughly illustrated in Fig. 1.

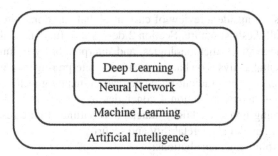

Fig. 1. Relationship diagram

Neural networks are a form of implementation for deep learning; in other words, deep learning is an advanced machine learning method built on the foundation of neural networks. In simple terms, a neural network is a mathematical model that processes and learns from data efficiently by simulating the complex connections and signal interactions between biological neurons. Deep learning uses multi-layer neural networks to learn latent features and patterns in input data, enabling tasks such as data classification and regression. Compared to shallow neural networks with only a few hidden layers, deep learning models have enhanced performance due to their multiple hidden layers. This deep architecture provides deep learning models with the ability to handle intricate non-linear problems and significantly improves the model's expressive power and generalization ability.

The uniqueness of deep learning models lies in their capacity to automatically extract and analyze higher-level abstract features from raw data. Moreover, through the backpropagation algorithm, deep learning models can accurately train their parameters to minimize the loss function, achieving efficient representation and precise prediction of input data. Therefore, deep learning is an advanced machine learning method based on neural networks. It constructs multi-layer neural networks to deeply explore latent features and intrinsic patterns of input data, efficiently performing complex tasks such as data classification and regression, and demonstrating powerful learning and prediction capabilities [8].

In order to address the problem of gradient vanishing or exploding as the number of model layers increases, researchers have conducted extensive research, with the representative achievement being residual networks. The basic component of a residual network is the residual module, which is a unique design that includes two or more convolutional layers and incorporates an innovative skip connection. The function of this skip connection is to directly add the input of the module to the processing result of the convolutional layer, constructing a structure called residual connection.

Specifically, if we assume that the input data is x and the output of the convolutional layer after processing is represented as $f(x)$, then the final output $H(x)$ of the residual module is the sum of $f(x)$ and the original input x, that is:

$$H(x) = f(x) + x.$$

In this equation, $f(x)$ represents the residual mapping processed by the convolutional layer, while x is the original input directly passed through skip connections. Figure 2 is a schematic diagram of a simple residual module. Note: Both convolutional layers and fully connected layers contain weight parameters, hence they are also referred to as weight layers.

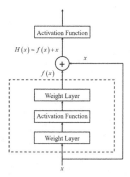

Fig. 2. Schematic Diagram of Residual Module

2.2 Backdoor Attack

Backdoor attacks in deep learning implant covert functionalities during model training. Activated by triggers, they alter outputs maliciously, complicating detection due to normalcy under usual conditions [10].

Figure 3 illustrates the process of a backdoor attack using poisoned datasets and model training, highlighting the insertion of triggers and their impact on model behavior. Specifically, the attacker first adds a trigger (a small white square in the bottom-right corner) to the original images of digits 1 and 3, poisoning the data to target a label of the attacker's choice. Then, they use these poisoned images along with other unpoisoned benign data to construct a training set, training a backdoored model. During the inference phase, when input data contains the trigger (such as the white square on digits 1 and 3), the backdoored model classifies it as the preset target label; whereas benign samples (such as untriggered digits 1 and 3) are classified accurately according to their true labels.

Backdoor scenarios manipulate datasets, platforms, or models, exploiting trust in third-party resources. Attack vectors include Bad Nets, Blended Attacks, Label-Consistent Attacks, and Trojan Net, undermining model integrity [11–15].

2.3 Interpretability

Grad-CAM (Gradient-weighted Class Activation Mapping) is an interpretability method used to explain model predictions after the model has been trained. It is a visualization technique suitable for deep learning, which helps to understand the model's decision-making process by analyzing the responses of various feature maps in a trained model, thus enhancing model interpretability [16, 17].

Grad-CAM determines the importance of each feature map by computing the gradient of the model's output with respect to each feature map. It first performs a forward pass to

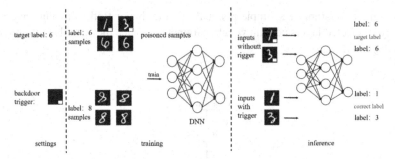

Fig. 3. BadNets Attack Flowchart

calculate the class probabilities for the model's output, and then computes the gradient of the class score of interest with respect to each feature map during the backward pass. After obtaining the gradients for each feature map, global average pooling is applied to spatially average these gradients, resulting in weights for each feature map channel. These weights reflect the contribution of each feature map to the target class. Finally, these weights are applied to the feature maps, multiplied channel-wise, and summed to produce the final Grad-CAM image [18]. In the Grad-CAM image, regions deemed important by the model appear as brighter areas.

To further refine the heatmap, the ReLU function is typically applied to threshold the heatmap, keeping only pixel values greater than zero; bilinear interpolation is used to resize the heatmap to match the dimensions of the input image; and pixel values are normalized to ensure they fall within the range of 0 to 1. These steps generate the final Grad-CAM image, as shown in Fig. 4.

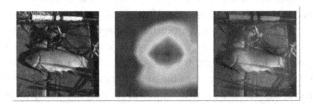

Fig. 4. An example of Grad-CAM

3   Experiment

In today's widespread application of neural networks, the security of models directly impacts social stability and the safety of people's lives and property. Faced with the threat of backdoor attacks, targeted defense measures are essential. Current backdoor attacks exploit the opacity of neural network models, making it crucial to enhance their interpretability as a strategy against such attacks. Visualization techniques are common methods used to enhance model interpretability. Therefore, the next step involves conducting backdoor attacks on deep learning models and applying visualization techniques to identify and defend against these attacks [19, 20].

The primary objective of the experiments is to understand and practice the training process of deep learning models, evaluate their performance on normal data versus data injected with backdoors, and use visualization techniques to understand the differences in decision-making processes between backdoored and clean models [21]. Through these experiments, we aim to achieve the goal of identifying and defending against backdoor attacks. This experiment is based on deep learning principles and utilizes two models, ResNet-9 and ResNet-18, trained on specific datasets.

The experiments involve evaluating the trained models, comparing the accuracy of the backdoored models when tested on normal versus injected backdoor data. Simultaneously, by enhancing the interpretability of models through visualization techniques, we aim to understand the logic and processes behind model decisions effectively, thereby enabling effective identification and defense against backdoor attacks.

3.1 Experimental Setup

This paper employs Residual Neural Networks (ResNets), specifically ResNet9 and ResNet18. Here's an overview of each:

ResNet9 utilizes Basic Block as its core unit, forming two-layer groups, layer1 and layer2, each comprising stacked Basic Block residual blocks. These blocks facilitate down sampling of feature maps while preserving their dimensions. The model concludes by flattening the feature maps and processing them through two fully connected layers: the first reduces feature map dimensions followed by a non-linear activation, and the second maps processed features to the final classification output.

ResNet18, named for its 18 trainable layers, begins with RGB images of size 224 × 224. It initiates feature extraction through four independent convolutional layers, each equipped with a 3 × 3 convolution kernel and ReLU activation. To address training challenges like gradient issues, ResNet18 incorporates eight residual blocks. Each block integrates two convolutional layers and a skip connection, ensuring stable gradient propagation and enhancing training efficiency. After feature extraction, global average pooling transforms high-dimensional features into a one-dimensional vector, retaining global image details [22–25]. A fully connected layer with 1000 neurons maps the pooled feature vector to the final classification space, followed by an output layer using SoftMax activation for generating class probabilities [26–30].

The experiments primarily use the CIFAR-10 dataset, consisting of 60,000 color images at 32 × 32 pixels. These images span ten classes like airplanes, cars, birds, facilitating advancements in image recognition. CIFAR-10 is split into five training batches and one test batch, ensuring rigorous model evaluation. Its balanced class distribution and manageable size make it ideal for evaluating machine learning and deep learning algorithms in image classification and computer vision.

In the experimental setup, a poisoning rate of 0.1 is applied, where 10% of dataset images are "poisoned" by placing a 2 × 2 white square in the bottom right corner of each image channel. This white square, set by pixel values to 1 in normalized [0, 1] range, acts as a trigger, depicted in Fig. 6 for adulterated data processing.

Figure 5 shows processed images from the CIFAR-10 dataset.

Fig. 5. Normal Dataset Images

Fig. 6. Poisoned Dataset Images

3.2 Experimental Results and Analysis

Using the Torch tool's data loader, three datasets were encapsulated: the poisoned training dataset, the normal test dataset, and the test dataset with the trigger. The batch size was set to 128, and the entire training dataset was iterated over 200 times. The learning rate was set to 0.001, and the transparency of the trigger in the data was set to 0.2. CUDA device GPU acceleration was used for training. The attack results were obtained, and the last 10 sets of data from the two models are provided as examples. Table 2 is for ResNet9, and Table 3 is for ResNet18 (Table 1):

Table 1. Experimental Environment Configuration

environment configuration	version	environment configuration	version
Cuda	11.8	Tqdm	4.66.2
torch vision	0.17.1	pillow	10.2.0
pandas	2.2.1	scikit_learn	1.4.1
NumPy	1.24.3	Torkham	0.4.0
Torch	2.2.1	OpenCV	4.6.0
matplotlib	3.8.3		

In both models, the loss function used is cross-entropy loss, and the optimization algorithm is stochastic gradient descent. From the data in Table 2 and Table 3, we can see

Table 2. Last 10 Sets of Data for ResNet9

epoch	loss	train_acc	test_ori_acc	test_tri_acc
190	295.972	0.7377	0.7317	0.9062
191	293.159	0.74738	0.7435	0.9082
192	293.353	0.74276	0.7391	0.9184
193	293.496	0.74702	0.7475	0.8987
194	292.058	0.73646	0.7331	0.8881
195	293.128	0.74928	0.7439	0.8967
196	292.093	0.74892	0.7463	0.8796
197	289.882	0.75182	0.7425	0.9043
198	289.588	0.74244	0.7402	0.8973
199	288.706	0.74258	0.7405	0.8969

Table 3. Last 10 Sets of Data for ResNet18

epoch	loss	train_acc	test_ori_acc	test_tri_acc
190	10.790	0.99332	0.8846	0.9377
191	9.290	0.9913	0.8833	0.9177
192	9.346	0.99268	0.8783	0.9175
193	9.350	0.99336	0.8817	0.9023
194	9.002	0.99406	0.8789	0.919
195	9.237	0.99468	0.8827	0.9136
196	8.504	0.99364	0.8852	0.8939
197	10.113	0.99344	0.8817	0.9321
198	9.404	0.9939	0.8822	0.9194
199	9.089	0.99172	0.8805	0.912

that the loss for ResNet9 ranges from 288 to 296, whereas for ResNet18, it ranges from 8 to 11. Additionally, considering the accuracy rates, we can determine that ResNet18 has better performance and stronger generalization capability compared to ResNet9. The data has been better trained, and there is no sign of overfitting.

The following two charts visualize the changes in experimental data:

- The Training curve represents the accuracy on the training data.
- The Testing-ori curve represents the accuracy on the original test data.
- The Testing-tri curve represents the accuracy on the test data with the trigger.

In Fig. 7 and Fig. 8, three different scenarios are depicted showing how accuracy changes with the number of training epochs: accuracy on the training data (blue line),

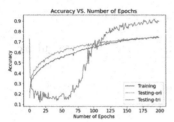
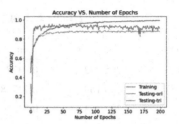

Fig. 7. Accuracy for ResNet9   **Fig. 8.** Accuracy for ResNet18

accuracy on the original test data (orange line), and accuracy on test data with triggers (green line). In both figures, as epochs increase, accuracy trends upward, except for initial confusion impacting triggered test data accuracy. This suggests continuous model learning and optimization. Training and original test data accuracies are kept high with minimal difference, indicating avoidance of overfitting or underfitting issues.

Early training stages in both graphs show rapid accuracy rise, indicating quick feature learning. Later, accuracy growth slows, nearing learning capacity or impacted by data noise.

In Fig. 7's first half, the model typically performs better on training data than unseen test data—a common occurrence. In backdoored models, test data with triggers may exceed both, seen towards Fig. 7's end due to ResNet9 flaws in image recognition. Figure 8 shows training data accuracy starting lower than trigger test data, improving later as ResNet18 trains adequately. In both figures, test data with triggers (green line) accuracy notably differs, reflecting backdoor attack impact on model behavior. This results in higher trigger test data accuracy than original test data, misleadingly boosted by the attack's manipulation.

From a security viewpoint, relying on outcome data alone to detect backdoors is unreliable. Methods like Grad-CAM for model decision visualization are crucial for defense.

Initially, input data undergoes preprocessing per the model training code: images are converted to tensors, normalized, and fed into the model. Hooks in the model's forward and backward propagation capture output feature maps and gradients from specific layers. Subsequently, steps such as reverse normalization, color channel conversion, and heatmap generation convert tensors back into image format for visualization.

Here are the Grad-CAM visualization results comparing the backdoored and clean models of ResNet18 using images from the bird class in the CIFAR-10 test set: bird1 (left), bird51 (right).

Fig. 9. Clean Model with Clean Data

Fig. 10. Clean Model with Trigger

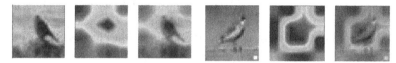

Fig. 11. Backdoor Model with Clean Data

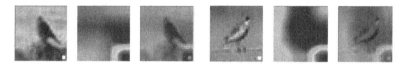

Fig. 12. Backdoor Model with Trigger

This paper uses malicious networks for backdoor attacks. Figure 9 and Fig. 10 use models trained on clean CIFAR-10 datasets, while Fig. 11 and Fig. 12 use models trained on CIFAR-10 data with triggers added to the lower-right corner of images (depicted as small white squares). Visualization experiments were conducted using CIFAR-10 test data with Grad-CAM.

In Fig. 9, after training with the clean model, image recognition focuses primarily on main objects, reflecting selected features during recognition. Figure 10 shows minimal alteration in image recognition when triggers are added to the clean model, with slight changes observed, such as blunting of heatmaps and the disappearance of weaker hotspots in certain images like bird1 (top-left) and bird118 (bottom-right).

Figure 11 demonstrates how the backdoored model's attention shifts towards corners during recognition of regular images. This shift results from preprocessing during training, such as random flips and cropping, potentially altering trigger positions to edge areas.

Figure 12 highlights that after adding triggers, the model's attention notably centers on trigger positions. Interestingly, visualizations for images like bird51 in both Fig. 11 and Fig. 12 remain nearly identical despite trigger variations, due to similarities between trigger colors and surrounding areas, impacting the model's recognition.

These Grad-CAM visualizations visually illustrate poisoning effects on the model. In summary, the backdoored model shifts attention to trigger regions during testing, unlike the clean model. Backdoor attacks condition models to recognize triggers as significant features, impacting operational results subtly but discernibly.

Visualization techniques like Grad-CAM play a crucial role in identifying and defending against deep learning backdoor attacks. Upon detection, steps such as dataset inspection, replacement, model reconstruction, or dataset augmentation can effectively mitigate these attacks and ensure normal model operation.

3.3 Feasibility Analysis

The effectiveness of Grad-CAM technology lies in its ability to generate heatmaps by calculating the gradient weights of each layer in the model during classification, thereby revealing the model's decision-making basis. Widely used in image classification tasks, Grad-CAM helps observe differences in model attention when processing images with and without triggers, making it a viable tool for detecting backdoor attacks. By comparing Grad-CAM results for clean models and backdoored models, it is evident that backdoored models focus on trigger areas, while clean models concentrate on the main subject of the image, effectively indicating the presence of backdoor attacks.

Furthermore, Grad-CAM analysis can guide the implementation of defense strategies such as dataset replacement, model retraining, or data augmentation to mitigate the impact of poisoned data. Known for its interpretability and ease of use, Grad-CAM is highly feasible for practical application and, when combined with other defense techniques, can form a comprehensive defense system to enhance model security and reliability.

4   Related Work

In recent years, significant progress has been made in the study of backdoor attacks and defenses in deep learning models, both domestically and internationally. Wu et al. introduce the Backdoor Bench benchmark [31], a comprehensive platform designed for the standardized evaluation of backdoor attacks and defenses. The BackdoorBench benchmark was presented at the NeurIPS 2022 conference, highlighting its contribution to the field. Li et al. have conducted substantial research on backdoor attacks, sharing their findings with the TechNet AI community. His work includes an introduction to the fundamentals and classic methods of backdoor attacks, along with Tsinghua University's research contributions. Furthermore, Li et al. developed the Backdoor Box toolkit [32], which offers a valuable resource for domestic researchers to advance their studies. Nguyen et al. proposed the Wanet-imperceptible warping-based backdoor attack [33]. Hossein et al. introduced the Sleeper agent: Scala attack method [34].

5   Conclusion and Outlook

Backdoor attacks exploit the inherent opacity of deep learning models, where their internal operations are often inscrutable. In this article, we have utilized Gradient Class Activation Mapping (Grad-CAM) to enhance the interpretability of these models. By visualizing the decision-making processes, Grad-CAM enables us to distinguish between clean models and those compromised by backdoors, thus facilitating the identification and mitigation of such attacks.

In conclusion, visualization methods are pivotal in defending against deep learning backdoor attacks by enhancing model interpretability and fortifying defense strategies. Future efforts should focus on technological advancements, practical implementations, and interdisciplinary collaborations to effectively address evolving and emerging security challenges in deep learning.

Acknowledgments. This work is funded in part by the Philosophy and Social Sciences Research Project of Universities in Jiangsu Province (No. 2024SJYB0345) and the Cyberspace Security construction project of key disciplines in Jiangsu Province during the 14th Five-Year Plan.

References

1. Ying, Z., Wu, B.: A survey of backdoor attacks in deep learning models. Comput. Sci. **50**(03), 333–350
2. Wu, B., Chen, H., Zhang, M., et al.: BackdoorBench: A Comprehensive Benchmark of Backdoor Learning. arXiv:2206.12654
3. Li, Y., Ya, M., Bai, Y., et al.: Backdoorbox: A Python Toolbox for Backdoor Learning. arXiv: 2302.01762
4. Nguyen, A., Tran, A.: WaNet -- Imperceptible Warping-based Backdoor Attack. arXiv:2102. 10369 (2021)
5. Souri, H., Fowl, L., Chellappa, R., et al.: Sleeper Agent: Scalable Hidden Trigger Backdoors for Neural Networks Trained from Scratch. arXiv:2106.08970 (2022)
6. Saito, Y.: Introduction to Deep Learning. People's Posts and Telecommunications Publishing House, 37–40 (2018)
7. Li, C.J., Yang, S.Y., Liu, F., et al.: Seventy years of neural networks: retrospect and prospect. J. Comput. Res. Dev. **39**(08), 1697–1716 (2016)
8. Qiu, X.: Neural Networks and Deep Learning, pp. 4–20. Machinery Industry Press (2020)
9. He, K., Zhang, X., Ren, S., et al.: Deep Residual Learning for Image Recognition. arXiv: 1512.03385 (2015)
10. Liu, Q., Zhang, T., Lu, X., et al.: A pre-trained model-assisted defense method for backdoor sample self-filtration. Comput. Technol. Dev. **33**(01), 121–129 (2023)
11. Yu, G.: Research and Application of Attack Methods in the Training and Inference Stages of Neural Networks. University of Electronic Science and Technology of China (2023)
12. Gu, T., Dolan-Gavitt, B., Garg, S.: Badnets: Identifying Vulnerabilities in the Machine Learning Model Supply Chain. arXiv:1708.06733 (2017)
13. Chen, X., Liu, C., Li, B., et al.: Targeted Backdoor Attacks on Deep Learning Systems Using Data Poisoning. arXiv:1712.05526 (2017)
14. Turner, A., Tsipras, D., Madry, A.: Label-consistent Backdoor Attacks. arXiv:1912.02771 (2019)
15. Tang, R., Du, M., Liu, N., et al.: An Embarrassingly Simple Approach for Trojan Attack in Deep Neural Networks. arXiv:2006.08131 (2020)
16. Lin, Y.: Research on Interpretable Ensemble Learning for Image-based Malware Detection. Beijing Jiao Tong University (2023)
17. Chen, J., Zhan, D., Xia, S., et al.: Research on explainability of malware detection based on deep learning. J. Nanjing Univ. Sci. Technol. **47**(03), 343–351 (2023)
18. Lin, Z.: Research on Interpretable Machine Learning and Applications. South China University of Technology (2023)

19. Papernot, N., McDaniel, P., Jha, S., Fredrikson, M., Celik, Z.B., Swami, A.: The limitations of deep learning in adversarial settings. In: Proceedings of IEEE European Symposium on Security and Privacy (EuroS&P), pp. 372–387 (2016)
20. Kurakin, A., Goodfellow, I., Bengio, S.: Adversarial machine learning at scale. In: Proceedings of International Conference on Learning Representations (ICLR) (2017)
21. Kurakin, A., Goodfellow, I.: Adversarial examples in the physical world. In: Proceedings of International Conference on Learning Representations (ICLR) (2017)
22. Su, D., Zhang, H., Chen, H., Yi, J., Chen, P.Y., Gao, Y.: Is robustness the cost of accuracy? A comprehensive study on the robustness of 18 deep image classification models. In: Proceedings of European Conference on Computer Vision (ECCV), pp. 631–648 (2018)
23. Rozsa, A., Gunther, M., Boult, T.E.: Are accuracy and robustness correlated?. In: Proceedings of the 15th IEEE International Conference on Machine Learning and Applications (ICMLA), pp. 227–232 (2016)
24. Carlini, N., Wagner, D.: Defensive Distillation is Not Robust to Adversarial Examples (2016). arXiv:1607.04311
25. Fawzi, A., Fawzi, O., Frossard, P.: Analysis of classifiers robustness to adversarial perturbations. Mach. Learn. **107**(3), 481–508 (2018)
26. Tramer, F., Papernot, N., Goodfellow, I., Boneh, D., McDaniel, P.: The' Space of Transferable Adversarial Examples (2017). arXiv:1704.03453
27. Liu, Y., Chen, X., Liu, C., Song, D.: Delving into Transferable Adversarial Examples and Black-box Attacks (2016). arXiv:1611.02770
28. Wu, L., Zhu, Z., Tai, C., W.E.: Understanding and Enhancing the Transferability of Adversarial Examples (2018). arXiv:1802.09707
29. Wang, Z., Bovik, A.C., Sheikh, H.R., Simoncelli, E.P.: Image quality assessment: from error visibility to structural similarity. IEEE Trans. Image Process. **13**(4), 600–612 (2004)
30. Rozsa, A., Rudd, E.M., Boult, T.E.: Adversarial diversity and hard positive generation. In: Proceedings of IEEE Computer Society Conference on Computer Vision and Pattern Recognition Workshops (CVPRW), pp. 25–32 (2016)

Attribute-Based Secret Key Signature Scheme

Chengtang Cao[✉][iD], Zongzheng Huang, and Shupei Mo

Department of Big Data and Information Engineering, Guizhou Industry Polytechnic
College,, Guizhou 550008 Guiyang, China
caochengtang@163.com

Abstract. In response to the drawbacks of low portability of secret key
in signature algorithms, an attribute-based secret key signature algorithm (ASKS) is constructed in this paper. In the process of generating
user public keys using attributes, polynomial based on the secret sharing
technology and the fuzzy vault idea are used to protect user attribute features. Because ASKS does not require users to store attribute features, it
does not require users to store keys, which eliminates the communication
overhead of the secret key.

Keywords: Attribute-Based Secret Key · Signature · Polynomial
Reconstruction

1 Introduction

In 2011, Maji et al. [1] proposed an attribute-based signature scheme. In the
attribute signature, the user obtains a set of attribute certificates from an
authority called the attribute authentication [2]. In the attribute-based signature schemes [3–6], the public key and secret key of the signer are generated
by a set of attributes, and the key generation center generates the signature
secret key for the signer based on the associated attributes. The signer uses the
security key to generate a verifiable signature on the message. These signature
schemes utilize attributes to generate the corresponding public key and secret
key. Recently, Kang et al. [7] have constructed a signature scheme that supports traceable and forward-secure attributes with flexible thresholds. Xu et al.
[8] have constructed an attribute-based signature scheme by obfuscating users'
private keys with fuzzy factors to protect their identity privacy.

In 2002, Juels and Sudan [9] first proposed a method called the fuzzy vaults
for preserving secret information. The fuzzy vaults is the process of adding confusing information to real information to protect it from being obtained by opponents. An attribute-based secret key signature algorithm (ASKS) is constructed
in this paper. The ASKS utilizes the idea of fuzzy vaults to generate corresponding public key by selecting attributes in the attribute set. The user does
not need to generate a secret key, which is an attribute of the user. Then, we
use the signature algorithm structure to construct in reference [10] signature.

W. Li et al. (Eds.): EISA 2024, CCIS 2266, pp. 99–106, 2025.
https://doi.org/10.1007/978-3-031-80419-9_7

1.1 Contributions

• Regarding the high communication cost of the secret key in the signature algorithm, the user attribute is used as its secret key for signature to reduce its communication cost.

  • In response to the low portability of the signature secret key, the ASKS uses attributes as the secret key, and the users do not need to store the secret key, which eliminates the need for tools to save the secret key, thus improving the portability of the secret key.

2 Preliminaries

The $d-1$ degree Lagrange interpolation polynomial over $\mathbb{Z}_n$ is denoted as

$$l(u) = \sum_{i=0}^{d-1} l(u_i)\triangle_{u_i,\{u_0,u_1,...,u_{d-1}\}}(u)$$

where $\triangle_{u_i,\{u_0,u_1,...,u_{d-1}\}}(u) = \prod_{u_j \in \{u_0,u_1,...,u_{d-1}\},u_j \neq u_i} \frac{u-u_j}{u_i-u_j}$.

Definition 1 ([11] The elliptic curve discrete logarithm problem(ECDLP)). *For the prime number n, the n order group is $\mathbb{G}$ generated by generator G on elliptic curve E. Give Q (where $Q = aG, a \in \mathbb{Z}_n$), the elliptic curve discrete logarithm problem is to find $a \in \mathbb{Z}_n$ satisfying $Q = aG$.*

Theorem 1 ([11] ECDLP assumption). *There is no probabilistic polynomial time (PPT) algorithm to solve ECDLP with a non negligible probability.*

3 Formal Model of ASKS Scheme

ASKS includes four PPT algorithms.

- **SetUp**: Input l and output $\mathbb{P}$, where l is the security parameter and $\mathbb{P}$ is the system parameter.
- **KeyGen**: Input $\mathbb{P}$, $(x_1, x_2, \ldots, x_l)$ and output pk, where $(x_1, x_2, \ldots, x_l)$ is the attribute and pk is a public key.
- **Sign**: Input $\mathbb{P}$, the pk, the $(x_1, x_2, \ldots, x_l)$, a message m, and output a signature σ.
- **Verify**: Input σ, and output "1" or "0".

  The correctness of **ASKS** is that **ASKS-Verify** outputs "1" for the legal signature.

Definition 2 (Unforgeability). *If the PPT $\mathcal{A}$ is nonexistent to win the following game with the non negligible probability, then **ASKS** is unforgeable.*

  *Setup: $\mathcal{C}$ runs **ASKS-SetUp** to get the parameter $\mathbb{P}$ and runs **ASKS-KeyGen** to get the public key pk, then gives $(\mathbb{P}, pk)$ to the adversary $\mathcal{A}$.*

  Query: $\mathcal{A}$ can execute polynomial queries.

  Forgery: $\mathcal{A}$ gives (pk^*, m^*, σ^*), when the following hold:

(1) $\mathcal{A}$ hasn't searched the attribute of pk^*;
(2) $\mathcal{A}$ hasn't searched (pk^*, m^*)'s signature, then $\mathcal{A}$ will win the game.

4   Construction of ASKS

ASKS includes four PPT algorithms: SetUp, KeyGen, Sign, Verify.
- ASKS-SetUp
  Step 1. Pick the group $\mathbb{G}$ of prime order $n \approx 2^l$, and generator G.
  Step 2. Set the threshold t.
  Step 3. Set the attribute set $A = \{a_1, a_2, \ldots, a_{6l}\} \subseteq \mathbb{Z}_n$ and $|A| = 6l$.
  Step 4. Pick Hash functions $H : \{0,1\}^* \to \mathbb{Z}_n$.
  Step 5. Output the system parameter $\mathbb{P} = (q, G, \mathbb{G}, n, H, t, A)$.
- ASKS-KeyGen
  Step 1. Pick $f_0 \in \mathbb{Z}_n$, $t-1$ degree polynomial f and $f(0) = f_0$.
  Step 2. Compute $P_{l+1} = f_0 G$.
  Step 3. Pick attributes $(x_1, x_2, \ldots, x_l) \in (\mathbb{Z}_n)^l$ and computer

$$P_1 = f(x_1)G, P_2 = f(x_2)G, \ldots, P_l = f(x_l)G.$$

  Step 4. Output the public key $(P_1, P_2, \ldots, P_{l+1})$.
- ASKS-Sign
  Step 1. Input a message m, the public key $(P_1, P_2, \ldots, P_{l+1})$ and the attribute $(x_1', x_2', \ldots, x_l')$.
  Step 2. Select $(x_1'', x_2'', \ldots, x_t'')$, where $\{x_1'', x_2'', \ldots, x_t''\} \subseteq \{x_1', x_2', \ldots, x_l'\}$ and computer $l_j = \prod_{1 \le j \le t, j \ne i} \frac{x - x_j''}{x_i'' - x_j''}$ to obtain $f(x) = \sum_{j=0}^{t-1} l_j(x) = \sum_{j=0}^{t-1} f_j x^j$.
  Step 3. Compute $f_0 G$. If $f_0 G = P_{l+1}$, then continue, otherwise to go step 2.
  Step 4. Select $\alpha, s_1, s_2, \ldots, s_l \in \mathbb{Z}_n$ and compute

$$L_{l+1} = \alpha G$$
$$c_1 = H(m, L_{l+1})$$
$$L_1 = s_1 G + c_1 \cdot P_1$$
$$c_2 = H(m, L_1)$$
$$L_2 = s_2 G + c_2 \cdot P_2$$
$$c_3 = H(m, L_2)$$
$$\ldots$$
$$L_l = s_l G + c_l \cdot P_l$$
$$c_{l+1} = H(m, L_l).$$

  Step 5. Compute $s_{l+1} = \alpha - c_{l+1} \cdot f_0 \bmod n$.
  Step 6. Output $\sigma = (s_1, s_2, \ldots, s_{l+1}, c_{l+1})$.
- ASKS-Verify
  Step 1. Input the signature $\sigma = (s_1, s_2, \ldots, s_{l+1}, c_1)$, the public key $(P_1, P_2, \ldots, P_{l+1})$ and the message m.

Step 2. Compute

$$L_{l+1} = s_{l+1}G + c_{l+1} \cdot P_{l+1}$$
$$c_{l+2} = H(m, L_{l+1})$$
$$L_{l+2} = s_1G + c_1 \cdot P_1$$
$$c_{l+3} = H(m, L_{l+2})$$
$$L_{l+3} = s_2G + c_2 \cdot P_2$$
$$c_{l+4} = H(m, L_{l+3})$$
$$\cdots$$
$$L_{2l+1} = s_lG + c_l \cdot P_l$$
$$c_{2l+2} = H(m, L_{2l+1}).$$

Step 3. If $c_{2l+2} = c_{l+1}$, output "1" or else output "0".
• ASKS-Correctness
We need to show $L_{l+1} = s_{l+1}G + c_{l+1} \cdot P_{l+1}$. Since $L_{l+1} = \alpha G$, $P_{l+1} = f_0 G$ and $s_{l+1} = \alpha - c_{l+1} \cdot f_0$, we have

$$
\begin{aligned}
s_{l+1}G + c_{l+1} \cdot P_{l+1} &= (\alpha - c_{l+1} \cdot f_0)G + c_{l+1} \cdot P_{l+1} \\
&= \alpha G - c_{l+1} \cdot f_0 G + c_{l+1} \cdot P_{l+1} \\
&= \alpha G - c_{l+1} \cdot f_0 G + c_{l+1} \cdot f_0 G \\
&= \alpha G \\
&= L_{l+1}.
\end{aligned}
$$

5 Security Analysis

Theorem 2 (Unforgeability). *If the **ASKS** signature can be forged by a PPT $\mathcal{A}$ with probabilistic ε at most Q times random oracle. Then the ECDLP can be solved a PPT $\mathcal{C}$ with probability at least*

$$(\varepsilon - 2^{-l})(\frac{\varepsilon - 2^{-l}}{Q} - 2^{-l}).$$

Proof. $\mathcal{C}$ picks $x \xleftarrow{\$} \mathbb{Z}_n$ and calculates the $P = xG$.
$\mathcal{C}$ sets two empty forms F_1, F_2 to record adversary $\mathcal{A}$'s inquiry.
Setup: Running the **ASKS-SetUp**, $\mathcal{C}$ sends $\mathcal{A}$ the system parameters

$$\mathbb{P} = (q, E, G, n, H, t, A).$$

Query: For the public key $(P_1, P_2, \ldots, P_{l+1})$, where $P_{l+1} = P$.
Hash query:

1. $\mathcal{A}$ gives message m to $\mathcal{C}$. For $i \in \{1, 2, \ldots, l\}$, $\mathcal{C}$ selects $s_i \in \mathbb{Z}_n$ and queries F_1, then $\mathcal{C}$ sends the same value if them have been existence;

2. Or else, $\mathcal{C}$ selects $c_{l+1} \in \mathbb{Z}_n$ and sends it to $\mathcal{A}$. $\mathcal{C}$ saves

$$(m, pk, (s_1, s_2, \ldots, s_l), c_{l+1})$$

to F_1.

Extract query:

1. $\mathcal{C}$ seeks F_2. When (P_{l+1}, x_i) have been existence, $\mathcal{C}$ sends (P_{l+1}, x_i) to $\mathcal{A}$;
2. Or else, $\mathcal{C}$ selects $x_i \in \mathbb{Z}_n$ and sends it to $\mathcal{A}$. $\mathcal{C}$ saves (P_{l+1}, x_i) to F_2.

Sign query:
   $\mathcal{A}$ gives message m and the public key $(P_1, P_2, \ldots, P_{l+1})$ to $\mathcal{C}$, where $P_{l+1} = P$.

1. $\mathcal{C}$ seeks F_1. When $(m, pk, (s_1, s_2, \ldots, s_l), c_{l+1})$ was nonexistent, $\mathcal{C}$ goes to Hash query and saves $(m, pk, (s_1, s_2, \ldots, s_l), c_{l+1})$ to F_1.
2. $\mathcal{C}$ seeks F_2. When (P_{l+1}, x_i) was nonexistent, $\mathcal{C}$ goes to Extract query and saves (P_{l+1}, x_i) to F_2.
3. $\mathcal{C}$ seeks the $(m, pk, (s_1, s_2, \ldots, s_l), c_l)$ in F_1 and seeks (P_{l+1}, x_i) in F_2;
4. $\mathcal{C}$ computers $s_{l+1} = \alpha - c_{l+1} \cdot x_i$ and returns the signature $(s_1, s_2, \ldots, s_{l+1}, c_{l+1})$.

Forgery:
   $\mathcal{A}$ gives a message m^*, the public key

$$pk^* = (P_{i1^*}, P_{i2^*}, \ldots, P_{i(l+1)^*}) \in (\mathbb{G})^l$$

and forges signature $(s_1^*, s_2^*, \ldots, s_{l+1}^*, c_{l+1}^*)$ to $\mathcal{C}$, the following meet:

1. $\mathcal{A}$ hasn't searched the attribute of pk;
2. $\mathcal{A}$ hasn't searched the (pk^*, m^*)'s signature.

Suppose (m^*, pk^*)'s legal signature is $(s_1^*, s_2^*, \ldots, s_{l+1}^*, c_{l+1}^*)$. Firstly, $\mathcal{C}$ seeks

$$(m^*, pk^*, (s_1^*, s_2^*, \ldots, s_l^*), c_{l+1}^*)$$

in F_1 and $(P_{i(l+1)^*}, x_{il^*})$ in F_2. If

$$(m^*, pk^*, (s_1^*, s_2^*, \ldots, s_l^*), c_{l+1}^*)$$

isn't in F_1, the game over. Otherwise, From $(s_1^*, s_2^*, \ldots, s_{l+1}^*, c_{l+1}^*)$ is legal signature, we get

$$s_{l+1}^* = \alpha - c_{l+1}^* \cdot x_{il^*} \bmod n. \tag{1}$$

From Lemma 3.1 in [12], $\mathcal{C}$ responses $\mathcal{A}$'s query again and responses all inquiries consistently except c_{l+1}, we get that $\mathcal{A}$ can get another forged signature $(s_1', s_2', \ldots, s_{l+1}', c_{l+1}')$. Then

$$s_{l+1}' = \alpha - c_{l+1}' x_{il^*} \bmod n \tag{2}$$

is obtained.

Because of (1) and (2), $x_{il^*} = \frac{s^*_{l+1} - s'_{l+1}}{c^*_{l+1} - c'_{l+1}}$ is obtained.

If C can successfully to solve ECDLP that the probability is ε'.

When $(m^*, pk^*, (s^*_1, s^*_2, \ldots, s^*_l), c^*_{l+1})$ isn't in L_1, then c^*_{l+1} get through the **ASKS-Verify** that the probability is $\frac{C^t_l + C^{t+1}_l + \cdots + C^l_l}{C^l_{6l}}$.

From $C^t_l + C^{t+1}_l + \cdots + C^l_l < 2^l$ and

$$C^l_{6l} = \frac{6l(6l-1)\cdots(l+1)}{5l(5l-1)\cdots 1}$$

$$= (\frac{6l(6l-1)(6l-2)(6l-3)}{5l(5l-1)(5l-2)(5l-3)} \cdots \frac{(2l+4)(2l+3)(2l+2)(2l+1)}{(l+4)(l+3)(l+2)(l+1)})$$

$$\cdot(\frac{l+l}{l} \cdots \frac{l+1}{1})$$

$$> (6/5)^{4l} \cdot 2^l$$

$$> 2^l \cdot 2^l,$$

we obtain $\frac{C^t_l + C^{t+1}_l + \cdots + C^l_l}{C^l_{6l}} < \frac{2^l}{2^l \cdot 2^l} < \frac{1}{2^l}$.

From Lemma 3.1 in [12], the Eq. (2) is obtained that the probability is

$$(\varepsilon - \frac{C^t_l + C^{t+1}_l + \cdots + C^l_l}{C^l_{6l}})(\frac{\varepsilon - \frac{C^t_l + C^{t+1}_l + \cdots + C^l_l}{C^l_{6l}}}{Q} - \frac{C^t_l + C^{t+1}_l + \cdots + C^l_l}{C^l_{6l}}).$$

Let $u = \varepsilon - \frac{C^t_l + C^{t+1}_l + \cdots + C^l_l}{C^l_{6l}}$, then

$$(\varepsilon - \frac{C^t_l + C^{t+1}_l + \cdots + C^l_l}{C^l_{6l}})(\frac{\varepsilon - \frac{C^t_l + C^{t+1}_l + \cdots + C^l_l}{C^l_{6l}}}{Q} - \frac{C^t_l + C^{t+1}_l + \cdots + C^l_l}{C^l_{6l}})$$

$$= u(\frac{1}{Q}u + u - \varepsilon).$$

From $u(\frac{1}{q}u + u - \varepsilon)$ in $[\varepsilon/2, \varepsilon]$ increase and $\varepsilon/2 < \varepsilon - \frac{1}{2^l} < \varepsilon - \frac{C^t_l + C^{t+1}_l + \cdots + C^l_l}{C^l_{6l}} < \varepsilon$, we obtain

$$(\varepsilon - \frac{C^t_l + C^{t+1}_l + \cdots + C^l_l}{C^l_{6l}})(\frac{\varepsilon - \frac{C^t_l + C^{t+1}_l + \cdots + C^l_l}{C^l_{6l}}}{q} - \frac{C^t_l + C^{t+1}_l + \cdots + C^l_l}{C^l_{6l}})$$

$$> (\varepsilon - 2^{-l})(\frac{\varepsilon - 2^{-l}}{Q} - 2^{-l}).$$

So

$$\varepsilon' > (\varepsilon - 2^{-l})(\frac{\varepsilon - 2^{-l}}{Q} - 2^{-l}),$$

and we get that the ECDLP is solved with probability at least $(\varepsilon - 2^{-l})(\frac{\varepsilon - 2^{-l}}{Q} - 2^{-l})$. Contradiction with Theorem 1.

6   Efficiency Comparison

As Table 1 compares the key length, signature length, time cost of signing, and time cost of verification between **ASKS** and the schemes proposed in Liu [10] and Maji [1]. Here, l represents the number of attributes in the attribute set or the number of ring members in a ring signature. $|\mathbb{G}|$ denotes the length of the generator. Pow stands for the time consumption of exponentiation in a multiplicative group or the time consumption of the multiplication in an additive group. Bil represents the time consumption of the bilinear pairing operation.

Table 1. Comparison of Communication and Storage Costs

Scheme	Private Key Size	Signature Size	Signing Cost	Verification Cost
Liu [10]	$|\mathbb{G}|$	$(l+2)|\mathbb{G}|$	$6l$Pow	4Pow
Maji [1]	$(l+2)|\mathbb{G}|$	$(2l+2)|\mathbb{G}|$	$2l$Pow$+(l+1)$Bil	$2l$Pow$+(l+1)$Bil
ASKS	$\times$	$(l+2)|\mathbb{G}|$	$2l$Pow	$2l$Pow

As can be seen from Table 1, the verification time of the scheme in Liu [10] is the shortest, while the **ASKS** scheme has the shortest signature length and signing time. The signature length of the scheme in Liu [10] is the same as that of **ASKS**, and it is shorter than that of the scheme in Maji [1].

7   Conclusions

In this paper, we design a signature algorithm using users' attribute features as private keys based on the idea of fuzzy vaults. Generating a secret key using users' attributes does not require users to store the secret key, making it more convenient. Our signature setting eliminates the need for the signer to save the secret key. Currently, in blockchain technology, electronic authentication requires users to protect and store their secret keys. Due to the re-input of attributes, users do not require it as the secret key during the signing process, which does not generating communication overhead. The ASKS uses users' attributes as their keys, which can effectively reduce communication overhead and improve the portability of keys.

Acknowledgement. This research is supported by Doctoral Fund of Guizhou Industry Polytechnic College (No. 2024-rc-01).

References

1. Maji, K., Prabhakaran, M., Rosulek, M.: Attribute-based signatures. In: Proceedings of the 11th International Conference on Topics in Cryptology, pp. 376–392. Springer, Berlin, Heidelberg: Germany (2011)

2. Sakai, Y., Attrapadung, N., Hanaoka, G.: Attribute-based signatures for circuits from bilinear map. In: 19th IACR International Conference on Practice and Theory in Public-Key Cryptography, pp. 283–300. Springer, Berlin, Heidelberg: Germany (2016)
3. Hou, H., Ning, J., Huang, X., Zhao, Y.: Verifiable attribute-based timed signatures and its applications. J. Softw. Sci. **34**(5), 246–2481 (2023)
4. Okamoto, T., Takashima, K.: Efficient attribute-based signatures for non-monotone predicates in the standard model. In: Proceedings of the 16th International Conference on, pp. 125–142. Springer, Berlin, Heidelberg: Germany (2013)
5. Li, J., Chen, Y., Han, J., et al.: Decentralized attribute-based server-aid signature in the internet of things. IEEE Internet Things J. **9**(6), 4573–4583 (2021)
6. Li, J., et al.: Efficient attribute-based server-aided verification signature. IEEE Trans. Serv. Comput. 3096420 (2021)
7. Kang, Z., Li, J., Shen, J., et al.: TFS-ABS: traceable and forward-secure attribute-based signature scheme with constant-size. IEEE Trans. Knowl. Data Eng. **35**(9), 9514–9530 (2023)
8. Tao, Q., Cui, X., Iftekhar, A.: A novel lightweight decentralized attribute-based signature scheme for social co-governance. Inf. Sci. 110839 (2024)
9. Juels, A., Sudan, M.: A fuzzy vault scheme. In: Proceedings of IEEE International Symposium on Information Theory, 408. IEEE (2002)
10. Liu, J. K., Wei, V.K., Wong, D.S.: Linkable spontaneous anonymous group signature for ad hoc groups. In: Proceedings of the Australasian Conference on Information Security and Privacy, pp. 325–335. Springer, Berlin, Heidelberg: Germany (2004)
11. Koblitz, N.: Elliptic curve cryptosystem. Math. Comput. **1987**(48), 203–209 (1987)
12. Bellare, M., Neven, G.: Multi-signatures in the plain public-key model and a general forking lemma. In: Proceedings of the 13th ACM conference on Computer and communications security, Association for Computing Machinery, pp. 390–399. Association for Computing Machinery: USA (2006)

Digital Token Transaction Tracing Method

Ling-Ling Xia[1,2]([✉]) [iD], Qun Wang[1,2], Zhuo Ma[1,2] [iD], and Bo Song[3]

[1] Department of Computer Information and Cyber Security, Jiangsu Police Institute,
Nanjing 210031, People's Republic of China
xll.njit@gmail.com
[2] Jiangsu Province Electronic Data Forensics and Analysis Engineering Research Center,
Nanjing 210003, People's Republic of China
[3] College of Modern Posts, Nanjing University of Posts and Telecommunications,
Nanjing 210003, People's Republic of China

Abstract. The digital currency, led by Bitcoin and USDT, has the characteristics of decentralization and anonymity, which makes the identity of traders difficult to identify, thus providing a hiding space for illegal activities, such as drug trafficking, money laundering, cyber fraud, terrorism, etc. Focusing on the USDT-TRC20 token on the Tron blockchain, we propose a transaction tracing method to trace the transaction path for digging out hidden addresses and encrypted assets. Specifically, we first construct a two-layer transaction network, where the top layer network describes the flow of USDT-TRC20 between on-chain addresses over time, and the bottom layer network represents the flow of TRX between on-chain addresses over time. Secondly, we propose a digital token transaction tracing method based on the constructed two-layer transaction network to identify the hidden on-chain address and different addresses belonging to the same user or group. Finally, we describe the acquisition of transaction records queried from the blockchain browser, and then the validity of the proposed tracing method is verified by empirical data.

Keywords: Blockchain · Digital token · Transaction tracing method · USDT-TRC20

1 Introduction

With the rapid development of blockchain [1] technology, the scale of cryptocurrency transactions continues to expand. The cryptocurrency, led by Bitcoin [2], has the characteristics of decentralization and anonymity, which makes the identity of traders difficult to identify. It is widely used in criminal activities, such as crimes using cryptocurrency as a payment tool, money laundering and terrorist financing crimes using cryptocurrency, crimes aimed at cryptocurrency, fraud and pyramid selling under the guise of investing in cryptocurrency and so on. According to the concept of cryptocurrency, the cryptocurrency can also be called decentralized digital currency. On January 16th, 2023, the 2022 research report on cryptocurrency crimes released by SAFEIS security research institute points out that the crimes involving digital currency in 2022 show a new trend of scale and organization and the currencies involved in digital currency crimes are still mainly Tether United States Dollar (USDT). Nowadays, USDT has been one of the most widely used stablecoins [3] on the digital currency market. As a stablecoin, USDT was originally issued on Bitcoin's Omni protocol and was later issued on the Ethereum network using the ERC20 token standard. With the development of different blockchain networks, USDT has successively existed in different token standards on other public chains, such as in the form of TRC20 token standard on the Tron blockchain. Users can choose which blockchain network to transact on using USDT based on their needs and preferences. In digital currency trading, stablecoins act as a bridge between digital currency and fiat currency, which is often used as a low-cost exit from the digital currency market.

As more and more crimes involve digital currency transactions, it is essential to supervise digital currency, track the source transaction and analyze the trading routes.

1.1 Related Work

At present, there are relatively few studies on digital currency transaction traceability both at home and abroad, and the existing studies are mainly classified into two categories: network layer traceability technology [4] and transaction data analysis technology. Take the Bitcoin for instance. Network layer traceability technology refers to collecting the information transmitted by the Bitcoin network layer, analyzing the transmission path of Bitcoin transactions in the network, and tracking the IP information of the server that generating the transaction, which can directly associate the anonymous transaction with the IP address of the node from which the transaction originated or the node that initiated the transaction, so as to achieve traceability [5]. In 2014, Koshy et al. [6] summarized the propagation patterns of broadcast message monitored in a period of time and proposed four modes of message propagation in the blockchain network. This tracing method monitors the message propagation mode, analyzes the real initiating node and matches the IP address with the on-chain address contained in the message, threatening the privacy of communication and user identity. Nowadays some users use proxy servers or virtual private network (VPN) to hide their real IP for avoiding tracking. Thus, the existing network layer traceability technology has low accuracy, and more computing and storage resources are required, resulting in poor practicability. Aiming at this problem, Gao et al. [5] proposed a new Bitcoin transaction traceability mechanism by utilizing neighbor node identification based on deploying probe nodes. Since the user's private information such as IP address can be accessed by tracking the transactions, the Bitcoin transactions are not truly anonymous. Xiao et al. [7] designed a mixing scheme with decentralized signature protocol to protect privacy in Bitcoin blockchain.

Transaction data analysis technology on the basis of analyzing transaction records is to deduce the relation and transfer path between different transaction addresses, such as trading patterns and fund flow. By analyzing ransom payment timestamps both longitudinally across CryptoLocker's operating period and transversely across times of day, Liao et al. [8] analyzed the ransom process of CryptoLocker and identified 795 ransom payments totalling 1,128.40 BTC on the basis of a cluster of 968 Bitcoin addresses belonging to CryptoLocker. Yousaf et al. [9] investigated tracing transactions across cryptocurrency ledges and distinguished various patterns of cross currency trades and of the general usage of these platforms to understand whether they serve a criminal or other profit-driven groups. Li et al. [10] presented a traceable Monero system and gave a detailed construction of traceable Monero by overlaying Monero with two types of tracing mechanisms. To characterize key agents in the cryptocurrency economy, Liu et al. analyzed Ethereum token transactions, and explored their identifiability through interpretable machine learning models [11]. In 2023, Dearden et al. [12] provided a structured method to quantitatively examine the Bitcoin blockchain ledger. Their results show that cryptocurrency transactions are generally identifiable (90%). These studies revealed that analyzing and mining transaction information from the transaction records can help track cryptocurrency transactions and find out illegal activities.

Moreover, some other researchers investigate new traceability schemes based on consensus algorithm or proof method from a perspective of supervision of blockchain. Ma et al. [13] designed a blockchain traceable scheme: SkyEye, using chameleon hash [14] and zero-knowledge succinct noninteractive arguments of knowledge (zk-SNARKs) [15]. In their design strategy, they added identify proofs associated with the users's private information to the blockchain data and demonstrated the security of SkyEye under specific cryptographic assumptions. Later, they proposed another efficient identify tracing scheme and implemented it with a simple proof method to address the supervision issues of blockchain [16]. In their scheme, only the trusted supervision center can track operations and users, and the user only needs to register once with the supervision center. As the transaction process lacks supervision, making it difficult to meet the actual demand, Xiao et al. [17] presented a secure multi-party payment channel on-chain and off-chain supervisable scheme from multiple perspectives of positive and negative, active and passive, and multiple layers of on-chain and off-chain. To realize the supervision of digital assets and strengthen the security, a dynamic delegated practical byzantine fault tolerance (DDPBFT) algorithm is proposed and an evaluation model for digital asset is constructed with deep learning [18].

Although the researches above can help trace virtual currency, it is not practicable to track virtual currency transactions from the perspective of network layer traceability or supervision of blockchain in the practical cases investigated by public security organs. Once a criminal incident has occurred, it is too late to collect the information transmitted by the network layer of cryptocurrency by deploying probe nodes or track operations and users by designing new proof method based on blockchain. Thus the transaction data analysis technology on the basis of transaction records has become an important means to trace the transaction path for digging out hidden encrypted assets and suspects and prevent crimes involving digital currency.

1.2 Our Contribution

It can be seen from the existing practical cases that the flow of TRX is very important to find the suspect's hidden on-chain address, while existing transaction data analysis methods only focus on the flow of USDT-TRC20 and ignore TRX.

In this paper, taking USDT-TRC20 token on the Tron blockchain as an example, we propose a digital token transaction tracing method based on two-layer transaction network derived from public transaction records. The top layer network describes the flow of USDT-TRC20 between on-chain addresses over time, and the bottom layer network represents the flow of TRX between on-chain addresses over time.

1.3 Paper Organization

The remainder of this paper is arranged as follows. In Sect. 2 we describe the characteristics of USDT-TRC20 transactions and the construction of the two-layer network. In Sect. 3, we provide a transaction tracing method based on two-layer transaction network. In Sect. 4, the validity of the proposed tracing method is verified. The conclusions are given in Sect. 5.

2 Two-Layer Transaction Network

Currently, among the major public chains, the stablecoin USDT has the highest liquidity and has become an important channel for money laundering. The market capitalization of USDT has surged to a record high, from about $66 billion at the beginning of 2023 to $94.9 billion in January, 2024. According to the report of on-chain research institutions, centralized exchanges are the main use scenario of USDT, and more than 50% of cryptocurrency transactions are brokered by USDT. Nowdays, most of the newly issued USDT is on the Tron blockchain. In this paper, we focus on the virtual currency traceability of USDT based on Tron TRC20 protocol (i.e. USDT-TRC20). During the actual transfer payment, users using the virtual currency wallet software to transfer USDT need to consume a certain amount of TRX, which makes the source of TRX (i.e. TRX transfers between users) important.

The digital token object investigated in this paper is USDT-TRC20 based on the Tron blockchain, and the transaction data includes records of both USDT-TRC20 and TRX transfers. The transaction network composed of USDT-TRC20 and TRX transactions can be abstracted into a complex two-layer network, where virtual currency addresses can be considered as nodes and TRC20 or TRX transactions between addresses can be regarded as edges. The two-layer network is depicted in Fig. 1.

The top layer (denoted by layer A) denotes the USDT-TRC20 transaction network, and the bottom one (denoted by layer B) denotes the TRX transaction network. In the upper layer A, there are n nodes and m_A directed edges, which represent n on-chain addresses and m_A USDT-TRC20 transactions between these addresses. In the bottom layer B, there are n nodes and m_B directed edges, which represent n addresses and m_B TRX transfers between these addresses. The each directed edge between a source and a target in each layer represents a single transaction including trading amount and date time from output address to input address. Since the number of USDT-TRC20 transactions typically exceeds that of TRX transactions, it can be seen from the Fig. 1 that the number of links between nodes in layer A is larger than that in layer B. In the two-layer network, the type of node denoting virtual currency address started with capital T in layer A is the same as that in layer B, and the nodes are one-to-one correspondence in the upper layer A and the bottom layer B.

Next, we abstract the two-layer network into a directed graph $G = (V, E^A \cup E^B)$ to describe the coupled relation between USDT-TRC20 and TRX transaction networks,

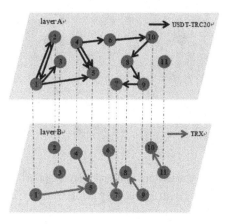

Fig. 1. The two-layer transaction network composed of USDT-TRC20 and TRX transactions.

where V is the set of nodes denoting the virtual currency addresses started with capital T and E^x, $x \in \{A, B\}$ is the set of edges in layer x. If there are single or multiple transactions from source node (output address) i to destination node (input address) j in layer A (i.e. $(i,j) \in E^A$), then we set $e_{ij}^A = m1(m1 \neq 0)$ and $e_{ij}^A = 0$ otherwise, where $m1$ denotes the number of transactions from node i to node j in layer A. Similarly, if there are single or multiple transactions from source node i to destination node j in layer B (i.e. $(i,j) \in E^B$), then we will set $e_{ij}^B = m2(m2 \neq 0)$ and $e_{ij}^B = 0$ otherwise, where $m2$ denotes the number of transactions from node i to node j in layer B. If $e_{ij}^x = 0, x \in \{A, B\}$, no transaction will exist from node i to node j neither USDT-TRC20 nor TRX in layer x. If $e_{ji}^x = 0, x \in \{A, B\}$, no transaction will exist from node j to node i neither USDT-TRC20 nor TRX in layer x. It can be seen that the coupled relation between USDT-TRC20 and TRX transaction networks is characterized by a pair of values consisting of e_{ij}^A and e_{ij}^B. In terms of the connected pair of nodes (i,j), there are four pairs values of e_{ij}^x, which are listed below,

$$\text{(a)} \begin{cases} e_{ij}^A = 0 \\ e_{ij}^B = 0 \end{cases} \text{(b)} \begin{cases} e_{ij}^A = 0 \\ e_{ij}^B = m2 \end{cases} \text{(c)} \begin{cases} e_{ij}^A = m1 \\ e_{ij}^B = 0 \end{cases} \text{(d)} \begin{cases} e_{ij}^A = m1 \\ e_{ij}^B = m2 \end{cases} \quad (1)$$

where $m1(m1 \neq 0)$ and $m2(m2 \neq 0)$ represent the number of transactions from node i to node j in layers A and B respectively. Figures 2(a) to (b) show that these four groups of values correspond to four different node connections in the two-layer network.

Because transactions between two nodes may have opposite directions, e_{ij}^x is radically different from e_{ji}^x, i.e. the connected pair of nodes (i,j) and (j, i) are opposite directions. Similarly, the connected pair of nodes (j, i) correspond to four different kinds of node connections in the two-layer network, where only the nodes are connected in opposite directions compared with Figs. 2(a) to (d).

At this point, the multi-relationship network graph has been constructed. In order to facilitate subsequent topological structure analysis, the graph will be abstracted into a two-layer network.

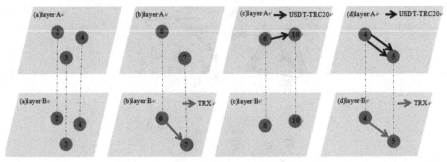

Fig. 2. The four different node connections in A and B layers. (a) $e_{2,3}^A = 0$, $e_{2,3}^B = 0$ (b) $e_{6,7}^A = 0$, $e_{6,7}^B = 1$ (c) $e_{6,10}^A = 1$, $e_{6,10}^B = 0$ (d) $e_{4,5}^A = 2$, $e_{4,5}^B = 1$.

3 Transaction Tracing Method

Next, focusing on the USDT-TRC20 token on the Tron blockchain,we propose a digital token transaction tracing method. The steps of the proposed transaction tracing method are summarized as follows:

Step 1: Transaction data acquisition. Starting from a suspect's USDT address, we use the data acquisition method described in Sect. 4 to recursively retrieve the counterparties of the address from the blockchain explorer, which can obtain all the transaction records between the upstream and downstream nodes associated with that address, until encountering so-called exchange large accounts or platform addresses.

Step 2: Two-layer network construction. Based on the summarized transaction table obtained in the first step and the two-layer network construction method described in Sect. 2, the two-layer direction graph $G = (V^A \cup V^B, E^A \cup E^B)$ can be represented by real USDT-TRC20 and TRX transaction data. We denote the set of nodes in layer A as V^A, where $|V^A|$ is the number of on-chain addresses involved in USDT-TRC20 transactions in the layer A. The set of nodes in layer B is denoted as V^B, where $|V^B|$ represents the number of on-chain addresses involved in TRX transactions in the layer B. The graph G can also be denoted as $G = (V, E^A \cup E^B)$, where $V = V^A \cup V^B$ is the union of the node sets from layers A and B, and $|V|$ is the number of nodes in this union. Similarly, $E^A = (e_{ij}^A)_{|V| \times |V|}$ and $E^B = (e_{ij}^B)_{|V| \times |V|}$ represent the set of USDT-TRC20 transactions (edges) in layer A and the set of TRX transactions (edges) in layer B respectively. As there are single or multiple transactions from source node (output address) i to destination node (input address) j in layer x, $x \in \{A, B\}$ (i.e. $(i, j) \in E^x$), we set $e_{ij}^x = m(m \neq 0)$ and $e_{ij}^x = 0$ otherwise, where m denotes the number of transactions from node i to node j in layer x. In these m transactions, each transaction amount is represented by $e_{ij}^x(t)$, $t \in \{t_1, t_2...t_m\}$ with the transaction time stamp t. If no transaction exists from node i to node j, we will set $e_{ij}^x = 0$ and $e_{ji}^x = 0$ corresponds to no transaction from node j to node i.

Step 3: Transaction flow analysis. To conduct a more effective traceability analysis of transactions between on-chain addresses, we propose two new metrics for assessing the strong relationship between addresses.

Metric 1. To measure the frequency of mutual transfer transactions between on-chain addresses in layer x, we defined a new metric m_{ij}^x based on the revised harmonic mean. The mutual-transfer metric m_{ij}^x is denoted as

$$m_{ij}^x = \frac{e_{ij}^x * e_{ji}^x}{e_{ij}^x + e_{ji}^x} \left(\text{and} \min(e_{ij}^x, e_{ji}^x) \geq thr \right) \tag{2}$$

where $thr(thr \geq 1)$ represents the threshold for the number of round-trip transfers, which can be set to a nonzero integer as needed, and $\min(e_{ij}^x, e_{ji}^x) \geq thr$ represents that the minimum number of transfers between node i and node j must be greater than or equal to the set threshold thr. It should be noted here that why the harmonic mean was chosen to design the indicator. Considering that the harmonic mean is sensitive to extreme values, it is more affected by extremely small values than by extremely large values. For example, if there are two pairs of node pairs, one pair with $e_{ij}^A = 215$ and $e_{ji}^A = 74$, and other pair with $e_{ij}^A = 39$ and $e_{ji}^A = 6$, then the values of m_{ij}^A are 55.05 and 5.2, respectively. If there is no round-trip transfer between node i and node j (i.e. $e_{ij}^x = 0$ or $e_{ji}^x = 0$), then the condition $\min(e_{ij}^x, e_{ji}^x) \geq thr$ is not satisfied, and there is no need to calculate the value of m_{ij}^x. From Eq. (2) we can see that when m_{ij}^x is non-zero, the larger the value, the greater the probability of mutual transfer of funds between node i and node j. That is, the greater the possibility that node i and node j belong to the same user or accomplices.

Metric 2. Based on the mutual-transfer metric, considering both USDT-TRC20 and TRX transactions, an improved metric is introduced to measure the shared ownership relationships between addresses. The shared ownership metric is denoted as

$$hij = \frac{e_{ij}^A * e_{ji}^A}{e_{ij}^A + e_{ji}^A} * [e_{ij}^B + e_{ji}^B + 1] = m_{ij}^A * (e_{ij}^B + e_{ji}^B + 1) \left(\text{and} \min(e_{ij}^A, e_{ji}^A) \geq thr \right) \tag{3}$$

where A and B represent the upper layer (USDT-TRC20 transactions) and the lower layer (TRX transactions) in the two-layer network respectively, m_{ij}^A denotes the round-trip transfer indicator of USDT-TRC20 transactions between addresses in layer A, and $thr(thr \geq 1)$ carries the same meaning as in Eq. (2) above. From the Eq. (3), we can see that when both the values of e_{ij}^B and e_{ji}^B are zero at the same time, the metric 2 degenerates into metric 1 (i.e. $h_{ij} = m_{ij}^A (e_{ij}^B = e_{ji}^B = 0)$). In the case, both e_{ij}^B and e_{ji}^B are zero, it means there is no TRX transfer between nodes i and j, and the strength of the common social relationship between nodes i and j is still measured by the metric 1.

In this step, we calculate the values of h_{ij} according to Eq. (3), sort it in descending order based on the values and output the corresponding addresses i and j, along with the values of $e_{ij}^x (x \in \{A, B\})$ and $e_{ji}^x (x \in \{A, B\})$. Clearly, if there are round-trip transfers of USDT-TRC20 and TRX transfers exist in the two-layer transaction network, the relationship between addresses i and j is closer with the larger value of h_{ij}.

Following the above steps, we can uncover address pairs belonging to common social relationships in the transaction records, and visualize the transaction topology between addresses on the basis of Neo4j.

4 Experiments

The transaction data including USDT-TRC20 and TRX trading records are obtained in the following way. First, we started with an USDT-TRC20 address of a suspect in a money laundering by virtual currency case and downloaded its transaction records through OKLink, a blockchain browser. Then, from its counterparty, continue to retrieve and download the counterparty's trading records, and repeat this process until the counterparty is the exchange address or the platform address. Follow the above steps to do the same for all suspects' USDT-TRC20 addresses. Finally, all transaction records are merged together in a table, and the records are cleaned to remove invalid records, such as non-USDT, non-TRX, and the amount transacted less than 0.01. The table contains transaction hash, block height, date time, from, to, token, trading amount, where from and to represent the output address and input address of the transaction, respectively. The dataset comprises 769 addresses and 4862 transactions between these addresses, where the number of addresses involved in the USDT-TRC20 and TRX transactions is 747 and 93, respectively. The number of USDT-TRC20 transactions between 747 addresses is 4670, and the number of TRX transactions between 93 addresses is 192.

According to the transaction tracing method described in Sect. 3, the set of digital token addresses is represented by $V = V^A \cup V^B$, and the number of addresses in the set is 769 (i.e. $|V| = 769$). The adjacency matrix $E^A = (e_{ij}^A)_{|V| \times |V|}$ can be populated by the output addresses, input addresses, and the number of transfers in USDT-TRC20 transactions, where addresses serve as nodes i and j and the transaction counts serve as matrix elements e_{ij}^A or e_{ji}^A. Similarly, the adjacency matrix $E^B = (e_{ij}^B)_{|V| \times |V|}$ can be populated by the output addresses, input addresses, and the number of transfers in TRX transactions, where addresses serve as nodes i and j and the transaction counts serve as matrix elements e_{ij}^B or e_{ji}^B.

Then, we calculate the metrics 1 and 2, and list the address pairs with the calculated metric values greater than 1 and 2 respectively. During the computation process, we set the threshold *thr* to 1 to ensure that each pair of nodes has transferred to each other at least once. Then, the address pairs along with their corresponding USDT-TRC20 and TRX transfer counts, and the calculated metric values are shown in Table 1 and Table 2. As the number of USDT-TRC20 transactions far exceeds the number of TRX, we only calculate the value of m_{ij}^A in the layer A.

From Table 1 and Table 2, it can be observed that the highest metric values correspond to the same node pairs, denoted as address ***QfoH and ***oLYW, which is verified by the digital currency wallet company. In Table 1, for addresses ***QfoH and ***oLYW, e_{ij}^A is 215, and e_{ji}^A is 74, both of which are quite high. This implies a high frequency of round-trip transfers between the addresses, and a higher probability that they belong to the same group. In this case, it could indicate that addresses ***QfoH and ***oLYW belong to accomplices participating in gambling together. In Table 2, the address pair ***QfoH and ***oLYW still ranks first, indicating a higher probability that the address pair belongs to the same entity. In this case, one address is specifically used to receive withdrawals from exchanges and transfer them to another address, which is then used for outward transfers, such as money laundering and other criminal activities. It's also possible that addresses ***QfoH and ***oLYW are involved in mutual transfers due to round-trip borrowing between each other. Even if it is indeed borrowing, the high

Table 1. The value of mutual-transfer metric with consideration of USDT-TRC20 transfers.

Address1	Address2	e_{ij}^A	e_{ji}^A	m_{ij}^A
***QfoH	***oLYW	215	74	55.05190311
***QCfG	***QfoH	6	39	5.2
***Shka	***QfoH	26	5	4.193548387
***zj7k	***QfoH	3	16	2.526315789
***RRsj	***QfoH	2	28	1.866666667
***wpWe	***QfoH	4	3	1.714285714
***wVW3	***QfoH	3	2	1.2
***nxtp	***oLYW	2	2	1
***Pj9V	***di28	2	2	1

Table 2. The value of shared ownership metric with consideration of both USDT-TRC20 and TRX transfers.

Address1	Address2	e_{ij}^A	e_{ji}^A	e_{ij}^B	e_{ji}^B	h_{ij}
***QfoH	***oLYW	215	74	9	1	605.5709343
***QfoH	***wVW3	2	3	11	11	27.6
***QfoH	***QCfG	39	6	1	1	15.6
***di28	***Pj9V	2	2	2	3	6
***QfoH	***Shka	5	26	0	0	4.193548387
***nxtp	***oLYW	2	2	0	3	4
***zj7k	***QfoH	3	16	0	0	2.526315789
***95K4	***rYvh	1	1	2	1	2

frequency of round-trip borrowing suggests a highly trusted relationship, such as a close friendship. Certainly, if it occurs in the context of money laundering activities, explaining such frequent round-trip transfers as repayments and refunds is clearly unreasonable. In addition, we can see that the metric 2 with consideration of both USDT and TRX transfers between addresses, leads to a higher probability that the node pairs listed at the top belong to a shared ownership relationship compared to those in Table 1. That is to say, a higher value of m_{ij}^A may represent a higher probability that a pair of addresses belong to the same user or group, and a higher value of h_{ij} may represent a higher probability that a pair of addresses belong to the same entity.

Therefore, the metrics 1 and 2 can assist us in uncovering hidden addresses and identifying pairs of nodes belonging to the common social relationships, which holds significant implications for the traceability of virtual currencies.

5 Conclusions

This work is mainly focused on the tracing method of digital token (USDT) transaction. We have constructed a two-layer network composed of the transactions of USDT-TRC20 and TRX. Based on the constructed two-layer transaction network, a digital token transaction tracing method is proposed, along with two new metrics for measuring the strength of common social relationships between two addresses. These two metrics are named the mutual-transfer metric and the shared ownership metric, respectively. The former is used to measure the strength of common social relationships between two addresses, and the latter measures the strength of shared ownership between two addresses with consideration of two-layer transaction network. The larger the value of the mutual-transfer metric, the higher the probability of round-trip transfers between addresses, suggesting a higher likelihood of the addresses belonging to the same group. The larger the value of shared ownership metric is, the higher probability of addresses belonging to the same user, as the shared ownership metric not only considers the mutual transfer of USDT-TRC20 but also the TRX transfers between addresses. The experiments are performed to demonstrate the effectiveness of the digital token transaction tracing method, and the proposed metrics can reliably identify address pairs belonging to the same user or group with a high probability.

Acknowledgments. This research has been supported by the National Natural Science Foundation of China (Grant Nos. 62202209,61802155 and 62203229), the Key Disciplines in Jiangsu Province during the 14th Five Year Plan period (Public Security Technology, Cyberspace Security), the Excellent Science and Technology Innovation Team in Jiangsu Province (Forensic Analysis of Electronic Data, Excellent Technological Innovation Team in Forensic Toxicology under the Framework of Artificial Intelligence), and the Science and Technology Project of Market Supervision Administration of Jiangsu Province (Grant No. KJ21125027).

Declaration of Competing Interest. The authors declare that they have no competing financial interests or personal relationships that could have appeared to influence the work reported in this paper.

References

1. Zheng, Z., Xie, S., Dai, H.N., Chen, X., Wang, H.: Blockchain challenges and opportunities: a survey. Int. J. Web Grid Serv. **14**(4), 352–375 (2018)
2. Nakamoto, S.: Bitcoin: A peer-to-peer electronic cash system [EB/OL]. https://bitcoin.org/bitcoin.pdf (2008)
3. Thanh, B.N., Hong, T.N.V., Pham, H., Cong, T.N., Anh, T.P.T.: Are the stabilities of stablecoins connected? J. Ind. Bus. Econ. **50**, 515–525 (2022)
4. Wu, J., Liu, J., Zhao, Y., Zheng, Z.: Analysis of cryptocurrency transactions from a network perspective: an overview. J. Netw. Comput. Appl. **190**, 103139 (2021)
5. Gao, F., Mao, H., Wu, Z., Shen, M., Zhu, L., Li, Y.: Lightweight transaction tracing technology for bitcoin. Chin. J. Comput. **41**(5), 989–1004 (2018)
6. Koshy, P., Koshy, D., McDaniel, P.: An analysis of anonymity in bitcoin using P2P network traffic. In: Christin, N., Safavi-Naini, R. (eds.) Financial Cryptography and Data Security. FC 2014, LNCS, vol. 8437, pp. 469–485. Springer, Berlin, Heidelberg (2014). https://doi.org/10.1007/978-3-662-45472-5_30

7. Xiao, R., Ren, W., Zhu, T., Choo, K.-K.R.: A mixing scheme using a decentralized signature protocol for privacy protection in bitcoin blockchain. IEEE Trans. Dependable Secure Comput. **18**(4), 1793–1803 (2021)
8. Liao, K., Zhao, Z., Doupé, A., Ahn, G-J.: Behind closed doors: measurement and analysis of cryptolocker ransoms in bitcoin. In: Proceedings of the APWG Symposium on Electronic Crime Research (eCrime), pp. 1–13. IEEE, Toronto, ON, Canada (2016)
9. Yousaf, H., Kappos, G., Meiklejohn, S.: Tracing transactions across cryptocurrency ledgers. In: Proceedings of the 28th USENIX Conference on Security Symposium, pp. 837–850. Santa Clara, CA, USA (2019)
10. Li, Y., Yang, G., Susilo, W., Yu, Y., Au, M.H., Liu, D.: Traceable Monero: anonymous cryptocurrency with enhanced accountability. IEEE Trans. Dependable Secure Comput. **18**(2), 679–691 (2021)
11. Liu, X.F., Ren, H.-H., Liu, S.-H., Jiang, X.-J.: Characterizing key agents in the cryptocurrency economy through blockchain transaction analysis. EPJ Data Sci. **10**(21) (2021)
12. Dearden, T.E., Tucker, S.E.: Follow the money: analyzing darknet activity using cryptocurrency and the bitcoin blockchain. J. Contemp. Crim. Justice **39**(2), 257–275 (2023)
13. Ma, T., Xu, H., Li, P.: SkyEye: a traceable scheme for blockchain[EB/OL]. IACR Cryptology ePrint Archive (2020). https://eprint.iacr.org/2020/034
14. Krawczyk, H., Rabin, T.: Chameleon hashing and signatures[EB/OL]. IACR Cryptology ePrint Archive (1998). https://eprint.iacr.org/1998/010
15. Gennaro, R., Gentry, C., Parno, B., Raykova, M.: Quadratic span programs and succinct NIZKs without PCPs. In: Johansson, T., Nguyen, P. (eds.) EUROCRYPT 2013, LNCS, vol. 7881, pp. 626–645. Springer, Berlin, Heidelberg (2013). https://doi.org/10.1007/978-3-642-38348-9_37
16. Li, P., Xu, H., Ma, T.: An efficient identity tracing scheme for blockchain-based systems. Inf. Sci. **561**, 130–140 (2021)
17. Xiao, K., Li, J., He, Y., Wang, X., Wang, C.: A secure multi-party payment channel on-chain and off-chain supervisable scheme. Futur. Gener. Comput. Syst. **154**, 330–343 (2024)
18. Fan, H.: The digital asset value and currency supervision under deep learning and blockchain technology. J. Comput. Appl. Math.Comput. Appl. Math. **407**, 114061 (2022)

GPT-Based Wasm Instruction Analysis for Program Language Processing

Liangjun Deng[1], Qi Zhong[2]([✉]), Hang Lei[1], Yao Qiu[3],
and Jingxue Chen[4]

[1] School of Information and Software Engineering, University of Electronic Science
and Technology of China, Chengdu 610054, China
dengliangjun@skycto.com, hlei@uestc.edu.cn
[2] Faculty of Data Science, City University of Macau, Macau, China
qizhong@cityu.edu.mo
[3] Ningbo Polytechnic College,, Zhejiang Ningbo 315800, China
2014061@nbpt.edu.cn
[4] School of Mathematical and Physical Sciences, University of Technology Sydney,,
NSW Sydney 2007, Australia
jingxue.chen@uts.edu.au

Abstract. Capturing the logical structure of programming languages poses a significant challenge for program analysis. Given the complex syntax rules, subjective code vulnerabilities, irrelevant statements, code annotations, and intricate structural information, related studies have explored various semantic comprehension and intermediate representation approaches to extract precise information for program analysis. However, most research in the generic domain ignores defective and non-defective program code, putting them in the same category. In this paper, we introduce a new program analysis method that combines WebAssembly (Wasm) instructions with a 20-billion-parameter transformer model and natural language processing. This approach aims to advance the capabilities of program analysis tools in computer science by jointly embedding Wasm instructions and natural language for more effective program analysis. Our experiments demonstrate that this fused embedding approach achieves state-of-the-art performance, and the accuracy reaches approximately 98 percent, better than traditional small-scale weight models based on intricate conversion tasks such as abstract syntax trees(AST). Moreover, it is more valuable to classify potential vulnerable and non-vulnerable programs in the formal verification special field. Our exploration enhances traditional program classification methods in software security and introduces the application of GPT to offer a more straightforward, convenient, and high-performance approach.

Keywords: WebAssembly · formal verification · deep learning · program analysis

Supported by Key Science and Technology R&D Plan of Ningbo in 2023 and The Third Batch of Approval Projects.

W. Li et al. (Eds.): EISA 2024, CCIS 2266, pp. 118–136, 2025.
https://doi.org/10.1007/978-3-031-80419-9_9

1   Introduction

Generative pre-trained transformer(GPT) models [1,2] achieve significant success across various natural language processing (NLP) [3] tasks and applications. These models not only consistently achieve state-of-the-art performance on a wide range of benchmark NLP tasks, but also sparked significant research advancements in the field of NLP, leading to the development of more sophisticated models and techniques. Researchers continue to explore ways to enhance the capabilities of GPT and address its limitations. Over time, The emergence of applications such as Code-llama [4], Code-QWen [5], and other GPT-based programs indicate that GPT can already read and write programming language code. This article attempts to introduce GPT in program analysis to improve the performance of the highest-level tasks in the code detection task. Program analysis is critical for understanding, improving, and maintaining software systems. It involves analyzing the software's behavior, structure, and performance to identify its strengths, weaknesses, and opportunities for improvement. It can also be used in software engineering tasks such as program comprehension, program testing, functionality classification, and code clone detection. The earliest research [6–8] on program analysis has succeeded in improving the quality of software development and maintenance. The pioneers usually focused on methodologies such as string-based pattern matching, rule-based model recognition, and a bag of words (BoW) [9]. However, these approaches treat code fragments as plain texts, ignoring the underlying semantic information in source code and resulting in poor performance.

In recent years, researchers have been exploring the intersection of program analysis and deep learning, to develop more effective techniques for analyzing and understanding software. For example, deep learning has been used to improve bug detection and program repair, as well as to assist with code recommendation and optimization. There is ongoing research into the best ways to combine program analysis and deep learning techniques to achieve the best results. For instance, TBCNN [10,11] classify program code according to functionality based on AST convolutional neural network(CNN). codeBERT [12] analyzes the relation between program language and natural language with deep learning to generate program code documentation. code2seq [13] makes use of compositional paths in its AST. UAST [14] unifies AST models to learn cross-language program classification. Although deep learning [15,16] holds great promise for advancing the field of software engineering, Our findings argue that existing research on program analysis and deep learning has certain limitations in dealing with specific scenarios. For instance, the naming conventions of developers can significantly affect the outcomes of source-code-based analysis. Furthermore, unoptimized code with redundant sections and different orders can lead to inaccurate program analysis results. Despite the effectiveness of ASTs in representing the organizational structure of codes, they may not fully capture the logical structure of the code, especially when irrelevant and redundant codes are present in the source code files. Logically unreachable code, code annotations, or commented-out functions can pose challenges for deep learning program analysis. Especially, high-accurate analysis is one of the important challenges in the software vulnerability detection project, the principle of equivalence verification in formal verification is based on the concept of logical equivalence of mathematical formulas. The verified program usually has potential defects, which may be caused by some very subtle code logic, common examples such as equal erroneously written not equal in the branch condition, then the previous program analysis method can not adapt to the work in formal verification project.

These limitations underscore the need for further research to enhance the robustness and accuracy of program analysis using deep learning techniques. Despite related research, challenges in this field remain unresolved. Hence, we propose a deep learning method for program instructions in formal language processing, which leverages the power of deep learning to automatically learn and extract features from program instructions, and supplement functionality equality detection tasks in the software security field. In this paper, We chose WebAssembly as the intermediate representation instructions for analysis. Instruction analysis involves the direct analysis of compiled program instructions, which vary across different compilers and CPUs produce differences, increasing the difficulty of instruction-based program analysis. Wasm serves as a low-level programming language, solving the problem well. Particularly, Wasm does not target specific hardware architectures as traditional assembly languages do, it provides a cross-platform solution that can run in various environments. Its design enables high-performance code execution across different systems, allowing developers to write code close to the hardware level. Developers can compile codes from various programming languages, including C, C++, Rust, and even high-level languages like JavaScript, into Wasm modules. Therefore, the instruction level program analysis based on Wasm language can realize multi-language program analysis, unified instruction, and cross-platform analysis, which greatly improves the practicability of this research work in the real world.

Our contributions to the field are outlined as follows:

- We present an approach for Wasm instruction analysis that combines deep learning with program analysis techniques, offering versatility across various programming languages.
- We introduce an innovative methodology that integrates natural language processing with binary data, aiming to facilitate GPT's comprehension of Wasm binaries.
- We introduce a novel approach to instruction analysis, potentially advancing deep neural network research within the domain of program analysis.

Section 2 introduces the background of program instruction analysis. Methodology in Sect. 3 details the embedding of Wasm binary files and natural languages. Experimental Sect. 4 shows the whole progress and evaluations, demonstrating the feasibility of this method. The final section is the conclusion.

2   Motivation and Background

2.1   Motivation

In formal verification, source code analysis and instruction analysis is a dilemma, whereas source code analysis and AST analysis pose significant challenges. Among them, when a CNN is applied to this kind of method of ASTs, the attention mechanism of CNN is not long enough to process code comments, pre-variable declaration, pre-logic processing, and pre-data, which will lead to unstable convolution results of ASTs. In addition, TBCNN directly gives up pooling operations to maintain the position information of the code. Compared to plain text, the AST may become more complex. Therefore, information based on tree structure has to simplify the upper and lower relations and brother node relations. TBCC splits ASTs into sub-trees of abstract syntax, according to condition branch or function call, and constructs a new simplified AST. It uses the self-attention mechanism and multi-head attention mechanism of the transformer network structure to alleviate the long-distance dependency in the code logic and improve the performance of program analysis.

To illustrate this challenge with a real-world example, consider the Disturb−CodeExample function shown in Fig. 1. This code snippet is a blend of unoptimized, unreachable, irrelevant, redundant, and commented logic. The line 2 and 4 indicate that the line 5 is an unreachable logic path. Assuming that the UnReachFn function organizes a complex program logic path, AST-based program analysis methods will be easily confused by this logic branch and get the wrong analysis results. Similarly, the line 7 is a snippet of comment statements, which also interferes with model identification. Additionally, if program analysis deeps into the line 11 involving condition variables "input" and "a", we discover the lines 8 to 10 are irrelevant codes, which do not affect the result of the DisturbCodeExample function. When program analysis focuses on condition variable "a" in the 11th line, It is clear that condition-if will get false forever in terms of the variable "a" leading to an invalid unreachable logic path in the 12th "LogicErrFn" line.

The DisturbCodeExample function code can be simplified drastically through the program analysis above mentioned. The function is equivalent to "LogicAFn(5)" regardless of the variable "input", "LogicBFn", "UnReachFn", or "LogicErrFn" is. Unfolding the irrelevant functions may cause a lot of code snippets or several enormous ASTs, and the corresponding program analysis of those irrelevant parts is vain, what's worse is that it may even mislead the analysis result of the program in a large probability. Though the AST can represent more structured information of programs compared with traditional methods, the real logic information under the source code structure is still difficult to capture for the analyzer. Particularly, the same source codes denote different logic caused by variables influencing factors. These similar code situations are common in software engineering practice, and greatly affect the recognition accuracy of program analysis based on source codes or ASTs.

```
01. void DisturbCodeExample(int input){
02.     int a=5;
03.     //logic statements
04.     if(a==907)
05.         a=UnReachFn(a);
07.     //for(int i;i<100;i++){++a;}
08.     int b=22;
09.     //logicB calcuate b
10.     b=LogicBFn(b);
11.     if(input > 0 && a == 10) {
12.         LogicErrFn(a);
13.     }else{
14.         LogicAFn(a);
15.     }
16. }
```

(a)

```
(module
  (type (;0;) (func (param i32) (result i32)))
  (type (;1;) (func))
  (type (;2;) (func (param i32)))
  (type (;3;) (func (param i32 i32) (result i32)))
  (type (;4;) (func (result i32)))
  (import "env" "printf" (func $printf (type 3)))
  (import "env" "__memory_base" (global (;1;) i32))
  (import "env" "__table_base" (global (;2;) i32))
  (import "env" "memory" (memory (;0;) 1))
  (func $LogicAFn (type 2) (param i32) )
  (func $LogicBFn (type 0) (param i32) (result i32))
  (func $LogicErrFn (type 0) (param i32) (result i32))
  (func $UnReachFn (type 0) (param i32) (result i32))
  (func $DisturbCodeExample (type 2) (param i32))
  (func $main (type 3) (param i32 i32) (result i32)
  (global (;3;) i32 (i32.const 0))
  (export "LogicAFn" (func $LogicAFn))
  (export "LogicBFn" (func $LogicBFn))
  (export "LogicErrFn" (func $LogicErrFn))
  (export "UnReachFn" (func $UnReachFn))
  (export "DisturbCode" (func $DisturbCodeExample))
  (export "main" (func $main))
  (data (;0;) (global.get 1) "Logic A Fn:%d\00"))
```

(b)

Fig. 1. Code vulnerability example includes unoptimized, unreachable, irrelevant, redundant, commented logic code snippet.

One possible solution is to generate binary files through compilation optimization, which in turn creates cross-platform instruction incompatibilities. Assuming instruction analysis, the executable program is specific to a certain platform, as a result, analysis software is not versatile. In software security verification, external modules without source code are also encountered at the boundaries of software API access. So it seems that instruction-based analysis is a more suitable approach for software verification. Wasm as a new assembly language unifies a set of instructions that can run any platform or CPU. It seems that Wasm is ideal for instruction analysis. The example codes have been compiled to readable Wasm bytecode as shown in Fig. 2 (b). Our motivation is to explore an analytical approach where natural language coexists with program instructions, based on the reasoning power of large-scale language models. Beyond all questions, people should do program analysis, meanwhile, it also brings new challenges. In the following section, this paper introduces base background information of Wasm and analyzes the Wasm module byte by byte using a transformer network to learn features.

2.2 Wasm

It is commonly acknowledged that each high-level programming language has its unique syntax sugar for code writing. The disparity in syntax features among different high-level programming languages results in a reduced universality of program analysis in comparison to low-level languages. Nonetheless, low-level machine language suffers from a lack of portability that is inextricably tied to the underlying hardware architecture, and thus they can only be executed on CPUs of the exact type for which they were compiled, in this case, program analysis work also faces the same difficulties. To address this issue, Wasm instructions have been suggested to provide a layer of abstraction between the hardware and the software. The advantages of this for program analysis are shown as follows:

- Fine-grained analysis: Instruction analysis provides a fine-grained analysis of the program, as it operates at the level of individual instructions. This allows us to capture a very detailed view of the program's behavior and identify subtle issues that might be missed by higher-level analyses.
- Language independence: Instruction analysis is language-independent, as it operates on the low-level instructions that are common to all programming languages. This makes it possible to analyze programs written in any language, without the need for language-specific tools or techniques.
- High performance: Instruction analysis is typically faster than higher-level analyses, as it operates on a lower-level representation of the program. This makes it possible to analyze large programs and datasets in a reasonable amount of time.

Wasm [11,13,17] applications are evolving rapidly. As an efficient and lightweight instruction set, Wasm provides excellent support for all types of central processing units (CPU), On the other side, Wasm as an official standard of the World Wide Web Consortium (W3C) [18] is the next generation instruction. The Wasm core specification defines the semantics of Wasm modules independent from a concrete embedding. It is a safe, portable, low-level code format designed for efficient execution and compact representation [18]. Wasm's fast startup, high-performance execution, and cross-CPU architecture make it a superior containerization or sandbox technology, the Wasm technology has been widely used in various fields, such as encryption, blockchain, simulation, deep learning, embedded microcontrollers, autonomous driving, and medical field, and has achieved good performance results. Haas [19] considers Wasm brings the web up to speed, meanwhile, Lehmann [20] argues that everything old is new again for Wasm, including binary security [21], program analysis [22,23], edge computing, IoT [24], containerization, microservices and serverless architectures. Hilbig advises an empirical study of real-world Wasm binaries security, languages, and use cases. Program analysis of Wasm presents many challenges to researchers.

2.3 Wasm and Wat

The module is the smallest unit in which a Wasm program is compiled, transferred, and loaded. The Wasm specification specifies two module formats, called Wasm and wat. The Wasm is a binary format, while the wat is a human-readable text format. Wasm Module structure can be expressed by grammar Eq. (1).

$$Module \Leftrightarrow magic \mid version \mid type_{sec?} \mid import_{sec?}$$
$$\mid func_sec? \mid table_sec? \mid mem_sec?$$
$$\mid global_sec? \mid export_sec? \mid start_sec? \tag{1}$$
$$\mid elem_sec? \mid code_sec? \mid data_sec?$$

In addition to magic and version, other else sections in the Wasm module are optional. There are 12 sections in a Wasm module according to the order 0 to 11. The instruction of the Wasm module is stored in order by section ID according to the dependency between the sections. Unlike the traditional binary program, the Wasm interpreter can parse Wasm programs as we read them from the IO stream without reading the whole program. Neither binary nor source code structures represent the logic of a program directly. Program analysis necessarily requires a deep dive into the instruction structure of the Wasm module. The overall structure of the Wasm binary format is shown in Fig. 2 (a), and a piece of Wasm binary instruction code is illustrated in Fig. 2 (b). Because any instruction can be represented in a single byte in Wasm and data is stored by byte using the LEB128 compression algorithm, Fig. 2 (b) is translated byte-by-byte to readable Fig. 2 (c).

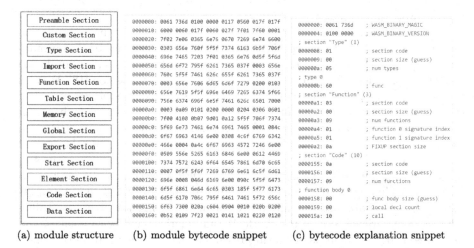

(a) module structure   (b) module bytecode snippet   (c) bytecode explanation snippet

Fig. 2. (a) is the overall structure of the Wasm module. (b) shows a piece of Wasm instruction code based on hex value. (c) is a readable instruction explanation based on (b).

Compared with the traditional binary program analysis, Wasm uses a data storage format called LEB128 (Little-Endian Base 128) to store data in a stacked memory space. LEB128 is a highly efficient encoding format that offers variable-length encoding, space efficiency, low CPU latencies, endianness support, ease of integration, and extensibility. LEB128 is a compression format based on encoding and decoding in comparison to common data storage. In addition, the LEB128 format also requires fewer CPU cycles to decode and encode than other encoding formats, resulting in lower CPU latencies and improved overall system performance. LEB128 allows for encoding numbers of variable length, making it more space-efficient than fixed-length encoding formats. LEB128 can encode numbers as small as 1 byte or as large as 128 bytes, allowing for efficient storage of both small and large integers. As a result, the traditional binary program analysis methodology cannot be applied to Wasm module analysis. To analyze the Wasm program, module sections have to be interpreted section by section as follows Table 1 demonstrated. More detailed work is elaborated in the methodology section.

Table 1. Section information of Wasm module

Section	ID	Description
Preamble		Preamble information, which stores version information.
Custom	0	Custom information, including debugging information, etc.
Type	1	A unique list of function signatures used in a Wasm module.
Import	2	Data and functions imported from external modules.
Function	3	A list of all functions in a Wasm module.
Table	4	A reference table to the address of the function.
Memory	5	All memory blocks without initialization are defined.
Global	6	Global variable
Export	7	Variables or functions exported to external modules.
Start	8	The entry function of a wasm program.
Element	9	Initialize the data of the Table Section.
Code	10	The implementation code for each Function.
Data	11	Initialize the data of the Memory Section.

2.4   Generative Pre-Trained Transformer Network

The architecture of the generative pre-trained transformer network is based on the Transformer model, which is introduced in the paper "Attention is All You Need" in 2017 [25]. The GPT builds upon this architecture, enhancing it for natural language understanding and generation tasks. The GPT consists of multiple layers of Transformer blocks. Each block typically contains two main subcomponents. Multi-head self-attention mechanism allows the model to focus on different parts of the input sequence simultaneously. It computes attention scores between all pairs of words in the input sequence, allowing the model to weigh the importance of each word based on its relevance to other words in the sequence. After the attention mechanism, each position in the sequence is passed through a feed-forward neural network independently. This network consists of multiple layers of linear transformations followed by non-linear activation functions, such as ReLU (Rectified Linear Unit). Unlike the original Transformer model, which is commonly used for both encoder and decoder tasks in sequence-to-sequence models, the GPT uses a decoder-only architecture. This means it generates output tokens autoregressively, one token at a time, without access to future tokens during generation. Figure 3 shows the network structure of the GPT model, which lacks the encoder module compared to the original Transformer architecture. Due to the stackable design of the decoder modules, the GPT can effectively share parameters. This means that many of the parameters in the model are used multiple times during training, which improves the utilization of the parameters and makes it possible to train a better model on a limited dataset. Since the GPT is pre-trained in an unsupervised manner, the structure of the decoder module enables the GPT to perform transfer learning on a variety of NLP tasks. By fine-tuning specific tasks, the GPT can adapt to new tasks and domains and achieve better performance Table 2.

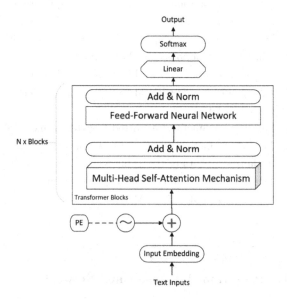

Fig. 3. The architecture of the generative pre-trained transformer network

In principle, the Transformers cannot implicitly learn the positional information of sequences. To address this issue of sequence processing, the solution proposed by the creators of Transformers is to use positional encoding (PE). It combines the position index and dimension index leading to each tensor element's position independence. PE can adapt to sentences that are longer than all the sentences in the training set. Suppose that the longest sentence in the training set has 100 words, the formula calculation method can be used to calculate

Table 2. Components of GPT

Components of GPT	Description
Embedding Layers	These embeddings capture semantic information about the tokens and serve as the input Transformer blocks.
Positional Encoding	Positional encoding are added to provide the model with information about token order.
Multi-head Attention	It captures dependencies between words non-sequentially and helps in understanding contextual relationships
Position-Wise FFN	Each token's representation is fed through a position-wise fully connected feed-forward neural network.
Transformer Blocks	GPT consists of multiple layers of Transformer blocks, typically organized in a stack.
Layer Normal	Layer Normalization help stabilize training, and residual connections mitigate the vanishing gradient problem, allowing for easier training of deep models.
Output Layer	A linear transformation followed by a softmax activation function. This produces a probability distribution over the vocabulary, allowing the model to generate the next token in the sequence.

the embedding at the 101st position. The final input of each word is obtained by adding the word vector and position vector, and the dense matrix is obtained by embedding matrix compression.

3   Methodology

The goal of the method proposed in this paper is to enable a large model to directly analyze the Wasm binary file according to the prompt words. The whole process is designed as shown in Fig. 4. The input includes two parts: the prompt words and the Wasm binary file. After word embedding and instruction embedding, the features are concatenated, and the input is sent to the GPT model for subsequent training. The specification of Wasm encapsulates 178 distinct instructions. Because static single assignment allows each variable to have a unique definition, data flow analysis and optimization algorithms for Wasm programs can be much simpler. In the Wasm program, several unrelated uses of the same variable in the source program can be converted into different uses of different variables in the SSA form, thus eliminating many unnecessary dependencies.

In this paper, we use Octopus to easily analyze control and function call flows of a Wasm program, thus cutting out irrelevant variables, statements, and functions that the compiler has not optimized. In the control flows, when encountering conditional instructions like "if", "while", "switch", "for" and the ternary operator "select", the method extracts conditional variables to identify

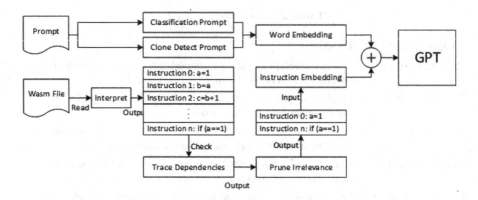

Fig. 4. The workflow of nature language and Wasm module combination analysis based on GPT

a sequence of code instructions related to the condition. By tracing dependencies with conditional variables, removing irrelevant instructions from the code flow can avoid the analysis of meaningless instruction regions that are unreachable. In the function call flows, other functions that have no call relationship to the analysis functions are common in modular programs. These functions are identified and filtered out to focus the analysis on relevant parts of the code.

Generally speaking, Wasm programs include many independent functions without dependencies that are used as external libraries. Therefore, irrelevant functions can be filtered before instruction embedding. In program analysis, the most challenging aspect lies in deciphering the underlying logic of the code. As demonstrated by the DisturbCodeExample in Fig. 1, if a significant portion of the code we analyze exists in regions where conditions render it unreachable (e.g., Line 5), precise analysis becomes meaningless. Similarly, if the vast code region we analyze is unrelated to the logic (e.g., Line 10), the analysis results are highly likely to deviate from the true intent. Furthermore, the complex conditional statement in the line 11 can lead to ambiguous branch path determination during program analysis. All these issues can severely impact the performance of program analysis. The pruning method proposed in this paper not only increases the scale of program analysis but also enables more precise analysis. As illustrated in Fig. 2 (b), all characters are meticulously represented using ASCII codes, while numerical values are encoded using LEB128, with larger values spanning continuous bytes. Alternatively, we have explored the parsing of LEB128-encoded data into decimal representations, subsequently converting these numbers into strings and mapping them again to ASCII codes to generate input vectors. Experimentally, it is observed that reading LEB128 encoding, whether directly or post-conversion to human-readable decimal strings, yields the same effectiveness.

In the stage of instruction embedding, the transformation of any binary Wasm program into an input vector only mandates a straightforward procedure of reading one byte at a time and converting it directly into the corresponding index within the dictionary. Concatenating prompts text and Wasm instructions, the final input vector identifies the start of Wasm using "<sow>", and the end of Wasm using "<eow>". The whole algorithm is shown as follows.

Algorithm 1: Combination Embedding of Wasm Instructions and Prompt Text

---

Input: Wasm file, prompt text, and label
Output: Tensor input for training

Step 1: Load Wasm module, extract the control flow graph (CFG) and function call graph (FCG);
(module, cfg, fcg) = OctopusExtract(Wasm_input);

Step 2: Filter out irrelevant variable operands and functions in the Wasm module if some compilers ignore certain optimizations;
module = filter(module, cfg, fcg);

Step 3: Read byte code according to Wasm instruction from the default export function main;
byte_array_instructions = ReadWasmInstruction(module);

Step 4: Convert Wasm byte instructions into token IDs;
Wasm_token_ids = Token(" < sow > ") + Token(byte_array_instructions)+ Token(" < eow > ");

Step 5: Concatenate IDs of Wasm and prompt text;
input_ids = Token(prompt) + Token("\n") + Wasm_token_ids;

Step 6: Assemble autoregressive training corpus;
tensor_input = Token(" < human >: ") + input_ids + Token("\n < bot >: ")+ Token(label);

Program language is a kind of language with strong structure and careful logic. The diversity of its expression makes program logic influenced by different coding methods. When writing a program, developers can choose different coding methods and styles according to their needs and personal preferences. For example, some programming languages allow different syntax rules and idioms to express the same logic, and this flexibility allows developers to make choices based on specific contexts and needs. Therefore, In the stage of positional encoding, rotary position embedding which is more in line with programming language processing is adopted. RoPE combines relative positional encoding with absolute positional encoding to obtain the complete positional encoding for each position. Specifically, the relative positional encoding is added to the word embeddings to obtain the complete positional encoding for each position. RoPE is a way to represent relative positions using absolute position encoding, preserving not only the position encoding but also the relationship between relative positions. RoPE enables the Transformer model to better capture the relative relationships between different positions in a sequence, thereby improving performance and efficiency when dealing with long sequences in program languages.

4   Experiment and Evaluation

4.1   Dataset

This paper considers two data sets for evaluation. The first dataset is the Big-CloneBench [26], a popular code clone benchmark collected from 25,000 Java software systems, which contains 6,000,000 clone pairs and 260,000 non-clone pairs. The second dataset is the open judge (OJ) dataset [27], a pedagogical online judge system that contains 104 different C coding problems. The system allows students to submit their source codes as solutions to certain problems, and the OJ system judges the validity of the submitted source code automatically according to the 104 problems that are labeled as code classes. After empirical evaluations, our datasets were mainly extracted from the OJ datasets, the reasons are due to the limitation of Java Wasm compilers such as JWasm and TeaVM, the BigCloneBench is based on Java code snippets, which are incomplete for compilation. In particular, when the source codes include thread, socket, AWT, and unknown imports, it is difficult to successfully compile Wasm programs. Initially, we gathered 52,000 original C/C++ classification codes, and approximately 50% of them are effortlessly compiled into Wasm modules using Clang. Among them, we ignored warnings of main-return-type and return-type as possible as we can to generate more Wasm programs, such as return type of main is not int(files: 3942.c,1958.c), or no return value in a main function(files: 3659.c, 3656.c, 1483.c). Certainly, the amount of each problem that can be compiled directly is different. We obtain 182 Wasm programs from the first 500 solutions, The rate of success compilations is approximately 36%. 500 solutions of the third problem between 1000 and 1500 generate 385 Wasm programs, occupying 77%.

The source code that cannot be compiled is mainly due to the inclusion of the C++ iostream library. Although these files have a ".c" extension indicating they are C language files, they use C++ libraries, such as cin and cout. Some files not only lack the inclusion of iostream but also do not declare the C++ std namespace. As a result, these files cannot be compiled properly even with gcc. Therefore, the Wasm compiler treats functions from the iostream library as unknown functions without special handling, and they are not supported. Consequently, these source code files were directly eliminated from the experiment. After compiling the first round of screening, the total training corpus reaches about 28,158. When compiling, we adopt the standalone mode to optimize the size of the compiled Wasm application as much as possible. The smallest Wasm module is just over 300 bytes and includes a complete function definition, function import, and function export module. Surprisingly, in the 878th file, the generated Wasm file size exceeded 100M, and we go on to filter out similar Wasm files from the corpus. It is observed that the real logic instructions in the 878th file are less than 400 bytes, however, the source codes allocate 100M array in the global section leading to a big compilation result. The algorithm implementation of the 56th problem in the 878th file is a special case. the 3878th file also completes the same work for the 56th problem, but its Wasm program occupies only 1668 bytes. In this experiment, 200 tokens are reserved for prompt text, and 56 tokens are for model responses, so our corpus is sifted again, this time reduced to 24,779 pieces with a size is less than 1750 bytes. The training corpus is divided into a ratio of 8:1:1 for training, validation, and testing, respectively, according to each problem.

4.2   Implementation Details

Our experiment is based on GPT-NeoX [28], namely, a 20 billion parameter auto-regressive language model, developed primarily for research purposes. The word embedding size in the transformer block is set to 6144, the number of layers N is set to 44, the head number of multi-head attention is set to 64, and the learning rate is set to 1e-6. All the experiments are conducted on a server with 9 NVIDIA RTX 8000 GPUs. All 44 layers are evenly distributed across 9 GPUs, except the last one, which consists of 4 layers. The first GPU allocates 44.5G of memory, while the last GPU occupies 45.0G of memory. The other remaining GPUs utilize approximately 42.39G of memory. Because of the gather-reduce operation, when the batch size is over 18, the memory of peak occurs overflow. In the experiment, we trained 18 pieces of data per batch, and when the gradient accumulation is set to 6, we can train 85,320 pieces of data in 24 h. We spent 7 d training 30 epochs, the total steps are 33,000.

4.3   Evaluation and Analysis

To demonstrate as much as possible the effect of comparing source-based and instruction-based analysis, we interfere with the source code of the test dataset to simulate the common program vulnerabilities that might be encountered in the software security field, as shown in the code example in Fig. 1. These disturbances include adding logically unreachable branches, dead loops, zero division error, null pointers, out of bound of the array, introducing if conditionals without altering the logic, and adding function calls for computing unrelated variables. We clone the TBCC project from GitHub [27] and test the code classification tasks on the same datasets. These datasets take into account specific scenarios, which significantly increases the difficulty of classification for TBCC. In addition to the reason for the datasets, the reproduction of TBCC training may also have

Table 3. Comparison with TBCC model for code classification with logic disturbances

Tool	$ACC(\%)$
TBCC	90.2
Our study	98.1

a certain factor, including training duration. The multi-head attention mechanism facilitates the learning of tasks by deep neural networks. Programming languages constitute structured information, ASTs represent structured information, and assembly instructions are also a form of structured information Table 3. In previous deep learning approaches, the representation of programming language features, whether in the form of plain text convolution or ASTs, was not adequately captured due to the absence of sufficiently large models like GPT and corresponding attention mechanisms. We summarize the three stages of program analysis as illustrated in Table 4.

Table 4. Feature analysis of source programs

Program Form	Feature Description
Plain Texts	Sequence dimension and syntax sugar.
ASTs	ASTs include syntax, structure, and sequence dimension.
Instructions	Semantic symbols, sequence dimension without syntax sugar.

In general, plain texts, ASTs, and instructions are common three forms of program analysis. They are also the key phases from source code to compilation results. In the past, limited to the simple dimension of sequences, plain texts, and instructions were difficult to analyze. However, ASTs contain more features, involving syntax, structure, and sequences. Therefore, AST-based methodologies achieve higher performances. Next, we make an in-depth analysis from the perspective of methods shown in Table 5.

Table 5. Feature of program analysis methodologies

Model	Features
BoW	Bag of words.
RNN	Long-short term memory and forget.
CNN	Partial feature extraction and discard feature.
Transformer	Feature extraction and attention mechanism.
GPT	Large-scale embedding dimension and attention mechanism.

As well as known, except for the simplest algorithm like BoW, RNN needs to set an input feature matrix in advance, through embedding matrix outputting a dense matrix. Moreover, the dimensions of the output matrix are commonly less equal than 512. CNN discards partial features during the pooling operation. The loss of this feature may not matter in an image task, but it is a fatal flaw in a software program. Therefore, feature loss is an inadvisable behavior for the program analysis. Transformer-based methods retain the whole features of the target program from ASTs. Among them, transformer-encoder components look like a complex feature conversion. On the contrary, GPT models cut encoder components, and end-to-end high-dimension matrix replaces encoder components. The essence of this performance improvement comes down to the matrix dimensions, which contain massive features.

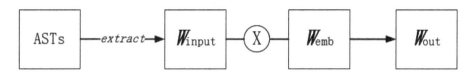

Fig. 5. Low dimension matrix needs to extract input features to capture more information in the traditional neural network.

When applying BPE segmentation to the GPT, tokens are merely indexes used to reference rows in the word embedding matrix. The inherent meaning of tokens is conveyed by the multidimensional complex tensor of the embedding matrix, surpassing the dimensionality of previous model representations. This is why the model can "understand" the combination of assembly instructions and natural language. We do not repeat more historical methods because reading Wasm instruction programs like a human is just the beginning, and we suspect that there is much more scope for large models to be explored, for deep neural networks to understand learning programs, even detect security vulnerabilities, maintain software, and so on.

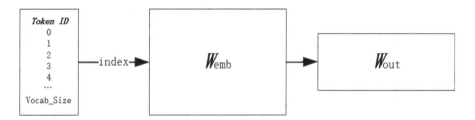

Fig. 6. A learnable embedding matrix, high-dimension(6144) weight matrix of GPT model adequately represent semantic information of program analysis.

4.4   Threat for Validations

GPT-NeoX is only a pre-training model trained on the Pile data sets [29]. To improve the generality of this model, we fine-tune the model Fig 5. The training data sets are easily obtained from hugging face [30], including multiple languages and multiple downstream tasks such as OIG [31], COIG [32], alpaca, moss, and so on. We also remove the number merging from the vocabularies so that all the numbers are a single number from 0–9 to better compare the size of the numbers. We continue to train for more than 6 months with a learning rate of 1e-6, and the loss value of related downstream tasks was less than 0.2 percent, while the minimum loss value could reach 0.02 percent. Each of these basic conditions may slightly affect the outcome of the experiment. Moreover, due to the stochastic gradient descent, the actual training consumption duration will also be biased. However,the conclusions are positive, because we also reach unprecedented achievement in another text embedding experiment Fig 6.

5   Conclusion

In this paper, we propose an approach based on GPT for Wasm instruction analysis, fused with nature language. Unlike previous studies, one novel aspect lies in the form of embedding, which consists of two distinct inputs. The other is an interesting instruction analysis experiment, based on the characteristics of Wasm, the feasibility of program analysis is greatly expanded for multiple program languages. In this work, Our primary target is to investigate how to apply GPT to program analysis, offering more easier, convenient, and high-performance methodology. It is still worth mentioning that our subsequent research may focus on embedding experiments. For instance, program analysis based on an AST is limited by a necessary lexical parser, certainly, our approach has its limitations, and instruction analysis needs to be based on a complete compilation environment. However, our endeavor to directly embed Wasm instructions into natural language offers a novel approach for exploring other embedding methods. In the future, It may eliminate the need for complex intermediate conversions and analyses. By embedding codes of any form and natural language together, it bypasses the requirement for various intricate conversion tasks, enabling the comprehension of source codes, ASTs, or instructions in a manner akin to human understanding-directly and intuitively.

Acknowledgements. This work is supported by the Research and Development of the digital Twin Paas Platform based on the frame of narrow meta-universe technology(Key Science and Technology R&D Plan of Ningbo in 2023 and The Third Batch of Approval Projects).

References

1. Floridi, L., Chiriatti, M.: Gpt-3: its nature, scope, limits, and consequences. Mind. Mach. **30**, 681–694 (2020)
2. Liu, X., et al.: Gpt understands, too. AI Open (2023)
3. O'Connor, J., McDermott, I.: *NLP*. Thorsons (2001)
4. Roziere, B., et al.: Code llama: Open foundation models for code. *arXiv preprint*arXiv:2308.12950 (2023)
5. Bai, J., et al. Qwen technical report. *arXiv preprint*arXiv:2309.16609 (2023)

6. Roy, C.K., Cordy, J.R.: Nicad: accurate detection of near-miss intentional clones using flexible pretty-printing and code normalization. In: 2008 16th IEEE International Conference On Program Comprehension, pp. 172–181. IEEE (2008)
7. Haiduc, S., Aponte, J., Marcus, A.: Supporting program comprehension with source code summarization. In: Proceedings of the 32nd ACM/IEEE International Conference on Software Engineering-vol. 2, pp. 223–226 (2010)
8. Frantzeskou, G., MacDonell, S., Stamatatos, E., Gritzalis, S.: Examining the significance of high-level programming features in source code author classification. J. Syst. Softw. **81**(3), 447–460 (2008)
9. Sajnani, H., Saini, V., Svajlenko, J., Roy, C.K., Lopes, C.V.: Sourcerercc: scaling code clone detection to big-code. In: Proceedings of the 38th International Conference on Software Engineering, pp. 1157–1168 (2016)
10. Mou, L., et al.: Natural language inference by tree-based convolution and heuristic matching. *arXiv preprint*arXiv:1512.08422 (2015)
11. Mou, L., Li, G., Zhang, L., Wang, T., Jin, Z.: Convolutional neural networks over tree structures for programming language processing. In: Proceedings of the AAAI Conference on Artificial Intelligence. vol. 30 (2016)
12. Feng, Z., et al.: Codebert: A pre-trained model for programming and natural languages. *arXiv preprint*arXiv:2002.08155 (2020)
13. Alon, U., Brody, S., Levy, O., Yahav, E.: code2seq: Generating sequences from structured representations of code. *arXiv preprint*arXiv:1808.01400 (2018)
14. Zhang, D., Fu, Y., Zheng, Z.: Uast: uncertainty-aware siamese tracking. In: International Conference on Machine Learning, pp. 26161–26175. PMLR (2022)
15. Kamilaris, A., Prenafeta-Boldú, F.X.: Deep learning in agriculture: a survey. Comput. Electron. Agric. **147** 70–90 (2018)
16. Chen, J., et al.: Industrial blockchain threshold signatures in federated learning for unified space-air-ground-sea model training. J. Ind. Inform. Integr. **39**, 100593 (2024)
17. Jain, S.M.: Webassembly introduction (2021). https://doi.org/10.1007/978-1-4842-7496-5-1
18. Webassembly core specification. World Wide Web Consortium (W3C). https://www.w3.org/TR/wasm-core-1/
19. Haas, A.: Bringing the web up to speed with webassembly. In: Proceedings of the 38th ACM SIGPLAN Conference on Programming Language Design and Implementation, pp. 185–200 (2017)
20. Lehmann, D., Kinder, J., Pradel, M.: Everything old is new again: binary security of webassembly. In: 29th USENIX Security Symposium (USENIX Security 20), pp. 217–234 (2020)
21. Deng, L., et al.: Formal verification platform as a service: webassembly vulnerability detection application. Comput. Syst. Sci. Eng. **45**(2) (2023)
22. Hilbig, A., Lehmann, D., Pradel, M.: An empirical study of real-world webassembly binaries: Security, languages, use cases. In: Proceedings of the Web Conference **2021**, 2696–2708 (2021)
23. Lehmann, D., Pradel. M.: Wasabi: a framework for dynamically analyzing webassembly. In: Proceedings of the Twenty-Fourth International Conference on Architectural Support for Programming Languages and Operating Systems, pp. 1045–1058 (2019)
24. Stiévenart, Q., De Roover, C.: Compositional information flow analysis for webassembly programs. In: 2020 IEEE 20th International Working Conference on Source Code Analysis and Manipulation (SCAM), pp. 13–24. IEEE (2020)

25. Vaswani, A.: Attention is all you need. Adv. Neural Inform. Proce. Syst. (2017)
26. Svajlenko, J., Roy, C.K.: Evaluating clone detection tools with bigclonebench. In: 2015 IEEE International Conference on Software Maintenance and Evolution (ICSME), pp. 131–140. IEEE (2015)
27. Tbcc project in github. *GitHub.* https://github.com/preesee/tbcc
28. Black, S., et al.: Gpt-neox-20b: an open-source autoregressive language model (2022)
29. Gao, L., et al.: The Pile: An 800gb dataset of diverse text for language modeling. *arXiv preprint*arXiv:2101.00027 (2020)
30. Hugging face datasets. *Hugging Face.* https://huggingface.co/datasets
31. Open instruction generalist (oig) dataset. *LAION-AI.* https://github.com/LAION-AI/Open-Instruction-Generalist
32. Zhang, G., et a.: A preliminary release, Chinese open instruction generalist (2023)

Research on Key Technologies of Fair Deep Learning

Xiaoqian Liu$^{(\boxtimes)}$ and Weiyu Shi

Department of Computer Information and Cyber Security, Jiangsu Police Institute,
Nanjing 210031, China
lxqlara@163.com

Abstract. Deep learning is an important field in machine learning research. It has strong feature extraction ability and shows advanced performance in many applications including computer vision, natural language processing and speech recognition etc. Therefore, it has a wide-ranging impact on all aspects of data-driven life. However, existing studies have shown that unfairness in deep learning has increasingly damaged people's interests in deep learning. Seeking methods that can effectively improve fairness has become one of the mainstream development directions of deep learning. This work reviews the tasks and fairness measurement methods of deep learning. In addition, we conduct experiments on typical fair deep learning datasets to implement individual fairness. The experimental results show that a balance is achieved between accuracy and fairness of classification tasks.

Keywords: Deep Learning · Algorithmic Bias · Individual Fairness

1 Introduction

In recent years, AI technologies such as deep learning have developed rapidly. Deep learning can effectively process massive amounts of data while forming multi-level feature representations, with end-to-end learning capabilities. It can automatically complete the mapping from input to output without manually designing features and rules [1]. Based on the above characteristics, deep neural networks have demonstrated superior performance in many applications. In these complex tasks that were previously difficult to handle manually and generally required high levels of expertise, the performance of deep learning has reached or even exceeded the level of human decision-making, achieving higher accuracy than traditional machine learning. For example, in the case of convolutional neural networks used for facial recognition, the performance of facial recognition has been further improved. In addition, the recognition process often requires only a few seconds [2].

Despite high accuracy and performance, deep learning also learns biases and discrimination in human behavior, especially when sensitive attributes such as race, age, and criminal record exist in the dataset. Fair deep learning motivates to ensure that machine learning models are designed and implemented in a way that minimizes biases and promotes fairness across various demographics. This motivation stems from several

© The Author(s), under exclusive license to Springer Nature Switzerland AG 2025
W. Li et al. (Eds.): EISA 2024, CCIS 2266, pp. 137–152, 2025.
https://doi.org/10.1007/978-3-031-80419-9_10

key factors, including justice and mitigating bias, legal and technical considerations, and long-term sustainability etc. The most famous example is the COMPAS system developed by North Pointe, which has been widely used as a judicial judgment aid in the United States [3]. The system predicts the likelihood of recidivism by analyzing the background information of relevant personnel to guide the degree of conviction, that is, higher crimes may lead to recommendations for heavier punishment behaviors in the system. However, it is found that in the actual application of the system, the probability of judging the high-risk possibility of similar white defendants was 77% lower than that of black defendants.

The bias and discrimination issues that exist in artificial intelligence related technologies such as deep learning not only have adverse consequences that harm the interests of individual services in the short term, but also have the potential to trigger social conflicts such as gender discrimination, racial discrimination, and occupational bias in the long term. Therefore, it is necessary to give fair attention to deep learning.

The European Union has formulated regulations such as the General Data Protection Regulation (GDPR), which require compliance with data protection and privacy regulations in artificial intelligence systems. The policy priorities of the United States on the issue of fairness in artificial intelligence include the Fair and Transparent Artificial Intelligence Act, aimed at ensuring that AI systems do not cause discrimination or unfair treatment in decision-making and application. China has also released the "Development Plan for the New Generation of Artificial Intelligence", emphasizing the need to abide by ethical norms in the research and application of artificial intelligence, and proposing to ensure the fairness and transparency of artificial intelligence technology.

At present, in the field of deep learning, the focus is on defining model fairness [4], debiasing algorithms [5], and bias detection [6] in terms of algorithm fairness and output result fairness. According to different data processing objects, fairness can be divided into individual fairness and group fairness. Multiple research areas have emerged regarding these fairness definitions, including preprocessing, training optimization, and property validation. There are already many models with fairness improvement schemes to alleviate bias in artificial intelligence models. According to the applicable stages of the methods, they can be mainly divided into three categories, including data processing stage, model training stage, and post-processing stage [7]. Normally, fair deep learning introduces fairness constraints directly into the optimization process, allowing the model to balance performance with fairness objectives.

In the research field, many researchers at home and abroad have conducted extensive research on fair deep learning. As fairness is an evaluation index based on the social behavior consequences generated by human profit activities, there is no inherent physical definition. Therefore, to measure whether the technology is fair, some fairness indicators must be defined first to evaluate it. In general, if there is no statistical difference in the prediction results of artificial intelligence models for different groups, and there is no discriminatory prediction result for specific sensitive attribute groups, it can be said that a model is relatively fair. From a quantitative perspective, evaluating the fairness of a model can be achieved by using group fairness indicators to measure the differences in predicted strengths between different groups and calculate the fairness of the model. As research continues to progress, it is likely that more novel approaches will emerge to address fairness issues.

2 Related Work

To evaluate the fairness of the model, the deep learning field first explores the definition of fairness. The current two main definitions of fairness are mainly divided into group fairness and individual fairness. Group fairness focuses on multiple protected attributes in the dataset, and by comparing and calculating group differences in model predictions [8]. Individual fairness focuses on similar individuals, striving to achieve that "similar individuals should be treated similarly". The mainstream research directions are divided into two directions including model optimization and similar individual judgment. Deep learning researchers need to consider both individual and group fairness to more effectively mitigate biases and unfairness in their models.

2.1 Fair Deep Learning

Fair deep learning algorithms are committed to developing models that are both accurate and meet fairness standards. When improving the fairness of deep learning algorithms, researchers often use fairness customized regularization terms or strong constraint conditions to optimize the learning algorithm for both accuracy and fairness. These constraints can help algorithms better consider the fairness requirements between different groups or individuals during the learning process, avoiding bias or discrimination against certain groups. Meanwhile, these fairness customized regularization terms also provide guidance for algorithm design, ensuring that the model can obtain correct training feedback in practical applications. These fairness definitions not only provide a theoretical basis for fairness enhancement, but also ensure the fairness of algorithms in practical life. Based on specific tasks of the learning process, we provide an overview of deep/machine learning works from three aspects including fair representation task, fair modeling task, and fair decision-making task. The comparison can be seen in Table 1 [9–13].

Fairness Metrics. Fairness is a topic of interest in the humanities and social sciences. The issue of fairness in the technology field has attracted the interests of scholars since the 1960s. In the era of rapid development of computer technology, people were immersed in the convenience and efficiency of technology, but they also gradually became aware of the hidden concerns and began to pay attention to the bias and unfairness that may arise in the relevant auxiliary decision-making process.

The core concept of fairness is to ensure that everyone has an equal opportunity to obtain certain benefits, which is also called fair behavior. If a certain behavior or decision cannot ensure that everyone obtains the benefits they deserve equally, thereby damaging the interests of disadvantaged groups, then this behavior is considered unfair. Discrimination and prejudice are concepts closely related to unfairness. Unfair behavior is also called biased behavior or discriminatory behavior [13].

Common fairness definitions can be divided according to the group-individual perspective [14, 15]. Group fairness starts from the perspective of the sample group and requires that the prediction results of the model from the perspective of the group are relatively similar. Some group fairness indicators can be seen below.

Table 1. Main works of fair deep/machine learning

Fair deep/machine learning	Input	Output	Goal	Bias mitigation mechanism	Fairness
Fair representation task	Fairly synthesized dataset of training samples	Fair feature representation	Data representation learning	Preprocessing mechanism	Statistical fairness Causal fairness
Fair modeling task	Training samples related to the task	Fair machine learning model	Model improvement	Processing mechanism	Statistical fairness Causal fairness
Fair decision-making task	Training samples and decision results	Fair decision results	Decision result adjustments	Post-processing mechanism	Statistical fairness Causal fairness

1) Statistical parity. If the probability of samples from different groups being predicted as positive examples (Positive Rate, PR) is the same, then the model satisfies the principle of statistical parity. If they are not the same, the absolute value of the difference between the PRs of different groups can measure the degree of unfairness of the model in terms of statistical parity.

2) Predictive parity. Compare the model prediction value with the true label of the sample, requiring the false positive rate (False Positive Rate, FPR) of different groups to be the same.

3) Equality of opportunity, which requires that the True Positive Rate (TPR) of different groups is the same and has the same chance to obtain an advantageous prediction result.

4) Equalized odds, which covers the equal opportunity index and the equal prediction index, and measures whether both the equal opportunity and the equal prediction are satisfied.

Individual fairness starts from the perspective of the individual and requires the model to treat the input sample individuals fairly at the individual level. Some individual fairness indicators can be seen below.

1) Individual fairness. For similar individual samples, the model should return similar output results.

2) Counter factual fairness. The model should give the same prediction results for a sample and its corresponding counterfactual sample with only inconsistent sensitive attributes.

In this paper, we focus more on deep learning models for individual fairness because they have many applications in real life and a lot of research has been conducted in academia. The individual fairness rate IFP is used as a test indicator to evaluate the fairness of deep learning models.

Equation (1) shows the calculation of fairness score of each individual. For each individual i, the difference between its actual result A_i and the deserved result E_i is determined. In short, the fairness score of each individual is measured with the difference between the actual result and the deserved result.

$$F_i = |A_i - E_i| \tag{1}$$

Then the overall fairness rate is calculated as the average of all individual fairness scores, as shown in Eq. (2), where N is the total number of individuals.

$$F = \frac{1}{N} \sum_{i=1}^{N} F_i \tag{2}$$

Generation and Classification of Algorithmic Bias/Discrimination. The emergence of algorithmic discrimination or bias is a complex phenomenon caused by multiple factors, usually stemming from imbalanced datasets, unconscious preferences of algorithm designers, and deep influences from social and cultural backgrounds. The main reasons can be attributed to datasets, algorithm writers, evaluation metrics, and feedback mechanisms. If the dataset used for algorithm training is insufficiently representative of certain groups or has systematic historical biases, the algorithm may learn and replicate these inequalities, leading to unfair treatment of these groups. Algorithm designers may also inadvertently embed personal biases or societal biases into the logic and decision-making processes of algorithms, especially in design teams lacking diversity and inclusivity. In addition, if the evaluation process of algorithms fails to adopt comprehensive fairness indicators and only pursues technical indicators such as accuracy or efficiency, it may also overlook the adverse effects on specific groups. Sociocultural factors, such as stereotypes and historical inequalities, can also lead to discrimination in data collection and algorithm applications [16]. In one or more of the above complex situations, the feedback mechanism of the algorithm may continuously reinforce bias, forming a vicious cycle. The common categories of biases are shown in Fig. 1.

Discovering unfairness in machine learning is a prerequisite for correcting bias and eliminating discrimination. The main techniques for bias discovery include association rule mining, k-nearest neighbor classification, probabilistic causal network methods, privacy attack methods, etc. [17–20]. Table 2 introduces several bias identification cases and methods.

Researchers have defined the fairness of deep learning models from different perspectives and specific scenarios. With these fairness definitions, they can be applied in specific scenarios to measure whether a deep learning model is biased, and if it is biased, to evaluate the degree of model unfairness.

2.2 Fairness Improvement in Data Preprocessing

The goal of the fairness improvement research in the data processing stage is to discover the biases in the training datasets used by the relevant models of deep learning and

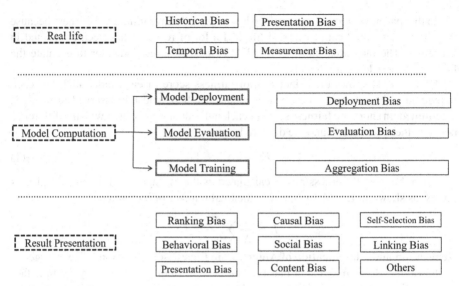

Fig. 1. Common bias categories.

use more fair and balanced data set preprocessing methods to enable the research to obtain models with better fairness. Improving fairness in the data preprocessing stage is a key step to ensure that machine learning models are fair and unbiased. At this stage, researchers need to take a series of measures to identify and reduce potential biases in the dataset to prevent these biases from being amplified during the model training process. Data cleaning, as a basic work, optimizes the quality of the basic data set by identifying and processing missing values, outliers, and mislabeled data. At the same time, researchers use feature selection as a personalized method for data preprocessing, selecting features that are helpful for prediction tasks but do not introduce or aggravate discrimination. In some special cases, related work may also create new features or transform existing features according to actual task requirements to reduce the correlation with sensitive attributes, such as race, gender, etc.

For processed data that meets specific fairness standards, introducing fairness constraints in the data preprocessing stage is also a direct method. In short, this method can be achieved by modifying the data or adding constraints in subsequent model training. Resampling is another commonly used method that reduces the bias of the model towards protected attributes by adjusting the proportion of each category in the dataset. Oversampling the protected attribute class can increase its weight in the training set, while undersampling the majority class can reduce the risk of it overly influencing the model. At the same time, combined with data perturbation technology, small random changes are introduced into the dataset to improve the generalization ability of the model, to achieve the purpose of reducing dependence on specific samples, such as using Generative Adversarial Networks (GANs) [21] to help analyze the diversity of enhanced datasets.

Table 2. Cases for identifying algorithmic biases.

Method Name	Basic Logic	Advantages
k-nearest neighbors classification [18]	Based on a similarity measure function, searches for test instances with similar features within the k nearest neighbors' range and tests using a given decision to reveal whether the decision involves discrimination	1) The model is straightforward and easy to understand, requiring no complex training 2) Overcomes the limitations of standard attributes, revealing data discrimination related to interval values
Probabilistic causal network [19]	Based on probabilistic causal theory and directed acyclic graphs, it comprehensively considers and clearly depicts the relationships between various attributes and their effects on decisions	1) Probabilistic causal networks can express complex dependencies between variables, including nonlinear and interaction effects 2) They support the assessment and inference of causal effects, including direct and indirect effects, helping to understand the causal mechanisms between variables
Privacy attack method [20]	Utilizes techniques like minimal attacks and inference control algorithms to obtain protected/unprotected attributes, further discovering discrimination based on background knowledge and applying the Frégier boundary theorem	Privacy attack methods can serve as an important tool for evaluating the effectiveness of existing privacy protection measures, helping to identify potential security vulnerabilities and exploring feasible technical approaches for discovering discrimination in privacy-protected data

2.3 Fairness Improvement in Model Training

Improving fairness during the model training phase is a key step in ensuring the fairness of deep learning algorithms. The goal of related research is to develop fair deep learning models that are highly generalizable across different groups, avoiding bias against any group or even harming their interests in real life. Related research shows that improving fairness during the model training phase can be achieved by introducing fairness regularization terms that constrain the model's performance on different groups and reduce the prediction differences between groups [22]. For example, a variation of the cross-entropy loss function can be used to penalize the model's unfair predictions for protected groups.

Improving fairness during the model training phase can also be achieved through techniques such as ensemble learning [23] and meta-learning [24]. Ensemble learning reduces bias by combining the predictions of multiple models. In general, each model analyzes different aspects of the data features in each dimension of the data and comprehensively feeds them back to the ensemble learning model, which then improves the fairness of the overall dataset by balancing performance and weighting. Meta-learning, also known as "learning to learn" is a learning method that enables models to quickly adapt to new tasks. In the research on improving fairness in the model training phase, meta-learning technology can balance the performance of the model on different subgroups by optimizing hyperparameters and can help the model pay more attention to task-related and non-biased features by adjusting the model architecture, such as using the attention mechanism. This method effectively improves the generalization ability of the model, making it more universal, and can better maintain output results with good fairness when facing datasets with different data features.

In the research on improving fairness in the model training phase, how to ensure that the decision-making process of the model is transparent and can be verified by a third party, and how to ensure the interpretability of the output results of the model is also one of the current mainstream research directions. Therefore, the research on improving fairness in the model training process also includes continuous monitoring and evaluation of the model. This idea can be achieved in practice by using interpretable machine learning models or integrating interpretable technologies in the model training process. For example, Google's "Fairness Indicators" project aims to develop a set of tools to help researchers and developers evaluate and improve the fairness of machine learning models. In addition, IBM's "AI Fairness 360" toolbox provides a comprehensive set of algorithms and methods for detecting and mitigating bias in machine learning models.

It is worth noting that the research on improving fairness in the model training phase is not a self-contained entity. In fact, the research on improving fairness in the model training phase is closely integrated with the data preprocessing and post-processing phases. Various factors in the data preprocessing and post-processing phases will have a significant impact on the fairness in the model training phase. For example, if bias is not effectively addressed in the data preprocessing phase, any efforts in the model training phase may be in vain. Similarly, even if the model performs fairly in the training phase, if positive feedback is not given in a timely manner in the post-processing phase, unfair situations may occur. Therefore, improving fairness in the model training phase is a multi-dimensional, cross-stage comprehensive project that requires a comprehensive approach to ensure that the fairness of machine learning models can be effectively improved in the model training phase.

2.4   Fairness Improvement in Post-Processing

Research on fairness improvement in the post-processing stage focuses on detailed review and evaluation of model outputs, including calculation and analysis of prediction performance indicators such as accuracy, false positive rate, and false negative rate between different groups. By comparing the differences in indicators between different groups, researchers can quickly identify potential biases and determine what adjustments need to be made. A common adjustment method is to adjust the classification threshold. By adjusting the threshold, the acceptance rate and rejection rate of different groups can be balanced to achieve fairness tasks required by practical tasks such as statistical equality or equal opportunity. In addition, the use of calibration techniques is also a common method at present. Researchers adjust the prediction probabilities of the model to ensure that they have the same distribution in different groups.

However, simply adjusting the classification threshold and calibrating the prediction probability may not have good universality. In some cases, the decision-making process often adopts more complex methods, such as cost-sensitive learning. Cost-sensitive learning is an effective strategy for improving fairness in machine learning systems. By integrating the costs of misclassifications into the modeling process, it provides a framework that can help mitigate biases and enhance equity across diverse populations. This method considers the different costs of different types of errors, allowing the model to reduce the adverse effects on specific groups while maintaining overall performance. For, example, a cost-sensitive approach can be employed where the costs of false negatives (denying loans to qualified individuals) for underrepresented groups are increased relative to others. This encourages the model to minimize these costly mistakes, leading to more equitable loan approvals.

Improving fairness in the post-processing stage is not a one-time process. It requires finding a balance between model accuracy and fairness. Excessive pursuit of fairness may lead to a decline in the overall performance of the model, while excessive pursuit of optimizing the performance indicators of the model may exacerbate unfairness. Therefore, in this stage of work, it is necessary to comprehensively consider various factors that actually exist in reality, such as business goals, ethical standards, and legal requirements. At the same time, in order to ensure that all adjustments and decision-making processes are traceable and explainable, fairness improvement research in the post-processing stage also requires the establishment of a transparent recording and reporting mechanism. This not only helps to improve the credibility of the model, but also provides necessary information for supervision and auditing. As data changes and the application scenarios of the model change, related research may also need to continuously monitor the performance of the model in actual applications and make corresponding adjustments based on feedback. This continuous optimization and improvement help ensure that the model remains fair in a changing environment.

This work aims to improve the fairness of the model's output results through judging similar individuals. First, for the classification task of deep learning, a method for calculating individual fairness was referred to. Attempts were made to reduce the prediction differences between similar individual samples to obtain good individual fairness. Based on the existing IIFR algorithm for improving individual fairness [25], this algorithm optimizes the learning fairness representation algorithm, which can simultaneously alleviate the two concepts of differences between different demographic subgroups in classification settings. We use cosine similarity in the training set to calculate the difference between samples and screen for similar sample pairs, followed by testing on the test set and reverse testing. Through in-depth research on optimizing feature representation learning methods and measuring the similarity between samples, fairness, interpretability and robustness of the model have been improved.

3   Fairness Improvement Algorithm Based on Similar Individuals

In this section, we refer to the IIFR algorithm and introduce cosine similarity as a metric to measure individual similarity, and screen out highly similar training sample pairs by setting a similarity threshold [25]. Then, we use these similar sample pairs to supplement and correct the model's training process, thereby ensuring that the model can take into account the influence of these similar individuals when predicting, and thus produce more reasonable and fair prediction results. The implementation of this method not only improves the accuracy of the model, but also effectively improves its fairness when dealing with different individuals. The process of the IIFR algorithm is shown Fig. 2.

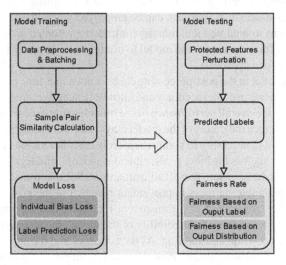

Fig. 2. Process of the IIFR algorithm.

1) Data preprocessing and batch processing. Perform necessary preprocessing on input data, such as standardization, normalization, etc., and divide it into batches of appropriate size.
2) Forward propagation. The preprocessed and batched data vectors are fed into a neural network model for forward propagation. Through the processing of each layer of the network, the preliminary prediction results of the samples are finally obtained in the output layer.
3) Calculate preliminary loss. Use the Cross Entropy Loss (CE) function to calculate the difference between the model's predicted results and the true labels and obtain the label prediction loss.
4) Similar sample recognition. Use cosine similarity, as shown in Eq. (3), to measure the similarity between each training sample and other samples and find another sample that is most like each training sample.

$$\cos\theta = \frac{a \cdot b}{||a|| \times ||b||} = \frac{\sum_{i=1}^{n}(x_i \times y_i)}{\sqrt{\sum_{i=1}^{n}(x_i)^2 \times \sum_{i=1}^{n}(y_i)^2}} \tag{3}$$

5) Determine similarity boundaries. Based on the features of the dataset, set a similarity threshold to determine which sample pairs are similar individuals.

6) Calculate individual fair loss. For all sample pairs that meet the similarity threshold, use JS divergence to calculate their differences in network output, and add these differences as the model's individual fair loss to the objective function. The label prediction loss is shown in Eq. (4), where $f(X^{(i)}, \theta)$ is the network output and $Y^{(i)}$ is the true label.

$$Loss = CE\left(f(X^{(i)}, \theta), Y^{(i)}\right) \tag{4}$$

7) Optimize objective function. The objective function consists of label prediction loss and individual fairness loss. By using optimization algorithms such as gradient descent to update the parameters of the model, the classification accuracy and individual fairness of the model can be improved simultaneously.

We optimize the objective function of feature selection to calculate the loss between similar individuals more reasonably and effectively. Specifically, we use Balance Error Rate (BER) as part of the loss function, as BER has good performance in ensuring classification accuracy, parity checking, and small joint errors across groups [26]. In addition, combining BER with condition aligned representations can achieve balanced odds and accuracy parity checks. When the equilibrium odds are met, BER can also serve as the upper limit of error for each subgroup, which further proves the rationality of using BER as the loss function.

By combining these strategies, the algorithm design aims to simultaneously optimize the classification accuracy and individual fairness of the model to meet the diverse needs in practical applications. This work mainly evaluates the performance of the model from two aspects including accuracy and fairness. Like previous work, this work uses ACC to measure the correctness of the model and demonstrate its predictive performance [25]. The correctness calculation is shown in Eq. (5):

$$ACC = \frac{TP + TN}{TP + TN + FP + FN} \tag{5}$$

Among them, TP refers to the number of correctly identified positive instances in the model prediction results, TN represents the number of correctly identified negative instances, FP and FN respectively represent the number of incorrectly identified negative and positive instances by the model.

In this section, we propose an optimized objective function with the BER function. This optimization process not only improves the model utility, but also pays special attention to ensuring individual fairness.

4 Experimental Results

4.1 Datasets and Experimental Setting

We conduct experiments on two popular real-world datasets in algorithmic fairness literature, including the Adult dataset and the COMPAS dataset [26]. Each dataset description is shown in Table 3.

Table 3. Adult dataset and COMPAS dataset description

Dataset	Number of samples	$P(A = 0)$	$P(Y = 1)$	$P(Y = 1 | A = 0)$	$P(Y = 1 | A = 1)$
Adult	45 222	0.675	0.248	0.312	0.114
COMPAS	6 172	0.48	0.455	0.383	0.523

Adult dataset (https://archive.ics.uci.edu/dataset/2/adult), refers to the adult popula-
tion in the 1994 US Census, including gender, education level, age, etc. In this dataset,
we use gender A as a sensitive attribute (A = 0 represents male, A = 1 represents
female), and the processed data contains 14 attributes such as occupation, gender, education level, etc. There are serious data biases in this dataset, such as 67.3% of the
data being male, and 31.2% of male data having an annual income of over 50k, while
only 11.4% of female data having an income of over 50k. The label distribution in the
Adult dataset is also uneven, with only 24.8% of people having higher salaries. COM-
PAS dataset (https://github.com/propublica/compas-analysis) is a collection of defendant
records from Broward County, Florida, United States. It records the prison, length of
imprisonment, demographic data, criminal history, and COMPAS risk score for each
defendant between 2013 and 2014, including 12 attributes such as prior criminal history,
race, and age. The protected attribute is race, including white (A = 0) and black (A =
1). Its task is to predict whether the defendant will commit another crime within two
years.

Individual fairness refers to the principle that similar individuals should receive
similar outcomes from a machine learning model or algorithm. For each dataset, we
conduct control experiments using a fixed baseline network architecture to facilitate
sharing among all fair representation learning methods. We adopt four models including
MLP, FAIR, CFAIR, and CFAIR-EO (a variant of CFAIR using BRE). The parameter
settings for the two datasets Adult and COMPAS are shown in Table 4.

Table 4. Parameter settings for experiments

Parameter	Adult	COMPAS
Benchmark model structure	[114, 30, 20, 15, 15, 10, 2]	[11, 30, 10, 5, 2]
Learning rate	1.0	1.0
Batch size	512	512
epochs	100	100
Adversarial classification loss coefficient	1.2	1.2

1) MLP. A feedforward artificial neural network, which is a multi-layer fully connected
network with ReLU activation function, trained using a supervised learning technique
called backpropagation, usually combined with gradient descent algorithm.

2) FAIR. It is a two-stage training framework aimed at enhancing the fairness of the model among different populations by reweighting the training samples. It does not require modifications to the original model architecture and can use sensitive information from the validation set to determine weights.

3) CFAIR. A multitask adversarial model, consisting of a shared hidden layer and $|A|+1$ classification layers. The classification layers include a fully connected layer that minimizes the prediction loss of classification tasks and $|A|$ fully connected layers that minimize the prediction loss of protected attributes within a certain population. The tasks of this model are trained using cross entropy loss.

4) CFAIR-EO. A variant of CFAIR using BER to calculate target loss, aiming to achieve balance between model accuracy and fairness across different populations [26].

4.2 Fairness Rate IFR

This section will introduce two metrics for calculating the individual fairness rate (IFR). IFR was set by Wang Yuying et al. for classification tasks in deep learning [25]. It is divided into label based individual fairness rate (IFR_b) and output distribution based individual fairness rate (IFR_p).

IFR_b refers to the proportion of test sample pairs that satisfy individual fairness to the total number of test samples. This calculation method considers whether similar samples have the same label in model prediction. Specifically, for each sample in the test set, a similar sample is generated by changing the protected attributes (such as gender, race, etc.) to form a pair of similar samples. If the predicted labels of similar sample pairs are the same, it is considered that this pair of samples satisfies individual fairness.

IFR_p refers to the proportion of similar sample pairs with predicted probability distribution differences within a certain threshold to the total number of test samples. This calculation method is more rigorous, as it not only considers whether the predicted labels are the same, but also whether the predicted probability distributions are close. Even if the predicted labels of two similar samples are the same, it is considered unfair if their predicted probability distributions differ significantly. To measure the differences between predicted probability distributions, JS divergence (Jensen Shannon Divergence) is commonly used.

4.3 Experimental Results Analysis

Table 5 shows the performance of MLP, FAIR, CFAIR, and CFAIR-EO in terms of individual fairness. We found that for models using the basic IIFR algorithm, there are many similar test sample pairs with consistent prediction labels but significantly different prediction probabilities in the trained prediction model. Taking the Adult dataset as an example, in the MLP model, there are 97.3% of similar test sample pairs with consistent labels, but only 61.4% of the samples have similar prediction probabilities, indicating that the MLP model still has discrimination when dealing with similar samples.

In addition, for imbalanced datasets such as the Adult dataset, using a simple error rate (BER) as an evaluation criterion in the loss function of the target variable may lead to the model overly focusing on the majority classes and neglecting the minority classes, thereby damaging the overall utility of the model. Therefore, when dealing with

Table 5. Comparison of model training performance

Dataset	Model	ACC	Individual fairness rate	
			IFRb	IFR$_p$
Adult	MLP	85.5	97.3	61.4
	FAIR	83.6	96.5	33.5
	CFAIR	84.4	97.1	41.5
	CFAIR-EO	84.1	97.0	45.5
COMPAS	MLP	68.4	93.7	73.5
	FAIR	67.0	79.9	59.4
	CFAIR	68.3	84.7	29.9
	CFAIR-EO	67.2	80.2	45.7

imbalanced datasets, it is necessary to adopt more appropriate evaluation metrics and optimization methods to ensure that the model can achieve better performance globally.

5 Conclusion

This work is based on the existing individual fairness rate model IIFR for feature representation optimization. The core of the IIFR model is to determine similar individuals through cosine similarity. In this experimental study on feature representation optimization, we adopt a new feature representation learning method aimed at further improving the performance and fairness of the model. Specifically, we introduce a new optimization strategy that aligns the conditional distribution of representations rather than the marginal distribution and combines the concept of balanced error rate to optimize the target variable and sensitive attributes, to improve the method of judging similar individuals [26]. The goal of this optimization method is to effectively improve the individual fairness level of the model while maintaining good group fairness. By balancing the fairness between individuals, this work aims to achieve a good balance between individual fairness and group fairness, thereby ensuring that the decision-making process effectively improves the individual fairness of the model while maintaining good group fairness.

In the actual operation of the experiment and testing phase, we have made detailed adjustments and optimizations to the model to ensure that it can more accurately identify similar individuals and consider the balance between target variables and sensitive attributes in the judgment process. Through this method, we expect to improve the predictive accuracy of the model while maintaining a high level of fairness. By comparing the performance of the model before and after optimization, we can clearly observe the fairness improvement.

Acknowledgments. We thank the editors and all reviewers for their valuable advice to improve this piece of work. This work is funded in part by the 2023 Jiangsu Provincial Higher Education Teaching Reform Research Project (No. 2023JSJG364), the Philosophy and Social Sciences

Research Project of Universities in Jiangsu Province (No. 2023SJYB0468) and the 2023 Jiangsu University "Blue Project" Outstanding Young Back-bone Teachers Project.

References

1. LeCun, Y., Bengio, Y., Hinton, G.: Deep learning. Nature **521**(7553), 436–444 (2015)
2. Benradi, H., Chater, A., Lasfar, A.: A hybrid approach for face recognition using a convolutional neural network combined with feature extraction techniques. IAES Int. J. Artif. Intell. (IJ-AI), **12**, 627–640 (2023)
3. Casillas, J.: Bias and discrimination in machine decision-making systems. Ethics Artif. Intell. 13–38 (2024)
4. Pessach, D., Shmueli, E.: A review on fairness in machine learning. ACM Comput. Surv. (CSUR) **55**(3), 1–44 (2022)
5. Alabdulmohsin, I.M., Lucic, M.: A near-optimal algorithm for debiasing trained machine learning models. Adv. Neural. Inf. Process. Syst. **34**, 8072–8084 (2021)
6. Verma, S., Ernst, M., Just, R.: Removing biased data to improve fairness and accuracy. arxiv preprint arxiv:2102.03054 (2021)
7. González-Sendino, R., Serrano, E., Bajo, J., et al.: A review of bias and fairness in artificial intelligence (2023)
8. Lohia, P.K., Ramamurthy, K.N., Bhide, M., et al.: Bias mitigation post-processing for individual and group fairness. In: ICASSP 2019–2019 IEEE International Conference on Acoustics, Speech and Signal Processing (ICASSP), pp. 2847–2851. IEEE (2019)
9. Zemel, R., Wu, Y., Swersky, K., et al.: Learning fair representations. In: International Conference on Machine Learning. PMLR, pp. 325–333 (2013)
10. Qian, S., Pham, V.H., Lutellier, T., et al.: Are my deep learning systems fair? an empirical study of fixed-seed training. Adv. Neural. Inf. Process. Syst. **34**, 30211–30227 (2021)
11. Grgic-Hlaca, N., Zafar, M.B., Gummadi, K.P., et al.: The case for process fairness in learning: feature selection for fair decision making. In: NIPS Symposium on Machine Learning and the Law, vol. 1, no. 2, p. 11 (2016)
12. Aghaei, S., Azizi, M.J., Vayanos, P.: Learning optimal and fair decision trees for non-discriminative decision-making. In: Proceedings of the AAAI Conference on Artificial Intelligence. **33**(01), 1418–1426 (2019)
13. Gu, T.L., Li, L., Chang, L., et al.: Fair machine learning: concepts, analysis, and design. Chin. J. Comput. **45**(5), 1018–1051 (2022)
14. Binns, R.: On the apparent conflict between individual and group fairness. In: Proceedings of the 2020 Conference on Fairness, Accountability, and Transparency, pp. 514–524 (2020)
15. Esmaeili, S., Duppala, S., Cheng, D., et al.: Rawlsian fairness in online bipartite matching: two-sided, group, and individual. In: Proceedings of the AAAI Conference on Artificial Intelligence, vol. 37, no. 5, pp. 5624–5632 (2023)
16. Vlasceanu, M., Amodio, D.M.: Propagation of societal gender inequality by internet search algorithms. Proc. Natl. Acad. Sci. **119**(29), e2204529119 (2022)
17. Tremblay, M.C., Dutta, K., Vandermeer, D.: Using data mining techniques to discover bias patterns in missing data. J. Data Inf. Qual. (JDIQ) **2**(1), 1–19 (2010)
18. Li, Y., Wang, J., Wang, C.: Certifying the fairness of KNN in the presence of dataset bias. In: Enea, C., Lal, A. (eds.) Computer Aided Verification. CAV 2023. Lecture Notes in Computer Science, vol. 13965, pp. 335–357. Springer, Cham (2023). https://doi.org/10.1007/978-3-031-37703-7_16

19. Madras, D., Creager, E., Pitassi, T., et al.: Fairness through causal awareness: Learning causal latent-variable models for biased data. In: Proceedings of the Conference on Fairness, Accountability, and Transparency, pp. 349–358 (2019)
20. Lyu, L., Yu, J., Nandakumar, K., et al.: Towards fair and privacy-preserving federated deep models. IEEE Trans. Parallel Distrib. Syst. **31**(11), 2524–2541 (2020)
21. Goodfellow, I., et al.: Generative adversarial networks. Commun. ACM **63**(11), 139–144 (2020)
22. Li, T., et al.: FAIRER: fairness as decision rationale alignment. In: International Conference on Machine Learning. PMLR (2023)
23. Iosifidis, V., Fetahu, B., Ntoutsi, E.: Fae: a fairness-aware ensemble framework. In: 2019 IEEE International Conference on Big Data (Big Data), pp. 1375–1380. IEEE (2019)
24. Zhao, C., et al.: Fair meta-learning for few-shot classification. In: 2020 IEEE International Conference on Knowledge Graph (ICKG). IEEE (2020)
25. Wang, Y.Y., Zhang, M., Yang, J.R., et al.: Research on fairness in deep learning models. J. Softw. **34**(9), 4037–4055 (2023). (in Chinese)
26. Zhao, H., Coston, A., Adel, T., et al.: Conditional learning of fair representations. arXiv preprint arXiv:1910.07162 (2019)

Adaptive Differential Privacy Based Optimization Scheme for Federated Learning

Qi Yuan[1], Ershuai Xu[1(✉)], Hao Yuan[1], and Shuo Zhao[2]

[1] Qiqihar University, Qiqihar 161000, China
xes457345355@163.com
[2] Network Information Center, Qiqihar University, Qiqihar 161006, China

Abstract. Federated learning has emerged as a promising solution to address privacy concerns in traditional machine learning models, which attracts significant attention from researchers. In this paper, we propose a federated learning optimization framework based on adaptive differential privacy (ALDP-FL) that dynamically adjusts privacy protection strategy to tackle key challenges in federated learning, such as accuracy degradation, difficulty in privacy quantification, and high communication overhead. We incorporate a local update mechanism with an adaptive gradient clipping strategy, while adding noise into the gradient transformation between clients and the central server. The impact of varying privacy levels on ALDP-FL model is analyzed on MNIST and CIFAR10 datasets. Simulation results demonstrate that ALDP-FL significantly enhances computational efficiency and reduces communication costs. Furthermore, the adaptive clipping threshold strategy maintains superior classification accuracy even under stringent privacy constraints and provides a balance between privacy and utility.

Keywords: Federated Learning · Differential Privacy · Gradient Transformation · Adaptive Noise

1 Introduction

In the era of big data, personal privacy protection has become increasingly crucial. In traditional centralized machine learning, data is transmitted to a central server or computing node for training. However, it can pose the significant risk of privacy leakage, especially when sensitive personal information is involved [1]. To address this issue, Google proposed the concept of federated learning in 2016. The core idea of federated learning is that the parties involved in model training do not need to exchange their original data, which can effectively resolve data privacy protection. Each participant stores data and trains model in local, and then only needs to upload trained parameters to the central server that is responsible for aggregating and updating global model parameters. Federated learning enables multi-party collaboration in training deep learning models without sharing original data, thereby it can reduce the risk of privacy leakage, release the potential value of data, and effectively alleviate the problem of "data silos" [2–6].

© The Author(s), under exclusive license to Springer Nature Switzerland AG 2025
W. Li et al. (Eds.): EISA 2024, CCIS 2266, pp. 153–164, 2025.
https://doi.org/10.1007/978-3-031-80419-9_11

For the privacy and security issues of federated learning, some research proposed solutions of potential security issues in FL to protect privacy information such as encryption, noise, etc. Meanwhile, lots of optimization solutions are proposed for FL. ABADI et al. [7] proposed a stochastic gradient descent algorithm in differential privacy which added noise to the gradient of each data batch to protect privacy. However, equal privacy budgets may lead to significant gradient distortion that can reduce data availability. LDP-Fed algorithm, proposed by TRUEX et al. [8], provided a stringent differential privacy guarantees for federated training. This algorithm collected model training parameters iteratively and combined selection with filtering technique that can achieve secure parameter update and sharing.

Further research in FL concentrates on optimizing algorithmic performance and selecting filter methodology to enhance both efficiency and accuracy. Additionally, Naseri et al. [9] introduced LDF algorithm to defend effectively backdoor attacks in FL. Moreover, this algorithm presented a comprehensive and reusable measurement for quantifying the balance between privacy and availability. Cai et al. [10] refined the tracking adversary used in the theoretical computer science for lower bounds, which improved existing min-max lower bounds for low-dimensional mean estimation and established new lower bounds for high-dimensional mean estimation and linear regression problems. The paper also devises a differential privacy algorithm to reach the minimum-maximum lower bound up to logarithmic factors, and a novel privacy iterative hard-thresholding algorithm is proposed especially for the high-dimensional linear regression. Furthermore, Wu et al. [11] presented an efficient training methodology under data perturbation which used finite communication costs.It mitigated overfitting and fluctuation through an adaptive learning rate algorithm. ZHANG et al. [12] introduced an adaptive decay noise based on the privacy protection algorithm, which reduced the introduction of noise by adding noise adjusted by linear decay rate into gradients during each iteration.

However, the impact of noise on model performance remains unresolved when DP is introduced to privacy protection of FL [13–17]. Therefore, these are bottlenecks to the self-regulation of FL models and the balance between privacy and availability in this field.

This paper proposes an adaptive local differential privacy based on federated learning model, named as (ALDP_FL). The main contributions encompass three aspects:

1) We propose a method for adaptive threshold clipping, which dynamically selects the clipping threshold based on the privacy budget and sensitivity of gradients. This approach aims to maximize model accuracy while it can satisfy differential privacy requirements. By protecting user data privacy, model accuracy and robustness are enhanced, while computational efficiency is improved and communication overhead is reduced.
2) The adaptive noise is introduced on the local client that can make a trade-off between privacy and model accuracy, and mitigate privacy attacks as well as inference risks, thus data privacy protection is enhanced.
3) Experimental validation of ALDP_FL is conducted using convolutional neural network models on the MNIST and CIFAR-10 datasets. Results demonstrate that the scheme achieves the higher average accuracy compared to DP-FL and LDP while effectively preserving local privacy.

2 Preliminaries

2.1 Federated Learning

Supposed there exists a federated learning framework comprising N participants, where D_i denotes the local dataset held by each participant C_i, $i \in \{1, 2, ..., N\}$. The objective is to train a global model W through federated learning such that it performs well on the data of all participants. Each participant i has a local loss function $L_i(W)$ to measure the performance of the model on their local data. Typically, the target is to minimize the average of local loss function for all participants, whicht is represented as shown below:

$$L(W) = \min_{W} \frac{1}{N} \sum_{i=1}^{N} L_i(W) \tag{1}$$

Participants compute their local gradients g_i and send them to the central server instead of transmitting original data. When the central server receives the gradients from all participants, it updates the parameters of the global model in some aggregation way, as showed below:

$$W \leftarrow W - \eta \frac{1}{N} \sum_{i=1}^{N} g_i \tag{2}$$

where η is a learning rate, which controls the step size of each parameter update.

2.2 Differential Privacy

Differential privacy [18] is a pioneering privacy-preserving technique on privacy leakage in statistical databases. It avoids the risk of individual privacy data disclosure by adding stochastic noise to statistical outputs.

Definition 1. (ε, δ)- Differential privacy [19]. Let $M : D \rightarrow R$ be a random mechanism, where the domain is D and the range is R. If for any d, d' in the domain D and for $S \subseteq R$:

$$\Pr[M(d) \in S] \leq e^{\varepsilon} \Pr[M(d') \in S] + \delta \tag{3}$$

The privacy mechanism M is called satisfying (ε, δ)-differential privacy. Here, $\Pr[x]$ denotes the probability of data x being leaked. The parameter ε is named as the privacy budget, which is used to measure the degree of privacy protection.where a smaller ε indicates a higher level of privacy protection.

Definition 2. Global Sensitivity [20]. For a set of query functions $f_i = \{f_1, f_2, ..., f_k\}$, if there exists a sensitivity parameter S_f for any neighboring datasets D and D_i, and for all $d, d' \in D, D'$ respectively.The following condition holds:

$$S_f \geq |f_i(d) - f_i(d')|_{l_2} \tag{4}$$

This set of functions is called possessing global sensitivity S_f.

Definition 3. Gaussian Mechanism [21]. Let M be a randomized algorithm and let $f : D \rightarrow R^d$ be any function with sensitivity S_f. Given that the random noise follows a normal distribution $N(0, \sigma^2)$, then a randomized algorithm is defined as follows:

$$M(D) = f(D) + N(0, S_f^2 \sigma^2) \tag{5}$$

For $\delta \in (0, 1)$, when $\sigma^2 > 2\ln(1.25/\delta) \cdot (S_f^2/\varepsilon^2)$, Gaussian mechanism satisfy (ε, δ)-DP, in which the standard deviation of Gaussian distribution, denoted as σ, determines the scale of the noise, the parameter ε represents the privacy budget that is negatively correlated with the noise, and the parameter δ represents the relaxation term that indicates the tolerance for the probability of violating differential privacy. Hence, the magnitude of the noise depends on the l_2 sensitivity of the query function. In the same privacy budget allocation, the noise added by Gaussian Mechanism is less than that is added by Laplace Mechanism [22–24], so it can greatly preserve the availability of data.

3 ALDP-FL Scheme

3.1 Scheme Design

The specific steps of ALDP-FL algorithm are shown in Table 1 below:

Step 1. Initialize Model Parameters. Before the local training begin, the participating party needs to initialize a model w_0. The parameters of this model will be updated during the training process. Typically, model initialization can be random or based on the pre-trained model.

Step 2. Obtain Local Data. The participating party retrieves sample from their local data set which is required for training the model. Each participating party may have a different data distribution and a sample size.

Step 3. Compute the Loss Function. Using the local data, the participating party calculates the loss function, which measures the model fits about the local data under the current parameters. The loss function is typically showed as $L(w_t, D_t)$, where w_t represents the model parameter and D_t represents the local data set.

Step 4. Compute the Gradient. Calculating the gradient of the loss function. The gradient represents the rate that the loss function changes with the parameters under the current model parameters.

$$\nabla g = \nabla L(w_{t-1}, L_k^i) \tag{6}$$

Step 5. Add Noise. In the differential privacy, to protect privacy, random noise can be introduced when computing the gradient. However, traditional differential privacy noise addition schemes may not be flexible enough to adjust based on the gradient information, which can result in either redundant or insufficient noise. Therefore, we propose an adaptive noise mechanism where each local client perturbs the parameters by setting a global noise parameter σ_t. When the parameters change greatly, more noise is added, and vice versa. The formula for the noise factor is as follows:

$$\sigma_t = \frac{g_t}{\sqrt{L[g^2]_t + \delta}} \sigma \tag{7}$$

Table 1. ALDP-FL algorithm.

Algorithm 1: ALDP-FL

Input: w_0, S, η, ε

Output: w_t

1: Initialize global model parameters w_0

2: for each iteration $t = 1, 2, ..., T$ do

3: Randomly select a subset of clients: $S_t = \{C_1, ..., C_k\}$

4: for each user $C_k \in S_t$ do

5: Update the local model $w_{t-1} \leftarrow w$

6: for each iteration $i = 1, 2, ..., E$ do

7: for $L_k^i \in D_k$, where L_k^i represents a randomly selected non-repeating batch of data from dataset D_k

8: Compute gradients: $\nabla g = \nabla L(w_{t-1}, L_k^i)$

9: Calculate sensitivity: $\nabla f_t = \max\limits_{d, d' \in D} \| f(d) - f(d') \|_2$

10: Noise scale: $\sigma_t = \dfrac{g_t}{\sqrt{L[g^2]_t + \delta}} \sigma$

11: Noise magnitude: $\Delta w_t \ \square \ N(0, (\nabla f_t)^2 \sigma_t^2)$

12: Threshold selection: $\tau = \text{ATA}(\nabla f_t, \sigma_t, \varepsilon)$

13: Gradient clipping: $\Delta w_t' = \begin{cases} \Delta w_t, & \text{if} |\Delta w_t| \leq \tau \\ \tau \cdot \text{sgn}(\Delta w_t), & \text{otherwise} \end{cases}$

14: Adaptive noise addition: $w_{t+1} \leftarrow w_t + \Delta w_t'$, $\quad \Delta w_t' \ \square \ N(0, (\Delta f_t)^2 \sigma_t^2)$

15: end for

16: end for

17: Update the global model: $\overline{w}_{t+1} = \dfrac{1}{K} \sum_{k=1}^{k} \overline{w}_{t+1}^k$

18: Parameter broadcasting: Randomly select a subset of clients S_{t+1}, then transmit the updated model parameters $\overline{w}_{t+1}$

19: end for

where σ_t is a adjusted noise factor by the local client, ε_t can be calculated from σ_t as a privacy budget, $L[g^2]_t$ represents the average of the squared sum of gradients in the current iteration, and g_t represents the gradient in the current iteration. The range is set to control the magnitude of adaptive noise to meet the noise requirements in different scenarios.

Local parameter is updated after the clipping step, and then the update is applied to the model parameters, thus the model update is completed. During the clipping process, it is necessary to choose a suitable threshold τ based on the characteristics of the data and privacy requirements to clip the parts of the model update that exceeds the threshold. This paper proposes an algorithm called Adaptive Threshold Adjustment (ATA) to calculate an appropriate threshold for the clipping of model update, as shown in Table 2:

Table 2. Adaptive Threshold Adjustment algorithm

Algorithm 2: Adaptive Threshold Adjustment (ATA)
Input: ∇f_t, σ, ε
Output: τ
1: Function ATA($\nabla f_t, \sigma_t, \varepsilon$)
2: Dynamic threshold: $\tau = k \cdot \sigma \cdot \dfrac{\nabla f_t}{\varepsilon}$
3: return τ
4: end Function

This algorithm integrates parameter sensitivity, distribution statistics of model update, and the privacy parameter of differential privacy to calculate adaptively threshold, which can ensure the most model update within an appropriate range. The algorithm can maximize model performance while protecting privacy. Once an appropriate threshold is obtained, it is necessary to clip the model parameter according to the threshold:

$$\Delta w_t' = \left\{ \begin{array}{ll} \Delta w_t, & |\Delta w_t| \leq \tau \\ \tau \cdot \mathrm{sgn}(\Delta w_t), & \text{otherwise} \end{array} \right\} \tag{8}$$

The noise added by the participant in the t-th communication round is denoted as $\Delta w_t \sim N(0, (\nabla f_t)^2 \sigma_t^2)$, where ∇f_t represents the sensitivity of the local data.

$$\nabla f_t = \max_{d,d' \in D} ||f(d) - f(d')||_2 \tag{9}$$

Step 6. Update Model Parameters. The model parameter is updated using the computed gradient. Typically, an optimization algorithm, such as gradient descent, is employed to perform the following step.

$$w_{t+1} = \overline{w}_t - \eta \Delta w_t' \tag{10}$$

where η represents the learning rate to govern the step size of parameter update.

Step 7. Output local model parameters. Eventually, each participant will obtain model parameters learned during the local training process.

Step 8. Aggregate model parameter. In each round, K clients are selected for model aggregation instead of all clients. The global model parameter aggregated during communication is depicted below:

$$\overline{w}_{t+1} = \frac{1}{K} \sum_{k=1}^{k} \overline{w}_{t+1}^k \tag{11}$$

Step 9. Broadcast parameter. The server randomly selects a non-repeating subset of clients and broadcasts the updated model parameters to them. Clients download the global model and update their local models. To reduce communication costs, only a part of clients is chosen for broadcasting.

3.2 Privacy Analysis

To demonstrate that the proposed ALDP-FL algorithm satisfies Definition 1. (ε, δ)-Differential privacy, the corresponding proof is provided as follows:

$$\left| \ln \frac{\Pr(M(D_i) = o_i)}{\Pr(M(D_i^i) = o_i)} \right| = \left| \ln \frac{\Pr(N = o_i - M(D_i))}{\Pr(N = o_i - M(D_i^i))} \right|$$

$$= \left| \ln \frac{e^{-\frac{x^2}{2\sigma_t^2}}}{e^{-\frac{(x + \Delta s_D)^2}{2\sigma_t^2}}} \right| = \left| \frac{1}{2\sigma_t^2} (2x \,\triangle\, s_D + \Delta s_D^2) \right| \tag{12}$$

It can be concluded that $x < \frac{\sigma_t^2 \varepsilon}{\Delta s_D} - \frac{\Delta s_D}{2}$. Assume $\frac{\sigma_t^2 \varepsilon}{\Delta s_D} - \frac{\Delta s_D}{2} = \eta$, and we need to demonstrate:

$$\Pr(|x| \geq \eta) < \delta \rightarrow \Pr(x \geq \eta) < \frac{\delta}{2} \tag{13}$$

Additionally, the boundary of $\Pr(x \geq \eta)$ is specified as follows:

$$\Pr(x > \eta) = \int_\eta^\infty \frac{1}{\sqrt{2\pi}} e^{-\frac{x^2}{2\sigma_t^2}} dx \leq \frac{\sigma_t}{\sqrt{2\pi} \eta} e^{-\frac{\eta^2}{2\sigma_t^2}} \tag{14}$$

Thus, it remains to prove:

$$\frac{\sigma_t}{\sqrt{2\pi} \eta} e^{-\frac{\eta^2}{2\sigma_t^2}} < \frac{\delta}{2} \Leftrightarrow \ln(\frac{\eta}{\sigma_t}) + \frac{\eta^2}{2\sigma_t^2} > \ln(\sqrt{\frac{2}{\pi}} \frac{1}{\delta}) \tag{15}$$

When the privacy scale of the participating users reaches the predetermined threshold, substituting $\sigma_t = \frac{c\Delta s}{\varepsilon}$ into Eq. (15) yields $c^2 \geq 2\ln(\frac{1.25}{\delta})$. Hence, the proof is established.

4 Experiment and Analysis

To evaluate the performance, we utilized two distinct datasets: MNIST and CIFAR10. MNIST comprises grayscale images depicting 10 handwritten digits, 60,000 training samples and 10,000 test samples, in which each image has a resolution of 28×28 pixels. CIFAR10 consists of RGB color images categorized into 10 classes, in which encompasses 50,000 training images and 10,000 test images that have a resolution of 32×32 pixels.

We employ a workstation running a 64-bit Windows 10 operating system, which configures with a 12th Gen Intel(R) Core(TM) i5-12400F @ 2.30 GHz CPU, an Nvidia GeForce RTX 3060 Ti 8 GB GPU, and 16 GB of RAM. The simulations are executed using Python 3.9, which can ensure a consistent environment for all experimental procedures.

4.1 Relationship Between Adaptive Noise and Model Accuracy

According to Definition 3, the magnitude of Gaussian noise depends on the noise scale σ, which is jointly determined by the sensitivity of the function Δf and the privacy budget ε. Δf dynamically changes with update of sample weight, and ε is inversely proportional to the noise level. When the number of clients K is 100, the client sampling rate is 30%, and the communication rounds N is 200, the overall trend of classification accuracy gradually improves as the value of σ decreases, as shown in Fig. 1(a). As the number of communication rounds is up to 10, the model accuracy under the conditions of $\sigma = 4, \sigma = 8$, and $\sigma = 10$ reaches 73.16%, 57.48%, and 49.03% respectively. It can be observed that under the same conditions, the smaller σ is, the higher the model accuracy. After the number of communication rounds is up to 50, the model tends to converge, in which a maximum accuracy approaches 94.02% when $\sigma = 4$, and a maximum accuracy is 92.36% when $\sigma = 10$.

Dimension of image data in CIFAR10 is higher than that in MNIST dataset, so the model accuracy of CIFAR10 is significantly lower than that of MNIST, and there is obvious oscillation in model accuracy. As shown in Fig. 1(b), when the communication rounds reach 50, the model tends to stabilize with a slow convergence trend. When $\sigma = 4$, the model achieves the highest accuracy of 43.83%, and when $\sigma = 10$, the highest accuracy also reaches 39.97%. Through experimental observation, it is found that ALDP-FL scheme exhibits a high stability when facing different kinds of noise. Additionally, testings on different datasets show that the ALDP-FL scheme achieves good performance on these datasets, which demonstrates its usability and generalization ability.

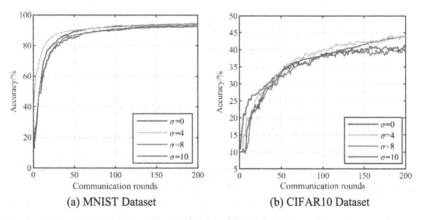

(a) MNIST Dataset   (b) CIFAR10 Dataset

Fig. 1. The relationship between adaptive noise and model accuracy

4.2 Relationship Between Cropping Ratio and Model Accuracy

This experiment covers two datasets, MNIST and CIFAR10. During the experiment, a noise factor $\sigma = 4$ is set, and 100 clients are involved in the federated learning process.

In each round, 30% of the clients are selected, and the local iteration number is set to 5 for model parameter update. The entire training process involves 200 communication rounds. Different clipping ratios $r = (0.2, 0.4, 0.6, 0.8)$ are set. Additionally, a experiment is designed without adding noise for comparison.

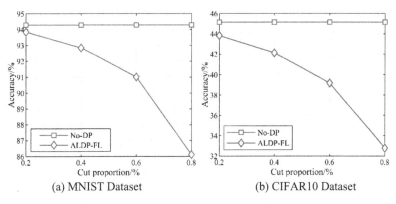

(a) MNIST Dataset   (b) CIFAR10 Dataset

Fig. 2. The effect of cutting ratio on model accuracy

As shown in Fig. 2(a), the model accuracy of the comparative experiment remains at the level of 94% and appears as a horizontal line. This reflects that the model can maintain relatively stable performance under different clipping ratios without differential privacy protection. Conversely, under differential privacy protection, as the clipping ratio increases, the model's accuracy shows a gradual downward trend, which is inversely proportional to the clipping ratio. This trend is also observed on different datasets, as shown in Fig. 2(b). This inverse relationship intuitively demonstrates that the accuracy of the model is significantly affected and exhibits a declining trend as the clipping ratio goes up.

4.3 Comparative Analyses of Model Performance

We contrast the performance variations of ALDP-FL, DP-FL [25] and LDP [26] in providing privacy protection to the model. In the experiment, privacy budgets are set to $\varepsilon = (0.5, 2, 4)$ on MNIST and CIFAR10 datasets. Both Fig. 3 and Fig. 4 show that accuracy of the model gradually improves as the privacy budget increases. Moreover, under the same privacy budget, ALDP-FL achieves significantly higher model accuracy than the other two schemes on both datasets. Specifically, when $\varepsilon = 4$, the average accuracy of ALDP-FL on the MNIST and CIFAR10 datasets reach 94.30% and 46.47%, respectively.

As shown in Fig. 3(c), DP-FL exhibits significant fluctuation when $\varepsilon = 4$, while ALDP-FL and LDP are more stable. On the MNIST dataset, with the increase of the privacy budget, the LDP scheme tends to converge after about 50 training rounds, while ALDP-FL converges about 20 rounds, and the DP-FL scheme requires about 100 rounds to barely reach convergence. The experiment demonstrates that ALDP-FL exhibits outstanding model classification accuracy under larger privacy budgets ε. In view of the

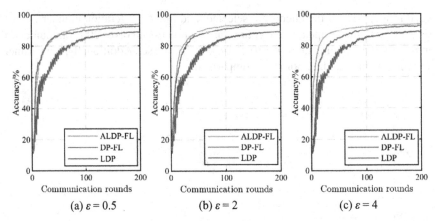

Fig. 3. Different privacy budgets on the MNIST datasets change with the change of training rings

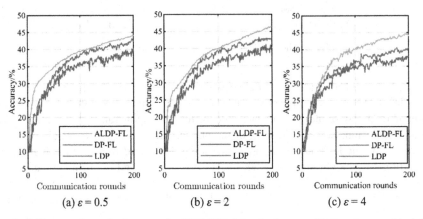

Fig. 4. Different privacy budgets on the CIFAR10 datasets change with the change of training rings

tradeoff between privacy protection and model performance, ALDP-FL scheme can meet the above two requirements to some extent and shows the significant performance advantage.

5 Conclusion

This paper proposes an adaptive differential privacy based federated learning scheme, where the model updates the clipping threshold for each iteration using an adaptive clipping threshold strategy during local training. Additionally, the adaptive noise is added during parameter uploading to ensure privacy security during the training process. Experimental results on the MNIST and CIFAR10 datasets demonstrate that this algorithm not only guarantees privacy and security for the data but also enhances model performance and makes the training process more stable. Future work will focus on conducting more comprehensive sensitivity analysis on parameters and exploring gradient clipping schemes to achieve more precise privacy protection as well as performance improvement, which can enhance the practicality of the scheme.

Acknowledgments. This work is supported by Heilongjiang Provincial Natural Science Foundation of China (LH2020F050), Fundamental Research Funds Heilongjiang Provincial Universities (145309213).

References

1. McMahan, H.B., Moore, E., Ramage, D., et al.: Federated learning of deep networks using model averaging. arXiv preprint arXiv,1602.05629 (2016)
2. Wang, D., et al.: Survey on model inversion attack and defense in federated learning. J. Commun. **44**(11), 94–109 (2023)
3. McMahan, B., Moore, E., Ramage, D., et al.: Communication-efficient learning of deep networks from decentralized data. Artif. Intell. Stat. PMLR, pp. 1273–1282 (2017)
4. Ghimire, B., Rawat, D.B.: Recent advances on federated learning for cybersecurity and cybersecurity for federated learning for internet of things. IEEE Internet Things J. **9**(11), 8229–8249 (2022)
5. Zhan, Y., et al.: A survey of incentive mechanism design for federated learning. IEEE Trans. Emerg. Top. Comput. **10**(2), 1035–1044 (2022)
6. Shi, W., et al.: Joint device scheduling and resource allocation for latency constrained wireless federated learning. IEEE Trans. Wireless Commun. **20**(1), 453–467 (2021)
7. Abadi, M., Chu, A., Goodfellow, I., et al.: Deep learning with differential privacy. In: Proceedings of the 2016 ACM SIGSAC Conference on Computer and Communications Security, pp. 308–318 (2016)
8. Truex, S., Liu, L., Chow, K.H., et al.: LDP-Fed: federated learning with local differential privacy. In: Proceedings of the Third ACM International Workshop on Edge Systems, Analytics and Networking, pp. 61–66 (2020)
9. Naseri, M., Hayes, J., De Cristofaro, E.: Local and central differential privacy for robustness and privacy in federated learning. arXiv preprint arXiv:2009.03561 (2020)
10. Cai, T.T., et al: The cost of privacy: optimal rates of convergence for parameter estimation with differential privacy, arXiv: Mach. Learn. **49**(5), 2825–2850 (2021)
11. Wu, X., Zhang, Y., Shi, M., et al.: An adaptive federated learning scheme with differential privacy preserving. Future Gen. Comput. Syst. 362–372 (2022)
12. Zhang, X., Ding, J., Wu, M., et al.: Adaptive privacy preserving deep learning algorithms for medical data. In: IEEE Winter Conference on Applications of Computer Vision (WACV), Waikoloa, HI, USA (2021)
13. Wang, X.F., Wang, C.Y., Li, X.H.: Federated deep reinforcement learning for internet of things with decentralized cooperative edge caching. IEEE Internet Things J. **7**, 9441–9455 (2020)
14. Zhao, Y., et al.: Correction to privacy-preserving blockchain-based federated learning for IoT devices. IEEE Internet Things J. **10**(1), 973 (2023)
15. Liu, Q., Tian, Y., Wu, J., et al.: Enabling verifiable and dynamic ranked search over outsourced data. IEEE Trans. Serv. Comput. (2019)
16. . Chai, Z.Y et al.: Communication efficiency optimization in federated learning based on multi-objective evolutionary algorithm. IEEE Trans. Neural Netw. Learn. Syst. **16**(3), 5 (2022)
17. Leng, J., Zhou, M., Zhao, J.L., et al.: Blockchain security: a survey of techniques and research directions. IEEE Trans. Serv. Comput. **15**(4), 2490–2510 (2020)

18. Kang, W., et al.: User-level privacy-preserving federated learning: analysis and performance optimization. IEEE Trans. Mob. Comput. **21**(9), 3388–3401 (2022)

19. Leng, J., Ye, S., Zhou, M., et al.: Blockchain-secured smart manufacturing in industry 4.0: a survey. IEEE Trans. Syst. Man Cybern. Syst. **51**(1), 237–252 (2020)

20. Xia, K., Wu, X., Mao, Y., et al.: Secure DNA motif-finding method based on sampling candidate pruning. ACM Trans. Internet Technol. (TOIT) **21**(3), 1–19 (2021)

21. Chen, M., Yang, Z., Saad, W., et al.: Performance optimization of federated learning over wireless networks. In: IEEE Global Communications Conference (GLOBECOM), pp. 1–6 (2019)

22. Hua, S., Yang, K., Shi, Y.: On-device federated learning via second-order optimization with over-the-air computation. In: IEEE 90th Vehicular Technology Conference (VTC2019-Fall), pp. 1–5 (2019)

23. Rodríguez-Barroso, N., Stipcich, G., Jiménez-López, D., et al.: Federated learning and differential privacy: software tools analysis, the Sherpa. ai FL framework and methodological guidelines for preserving data privacy. Inf. Fusion **64**, 270–292 (2020)

24. Wang, T., Huo, Z., Huang, Y., et al.: Review on privacy-preserving technologies in federated learning. J. Comput. Appl. **43**(2), 437 (2023)

25. Geyer, R.C., Klein, T., Nabi, M.: Differentially private federated learning: A client level perspective. arXiv preprint arXiv, 2017,1712.07557

26. Naseri, M., Hayes, J., De Cristofaro, E.: Local and central differential privacy for robustness and privacy in federated learning. In: Proceedings 2022 Network and Distributed System Security Symposium (2022)

Cascading Failures Model with Noise Interference in Supply Chain Networks

Bo Song[1]($\boxtimes$), Yi Qin[2] (ORCID), Yu-Rong Song[1]($\boxtimes$), and Xu Wang[3]

[1] School of Automation, Nanjing University of Posts and Telecommunications,
Nanjing 210003, China
`songbo@njupt.edu.cn`
[2] School of Modern Posts, Nanjing University of Posts and Telecommunications,
Nanjing 210003, China
[3] GBDTC, University of Technology Sydney, Sydney, NSW 2007, Australia

Abstract. Cascade failure is a common phenomenon in supply chain networks, where the environmental uncertainty injects a layer of significant complexity into the dynamics of the failures. This paper addresses this challenge by proposing a novel cascading failure model that incorporates noise interference. The model, grounded in complex network theory, aims to analyze the impact of environmental uncertainty on the propagation of cascading failures within supply chain networks. Simulation results demonstrate that noise disturbances exacerbate the cascading failure process by increasing the critical threshold and accelerating the decomposition of the network structures. Interestingly, the influence of noise diminishes as the heterogeneity of load redistribution increases. Additionally, the study delves into the impact of both initial load parameters and load redistribution parameters on the critical threshold. Our findings reveal that by strategically adjusting these two parameters, a minimum critical threshold can be achieved, potentially enhancing network resilience.

Keywords: Cascading failure · noise interference · supply chain network

1 Introduction

Supply chains, composed by a group of business entities, e.g., logistics providers, manufacturers, distributors and retailers, are gradually evolving from chained structure to networked structure with economic globalization [1]. The complex supply chain network structure enriches the dynamics on and of the businesses entities, on the one hand, the heterogeneity of entity nodes is highlighted, and on the other hand, trade flows are becoming increasingly abundant. With the help of complex network theory, models can be established to describe and analyze the dynamics of and on supply chain networks, e.g., the trade relations changing and propagation dynamics [2, 3].

The interconnectivity of components in supply chain networks renders them vulnerable to cascading failures, where localized disruptions can propagate through network couplings, potentially triggering widespread or even global breakdowns [4–6]. The ripple effects of such large-scale disruptions, often characterized by exponential propagation and unpredictable patterns, can generate profound negative effects on economic stability, and social cohesion. Consequently, the investigation and mitigation of cascading failure in supply chain networks has transitioned to a paramount research priority. Complex network theory provides a valuable framework for investigating the robustness of real-world systems against cascading failures, which enables researchers to model and predict dynamics governing diverse phenomena, thereby informing mitigation strategies and enhancing system robustness [4, 7, 8].

In supply chain networks, each node represents an entity in business, and edges denote business relations among them, involving commercial activities in material flows, capital flows and information flows. During the transmission process, the disturbance caused by complex environments permeates the entire risk propagation process. For example, government macroeconomic regulation, communication conditions, adverse weather conditions, and other disturbances can all have an impact on the transmission process. Positive factors such as macroeconomic control measures may restrain the risk propagation to some extent, while destabilizing factors such as cut-throat competitions and natural disasters will facilitate the risk propagation. Most of these disturbances occur during the risk propagation process of the network. For example, after the cascading failure occurs, the disturbances may intensify or slow down the process of load redistribution, which can affect the process of cascading failure.

By categorizing the disruptive influences on the cascading failure process as noise, we develop a cascading failure model incorporating noise interference induced by risk propagation within supply chain networks. We quantify the robustness of supply chain networks under various noise conditions by theoretical analysis and simulations. Simulation results indicate that the presence of noise elevates the critical threshold, necessitating increased redundancy to ensure supply chain network robustness. Our model offers a foundation for further research into risk propagation within supply chain networks, potentially contributing to advancements in supply chain management.

The remainder of this paper is structured as follows. Section 2 introduces the proposed cascading failure models incorporating noise interference. Section 3 presents a theoretical analysis of network robustness against cascading failures. Subsequently, simulation results are detailed in Sect. 4. Finally, Sect. 5 offers concluding remarks.

2 Related Work

Cascading failures characterize the dynamical processes of a network after the failure of nodes or edges, serving as a crucial method for studying network resilience [6]. In real world systems, very small fraction of elements' failure can lead to the redistribution of network load, triggering the failure of other nodes due to capacity constraints, and even causing a complete system collapse. The study of cascading failures in complex networks has been a focal point of research for scholars [7, 9–15]. In recent years, numerous models have been developed to better understand and address cascading failures, including load-flow models [7, 9–11], sandpile models [12], the CASCADE model [13], optimal power flow models [14], and coupled map lattice models [15]. Among these, load-capacity models, as the most common type of cascading failure model in complex networks, have been widely applied to real-world systems such as supply chain networks, power grids, and urban transportation networks to simulate cascading failure processes.

Research on cascading failure models based on load capacity primarily focuses on three processes, the initial load definition, the load capacity definition and the load redistribution strategy after a failure [16–21]. The definition of node initial load and the relationship between node capacity and initial load are key components in constructing load capacity models. Motter, Liu and other scholars defined capacity as being proportional to the initial node load [16, 17], resulting in a linear load capacity model. With the deepening of research, scholars have proposed and verified the feasibility of nonlinear load capacity models. As early as 2002, Holme et al. demonstrated that the capacity and initial load of four real-world networks-aviation, highways, power grids, and internet routers-exhibit a nonlinear relationship, providing a new perspective for the widespread application of nonlinear load capacity models [18]. In the same year, Kim et al. found that more capacity in networks is allocated to edges with smaller loads, leading to a small network load capacity, proving the existence of a negative linear relationship between load and capacity on power grids and the Internet [19]. Wang et al. applied nonlinear load capacity models to study cascading failures caused by edge failures and investigated the robustness of networks under cascading failures of the highest-loaded edges, finding that the impact of the remaining capacity of high-loaded edges on network robustness increases with the power-law exponent [20].

In load capacity models, different load redistribution strategies can also significantly affect the robustness of networks after cascading failures [22–25]. The load of failed nodes is transferred to their neighboring nodes according to certain redistribution mechanisms. To mitigate cascading failures, the load of failed nodes or edges is redistributed to their nearest neighbors, including redistribution strategies considering time-varying load and capacity, degree-based redistribution methods, clustering coefficient-based redistribution methods, redistribution strategies based on the initial load ratio of neighboring nodes, redistribution strategies based on the capacity ratio of neighboring nodes, and redistribution strategies based on the ratio of the difference between the capacity and initial load of neighboring nodes.

Cascading failures in supply chain networks refer to a series of chain reactions that occur throughout the entire system due to a failure at a specific link, thereby affecting the stability and operational efficiency of the entire network. In recent years, with the development of global economic integration and internet technology, supply chain networks have become increasingly complex, and the issue of cascading failures has received widespread attention. When studying cascading failures in supply chain networks, scholars often adopt the perspective of complex network theory to analyze the network's structural characteristics, the interdependence of nodes and edges, and the risk propagation mechanism. Studies have shown that the robustness of supply chain networks is closely related to the network's topology, the connection modes of nodes, and factors such as node capacity and load. To improve the robustness of supply chain networks, researchers have proposed a variety of models and strategies, including optimizing network structure, enhancing the fault tolerance of critical nodes, and developing effective risk management and response measures.

Researchers have constructed various supply chain network models, such as undirected informational layer networks, directed physical layer networks, and multi-layer supply chain network models, to simulate and analyze cascading failures in supply chain networks. These models not only consider the hierarchical nature of supply chain networks but also the coupling relationships between nodes and the diversity of failure modes. For instance, an overload cascading failure may occur in the upper-level supplier network, while an under load cascading failure may occur in the lower-level retailer network [26]. The coupling between the upper and lower layers can further expand the scope of failures. Moreover, the vulnerability analysis of supply chain networks is also a focal point of research. Researchers have conducted simulations and numerical simulations to analyze the iterative failure process and the scale of failures in supply chain networks under different attack modes and attack proportions, as well as the vulnerability and efficiency of networks under different node capacity parameters. These studies help identify potential risks in supply chain networks and provide a theoretical basis for developing effective risk prevention and mitigation measures.

3   Cascading Failures Models with Noise Interference

Consider a network of N nodes connected by L links as a supply chain network, where nodes symbolize entities and edges denote their relationships. Building upon the ML capacity-load model [16], this section presents a detailed description of the cascading failure model with noise interference in supply chain networks, encompassing initial load, load capacity, and the noise-influenced load redistribution process.

3.1   Initial Load

For a stable supply chain network, the number of neighboring entities of node i can to some extent represent its load situation, and we define the initial load of node i is proportional to its degree. The larger the degree value of node i, the greater the initial load. For simplicity, we assume that the network is at the static state initially where the initial risk load of each entity is less than its capacity and there are no failed nodes. In our model, the initial work load of node i is set as

$$L_i(0) = \beta_1 k_i^{\alpha_1}, \; i = 1, \, 2 \dots N \tag{1}$$

where k_i is the degree of node i, α_1 and β_1 are the adjustable parameters that govern the strength of initial loads.

3.2   Load Capacity

On account of finite cost and resources, the ability of node i against risks is limited. The load capacity of node i is defined as the minimum load in case of node failure. In general, the node load capacity is directly proportional to its importance in the network, such as its degree, betweenness, etc. Here, based on the definition of initial load, we can also define the load capacity of node i as

$$C_i = (1 + \beta_2)L_i(0) \tag{2}$$

β_2 ($\beta_2 > 0$) is the tolerance parameter and suggests the upper bound of ability that enterprises withstand risks. Beyond all doubts, if β_2 is larger, the supply chain networks will be more robust against cascading failures. Namely, if β_2 is large enough, the network will not collapse because each node possesses sufficient redundancy to take the risks from the failed node. However, the upper bound of ability of defense against risks is really confined and improving the ability regardless of costs is not reasonable. Therefore, we aim to investigate the minimum upper bound that we define as critical threshold β_m to reach the global robustness. That is, when β_2 is less than β_m, the supply chain networks will collapse due to the load propagation. On the contrary, there will no more newly generated failed nodes if β_2 goes beyond β_m. Strictly, minimizing critical threshold β_m is what we pursue.

3.3 Load Redistribution

Upon the failure of a network entity, its workload is redistributed among neighboring entities to maintain network functionality. Within supply chain networks, entities with a greater number of cooperative partners generally possess enhanced capacity and resources to mitigate redistribution-induced risks. Consequently, nodes with higher degrees exhibit increased resilience to risk propagation. Incorporating these factors, the workload redistribution is defined as follows

$$P_{i \to j} = \frac{k_j^{\alpha_2}}{\sum\limits_{m \in V_i} k_m^{\alpha_2}} \qquad (3)$$

where V_i is the set of failed node i's neighbors, and node j is one element of the set. The proportion depends on the degree. The larger the degree is, more loads the node will be redistributed. Parameter α_2 ($\alpha_2 \geq 0$) is tunable and governs the power of risk redistribution. Apparently, each pair of α_1 and α_2 corresponds to a certain β_m. By adjusting α_1 and α_2, we can obtain the optimal critical threshold β_m. The load that node j takes from failed node i can be defined as

$$\Delta L_{i \to j}(t) = L_i(t-1)P_{i \to j} \qquad (4)$$

In real world, the market environment is not always smooth, and sometimes it will be disturbed by some unpredictable incidents, such as wars, trade wars and malicious rumors etc. These market fluctuations caused by policies and regulations or unpredictable incidents are system noise in our model. Noise exists in the process of load propagation. Therefore, an entity in supply chain networks will not only take the risks from failed neighbors, but also bear the system noise at each time step. The load of node j at time t can be defined as.

$$L_j(t) = L_j(t-1) + \Delta L_{i \to j}(t) + n_j, \; n_j = \alpha_3 \cdot noise \cdot L_j(0) \qquad (5)$$

where α_3 is the variable parameter that govern the intensity of noise. In fact, the case of $\alpha_3 = 0$ corresponds to a smooth market environment without disturbance, and the proposed model degenerates to an absolutely idealized situation.

When node i breaks down, its risks will propagate along with the collaboration relations, then its neighbors will take the risks. After taking the extra work load from node i, node j will fail if the updated work loads go beyond the capacity ($L_j(t) > C_j$). In turn, risks of node j will propagate following Eqs. (3)-(5). The cascading failures will cease until the whole supply chain networks collapse or there are no newly generated failure nodes. Figure 1 depicts the whole process of the proposed cascade failure model.

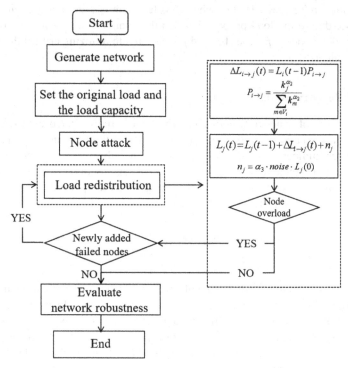

Fig. 1. The framework of cascading failure model with noise interference.

4 Theoretical Analysis

Based on the proposed model, we analyze the global network robustness in this section [22]. For simplicity, we firstly set $\alpha_1 = 1$ and $\beta_1 = 1$ and analyze the impact of α_2 on critical threshold β_m of the tolerance parameter. In the case of $\alpha_1 = 1$, the model can be described as

$$L_i(0) = k_i,$$
$$C_i = (1 + \beta_2)L_i(0),$$
$$P_{i \to j} = \frac{k_j^{\alpha_2}}{\sum\limits_{m \in V_i} k_m^{\alpha_2}},$$
(6)
$$\Delta L_{i \to j}(t) = L_i(t-1)P_{i \to j},$$
$$L_j(t) = L_j(t-1) + \Delta L_{i \to j}(t) + n_j, n_j = \alpha_3 \cdot noise \cdot L_j(0)$$

To guarantee the global robustness, the model ought to satisfy the following condition

$$L_j(0) + \Delta L_{i \to j}(1) + n_j \leq C_j$$
(7)

Based on the Eqs. (6)-(7), the critical threshold β_m can be derived. After a simple transformation, Eq. (7) can be rewritten as

$$(1 + \alpha_3 \cdot noise)k_j + k_i \cdot \frac{k_j^{\alpha_2}}{\sum\limits_{m \in V_i} k_m^{\alpha_2}} < (1 + \beta_2)k_j$$
(8)

The tolerance parameter β_2 of node j satisfied

$$\beta_2 > k_i \cdot \frac{k_j^{\alpha_2 - 1}}{\sum\limits_{m \in V_i} k_m^{\alpha_2}} + \alpha_3 \cdot noise$$
(9)

Therein, $\sum\limits_{m \in V_i} k_m^{\alpha_2} = \sum\limits_{k'=k_{min}}^{k_{max}} k_i \cdot P(k'|k_i)k'^{\alpha_2}$, in which $P(k'|k_i)$ is the conditional probability that node with degree k_i has neighbors with the amount of k'. Particularly, considering the degree-degree irrelevance [27], $P(k'|k_i)$ can be expressed as $P(k'|k_i) = \frac{k'P(k')}{<k>}$. The formula (9) can be expanded as

$$\beta_2 > k_i \cdot \frac{k_j^{\alpha_2 - 1}}{\sum\limits_{m \in V_i} k_m^{\alpha_2}} + \alpha_3 \cdot noise = \frac{k_i k_j^{\alpha_2 - 1}}{k_i \sum\limits_{k'=k_{min}}^{k_{max}} \frac{k'P(k')}{<k>} k'^{\alpha_2}} + \alpha_3 \cdot noise$$
$$= \frac{k_j^{\alpha_2 - 1} <k>}{<k^{\alpha_2 + 1}>} + \alpha_3 \cdot noise$$
(10)

Based on the Eq. (10), we can obtain the theoretical expression of the upper bound of critical threshold β_m^*.

$$\beta_m^* = \begin{cases} \dfrac{k_{min}^{\alpha_2 - 1} <k>}{<k^{\alpha_2 + 1}>} + \alpha_3 \cdot noise, & \alpha_2 < 1 \\[2ex] \dfrac{<k>}{<k^2>} + \alpha_3 \cdot noise, & \alpha_2 = 1 \\[2ex] \dfrac{k_{max}^{\alpha_2 - 1} <k>}{<k^{\alpha_2 + 1}>} + \alpha_3 \cdot noise, & \alpha_2 > 1 \end{cases}$$
(11)

where k_{min} and k_{max} are respectively the minimum degree and maximum degree.
When $\alpha_2 < 1$,

$$\beta_m^* = \frac{k_{min}^{\alpha_2-1} <k>}{<k^{\alpha_2+1}>} + \alpha_3 \cdot noise = \frac{k_{min}^{\alpha_2-1} <k>}{\frac{1}{N}\sum_{i=1}^{N} k_i^{\alpha_2+1}} + \alpha_3 \cdot noise$$

$$= \frac{<k>}{\frac{1}{N}\sum_{i=1}^{N} k_i^2(\frac{k_i}{k_{min}})^{\alpha_2-1}} + \alpha_3 \cdot noise \geq \frac{<k>}{\frac{1}{N}\sum_{i=1}^{N} k_i^2} + \alpha_3 \cdot noise \qquad (12)$$

$$= \frac{<k>}{<k^2>} + \alpha_3 \cdot noise$$

When $\alpha_2 > 1$,

$$\beta_m^* = \frac{k_{min}^{\alpha_1-1} k_{max}^{\alpha_2-\alpha_1} <k>}{<k^{\alpha_2+1}>} + \alpha_3 \cdot noise \geq \frac{k_{min}^{\alpha_2-1} <k>}{<k^{\alpha_2+1}>} + \alpha_3 \cdot noise$$

$$= \frac{k_{min}^{\alpha_2-1} <k>}{\frac{1}{N}\sum_{i=1}^{N} k_i^{\alpha_2+1}} + \alpha_3 \cdot noise = \frac{<k>}{\frac{1}{N}\sum_{i=1}^{N} k_i^2(\frac{k_i}{k_{min}})^{\alpha_2-1}} + \alpha_3 \cdot noise \qquad (13)$$

$$\geq \frac{<k>}{\frac{1}{N}\sum_{i=1}^{N} k_i^2} + \alpha_3 \cdot noise = \frac{<k>}{<k^2>} + \alpha_3 \cdot noise$$

We can see from Eqs. (11)–(13) that, when $\alpha_1 = \alpha_2 = 1$, the value of β_m^* is the smallest either with or without noise, i.e., the network shows strongest robustness. In addition, noise impacts the value of β_m^*, bad noise, such as malicious rumors, bad weather, can increase β_m^* and weaken network robustness, while good ones such as policy regulation of the government can enhance the network robustness. By using simulations, we continue to study the effect of different noise on the cascade failure process.

5   Simulation Results

Researchers have found that the topology structures of most supply chain networks compliant with scale-free characteristics [28, 29]. Considering the structural heterogeneity of supply chain networks, 50 different BA network models are applied to simulate and analyze the network robustness against cascading failures. In each of the networks, the number of nodes is $N = 1000$, and the average degree is $<k> = 6$. Simulations are performed on each network, and the average results are presented in our simulation results. For simplicity, we set $\alpha_1 = 1$.

In Sect. 3, we obtained the relationship between redistribution parameter α_2 and the upper bound of critical threshold β_m^*. Therefore, simulations on the BA scale-free network models are first implemented to verify theoretical analysis. Figure 2 shows the relation between critical threshold β_m and α_2 from simulations and the the upper bound of critical threshold β_m^* from theoretical analysis. We can see from Fig. 2 that there exists an optimal critical threshold when $\alpha_1 = \alpha_2 = 1$, which is is consistent with the theoretical analysis result. Namely, when the original work load and load redistribution are both linearly proportional to degree, networks can obtain global robustness with lowest costs.

We can also see from Fig. 2 that as α_2 grows, the heterogeneity of redistribution proportion is enhanced, which means nodes with larger degree will take more work loads from failed nodes. Under this condition, larger redundant capacity is required to keep global robustness. Therefore, when $\alpha_2 > 1$, the critical threshold increases with increase of α_2.

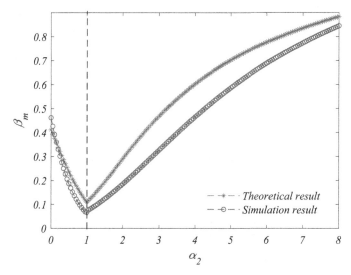

Fig. 2. The relation between critical threshold β_m and α_2.

Further, we investigate the effect of noise on the cascade failures. Two types of noise are considered in the simulation, one is uniform noise and the other is Gaussian noise. The uniform noise distribution follows $U(-0.5, 0.5)$, and the Gaussian noise distribution follows $N(0, 0.1)$. The range of noise values indicates both harmful and beneficial noise have been considered and the average value of both types of noise is 0. Figure 3 shows the influences of noise on critical threshold β_m. As showed in Fig. 3, the optimal critical threshold still appears at $\alpha_2 = 1$ whether the noise exists or not, as we conclude in Sect. 3. While noises do have clear influences on the value of critical threshold. First, critical threshold is enhanced in the case of noise, for guaranteeing sufficient redundant capacity to resist risks propagation due to the unstable market environment. Also, noises have the greatest impact on critical threshold at $\alpha_2 = 1$. As the increase of α_2, the heterogeneity of redistribution proportion is enhanced, and nodes with larger degree will be reassigned to more work loads from failed node and take more risk. Compared with the enormous increase of work loads, the impact of noise is increasingly smaller and gradually vanishes, as shown in Fig. 3.

174 B. Song et al.

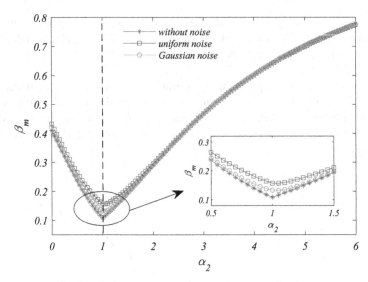

Fig. 3. The influences of noise on critical threshold β_m.

Cascading failures exacerbate network fragmentation, particularly in the context of intentional attacks [30]. Nodes with higher workloads, when removed along with their associated edges, are more likely to trigger large-scale cascading failures. Consequently, the structural robustness of networks against cascading failures emerges as a critical concern. The largest connected component (L_c), defined as the proportion of the largest connected subgraph remaining after the cascading failure, is a widely employed metric for assessing network robustness. A larger L_c indicates greater resilience to cascading failures.

By removing nodes in descending order of the work loads, the impact of noise on cascading failure process in BA networks is studied. Figure 4 shows the the changes of L_c as the number of nodes being attacked grows. We can see that as the noise parameter α_3 increases, the difference among curves is getting larger. Network robustness is diminished in the presence of noise compared to noise-free conditions. Furthermore, uniform noise poses a more significant threat to network robustness in our simulations. This disparity arises from the fact that while both noise distributions exhibit a mean of zero, the values associated with Gaussian noise exhibit greater proximity to zero. Consequently, for scenarios with minimal noise parameters (e.g., Fig. 4(a) and Fig. 4(b)), the curves representing Gaussian noise and the absence of noise exhibit near-perfect overlap. In contrast, uniform noise values are randomly distributed between -0.5 and 0.5, resulting in a more substantial impact on network robustness compared to Gaussian noise. This distinction can be attributed to the wider range of potential disruptions introduced by uniform noise.

Simulation results indicate that networks exhibit optimal global robustness when both initial workload and load redistribution scale linearly with node degree, irrespective of noise conditions. However, noise significantly influences the optimal critical threshold. Moreover, networks demonstrate decreased resilience in noisy environments compared

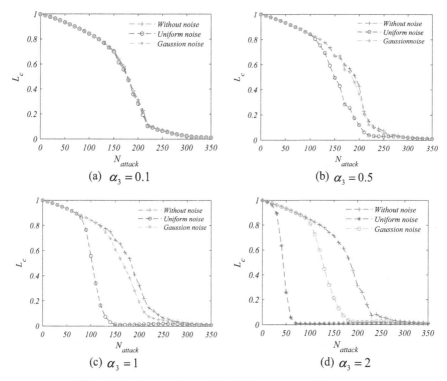

Fig. 4. The impact of cascading failures on network structure.

to noise-free conditions. Among the noise types simulated, uniform noise posed the most substantial threat to network robustness.

6   Conclusion

The intricate nature of supply chain networks renders enterprises susceptible to disruptions. Targeted attacks on a subset of enterprises can trigger cascading failures, a phenomenon exacerbated by environmental factors, policies, and other external influences. To investigate the impact of environmental uncertainty on cascading failure propagation within supply chain networks, a novel cascading failure model incorporating noise interference is proposed. Theoretical analysis and simulation results demonstrate that noise significantly undermines network robustness against cascading failures. Networks exhibit heightened fragility in noisy environments, with uniform noise posing the most substantial threat to network robustness in our simulations.

As real-world systems become increasingly complex and interconnected, cascading failures in interdependent networks have become a critical research focus. On one hand, in mutually dependent networks, the coupling relationship between networks can influence the dynamics of cascading failures at the node level. Therefore, when constructing cascading failure models, it is necessary to consider the role of complex coupling strengths and investigate their impact on the dynamics of edge cascading failures. On the other hand, different types of noise exist in different systems, which may have different impacts on cascading failures. Therefore, studying the propagation mechanism of cascading failures in interdependent networks, as well as prediction and control, will be the focus of our further research.

Acknowledgments. This study was funded by National Natural Science Foundation of China (grant number 62203229).

Disclosure of Interests. The authors have no competing interests to declare that are relevant to the content of this article.

References

1. Shi, X., Long, W., Li, Y., et al.: Robustness of interdependent supply chain networks against both functional and structural cascading failures. Phys. A Stat. Mech. Appl. **586** (2022)
2. Wang, Y., Zhang, F.: Modeling and analysis of under-load-based cascading failures in supply chain networks. Nonlinear Dyn. **92**, 1403–1417 (2018)
3. Kang, X., Wang, M., Chen, L L X.: Supply risk propagation of global copper industry chain based on multi-layer complex network. Resour. Policy, **85**(Pt.A) (2023)
4. Zhang, M.Y., Chen, S.W., Du, W.B., et al.: Risky cascading transitions in international relationships. PANS Nexus **2**(1), pgac289 (2023)
5. Artime, O., Grassia, M., De, D.M., et al.: Robustness and resilience of complex networks. Nat. Rev. Phys. **6**, 114–131 (2024)
6. Liu, X.M., Li, D.Q., Ma, M.Q., et al.: Network resilience. Phys. Rep. **971**, 1–108 (2022)
7. Yuan, Y.F., Shen, X.H., Sun, L., et al.: Modeling cascading failures and invulnerability analysis of underwater acoustic sensor networks based on complex network. IEEE Sens. J. **24**(5), 6942–6952 (2024)
8. Buldyrev, S.V., Parshani, R., Paul, G., et al.: Catastrophic cascade of failures in interdependent networks. Nature **464**, 1025–1028 (2010)
9. Gong, L.X., Liu, T.Q., He, C., et al.: Resilience of power system with integrated energy in context of low-carbon energy transition: review and prospects. Electr. Power Autom. Equip. **41**(09), 2735–2745 (2020)
10. Dong, A., Wu, Y.L., Ren, Y.G., et al.: Initial load definition of cascading failure model based on local entropy. Complex Syst. Complexity Sci. **20**(4), 18–25 (2023)
11. Duan, D-L., Wu, X-Y.: Cascading failure of scale-free networks based on a tunable load redistribution model. Acta Phys. Sin. **63**(3), 030501 (2014)
12. Turalska, M., Burghardt, K., Rohden, M., et al.: Cascading failures in scale-free interdependent networks. Phys. Rev. E **99**(3), 032308 (2019)
13. Kim, M.J., Kim, J.S.: A model for cascading failures with the probability of failure described as a logistic function. Sci. Rep. **12**, 989 (2022)
14. Lejeune, M.A., Dehghanian, P.: Optimal power flow models with probabilistic guarantees: a Boolean approach. IEEE Trans. Power Syst. **35**(6), 4932–4935 (2020)
15. Ye, H.N., Luo, X.: Cascading failure analysis on Shanghai metro networks: an improved coupled map lattices model based on graph attention networks. Int. J. Environ. Res. Public Health **19**(1), 204 (2022)
16. Motter, A.E., Lai, Y.C.: Cascade-based attacks on complex networks. Phys. Rev. E **66**(6), 065102 (2002)

17. Liu, J., Xiong, Q.Y., Shi, X., et al.: Load-redistribution strategy based on time-varying load against cascading failure of complex network. Chin. Phys. B **24**(7), 076401 (2015)
18. Holme, P.: Edge overload breakdown in evolving networks. Phys. Rev. E **66**, 036119 (2002)
19. Kim, D.H., Motter, A.E.: Resource allocation pattern in infrastructure networks. J. Phys. A Math. Theor. **41**(22), 4539 (2008)
20. Wang, L., Fu, Y., Chen, M.Z., et al.: Controllability robustness for scale-free networks based on nonlinear load-capacity. Neurocomputing **251**, 99–105 (2017)
21. Dong, R., Wang, Z., Liu, R.J., et al.: Robustness analysis of chemical process systems based on complex network non-linear load capacity model. Can. J. Chem. Eng. **101**(2), 953–966 (2023)
22. Song, B., Zhang, Z.H., Song, Y.R., et al.: Preferential redistribution in cascading failure by considering local real-time information. Physica A **532**, 121729 (2019)
23. Zhang, Z.H., Song, Y.R., Xia, L.L., et al.: A novel load capacity model with a tunable proportion of load redistribution against cascading failures. Secur. Commun. Netw. **2018**, 1–7 (2018)
24. Yu, R.B., Jiang, Y., Yan, Y.W., et al.: Research on robustness of interdependent networks considering dependent side load. J. Univ. Electr. Sci. Technol. China **51**(5), 774–785 (2022)
25. Song, B.O., Wu, H-M., Song, Y-R., et al.: Robustness of community networks against cascading failures with heterogeneous redistribution strategies. Chin. Phys. B **32**, 098905: 1–8 (2023)
26. Li, S., Yang, H., Song, B.: Study on co-evolution of underload failure and overload cascading failure in multi-layer supply chain network. Comput. Sci. **48**(10), 351–358 (2021)
27. Wang, J.-W., Rong, L.-L.: Cascading failures on complex networks based on the local preferential redistribution rule of the load. Acta Phys. Sin. **58**(6), 3714–3721 (2009)
28. Lu, Z., Dong, Z.: A gravitation-based hierarchical community detection algorithm for structuring supply chain network. Int. J. Comput. Intell. Syst. **16**, 110 (2023)
29. Wang, J., Zhou, H., Sun, X., et al.: A novel supply chain network evolving model under random and targeted disruptions. Chaos, Solitons Fractals Appl. Sci. Eng. Interdiscipl. J. Nonlinear Sci. **170** (2023)
30. Albert, R., Jeong, H., Barabási, A.L.: Attack and error tolerance in complex networks. Nature **406**(6794), 387–482 (2000)

DefMPA: Defending Model Poisoning Attacks in Federated Learning via Model Update Prediction

Mengya Guo[1], Bing Chen[1,2(✉)], Baolu Xue[1], and Jiewen Liu[1]

[1] Nanjing University of Aeronautics and Astronautics, Nanjing 210016, China
{guoguo,cb_china,xbl236,sx2216146}@nuaa.edu.cn
[2] Collaborative Innovation Center of Novel Software Technology and
Industrialization, Nanjing, China

Abstract. Federated learning, as a novel machine learning paradigm, achieves distributed model training while preserving client data privacy. However, under the distributed architecture, due to factors such as client manipulability and weaker aggregation algorithms, federated learning faces security threats at various stages. Among these, model poisoning attacks occur during the training phase, where attackers impersonate benign clients and upload malicious model gradients to the server for aggregation, resulting in a decline in global model performance. Existing aggregation methods for defending against model poisoning attacks only exhibit superior performance when the number of malicious clients is small or when targeting a specific attack method. To address this, we have designed a general defensive aggregation method, DefMPA, that does not rely on the number of malicious clients. DefMPA predicts model updates using the Cauchy mean value theorem, where malicious model updates will significantly differ from the predicted updates. Subsequently, the DBSCAN clustering method is employed to identify malicious model updates. Moreover, DefMPA implements a trust score mechanism that dynamically adjusts each client's contribution, weakening the influence of malicious model updates on the global model and reducing the attack's effectiveness. Extensive experiments demonstrate that DefMPA achieves an overall detection success rate of around 90% against three different attacks. Furthermore, as the number of malicious clients increases, DefMPA maintains more stable global model accuracy compared to five mainstream aggregation algorithms.

Keywords: Federated learning · Model poisoning attacks · Security

1 Introduction

Federated learning [12,16] is an innovative distributed computing paradigm. Unlike traditional machine learning, clients in federated learning do not need to upload their local data to the server. Instead, they use local data to train

W. Li et al. (Eds.): EISA 2024, CCIS 2266, pp. 178–191, 2025.
https://doi.org/10.1007/978-3-031-80419-9_13

local models and then upload the trained model updates to the server. Federated learning achieves distributed model training while protecting data privacy. Currently, federated learning has been widely applied in various fields such as computer vision, natural language processing, smart cities, and autonomous driving.

Despite avoiding the direct upload of client data, federated learning in a distributed architecture is susceptible to various malicious attacks at different stages due to factors like client manipulability and the inability of general aggregation algorithms to identify malicious model updates. Among these, model poisoning attacks [18] occur during the training phase, where attackers impersonate benign clients to upload malicious model updates to the server for aggregation, thus affecting the performance of the global model. Many model poisoning attack algorithms exist, for example, Shejwalkar et al. proposed an optimization-based framework [15] for model poisoning attacks that manipulate local model updates to attack Byzantine-robust federated learning algorithms, demonstrating their efficiency across various datasets. Bagdasaryan et al. employed a "constrain-and-scale" technique [2] to locally train models with backdoor data and adjust model parameters to evade anomaly detection.

Some robust aggregation methods have been proposed in recent research to prevent the global model from being compromised by attackers. For instance, Yin et al. proposed the Trimmed-Mean algorithm [20], which sorts the model updates for each coordinate or dimension, removes a certain proportion of the maximum and minimum values, and then computes the average of the remaining values to eliminate outliers. Cao et al.'s FLTrust [6] algorithm adjusts trust scores based on the deviation between local model updates and server-calculated updates using a validation dataset. Gupta et al. proposed MUD-HoG [9], which detects malicious and unreliable clients using long and short historical gradients. However, these defense algorithms only perform well when the number of malicious clients is small, require additional dataset support, or target specific attacks. Zhang et al. proposed FLDetector [21] to distinguish between benign and malicious model updates through model update consistency. This method predicts model updates using the Cauchy mean value theorem based on a universal Hessian matrix, capturing curvature information during the model update process rather than relying solely on simple historical model updates. Although this approach effectively filters out anomalous updates and enhances robustness, the universal Hessian matrix calculated from the historical gradients of the global model may not be suitable for predicting model updates for all clients in the case of Non-Independent and Identically Distributed (Non-IID) client data, leading to inaccurate predictions.

In this paper, we propose a defense aggregation method called DefMPA to defend against model poisoning attacks. This method does not require additional datasets for support, with its defense effectiveness being independent of the number of malicious clients or specific attack methods. DefMPA consists of three main components: model update prediction, clustering, and trust score mechanism. Specifically, we first calculate the personalized Hessian matrix using the client's historical gradient data to enhance prediction accuracy, employing the Cauchy mean value theorem to predict client model updates. Subsequently, the Euclidean distance between each client's actual uploaded model update and the predicted model update is calculated and normalized. The DBSCAN clustering algorithm is then employed to distinguish between malicious and benign model updates. Compared to methods that rely solely on averages or cosine similarities of local model update history, the approach utilizing the Cauchy mean value theorem leverages the consistency of model updates and captures the variations in model update history, thereby filtering out anomalous model updates more effectively. Experimental results demonstrate that this detection method has a detection success rate of about 90%.

Moreover, we introduce a trust score mechanism that reduces the trust score of malicious clients detected in each round, weakening their influence on the global model. All clients' trust scores are normalized and used as weights for aggregating local model updates. This mechanism not only suppresses the impact of malicious clients but also dynamically adjusts the contribution of each client, ensuring the robustness of the global model against model poisoning attacks. Experimental results indicate that in the presence of attacks, DefMPA improves model accuracy by at least 40% compared to the baseline aggregation algorithm FedAvg [13]. Even in scenarios without attacks, DefMPA does not affect the performance of the global model. We summarize our main contributions as follows:

- To defend against model poisoning attacks in federated learning, we propose a defense aggregation method named DefMPA, which identifies malicious model updates based on the distance between predicted and actual model updates. DefMPA does not require additional datasets, and its defense effectiveness is not dependent on the number of malicious clients or specific attack methods.
- DefMPA utilizes the Cauchy mean value theorem and personalized Hessian matrices to predict model updates. Compared to methods that depend solely on the averages or cosine similarities of local model update histories, this approach utilizes the consistency of model updates to capture variations in update histories, thereby more effectively identifying and filtering out anomalous model updates.
- We incorporate the DBSCAN clustering algorithm into the detection of malicious model updates by calculating and normalizing the Euclidean distance between each client's actual model updates and the predicted model updates. This method distinguishes between malicious and benign model updates. Additionally, we introduce a trust score mechanism that dynamically adjusts each client's contribution, further enhancing the defense effectiveness.

The remainder of this paper is organized as follows. Section 2 reviews the work on model poisoning attacks in federated learning and existing robust defense methods. Section 3 describes the problem definition. Section 4 elaborates on the principles of DefMPA in detail. Section 5 describes the experiments and parameter settings of DefMPA and presents the experimental results. Section 6 concludes the paper.

2   Related Work

2.1   Model Poisoning Attacks

While federated learning preserves user privacy, its distributed architecture presents security challenges at various stages due to the susceptibility of clients to manipulation by attackers and the inability of aggregation algorithms to effectively identify malicious clients. Model poisoning attacks predominantly occur during the training stage, where attackers upload malicious model updates to disrupt the global model. These attacks can be categorized into two types based on their targets: untargeted attacks and targeted attacks.

In untargeted attacks, the goal of the attacker is to degrade the overall performance of the global model. Fang et al. proposed a local model poisoning attack [8] on Byzantine-robust federated learning, where in each iteration, the compromised devices upload carefully crafted local models that cause the global model to deviate in the opposite direction of its intended update, thereby maximizing the performance degradation. Xie et al. [19] generated consistent and dynamically adjusted malicious model updates on fake clients, causing the global model to significantly deviate in random directions, thereby increasing the test error rate. In targeted attacks, also known as backdoor attacks, the attacker's goal is to insert specific data into the poisoned model to produce attacker-specified outcomes. For instance, Bagdasaryan et al. employed a "constrain-and-scale" technique [2] to train a backdoored model locally and adjust the model parameters to evade anomaly detection. In the Scaling Attack, attackers trained local models with trigger-embedded data and amplified the influence of these malicious updates, further enhancing the attack's impact.

2.2   Robust Defense Aggregation Algorithms

With the advancement of attack models, various defense aggregation algorithms have been proposed. These defense methods can be broadly categorized into two types based on their principles: robust fault-tolerant aggregation algorithms and malicious client identification aggregation algorithms.

In robust fault-tolerant aggregation algorithms, the server utilizes statistical analysis to filter or trim outlier model updates before aggregation. Blanchard et al. proposed the Krum algorithm [3], which selects the local model update closest to the other $n - m - 2$ local model updates among the uploaded models, thereby mitigating the impact of outliers. Yin et al. introduced the Trimmed-Mean and Median algorithms [20]. The Trimmed-Mean algorithm sorts the model updates for each coordinate or dimension, removes a certain proportion of the largest and smallest values, and then computes the average of the remaining values to eliminate extreme values. The Median method aggregates model updates by computing the median for each parameter dimension. Cao et al. proposed FLTrust [6], which assigns a lower trust score to local model updates if their update direction significantly deviates from the server model update direction computed based on a validation dataset. However, these algorithms often exhibit optimal defensive performance only when few malicious clients or additional datasets are available.

In aggregation algorithms that identify malicious clients, the primary principle is to detect malicious model updates before aggregation. Gupta et al. proposed MUD-HoG [9], which utilizes long-short history gradients to not only identify malicious clients but also unreliable ones. However, this method is designed for specific attacks and is only applicable in scenarios with malicious attacks. Awan et al. introduced CONTRA [1], which assesses the credibility of local gradients in each iteration using cosine similarity, but this approach may mistakenly identify benign clients with similar training data as malicious. Wang et al. [17] rely on validation sets to evaluate each client's model, aggregating only the model updates that perform well. Jagielski et al. proposed the TRIM [10] defense method, in each iteration, the subset of training samples with the smallest residuals is selected to estimate regression parameters, and a trimmed loss function is used to remove points with large residuals. Both methods require additional clean datasets with consistent data distribution, which is often not feasible in real-life scenarios. Therefore, we designed a general defense aggregation method to resist model poisoning attacks, which does not require additional datasets. Moreover, in the absence of attacks, this detection method does not affect the accuracy of the global model.

3   Problem Definition

In this section, we introduce the threat model and the objectives we aim to achieve. Finally, we briefly summarize the principles of each component in the DefMPA system architecture.

3.1   Threat Model

The attacker poses as a benign client and uploads malicious model updates to the server during the last fifty rounds of every one hundred rounds in the training process, and the server is unable to recognize which model updates are malicious. Malicious clients cannot access and modify the aggregation algorithm on the server, but they can access and modify their own data and model, as well as the data and models of other malicious clients.

3.2   Defense Goals

Our objective is to design a defense method, DefMPA, to defend model poisoning attacks in federated learning, achieving the following two goals: i) In attack scenarios, DefMPA can detect malicious model updates and mitigate their impact on the global model when the server aggregates model updates; ii) In non-attack scenarios, DefMPA does not affect the performance of the global model.

3.3   System Framework

As illustrated in Fig. 1, the DefMPA framework consists of three components. The first component utilizes the Cauchy mean value theorem to compute the approximate model update for each client based on model consistency. The Euclidean distance between the predicted and actual model updates is then calculated, resulting in K Euclidean distances, where K is the number of clients. The second component normalizes the K Euclidean distances and then uses DBSCAN to cluster them. Malicious model updates are characterized by significant deviations from the predicted model updates, thus model updates in clusters with larger Euclidean distances are identified as malicious. The third component reduces the trust scores of clients that upload malicious model updates, thereby diminishing their influence on the global model, which is finally aggregated to obtain the global model.

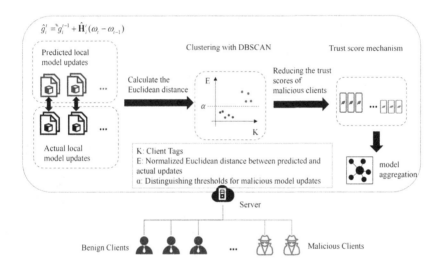

Fig. 1. The Design of DefMPA. The server receives model updates from clients and performs the following three steps: i) predicts the model updates and calculates the distance from the actual model updates, ii) classifies these distances using the DBSCAN algorithm, with larger distance clusters considered as malicious updates, and iii) reduces the trust scores of malicious clients. After these steps, the server aggregates the model updates.

4   Design of DefMPA

The DefMPA framework comprises three components: model update prediction, DBSCAN clustering, and the trust score mechanism. In this section, we provide a detailed explanation of the principles and design of these components.

4.1 Predicting Model Updates Using the Cauchy Mean Value Theorem

According to the Cauchy mean value theorem [11], the local model update for client i at round t can be calculated using Eq. 1.

$$g_i^t = g_i^{t-1} + \mathbf{H}_i^t(\omega_t - \omega_{t-1}), \tag{1}$$

where $\mathbf{H}_i^t = \int_0^1 \mathbf{H}_i(\omega_{t-1} + x(\omega_t - \omega_{t-1}))dx$ is an integrated Hessian matrix of client i at round t. g_i^{t-1} and g_i^t are the local model updates of client i at round t-1, and round t, respectively. ω_{t-1} and ω_t are the global models for round t-1, and round t, respectively. However, the integrated Hessian matrix is difficult to compute directly. Therefore, we use the L-BFGS algorithm [4] to compute the approximate Hessian matrix. Zhang et al. calculated an approximate universal Hessian matrix for all clients using the global model update history in each iteration. However, when client data is Non-IID, this approximate universal Hessian matrix may lead to unstable predictions of client model updates. To address this issue, we compute an approximate personalized Hessian matrix for each client based on their local model update history, thereby improving the accuracy of model update predictions. The experimental results shown in Fig. 2 validate that using the corresponding personalized Hessian matrix for each client results in predicted model updates that are closer to the clients' actual local model updates. Specifically, we define $\Delta\omega_t = \omega_t - \omega_{t-1}$ as the difference of the global model in round t, and $\Delta g_i^t = g_i^t - g_i^{t-1}$ as the difference of the local model update for client i in round t. In round t, we denote $\Delta W_t = \{\Delta w_{t-N}, \Delta w_{t-N+1}, ..., \Delta w_{t-1}\}$ as the difference in the global model over the past N rounds, and $\Delta G_i^t = \{\Delta g_i^{t-N}, \Delta g_i^{t-N+1}, ..., \Delta g_i^{t-1}\}$ as the difference in the local model updates for client i over the past N rounds. Then, based on the L-BFGS algorithm, we can use ΔW_t and ΔG_i^t to estimate the approximate personalized Hessian matrix $\hat{\mathbf{H}}_i^t = \text{L-BFGS}(\Delta W_t, \Delta G_i^t)$ for client i. Finally, we predict the model update for client i in iteration t as follows:

$$\hat{g}_i^t = g_i^{t-1} + \hat{\mathbf{H}}_i^t(\omega_t - \omega_{t-1}). \tag{2}$$

In our experiments, we set N to 10. To ensure that the computed approximate Hessian matrix is more stable, we start detecting malicious model updates from the 40th round. In each subsequent round, the server promptly updates ΔW_t and ΔG_i^t, and recalculates the personalized Hessian matrix for each client to predict the model update for that round. Based on the consistency of model updates, benign model updates have small differences from the predicted model updates, resulting in small Euclidean distances. In contrast, malicious model updates exhibit large differences from the predicted model updates, leading to large Euclidean distances. Therefore, we can leverage this discrepancy to distinguish between benign and malicious model updates.

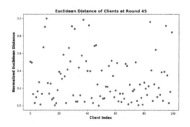 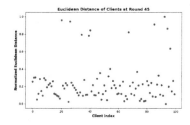

(a) Using an approximate universal Hessian matrix

(b) Using the corresponding approximate personalized Hessian matrix

Fig. 2. The Euclidean distance between the predicted and actual model updates of 100 clients over 45 rounds.

4.2 DBSCAN Clustering and Trust Score Mechanism

At round t, the server computes for each client the Euclidean distance between its actual uploaded model update and the predicted model update, normalizes these Euclidean distances, i.e., $D = \{d_1, d_2, ..., d_K\}$, where d_k is the normalized Euclidean distance for client k, and finally clusters D using DBSCAN [14]. DBSCAN categorizes data points into core, boundary, and noise points. Where noise points are separate points and all noise points are grouped together. Algorithm 1 describes the principle of DBSCAN clustering.

The clustering results are divided into two cases. Under normal circumstances, there is only one cluster category, aside from the noise points category. Due to factors such as equipment, environment, and data quality, benign clients may occasionally upload abnormal local model updates during training. When most data points are categorized into one class, the presence of a small number of noise points is considered normal. In the anomalous case, two or more clustering categories are identified, excluding the noise point category. We consider that the data D can be explicitly classified, at which point the average Euclidean distance is calculated for each category. If the maximum Euclidean distance significantly exceeds the minimum Euclidean distance, we mark the category corresponding to the maximum distance as malicious, indicating the presence of malicious updates. To ensure no malicious updates go unrecognized, we also consider all model updates corresponding to noise points as malicious model updates.

Upon detecting an anomaly, the trust score of the client corresponding to the malicious model update is halved to reduce its influence on the global model. To prevent an imbalance in the weights, the trust scores of all clients are normalized and used as weights for aggregating local model updates. This ensures that each client has a reasonable contribution to the global model update. This mechanism not only suppresses the impact of malicious clients but also dynamically adjusts the contribution of each client, thereby maintaining the robustness of the global model against model poisoning attacks.

Algorithm 1. DBSCAN Clustering

Input: Dataset D, neighborhood radius eps, minimum points $MinPts$
Output: Clustered dataset
1: $C \leftarrow 0$
2: **for all** point P in dataset D **do**
3:     **if** P is visited **then**
4:         **continue** to next point
5:     **end if**
6:     mark P as visited
7:     $NeighborPts \leftarrow$ all points within P's eps-neighborhood (including P)
8:     **if** $|NeighborPts| < MinPts$ **then**
9:         mark P as NOISE point
10:     **else**
11:         $C \leftarrow C + 1$
12:         add P to cluster C
13:         **for all** point P' in $NeighborPts$ **do**
14:             **if** P' is not visited **then**
15:                 mark P' as visited
16:                 $NeighborPts' \leftarrow$ all points within P''s eps-neighborhood (including P')
17:                 **if** $|NeighborPts'| \geq MinPts$ **then**
18:                     $NeighborPts \leftarrow NeighborPts$ joined with $NeighborPts'$
19:                 **end if**
20:             **end if**
21:             **if** P' does not belong to any cluster **then**
22:                 add P' to cluster C
23:             **end if**
24:         **end for**
25:     **end if**
26: **end for**
27: **return** Clustered dataset

---

5   Experiment

5.1   Experiment Setup

Datasets and Model: This paper uses two datasets, MNIST [7] and FEMNIST [5]. The data among the clients is Non-IID, which more closely reflects real-world scenarios. Both datasets utilize the same CNN model architecture: two convolutional layers, two pooling layers, a flatten layer, a fully connected layer with 512 neurons, and an output layer.

FL Settings: We compare DefMPA with five aggregation algorithms: FedAvg, Median, Krum, Trimmed-Mean, and Simple-Mean. Simple-Mean averages the local model updates from all clients to update the global model. In the federated learning architecture, there is a server and 100 clients, of which 28 are malicious. In each round, all clients participate in training. For the MNIST dataset, the learning rate is set to 0.0002 and the total number of training rounds is 100. For the FEMNIST dataset, the learning rate is set to 0.002 and the total number of training rounds is 300.

Attack Categories: This paper considers three model poisoning attacks: Partial Knowledge (PK) Attack [8], Gaussian Attack, and Scaling Attack [2]. Partial knowledge attack and Gaussian attack are two types of untargeted attacks, whereas scaling attack is a type of targeted attack. Specifically, Partial knowledge attack is used to modify the gradient according to the statistical properties of the aggregated gradient of the malicious client. Gaussian Attack involves adding Gaussian noise to the model update. In Scaling Attack, the attacker injects poisoned data with trigger conditions into the dataset and uses it to train the model. Here, the attacker's objective is to direct multiple sample labels to the same target label. The attacker amplifies the malicious model updates by a certain factor and then uploads them to the server.

Evaluation Metrics: We use Detection Success Rate (DSR), Benign Misclassification Rate (BMR), and Malicious Misclassification Rate (MMR) as detection evaluation metrics. DSR represents the proportion of clients correctly classified as benign or malicious, BMR represents the proportion of benign clients misclassified as malicious, and MMR represents the proportion of malicious clients misclassified as benign. Additionally, we use the accuracy of the global model as the performance evaluation metric, defined as the proportion of correct classifications on the test set.

Parameter Settings: To determine whether a model update is malicious, a threshold of 0.8 is set for the difference between the Euclidean distance of the largest and smallest clusters. If the difference exceeds this threshold, the model updates in the largest Euclidean distance cluster are considered malicious. In the MNIST dataset, the neighborhood radius ϵ for DBSCAN is set to 0.08, while for the FEMNIST dataset, it is set to 0.3. The number of samples in the neighborhood for both datasets is set to 10. Each client's initial trust score is set to 1.

5.2   Main Results

Detection Results: Table 1 demonstrates the feasibility of the detection mechanism (excluding the trust score mechanism). The experimental setup involves the server starting to detect malicious model updates after 40 training rounds, with the attackers launching one of the three types of attacks after 50 rounds. Terminate training upon detection of malicious model updates and record the detection results. As shown in Table 1, our method achieves a Detection Success Rate (DSR) of approximately 90% when combined with the Krum, Median, Trimmed-Mean, and Simple-Mean algorithms on the MNIST and FEMNIST datasets, successfully identifying most malicious model updates. However, the detection method combined with the Krum aggregation algorithm has a relatively lower detection success rate against the Partial Knowledge attack. This is because the malicious clients' updates are designed to closely resemble the benign clients' updates, causing the Krum algorithm to mistakenly select the malicious updates as the closest updates, thereby affecting the detection effectiveness.

Table 1. Detection results (DSR, BMR, MMR) of combined detection methods with four aggregation algorithms against three attacks on MNIST and FEMNIST datasets

Dataset	Attack	Simple-Mean			Krum			Trimmed-Mean			Median		
		DSR	BMR	MMR	DSR	BMR	MMR	DSR	BMR	MMR	DSR	BMR	MMR
MNIST	PK Attack	0.92	0.11	0.00	0.89	0.15	0.00	0.98	0.03	0.00	0.97	0.04	0.00
	Gaussian Attack	0.93	0.10	0.00	0.93	0.10	0.00	0.99	0.01	0.00	1.00	0.00	0.00
	Scaling Attack	1.00	0.00	0.00	1.00	0.00	0.00	0.97	0.04	0.00	0.91	0.13	0.00
FEMNIST	PK Attack	0.99	0.01	0.00	0.88	0.00	0.43	1.00	0.00	0.00	1.00	0.00	0.00
	Gaussian Attack	0.99	0.01	0.00	1.00	0.00	0.00	1.00	0.00	0.00	1.00	0.00	0.00
	Scaling Attack	1.00	0.00	0.00	1.00	0.00	0.00	0.99	0.01	0.00	1.00	0.00	0.00

Global Model Performance: Figure 3 illustrates the changes in global model accuracy for DefMPA and the other five aggregation algorithms under three different attacks as training rounds increase. The first row is based on the MNIST dataset, and the second row is based on the FEMNIST dataset. The first column corresponds to the Partial Knowledge Attack, the second column to the Gaussian Attack, and the third column to the Scaling Attack. Experimental results show that DefMPA demonstrates superior performance and higher robustness against model poisoning attacks compared to the other five aggregation algorithms. Although there is a decline in global model accuracy between rounds 150 and 200 under the Partial Knowledge Attack on the FEMNIST dataset, the accuracy recovers in subsequent rounds.

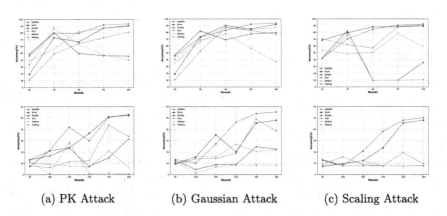

(a) PK Attack   (b) Gaussian Attack   (c) Scaling Attack

Fig. 3. Comparison of global model accuracy under different attacks using DefMPA and other aggregation algorithms on MNIST and FEMNIST datasets.

The Variation in the Number of Malicious Clients: Figure 4 demonstrates the global model accuracy obtained by DefMPA and the five aggregation algorithms under varying numbers of malicious clients, using the Partial Knowledge Attack as an example. The experimental results indicate that even as the number of malicious clients increases, the global model accuracy trained by DefMPA remains stable. In contrast, the accuracy of the global models trained with FedAvg, Median, Trimmed-Mean, and Simple-Mean algorithms shows a noticeable decline as malicious clients increase.

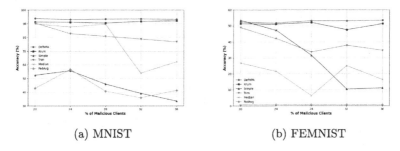

(a) MNIST   (b) FEMNIST

Fig. 4. Global model accuracy under varying numbers of malicious clients with Partial Knowledge Attack.

No Attack: In scenarios without attacks, the global model accuracy on the MNIST dataset using DefMPA and the simple-mean algorithm is 94.10% and 94.07%, respectively. On the FEMNIST dataset, the global model accuracy using DefMPA and the simple-mean algorithm is 52.43% and 52.78%, respectively. These results indicate that the detection method of DefMPA does not impact the performance of the global model in the absence of attacks.

6   Conclusion

This paper proposes a defense detection method called DefMPA, which determines the presence of malicious model updates in client uploads based on the consistency of model updates before server aggregation. It reduces the trust scores of clients identified as malicious, thereby diminishing the impact of malicious updates on the global model. Experiments demonstrate that our defense method can distinguish a large number of malicious updates. Compared to five aggregation algorithms, our method maintains the stability of global model performance even as the number of malicious clients increases, providing a practical solution for defending against model poisoning attacks. For future research, optimization based on DefMPA's defense method can be pursued to explore more sophisticated model update detection algorithms to counter increasingly complex and covert security threats.

Acknowledgement. This work is supported by the National Natural Science Foundation of China (Grant No.62176122), Research on Edge Federated Learning Security Mechanisms for Unmanned Swarm Systems, AI-Based Future IoT Technologies and Services, and National Natural Science Foundation project, A3 Foresight Program of NSFC(Grant No.62061146002).

References

1. Awan, S., Luo, B., Li, F.: Contra: defending against poisoning attacks in federated learning. In: Computer Security–ESORICS 2021: 26th European Symposium on Research in Computer Security, Darmstadt, Germany, October 4–8, 2021, Proceedings, Part I 26, pp. 455–475. Springer (2021)
2. Bagdasaryan, E., Veit, A., Hua, Y., Estrin, D., Shmatikov, V.: How to backdoor federated learning. In: International Conference on Artificial Intelligence and Statistics, pp. 2938–2948. PMLR (2020)
3. Blanchard, P., El Mhamdi, E.M., Guerraoui, R., Stainer, J.: Machine learning with adversaries: byzantine tolerant gradient descent. Adv. Neural Inf. Process. Syst. **30** (2017)
4. Byrd, R.H., Nocedal, J., Schnabel, R.B.: Representations of quasi-newton matrices and their use in limited memory methods. Math. Program. **63**(1), 129–156 (1994)
5. Caldas, S., et al.: Leaf: A benchmark for federated settings. arXiv preprint arXiv:1812.01097 (2018)
6. Cao, X., Fang, M., Liu, J., Gong, N.Z.: Fltrust: Byzantine-robust federated learning via trust bootstrapping. arXiv preprint arXiv:2012.13995 (2020)
7. Deng, L.: The MNIST database of handwritten digit images for machine learning research [best of the web]. IEEE Signal Process. Mag. **29**(6), 141–142 (2012)
8. Fang, M., Cao, X., Jia, J., Gong, N.: Local model poisoning attacks to {Byzantine-Robust} federated learning. In: 29th USENIX security symposium (USENIX Security 20), pp. 1605–1622 (2020)
9. Gupta, A., Luo, T., Ngo, M.V., Das, S.K.: Long-short history of gradients is all you need: detecting malicious and unreliable clients in federated learning. In: European Symposium on Research in Computer Security, pp. 445–465. Springer (2022)
10. Jagielski, M., Oprea, A., Biggio, B., Liu, C., Nita-Rotaru, C., Li, B.: Manipulating machine learning: poisoning attacks and countermeasures for regression learning. In: 2018 IEEE symposium on security and privacy (SP), pp. 19–35. IEEE (2018)
11. Lang, S.: A Second Course in Calculus. Addison-Wesley series in mathematics, Addison-Wesley Publishing Company (1968). https://books.google.com/books?id=ry7vAAAAMAAJ
12. Liu, B., Lv, N., Guo, Y., Li, Y.: Recent advances on federated learning: a systematic survey. Neurocomputing 128019 (2024)
13. McMahan, B., Moore, E., Ramage, D., Hampson, S., y Arcas, B.A.: Communication-efficient learning of deep networks from decentralized data. In: Artificial Intelligence and Statistics, pp. 1273–1282. PMLR (2017)
14. Schubert, E., Sander, J., Ester, M., Kriegel, H.P., Xu, X.: DBSCAN revisited, revisited: why and how you should (still) use DBSCAN. ACM Trans. Database Syst. (TODS) **42**(3), 1–21 (2017)
15. Shejwalkar, V., Houmansadr, A.: Manipulating the byzantine: optimizing model poisoning attacks and defenses for federated learning. In: NDSS (2021)
16. Shirvani, G., Ghasemshirazi, S., Beigzadeh, B.: Federated learning: Attacks, defenses, opportunities, and challenges. arXiv preprint arXiv:2403.06067 (2024)

17. Wang, Y., Zhu, T., Chang, W., Shen, S., Ren, W.: Model poisoning defense on federated learning: a validation based approach. In: International Conference on Network and System Security, pp. 207–223. Springer (2020)
18. Xia, G., Chen, J., Yu, C., Ma, J.: Poisoning attacks in federated learning: a survey. IEEE Access **11**, 10708–10722 (2023)
19. Xie, Y., Fang, M., Gong, N.Z.: Poisonedfl: Model poisoning attacks to federated learning via multi-round consistency. arXiv preprint arXiv:2404.15611 (2024)
20. Yin, D., Chen, Y., Kannan, R., Bartlett, P.: Byzantine-robust distributed learning: towards optimal statistical rates. In: International Conference on Machine Learning, pp. 5650–5659. Pmlr (2018)
21. Zhang, Z., Cao, X., Jia, J., Gong, N.Z.: Fldetector: defending federated learning against model poisoning attacks via detecting malicious clients. In: Proceedings of the 28th ACM SIGKDD Conference on Knowledge Discovery and Data Mining, pp. 2545–2555 (2022)

SDDRM: An Optimization Algorithm for Localized Differential Privacy Based on Data Sensitivity Differences

Li Bingbing, Shi Peizhong[(✉)], Gu Chunsheng, Zhang Yan, Jing Zhengjun, and Zhao Quanyu

Jiangsu University of Technology, Changzhou 213001, Jiangsu, China
spz0812@jsut.edu.cn

Abstract. Local Differential Privacy (LDP) has advantages of relying on no trusted third parties. However, if the sensitivity of data is not considered, which will lead to imbalanced privacy protection, lower data accuracy, and lower utility. For privacy sensitivity differences among the data, we propose an optimized algorithm called Sensitivity Dynamic Difference Report Mechanism (SDDRM). In SDDRM algorithm, the dynamic difference report mechanism is adopted to allocate different privacy budgets for sensitive and non-sensitive data, which can provide stronger privacy protection for sensitive data and effectively reduce noise interference for non-sensitive data. In other words, the accuracy of data is improved while the data privacy is satisfied. Finally, experiments are conducted on two real datasets, Stocks and Syn^B, and an optimal selection method is given through different Settings of privacy budget allocation, which can achieve the balance between data privacy protection and data accuracy. Comparative experiments show that the loss indicators are significantly reduced by the optimized SDDRM algorithm (compared with the DDRM algorithm, the percentage of reduction is between 5% and 45%), which confirm that the optimized SDDRM algorithm can improve the data accuracy while protecting the data privacy.

Keywords: Local Differential Privacy · Data Sensitivity · Dynamic Difference Report Mechanism · Privacy Budgets · Loss Indicators · Noise Addition

1 Introduction

With the rapid advancement of information technology and the proliferation of big data, data privacy has emerged as a critical issue in recent years. While data can provide valuable insights for machine learning [1–3], business analytics, and other applications, improper processing and use of data may lead to the disclosure of users' private information. Therefore, how to protect personal privacy in the process of mining and using data has become an urgent problem to be solved.

Differential privacy, first proposed by Dwork et al. [4] in 2006, has been widely recognized as a powerful privacy protection technology. Centralized Differential Privacy (CDP) is a common form of differential privacy. Its core idea is to confuse data by adding

W. Li et al. (Eds.): EISA 2024, CCIS 2266, pp. 192–207, 2025.
https://doi.org/10.1007/978-3-031-80419-9_14

random noise during the generation, distribution and use of data, so that attackers cannot accurately identify the private information of individuals or groups. However, in the CDP model, reliance on trusted third-party data collectors is unrealistic in many practical application scenarios. Local Differential Privacy (LDP [5]) means that data is directly noisy on the client side, ensuring that personal information is protected before it leaves the user's device, without the need to rely on trusted third-party data collectors.

LDP offers a robust and mathematically rigorous framework for privacy protection, which has been successfully designed and implemented in various practical scenarios [6]. Jain et al. [7] demonstrate that Local Differential Privacy (LDP) can be applied in various contexts, including healthcare [8] and health data analysis [9]. However, most existing LDP schemes fail to adequately address the sensitivity of the data [10] and usually provide uniform privacy protection for all data types. Murakami et al. [11] attempt to differentiate between sensitive and non-sensitive data by introducing Utility-optimized Local Differential Privacy (ULDP), applying distinct levels of privacy protection to each. But this approach is not suitable for scenarios where user data contains both sensitive and non-sensitive values. The Dynamic Difference Report Mechanism (DDRM) [12] is a data collection method supporting Localized Differential Privacy, which aims to provide valuable statistical information for data collectors while protecting user privacy. The DDRM algorithm follows the node selection process and does not allocate a privacy budget for insensitive data (i.e., 0 values), but instead randomly perturb these values to − 1 or 1 with a probability of 0.5. Conversely, for sensitive data (i.e., −1 or 1), the privacy budget is utilized, and the data is perturbed accordingly. A notable limitation of the algorithm is its treatment of 0 values, although these values do not consume the privacy budget, the addition of significant noise affects the accuracy of the data.

To solve the above problems, adapting the core idea of the suWheel algorithm [13], this paper proposes an optimization of Localized Differential Privacy algorithm called SDDRM (Sensitivity Dynamic Difference Report Mechanism) based on data sensitivity differences. The SDDRM algorithm employs a more flexible approach to noise addition, tailoring the perturbation strength to the actual sensitivity of the data. Specifically, data values of −1 and 1 are treated as sensitive, while value of 0 is considered as non-sensitive. Distinct privacy budgets are allocated to each data type, which can enhance data availability. The main contributions of this paper are summarized as following three aspects.

- We proposed an optimization of localized differential privacy algorithm SDDRM based on data sensitivity differences.
- The SDDRM algorithm is theoretically analyzed, and it is proved that SDDRM satisfies the conditions of local differential privacy protection.
- Experiments are performed on two real datasets, Stocks and SynB, where an optimal selection method is given for achieving the balance between data privacy protection and data accuracy. At the same time, compared with the DDRM algorithm, it is confirmed that the optimization SDDRM algorithm can protect data privacy and improve data accuracy.

2 Related Works

Dwork et al. [14] propose a systematic method for determining the amount of noise by adjusting the noise size based on the sensitivity of the data, although computing data sensitivity can be challenging, particularly in cases involving high-dimensional or complex data. Shiyu Yin et al. [15] explore methods to optimize the utility of joint distribution estimation for 2D data within an LDP framework by leveraging differences in data sensitivity, yet the coarse categorization of sensitivities may not adequately represent real-world scenarios. Minami et al. [16] study Gibbs' posterior with a convex and Lipschitz loss function that accommodates unbounded sensitivities, highlighting limitations in quantifying privacy preservation. Johnson et al. [17] introduce the elastic sensitivity approach to approximate the local sensitivity of queries and develope the FLEX system to implement differential privacy, though improvements are needed to generalize this approach across diverse database environments and query types. Kobbi Nissim et al. [18] investigate the application of differential privacy to establish that a query with high concentration bounds for sensitivity functions, proposing conditions for cases that satisfy these bounds under specific distributions and functions. Despite providing a theoretical framework, practical applications are often hindered by function specificity and conditionality. To address these challenges, Lee and Clifton [19] explore methods for selecting an appropriate privacy budget, providing suggestions and techniques for determining this budget, though the alignment with actual privacy protection standards remains ambiguous. Kifer and Machanavajjhala [20] introduce the Pufferfish framework, which designs a differential privacy protection mechanism tailored to varying needs based on data sensitivity and application characteristics. This mechanism primarily focuses on the analysis of the framework without detailing a concrete implementation for data sensitivity. Consequently, the optimization algorithm based on data sensitivity proposed is essential. The design and implementation process is outlined based on the DDRM algorithm [12], with its privacy protection and accuracy validated through experimental verification.

3 Preliminaries and Problem Definition

3.1 Local Differential Privacy

LDP [21] is a variation of differential privacy, which provides privacy protection for each data point at the data collection stage. The core idea is to allow users to locally add random noise to original data and send the obfuscated data to the data collector. Data collectors cannot obtain the original data from the beginning, providing stronger privacy protection for users. Such a mechanism enhances user privacy by ensuring that the collector receives only the altered dataset. The mathematical definition of LDP is as follows.

Definition 1. (ε-LDP [22]). *A randomized algorithm f satisfies ε-LDP, where $\varepsilon \geq 0$, if and only if for any pair of input values $x, x\prime \in X$ and for any possible output $S \subseteq Range(f)$.*

$$Pr[f(x) \in s] \leq e^{\varepsilon} Pr[f(x\prime) \in s]. \tag{1}$$

The parameter ε is a pivotal factor, which determines the privacy budget and makes a tradeoff between privacy protection and data utility. The smaller ε is involved with the addition of less noise, which can provide stronger privacy protection. For the larger ε, its privacy protection will become weaker. Compared with traditional differential privacy, LDP does not rely on a centralized trusted entity by adding noise, which reduces the risk of centralized data storage and processing, such as data leakage, insider attacks [23], or other security threats [24]. LDP provides stronger privacy protection, where each user adds noise locally and sends the perturbed data. Consequently, this prevents data collectors and analysts from accessing pristine data, which effectively provides privacy protection for users.

Property 1. (*Sequential Composition* [25]). *Given a dataset x and a set of m algorithms* $\{f_1, f_2, ..., f_m\}$, *where each algorithm* $f_i (1 \leq i \leq m)$ *satisfies* ε_i-*LDP. Then, when applying all m algorithms* $\{f_1, f_2, ..., f_m\}$ *to the same dataset x, the sequence of* $\{f_1(x), f_2(x), ..., f_m(x)\}$ *satisfies* $(\sum_{i=1}^{m} \varepsilon_i)$-*LDP.*

Table 1. Notations.

Notation	Description
ε	the privacy budget
n	total participants
u_i	user at position i
d_i	sequential data for user u_i
d_i^t	the true value at timestamp t for user u_i
$\tilde{v}_i^t$	the perturbed value at timestamp t for user u_i
$f^t, \hat{f}^t$	the true/estimated frequency of '1' at timestamp t
c_i^t	the interval difference between consecutive data entries
R_i^t	storage of key nodes in the timestamp indexed differential tree
h_i^t	index of node selected by user u_i in set R_i^t at timestamp t
k	parameter for distributing privacy budge

3.2 Problem Description

At timestamp t, the distance between the estimated frequency and the true frequency, denoted by $Dis(t)$, is minimized as follows:

$$Dis(t) = \sqrt{\sum_{m \in M} |\hat{f}_m^t - f_m^t|^2}, \tag{2}$$

where M is the domain of values. Under consideration for LDP and sensitivity difference, we aim to solve the problem of continuous frequency estimation for discrete data.
While ensuring the privacy of individual data, we discuss how to realize the frequency
estimation of data in the dynamic data environment. Our approach involves a setting
with individual users and an untrusted data collector. Each user $u_i (i \in [1, n])$ possesses
a private time series $d_i = [d_i^1, ..., d_i^t, ...]$,, with values restricted to (0, 1). The data collector aims to estimate the frequency of '1' across all users at each timestamp t. The
ultimate goal is to improve the accuracy of this frequency estimation. This ensures both
the privacy and security of user data. Table 1 summarizes the notations.

4   Sensitivity-Based Optimization Algorithm: SDDRM

4.1   SDDRM Algorithm Overview

Based on the dynamic differential reporting mechanism, we consider the difference in
data sensitivity and evaluate the sensitivity of data in terms of privacy protection [26]. For
example, some data with inherent importance and higher sensitivity compromise more
user privacy. Consequently, our approach enhances privacy protection by allocating a
smaller privacy budget, which adds more noise to sensitive data. For non-sensitive data, a
large privacy budget is allocated to reduce the impact of noise and improve the accuracy
of the data. Throughout the data aggregation process, the privacy budget designated for
sensitive data is utilized. This ensures comprehensive privacy maintenance.

4.2   Design of the SDDRM Algorithm

4.2.1   Optimization of the Perturbation Algorithm

For ensuring data privacy protection, data are classified as sensitive or non-sensitive based
on their attributes and sensitivity levels. Consider a node value denoted by v, where the
value range of v is $\{-1, 0, 1\}$. Data with $v = 0$ are considered non-sensitive, whereas data
with $v = 1$ or $v = -1$ are classified as sensitive. The privacy budget quantifies the degree of
privacy loss incurred during data release. The metric ensures protection of data privacy
and optimal utilization of constrained resources, which sets definitive boundaries on the
privacy budget. This facilitates efficient data querying and analysis. At the point of data
perturbation, privacy budgets are differentially allocated based on the classification of
data. For sensitive data, its own privacy value is higher, and the allocated privacy budget
is smaller to strengthen the protection (denoted by ε_1). Conversely, non-sensitive data,
with lower privacy value, is allocated with a larger privacy budget (denoted by ε_2). When
the sensitive data are perturbed to 1 (or -1), the probability is $\frac{1}{2} + \frac{v}{2} \cdot \frac{e^\varepsilon - 1}{e^\varepsilon + 1} (or \frac{1}{2} - \frac{v}{2} \cdot \frac{e^\varepsilon - 1}{e^\varepsilon + 1})$.
After the perturbation, the difference tree structure and its nodes are used to represent the
corresponding data. Each user sends the perturbed value $\tilde{v}_i^t$ along with its indexed position
in the difference tree h_i^t to the data collector. The optimized perturbation algorithm is
given in Algorithm 1, which ensures effective privacy protection without sacrificing data
quality.

Algorithm 1: Optimized Perturbation Algorithm

    Input   : Selected value $v \in \{-1, 0, 1\}$, privacy budgets $\varepsilon_1, \varepsilon_2$
    Output: Perturbed value $\tilde{v}_i^t$
1   **if** $v = 1 \; or \; -1$ **then**
2 | $\varepsilon = \varepsilon_1$
3   **else**
4 | $\varepsilon = \varepsilon_2$
5   **end**

6   $\tilde{v}_i^t = \begin{cases} 1, & \frac{1}{2} + \frac{v}{2} \cdot \frac{e^\varepsilon - 1}{e^\varepsilon + 1} & \text{// probability of perturbation being 1} \\ -1, & \frac{1}{2} - \frac{v}{2} \cdot \frac{e^\varepsilon - 1}{e^\varepsilon + 1} & \text{// probability of perturbation being -1} \end{cases}$

7   **return** $\tilde{v}_i^t$

4.2.2 Design of the SDDRM Algorithm

As shown in Algorithm 2, we give the an optimization for LDP based on data sensitivity differences. Before data collection, the overall privacy budget ε is evenly distributed to each operation, and its value of privacy budget is calculated as $\varepsilon_0 = \frac{\varepsilon_1}{k}$ (Line 1). During the initialization phase, each user u_i sets its respective $d_i^0 = 0, R_i^0[1] = 0[1] = 0$, and initializes a counter as $\alpha_i = 0$, which can count the number of perturbations that produce non-zero values (Lines 4-6). User u_i updates the difference tree, known as the R_i^t, by computing the data variance c_i^t (Lines 7-8). Subsequently, the node index h_i^t and its corresponding value v_i^t are received by the user as a result of the node selection procedure (Line 9). The procedure implements the optimized perturbation technique detailed in Algorithm 1. Specifically, the parameter ε is assigned to ε_2 when the node value equals zero (Line 11), and ε_0 when the node value is non-zero (Line 13). Decisions about counter updates and variable assignments are made contingent upon the values of a_i and v_i^t. The user updates counter a_i (Line 16), sets v_i^t to 0 (Line 18) and assigns ε_2 to ε (Line 19). The user u_i obtains the value v_i^t by applying the perturbation method described in Algorithm 1, with the designated privacy budget ε (Line 21). The user u_i forwards $\tilde{v}_i^t$ to the data collector alongside the node index h_i^t (Line 22). For the estimation of the frequency $\hat{f}^1, ..., \hat{f}^T$, the data collector employs the calibration factor $\frac{e^{\varepsilon_0}+1}{e^{\varepsilon_0}-1}$ to adjust the perturbed data (Line 25).

Algorithm 2: Optimization Algorithm SDDRM

Input : All users' time series datasets $\{d_1, ..., d_n\}$, privacy budgets ε_1 and ε_2, allocation parameter k, time series length T

Output: Estimated frequencies $\hat{f}^1, ..., \hat{f}^T$

1 Set $\varepsilon_0 = \frac{\varepsilon_1}{k}$
2 **for** t *from 1 to T* **do**
    // User side
3   **for** *each user u_i (where $i \in [1, n]$)* **do**
4   **if** $t == 1$ **then**
5 | Initialize d_i^0 to 0, $R_i^0[1]$ to 0, α_i to 0
6   **end**
7   Compute $c_i^t = d_i^t - d_i^{t-1}$
8   Use R_i^{t-1}, c_i^t, t to update R_i^t
9   Select node from R_i^t and t to get (v_i^t, h_i^t)
10   **if** $v_i^t == 0$ **then**
        // Non-sensitive data
11 | $\varepsilon = \varepsilon_2$
12   **else**
        // Sensitive data
13 | $\varepsilon = \varepsilon_0$
14   **end**
15   **if** $\alpha_i < k$ *and* $v_i^t \neq 0$ **then**
16 | $\alpha_i = \alpha_i + 1$
17   **else**
18 | Set v_i^t to 0
19 | $\varepsilon = \varepsilon_2$
20   **end**
21   Perturb v_i^t using the corresponding ε to obtain $\tilde{v}_i^t$
22   Report $\tilde{v}_i^t$ and h_i^t to the data collector
23   **end**
    // Collector side
24   **for** *each user u_i (where $i \in [1, n]$)* **do**
25 | Calibrate using v_i^t and ε_0 to get v_i^t
26   **end**
27   Estimate frequency to get $\hat{f}^t$
28 **end**
29 **return** $\hat{f}^1, ..., \hat{f}^T$

4.2.3 Selection of Parameter ε_2

The privacy budget ε reflects the extent of data privacy protection, where a lower value indicates enhanced protection. When dealing with sensitive and non-sensitive data, it is crucial to properly allocate the privacy budget to balance the privacy protection and utility of the data. This necessity arises from the need to achieve an optimal balance, which involves both safeguarding data privacy and maintaining the utility of the data.

Sensitive data is assigned a smaller privacy budget to provide stronger privacy safeguards. Non-sensitive data is afforded a larger privacy budget due to its lesser privacy concerns. A scaling factor α is employed to ensure that the privacy budget is allocated adequately between sensitive and non-sensitive data. So, the privacy budget ε_2 can be determined as follows:

$$\varepsilon_2 = \alpha * \varepsilon_1. \tag{3}$$

The privacy budget for non-sensitive data is α ($\alpha > 1$) times larger than that for sensitive data. Therefore, experiments with different α values can be set to analyze their impact on related performance indicators. The optimal α value is used for achieving a balance between privacy protection strength and data accuracy.

4.3 Privacy Analysis of the SDDRM Algorithm

An optimization strategy is employed to calibrate the trade-off between data accuracy and user privacy. This is achieved by differentially allocating the privacy budget. The allocation is based on data sensitivity. The differential privacy assurance that the SDDRM algorithm provides is formalized in Theorem 1.

Theorem 1. *Given privacy budgets ε_1 and ε_2, SDDRM satisfies localized differential privacy for continuous frequency estimation.*

Proof. Let v_i^t denote the node value selected by user u_i, and $\tilde{s} = \{(\tilde{v}^1, h^1), \cdots, (\tilde{v}^T, h^T)\}$ represent the set of perturbation reports obtained by users. Independently of v_i^t actual value, it will be reset to 0 if the set $\{v_i^1, \cdots, v_i^{t-1}\}$ already contains k non-zero values. For any two users u_i, u_j, the initial k values $v_i^1, \cdots, v_i^k$ for user u_i are non-zero,while the subsequent k values $v_j^{k+1}, \cdots, v_j^{2k}$ for user u_j are non-zero. Hence, $\frac{Pr\{f(x_i)=\tilde{s}\}}{Pr\{f(x_j)=\tilde{s}\}} = \frac{Pr\{\tilde{v}^1|v_i^1\}\cdots Pr\{\tilde{v}^k|v_i^k\}}{Pr\{\tilde{v}^{k+1}|v_j^{k+1}\}\cdots Pr\{\tilde{v}^{2k}|v_j^{2k}\}}$, When $\tilde{v}^a = v_i^a$, $a \in \{1, \cdots, k\}$, and $\tilde{v}^b \neq v_j^b$, $a \in \{k+1, \cdots, 2k\}$, the above probability can be maximized. The exact formula is stated for both sensitive and non-sensitive data in the following sections.

- For sensitive data, localized differential privacy at level ε_1/k safeguards each user's actions at every time step. Equation (4) demonstrates how localized differential privacy at level secures users' sensitive information. This security is maintained throughout the data collection process. This reflects the inherent crosstalk properties of differential privacy.

$$\frac{Pr\{f(x_i) = \tilde{s}\}}{Pr\{f(x_j) = \tilde{s}\}} \leq \frac{(\frac{1}{2} + \frac{1}{2} \cdot \frac{e^{\varepsilon_1/k}-1}{e^{\varepsilon_1/k}+1}) \cdots (\frac{1}{2} + \frac{1}{2}\frac{e^{\varepsilon_1/k}-1}{e^{\varepsilon_1/k}+1})}{(\frac{1}{2} - \frac{1}{2} \cdot \frac{e^{\varepsilon_1/k}-1}{e^{\varepsilon_1/k}+1}) \cdots (\frac{1}{2} - \frac{1}{2} \cdot \frac{e^{\varepsilon_1/k}-1}{e^{\varepsilon_1/k}+1})} = \frac{\frac{e^{\varepsilon_1/k}}{e^{\varepsilon_1/k}+1} \cdots \frac{e^{\varepsilon_1/k}}{e^{\varepsilon_1/k}+1}}{\frac{1}{e^{\varepsilon_1/k}+1} \cdots \frac{1}{e^{\varepsilon_1/k}+1}} = e^{\varepsilon_1}$$

(4)

- For non-sensitive data, *(T-k)* the user's operations at each time step are protected by localized differential privacy at level ε_2. According to the crosstalk nature of differential privacy, the user's sensitive information is protected. This protection is achieved by localized differential privacy, as shown in Eq. (5).

$$\frac{Pr\{f(x_i) = \tilde{s}\}}{Pr\{f(x_j) = \tilde{s}\}} \leq \frac{(\frac{1}{2} + \frac{1}{2} \cdot \frac{e^{\varepsilon_2}-1}{e^{\varepsilon_2}+1}) \cdots (\frac{1}{2} + \frac{1}{2}\frac{e^{\varepsilon_2}-1}{e^{\varepsilon_1}+1})}{(\frac{1}{2} - \frac{1}{2} \cdot \frac{e^{\varepsilon_2}-1}{e^{\varepsilon_2}+1}) \cdots (\frac{1}{2} - \frac{1}{2} \cdot \frac{e^{\varepsilon_2}-1}{e^{\varepsilon_2}+1})} = \frac{\frac{e^{\varepsilon_2}}{e^{\varepsilon_2}+1} \cdots \frac{e^{\varepsilon_2}}{e^{\varepsilon_2}+1}}{\frac{1}{e^{\varepsilon_2}+1} \cdots \frac{1}{e^{\varepsilon_2}+1}} = e^{(T-k)*\varepsilon_2}$$

(5)

Consequently, the SDDRM algorithm complies with the requirements of localized differential privacy.

5 Experiments and Results Analysis

5.1 Experimental Environment

This section details a series of experiments designed to evaluate the performance and effectiveness of our proposed SDDRM algorithm. Experimental Environment: The tests were conducted on a system equipped with an Intel(R) Core(TM) i7-7700HQ CPU @ 2.80 GHz and 8 GB RAM, and running Windows 10 operating system. All the compared algorithms are implemented in the MATLAB programming language.

5.2 Performance Metrics

For each time point t, the distance $Dis(t)$ between the true frequency and the estimated frequency is calculated by Eq. (2). To validate the effectiveness of the SDDRM and DDRM, three performance metrics are introduced [12]: l_1 loss, l_2 loss, and the infinite norm l_∞, as detailed in Eq. (6).

$$
\begin{aligned}
l_1 &= Dis(1) + ... + Dis(T) \\
l_2 &= \sqrt{Dis(1)^2 + ... + Dis(T)^2} \\
l_\infty &= \max(Dis(1), ..., Dis(T))
\end{aligned}
\tag{6}
$$

For robustness evaluation, the infinite norm l_∞ serves as the primary assessment of the algorithm's performance in the worst-case scenario. In contrast, the l_1 quantifies the absolute error between the model predictions and the true values. The l_2 evaluates performance from a global perspective by calculating the cumulative error across the entire time series T. These three metrics constitute a comprehensive evaluation framework, which can not only reflect the performance of correlative algorithms in a specific situation, but also provide their important information about the performance. In the experiments, the results of l_2 and l_∞ loss are mainly used for comparative analysis.

5.3 Experimental Setup

We compare SDDRM and DDRM on the real dataset Stocks and Syn^B by varying privacy budget. As shown in Table 2, 'Stocks' refers to a dataset of historical daily closing prices of stocks, 'Syn^B' pertains to a binary synthetic dataset, 'Time' denotes the time domain, and 'DB' indicates the time series data.

Table 2. Experimental datasets.

Dataset Name	Time(T)	DB
Stocks	16	169879
Stocks	32	169879
Syn^B	16	100000
Syn^B	32	100000

5.4 Analysis of Experimental Results

5.4.1 Analysis of ε_2 Optimal Selection

In the experiments, ε_2 denotes the privacy budget for non-sensitive data. Non-sensitive data requires a larger privacy allocation. Therefore, privacy budgets are adjusted accordingly. Specifically, budgets of 1.5 ε_1, 2 ε_1, 3 ε_1, and 4 ε_1 are utilized. For the Stocks and Syn^B datasets, the time step at $T = 16$ is selected as representative.

Figure 1 presents four plots that demonstrate the effects of varying multiples of the privacy budget. These variations impact the performance metrics l_∞ or l_2 for the Stocks and Syn^B datasets at $T = 16$. Each plot features four curves corresponding to different multiples of the privacy budget. The curves exhibit a downward trend as the privacy budget increases. This indicates that data accuracy improves as the intensity of privacy protection is reduced. As the privacy budget is further increased, the rate of decrease in performance metrics diminishes. As the privacy budget increases, the improvements in data accuracy show a trend of diminishing significance. The curve displays the lowest performance index at a privacy budget of 2 ε_1. This achieves an optimal balance between data privacy protection and accuracy. The experimental results indicate that the most effective balance is achieved at a privacy budget of 2 ε_1.

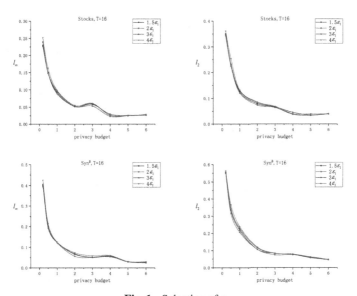

Fig. 1. Selection of ε_2

Table 3 shows the $l_0 + l_2$ loss values under different privacy budget multiples at $T = 16$ on the Stocks and Syn^B datasets. As shown in Figs. 2 and 3, at a multiple of 2 ε_1, the data show that the loss value is lower than that of 1.5 ε_1, 3 ε_1, and 4 ε_1. This indicates that a privacy budget of 2 ε_1 achieves the best balance between privacy protection and data accuracy in both datasets. Increasing the privacy budget beyond 2 ε_1 does not consistently reduce the $l_0 + l_2$ value. Higher privacy budgets do not significantly improve data accuracy. This may result in unnecessary privacy loss. Conversely, a smaller privacy budget (e.g., 1.5 ε_1) may compromise data accuracy through excessive privacy protection. A larger budget (e.g., 3 ε_1 or 4 ε_1) may weaken privacy protection. Therefore, 2 ε_1 is determined as the optimal privacy budget. It effectively balances utility and privacy considerations.

Table 3. Data on $l_\infty + l_2$ loss of different multiples of ε_1 in the dataset.

privacy budget ε_1	Stocks,$T = 16,l_\infty + l_2$				Syn^B,$T = 16,l_\infty + l_2$			
	1.5 ε_1	2 ε_1	3 ε_1	4 ε_1	1.5 ε_1	2 ε_1	3 ε_1	4 ε_1
0.2	0.5779	0.5702	0.5922	0.6134	1.1339	1.1202	1.1497	1.1778
0.5	0.3803	0.3728	0.3824	0.416	0.7148	0.688	0.7252	0.7819
1	0.2173	0.2105	0.2256	0.2317	0.4368	0.4179	0.4548	0.4713
2	0.1309	0.1258	0.1359	0.1412	0.2375	0.2315	0.2518	0.2611
3	0.1258	0.118	0.1258	0.1306	0.2094	0.1925	0.2084	0.2146
4	0.065	0.0614	0.0758	0.0678	0.1419	0.1369	0.1547	0.1463
5	0.06	0.0592	0.0611	0.0663	0.1186	0.1155	0.1206	0.1293
6	0.0677	0.0662	0.0694	0.0673	0.1133	0.1113	0.1154	0.1142

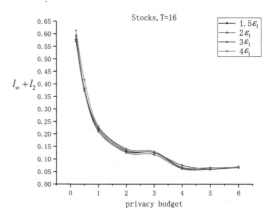

Fig. 2. Data on $l_\infty + l_2$ loss of different multiples of ε_1 on Stocks in the dataset.

5.4.2 Performance Comparison Analysis

Comparative experiments that involve SDDRM and DDRM are conducted on the Stocks and Syn^B datasets. These experiments cover timeframes $T = 16$ and $T = 32$, with privacy budgets ranging from 0.2 to 6. The results in terms of l_2 and l_∞ losses are shown in Figs. 4 and 5.

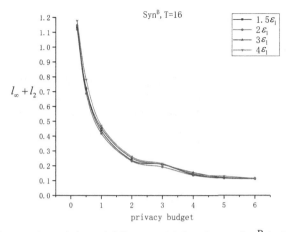

Fig. 3. Data on $l_\infty + l_2$ loss of different multiples of ε_1 on Syn^B in the dataset.

Figure 4 illustrates the impact of different privacy budgets on the l_2 performance metrics of the two algorithms. As the privacy budget is elevated, the l_2 losses of both SDDRM and DDRM decrease. The l_2 loss of SDDRM is lower than that of DDRM in all privacy settings. This difference is especially noticeable when the privacy budget is low. Although the loss values of both algorithms gradually converge with increasing budget, SDDRM consistently provides better utility. This is observed across the range

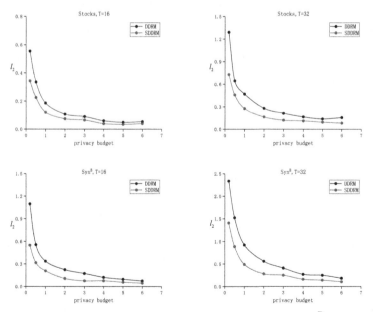

Fig. 4. l_2 loss of DDRM and SDDRM on Stocks and Syn^B.

of 0.2 to 6. Figure 5 shows the impact on l_∞ performance metrics, where SDDRM also outperforms DDRM.

From the aforementioned experimental results and analysis, it is evident that SDDRM has lower loss. This occurs under the same privacy budget, which is in comparison to DDRM. The l_2, l_∞ loss metrics demonstrate lower values across a privacy budget range of 0.2 to 6. This signifies that SDDRM affords enhanced data privacy protection with diminished errors. Consequently, SDDRM strikes a well-defined balance between user privacy protection and data accuracy. It simultaneously safeguards data privacy and enhances data utility. This achievement is largely attributed to the consideration of data sensitivity in SDDRM. Also, for the allocation of its privacy budget, it is beneficial to improve the accuracy of data and estimation results.

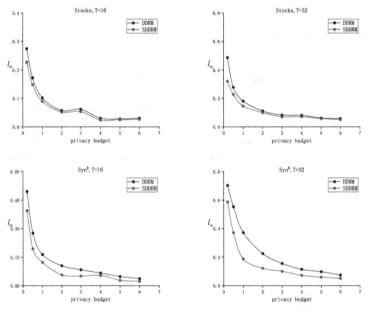

Fig. 5. l_∞ loss of DDRM and SDDRM on Stocks and Syn^B.

Compared with DDRM, SDDRM achieves significantly lower l_2, l_∞ loss metrics on both Stocks and Syn^B datasets. This performance improvement can be quantified in terms of loss reduction percentage, as shown in Table 4. The table shows the l_2, l_∞ loss percentage reduction for SDDRM compared to DDRM. This comparison is made under different privacy budgets. For instance, on the Stocks dataset when $T = 16$ and the privacy budget is 0.2, SDDRM shows significant reductions. It reduces by 38% in l_2 performance metric. In l_∞ performance metric, it reduces by 19% compared to DDRM. This indicates that SDDRM significantly lowers the mean errors. It also reduces the maximum errors compared to DDRM. Improvements in SDDRM are especially important for lower privacy budgets. This is because under lower privacy budgets, data privacy requirements are higher. SDDRM can make more efficient use of the limited privacy budget to maximize data accuracy. As the privacy budget increases, the performance difference between the two algorithms decreases, but SDDRM retains its advantage.

The results of the study show that the percentage reduction loss ranges from 5% to 45%. Compared with DDRM, SDDRM has better performance, because it safeguards data privacy and enhances data accuracy more effectively. SDDRM effectively addresses the balance problem of privacy protection and data accuracy.

Table 4. Percentage reduction in l_2, l_∞ loss of algorithm SDDRM compared to algorithm DDRM on Stocks and Syn^B.

privacy budget ε_1	Stocks				Syn^B			
	$T = 16$		$T = 32$		$T = 16$		$T = 32$	
	l_2	l_∞	l_2	l_∞	l_2	l_∞	l_2	l_∞
0.2	38%	19%	43%	34%	45%	20%	39%	16%
0.5	32%	14%	29%	18%	43%	29%	40%	33%
1	34%	11%	41%	18%	38%	25%	44%	45%
2	31%	10%	41%	10%	44%	44%	45%	45%
3	27%	13%	43%	14%	43%	39%	36%	35%
4	34%	22%	32%	12%	37%	18%	40%	37%
5	29%	11%	31%	5%	40%	41%	41%	39%
6	25%	12%	43%	13%	38%	36%	42%	30%

6 Conclusion

Combining the local differential privacy protection mechanism and the sensitivity differentiation, we aim to provide privacy protection and improve data accuracy by protecting data with different sensitivity with different intensities. In this paper, an optimized algorithm called SDDRM is proposed for sensitive and non-sensitive data by allocating different privacy budgets. Experiments on two real datasets (Stocks and Syn^B) show that the optimal selection method can achieve a balance between data privacy protection and data accuracy according to the privacy budget allocation. The loss indicators of the optimized SDDRM are better than those of DDRM. The percentage of reduction is between 5% and 45%. This confirms its performance in terms of data utility. The future work will include two aspects based on our optimization SDDRM algorithm: the data perturbation algorithm and frequency estimation. In the context of dynamic data change and sensitivity diversification, sensitive and non-sensitive sensitivity differences are further subdivided. This is done to further investigate privacy protection mechanism and improve data utility.

Acknowledgments. This study was supported in part by the National Natural Science Foundation of China (grant number 61602216 and 61672270), in part by the Jiangsu Province 'Qinglan Project'

Outstanding Young Backbone Teachers Training object (grant number KYQ22003), in part by the Natural Science Foundation of the Jiangsu Higher Education Institutions of China (grant number 24KJB520007 and 24KJB520008).

References

1. Kumbure, M.M., Lohrmann, C., Luukka, P., et al.: Machine learning techniques and data for stock market forecasting: a literature review. Expert Syst. Appl. **197**, 116659 (2022)
2. Amini, M., Sharifani, K., Rahmani, A.: Machine learning model towards evaluating data gathering methods in manufacturing and mechanical engineering. Int. J. Appl. Sci. Eng. Res. **2023**(15), 349–362 (2023)
3. Akhter, R., Sofi, S.A.: Precision agriculture using IoT data analytics and machine learning. J. King Saud Univ. Comput. Inf. Sci. **34**(8), 5602–5618 (2022)
4. Dwork, C.: Differential privacy. In: Bugliesi, M., Preneel, B., Sassone, V., Wegener, I. (eds.) Automata, Languages and Programming. ICALP 2006. Lecture Notes in Computer Science, vol. 4052, pp. 1–12. Springer, Berlin, Heidelberg (2006). https://doi.org/10.1007/11787006_11-12
5. Yang, M., Guo, T., Zhu, T., et al.: Local differential privacy and its applications: a comprehensive survey. Comput. Stand. Interfaces, 103827 (2023)
6. Ni, Y., Li, J., Chang, W., et al.: A LDP-based privacy-preserving longitudinal and multidimensional range query scheme in IOT. IEEE Internet of Things J. (2023)
7. Jain, P., Gyanchandani, M., Khare, N.: Big data privacy: a technological perspective and review. J. Big Data **3**, 1–25 (2016)
8. Verma, A., Bhattacharya, P., Patel, Y., Shah, K., Tanwar, S., Khan, B.: Data localization and privacy-preserving healthcare for big data applications: architecture and future directions. In: Singh, P.K., Kolekar, M.H., Tanwar, S., Wierzchoń, S.T., Bhatnagar, R.K. (eds.) Emerging Technologies for Computing, Communication and Smart Cities. Lecture Notes in Electrical Engineering, vol. 875, pp. 233–244. Springer, Singapore (2022). https://doi.org/10.1007/978-981-19-0284-0_18
9. Zia, M.T., Khan, M.A., El-Sayed, H.: Application of differential privacy approach in healthcare data–a case study. In: 2020 14th International Conference on Innovations in Information Technology, pp. 35–39. IEEE (2020)
10. Zhang, X., He, F., Chen, Q., et al.: A differentially private indoor localization scheme with fusion of WiFi and bluetooth fingerprints in edge computing. Neural Comput. Appl. **34**(6), 4111–4132 (2022)
11. Murakami, T., Kawamoto, Y.: {Utility-optimized} local differential privacy mechanisms for distribution estimation. In: 28th USENIX Security Symposium (USENIX Security 19), pp. 1877–1894 (2019)
12. Xue, Q., Ye, Q., Hu, H., et al.: DDRM: A continual frequency estimation mechanism with local differential privacy. IEEE Trans. Knowl. Data Eng. **35**(7), 6784–6797 (2023)
13. Cao, Y., Zhu, Y., He, X., et al.: Utility-optimized mechanism for frequency estimation of set data under local differential privacy. Comput. Res. Dev. **59**(10), 2261–2274 (2022). [In Chinese]
14. Dwork, C., McSherry, F., Nissim, K., et al.: Calibrating noise to sensitivity in private data analysis. J. Privacy Confidentiality **7**(3), 17–51 (2017)
15. Yin, S., Zhu, Y., Zhang, Y.:Utility-optimized mechanism for joint distribution estimation under local differential privacy. Comput. Sci. **50**(10), 315-326 (2023)
16. Minami, K., Arai, H.I., Sato, I., et al.: Differential privacy without sensitivity. Adv. Neural Inf. Process. Syst. **29** (2016)

17. Johnson, N., Near, J.P., Song, D.: Towards practical differential privacy for SQL queries. Proc. VLDB Endowment **11**(5), 526–539 (2018)
18. Nissim, K., Stemmer, U.: Concentration bounds for high sensitivity functions through differential privacy. J. Privacy Confidentiality, (1) (2019)
19. Lee, J., Clifton, C.: How much is enough? choosing ε for differential privacy. In: Lai, X., Zhou, J., Li, H. (eds.) Information Security. ISC 2011. Lecture Notes in Computer Science, vol. 7001. Springer, Berlin, Heidelberg (2011). https://doi.org/10.1007/978-3-642-24861-0_22
20. Kifer, D., Machanavajjhala, A.: Pufferfish: a framework for mathematical privacy definitions. ACM Trans. Datab. Syst. (TODS) **39**(1), 1–36 (2014)
21. Ye, Q., Meng, X., Zhu, M., et al.: A survey of localized differen-tial privacy. J. Softw. **29**(07), 1981–2005 (2018). [In Chinese]
22. Kasiviswanathan, S.P., Lee, H.K., Nissim, K., et al.: What can we learn privately? SIAM J. Comput. **40**(3), 793–826 (2011)
23. Hu, T., Xin, B., Liu, X., et al.: Tracking the insider attacker: a blockchain traceability system for insider threats. Sensors **20**(18), 5297–5315 (2020)
24. Ju, C., Gu, Q., Wu, G., et al.: Local differential privacy protection of high-dimensional perceptual data by the refined bayes network. Sensors **20**(9), 2516 (2020)
25. McSherry, F.D.: Privacy integrated queries: an extensible platform for privacy-preserving data analysis. In: Proceedings of ACM SIGMOD International Conference on Management of Data, pp. 19–30 (2009)
26. Laud, P., Pankova, A., Pettai, M.: A framework of metrics for differential privacy from local sensitivity. Proc. Privacy Enhancing Technol. **2020**(2), 175–208 (2020)

Blockchain-Based Key Management Scheme in Internet of Things

Zihan Wang[1], Jiqun Zhang[1], Jingcheng Song[1], Yongwei Tang[2], and Hongyuan Cheng[1]([✉])

[1] School of Information Science and Engineering, Linyi University, Linyi 267000, China
chenghongyuan@lyu.edu.cn
[2] Key Laboratory of Computing Power Network and Information Security, Ministry of Education, Shandong Computer Science Center, Qilu University of Technology (Shandong Academy of Sciences), Jinan 250014, China

Abstract. Based on the study of key management schemes and blockchain technology, a hierarchical IoT key management scheme using blockchain is proposed. This scheme encapsulates the key generation process in the blockchain as a smart contract, creating communication keys only for adjacent nodes that communicate. When the contract receives a key generation request, it automatically generates the key, ensuring the process is tamper-proof and reliable. The generated public key is output as the transaction result, which terminal nodes can obtain by viewing. Security analysis and experiments show that this scheme reduces the communication overhead of key distribution, ensures the security of key transmission, and improves the reliability of key management.

Keywords: Blockchain · key generation · Internet of Things (IoT)

1 Introduction

To safeguard the data transmitted and stored in the Internet of Things (IoT) [1, 2] from unauthorized access, leakage, or tampering, the industry and researchers have been exploring various technological schemes. Currently, Radio-Frequency Identification (RFID) encryption technology, as a commonly used method, has been widely applied. RFID [3, 4] encryption technology realizes the identification and encryption of objects and their related information by attaching an electronic tag with a unique identifier and password to each object. The RFID encryption technology enhances the security of IoT systems to a certain extent, as it ensures that only authorized devices can read or modify the data on the tags. However, despite its unique advantages, RFID encryption technology has some noteworthy drawbacks.

Firstly, implementing RFID technology requires a large number of electronic tags and readers, which are expensive and increase the overall cost of the system. Additionally, these devices' installation, deployment, and maintenance involve complex engineering operations. Such high costs and complexity may limit the promotion and application of RFID encryption technology in resource-constrained or budget-tight scenarios.

W. Li et al. (Eds.): EISA 2024, CCIS 2266, pp. 208–218, 2025.
https://doi.org/10.1007/978-3-031-80419-9_15

Secondly, with the continuous development of IoT technology, the amount of data in the system has proliferated, and the communication frequency has also increased significantly [5, 6]. Meanwhile, IoT application scenarios have become increasingly diverse, ranging from smart homes to industrial automation, from smart cities to intelligent transportation, with each scenario having unique needs and challenges. However, RFID encryption technology may find it difficult to adapt to these changes. As RFID technology relies on wireless radio-frequency signals for communication, its transmission range and communication capability are relatively limited, and it cannot meet the needs of large-scale, high-frequency communication. In addition, the storage capacity and computing power of RFID tags are also relatively limited, making it challenging to support complex data processing and security mechanisms. Therefore, we need to find a more advanced, flexible, and efficient IoT data protection method to address these challenges. This method should be able to overcome the limitations of RFID encryption technology while meeting the high requirements of IoT systems for security, reliability, and efficiency.

At the same time, we must recognize that the Internet of Things (IoT) is a vast and complex network system. It encompasses technologies and applications from sensors and actuators to cloud computing and big data [7, 8]. IoT applications involve various industries and fields, such as transportation, healthcare, energy, and environmental protection [9, 10]. These industries and fields exhibit strong cross-cutting and complementary characteristics, but they also face challenges like data silos and information barriers. Therefore, the IoT urgently needs a unified management platform that can integrate resources from various industries [11, 12]. This platform should possess robust data processing and analytical capabilities, enabling the centralized collection, storage, management, and analysis of IoT data. Furthermore, it should provide a diverse range of application interfaces and services, supporting data sharing and collaborative innovation across different industries and fields [13, 14]. We can achieve resource sharing, collaborative innovation, and maximize value by constructing a comprehensive IoT industry chain model. This can improve the overall performance and efficiency of IoT systems, promote cooperation and communication between different industries and fields, and promote the innovation and development of IoT technology.

Currently, blockchain has low throughput and immature technology, making it challenging to implement this system fully on the blockchain. Therefore, the key generation and negotiation, the core parts of the system, are implemented using smart contract technology and encryption algorithms to ensure security and efficiency.

The rest of this paper is organized as follows. Section 2 introduces the related work of this paper. Section 3 describes key management schemes. Section 4 proposes safety analysis. Section 5 conducts experimental analysis. Finally, Sect. 6 concludes the paper.

2 Network Model

2.1 Scenario Model

In this section, a hierarchical IoT topology is adopted, and the nodes that need to communicate are divided into three types: base stations, cluster heads, and standard sensor nodes.

Base station: The base station is static and trustworthy, that is, a visual terminal in the general sense. Its communication range covers the entire sensor network and has powerful computing, communication, and storage capabilities.

Cluster head: The cluster head is a wireless communication device with strong storage and computing capabilities and a long service life. It is responsible for collecting and forwarding data to the base station of the members in the cluster and maintaining the blockchain as a member node.

Common sensor nodes: The common sensor node is responsible for interacting with the surrounding environment, collecting data about the surrounding environment, and forwarding the data to the base station through the cluster head.

2.2 Blockchain Deployment Structure

This scheme uses a cloud-edge-end blockchain structure [15, 16] with three layers: the device, edge, and cloud blockchain layers. The specific description is as follows.

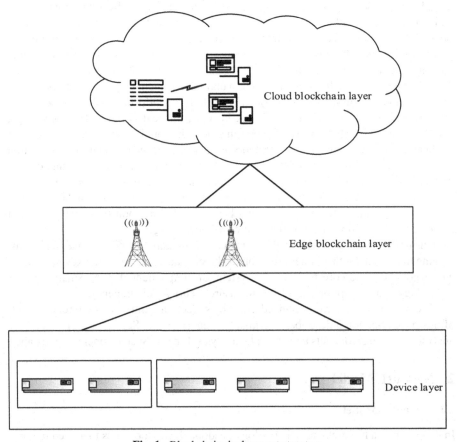

Fig. 1. Blockchain deployment structure

Device layer: The layer generally includes various essential device nodes, such as industrial sensors and terminal smart homes. This scheme mainly refers to ordinary nodes. Due to small devices' limited computing and storage capabilities, the data required for key negotiation between nodes can be sent to the cluster heads in the edge layer.

Edge blockchain layer: They are composed of edge node cluster heads. They generally have ample storage space and computing power, receive data from the device layer, and perform low latency collection, encapsulation, and other related processing on the data. A new block will be generated after reaching consensus with other nodes through consensus algorithms, and the random public key information of nodes within the cluster will be saved in the chain. The edge computing node is usually physically closer to the terminal device node, so it can effectively reduce the communication delay and improve the communication efficiency.

Cloud blockchain layer: The cloud blockchain layer ensures the integrity of information through its secure and verifiable computing capabilities in a trustless environment and its decentralized and tamper-proof features. This scheme mainly assists in information recovery, identity authentication, and message verification (Fig. 1).

3 Key Management Schemes

This section proposes a key management scheme for IoT networks, which is divided into three phases: key generation, group key negotiation, and node change. The scheme builds a blockchain-based IoT key generation system based on the authentication system and blockchain technology. The core idea is to combine the authentication system with smart contracts and use smart contracts to realize the generation and distribution of identity key pairs deployed in a blockchain block. When a terminal node in the network needs an identity key, it initiates a transaction to the smart contract to meet the preset conditions. The contract automatically generates a pair of public and private keys when executed and publishes the public keys throughout the network.

3.1 Key Generation

Taking advantage of the low consumption and fast computing speed of Elliptic Curve Cryptography (ECC) algorithm, a hierarchical intelligent key generation scheme based on ECC algorithm was proposed. The steps to generate a smart key are as follows: Table 1 shows the algorithm symbols and definitions used in this section.

The steps for generating a smart key are as follows.

Step 1: The ordinary node L_u generates a set of $(RASK, RAPK)$ according to the pre-selected work password algorithm ECC. In elliptic curves, not all elliptic curves with large order values can be applied to encryption systems. This article uses a secure elliptic curve for encryption.

Step 2: Node L_u sends a transaction to the contract to trigger the preset conditions of the contract;

Step 3: The contract obtains node information, including the node L_u random public key $RAPK_u$ and the node information identifier ID_u;

Table 1. Description of symbols

Notation	Description
L_u	Node numbered u
CH_i	The ith cluster head
RAPK	Nodes autonomously generate random private keys
IDPK	The public key of the flag generated by the contract
IDSK	The private key of the logo generated by the contract
RAPK	Nodes autonomously generate random public keys

Step 4: Review the information submitted for the contract, ensure its authenticity and uniqueness, and generate an identification key pair (*IDPK*, *IDSK*) based on the submitted information.

Step 5: The public key $IDPK_u$, random public key $RAPK_u$, and node information identifier ID_u are output to the entire network;

Step 6: The contract stores node information and the identification key pair $(IDPK_u, IDSK_u)$;

Step 7: The remaining nodes obtain the public key by viewing the transaction results and use the random public key for communication.

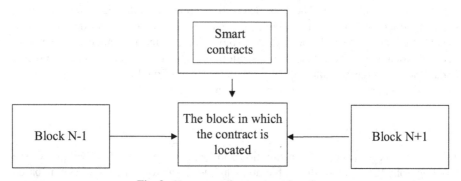

Fig. 2. Key generation contract location

As shown in Fig. 2, a program dedicated to generating key pairs is deployed on the blockchain using smart contract technology. The contract is embedded in a specific block of the blockchain and can only be activated if certain conditions are met. When a node in the network needs a new key pair, it can start a smart contract by initiating a transaction that satisfies the preset trigger conditions. The smart contract automatically generates a pair of public and private keys at runtime and broadcasts the public key throughout the network. This way, other nodes can get that public key by looking at the transaction history. The private key is sent to the requesting node through a secure and reliable key distribution mechanism. Since smart contracts run on the blockchain, they are immutable and non-stoppable. Therefore, there is no external force that can intervene or modify the content and results of the smart contract throughout the process.

3.2 Group Key Negotiation

3.2.1 Key Routing Network is Established

To route data to the base station, the cluster head directional routing network with the base station as the root is built as follows:

The base station sends a routing request message in a single-hop manner to the nearest cluster head. Set the routing level of the base station to 0, that is, $L(BS) = 0$. When cluster head CH_i receives the routing request message, it changes its routing level to one level higher than that of the base station, that is, $L(i) = L(BS) + 1$. Use the base station as your own parent node. Recursively, CH_i broadcasts the modified message. If cluster header Ch_j receives a message, and its routing level $L(j)$ is equal to or less than the routing level d of cluster header CH_i, i.e., $L(j) \leq L(i)$, then Ch_j drops the message directly. Otherwise, Ch_j updates its routing level to one more level than Ch_i, i.e., $L(j) = L(i) + 1$, and sets it as one of its parent nodes. This process takes place recursively in the network, and all cluster header broadcasts complete the establishment of the routing network. Similarly, an intra-cluster key routing network can be set up in the same way.

3.2.2 Execution Phase

Step 1: Suppose the group key communication initiator node is L_u and the communication parent node is L_v.

Step 2: L_u obtains the random public key $RAPK_v$ and node information identification ID_v of the parent node through the cloud blockchain;

Step 3: L_u uses the node information $ID_1 = RAPK_v || ID_v$ to obtain the control information h, the root input of the multilinear control selection function. Generate a meta based on h and the public key $IDPK_v$ to generate the flag public key

Step 4: Verify that the generated flag public key $IDPK_v$ is consistent with the flag public key exposed on the chain;

Step 5: After verifying consistency. L_u uses the random public key $RAPK_v$ of the parent node v to communicate with the L_v.

3.3 Node Updates

Because the endpoint is a small, untrusted device, the IoT system inevitably needs to add new IoT nodes to the cluster, and the damaged nodes will exit the cluster. Therefore, this section describes the specific process of node update in this scheme from two aspects: adding new nodes and adding old nodes.

3.3.1 New Node Joining

When a new node joins, the node is first configured with corresponding parameters. Then, the node spontaneously generates a public and private key according to the implementation of the selected cryptographic algorithm and broadcasts the public key in the cluster:

(1) To add the key information of the cluster. The new node spontaneously generates a random public-private key pair based on the selected algorithm. It broadcasts its unique identifier and public key to the cluster head node it wishes to join. Upon receiving the information about the new node, the cluster head automatically runs a smart contract, generates the identification key pair for the latest node, and broadcasts the relevant information within the cluster.

(2) Other clusters update key information. The cluster head node broadcasts information about the new node joining to other cluster head nodes..

(3) Store the information on the blockchain. Once consensus is reached among the nodes within each cluster, the cluster head node will record the public key information of all nodes in its cluster into a sub-blockchain and prompt the nodes in the cluster to update this sub-blockchain. Suppose all clusters achieve consensus within a given period. In that case, the central node will merge the sub-blockchains from each cluster into a primary blockchain based on their cluster numbers and synchronize this primary blockchain with each cluster head node.

3.3.2 Exit of the Old Node

When a node in the cluster is destroyed, you need to revoke all keys about the common node, update the routing structure about the node, and re-run the key generation process to update the cluster key. When the cluster head node detects that the node is damaged, the cluster head node is determined according to the position of the damaged node in the routing structure:

(1) When the node to be revoked is a leaf node, only one revocation message needs to be sent to its parent node.

(2) When the node to be revoked is the parent node and its child node has a standby parent node, the parent node of the damaged node is sent to the parent node

Send a revocation message to the child node and use the standby parent node for the subsequent communication.

(3) When the node to be revoked is the parent node and its child node does not have a standby parent node, the cluster head needs to re-establish a route for the child node of the damaged node and pass the revocation information and a new routing structure to the child node.

4 Security Analysis

The security of the key management scheme is a critical evaluation metric. This section discusses the security requirements that the proposed scheme can meet, specifically in the following aspects:

Attack resistance: All key management schemes must consider the issue of nodes being attacked. Assuming that the compromised node is Lu, its key and transmitted data will be stolen. However, the identity private key cannot be stolen because its generation process is related to the node's unique identifier. Attackers will only steal the key and cannot forge the identifier, and such attacks will be quickly detected. Moreover, the blockchain technology based on this scheme can fundamentally resist standard attack methods such as witch attacks, sniffing attacks, DDoS attacks, and replay attacks. In addition, node communication mainly occurs within the cluster, and attacks will not affect the entire network. Therefore, even in the presence of attacks, the scheme still has high availability.

Data integrity: In the blockchain-based key management scheme proposed in this chapter, sensitive data such as device identity and password information are stored on the blockchain. By leveraging the blockchain's distributed consensus mechanism and encryption algorithm, it is tough for attackers to modify the data on the chain. Because attackers need to have more than 1/2 of the entire network's computing power to tamper with the blockchain, the cost of doing so is much higher than the benefits they may obtain. This ensures the integrity and security of data in the network.

Identity verifiability: The key management scheme based on blockchain designed in this article utilizes smart contracts and edge blockchain technology to provide. We provide comprehensive public key management services. First, we use smart contracts to maintain the relationship between the device's identity information and the identifier's public key. The mapping relationship ensures each device has a unique identity identifier and corresponding public key. Secondly, we use the edge area. Blockchain is used to implement identity authentication services between devices; when two devices need to communicate, they will exchange their respective identity information sent to the edge blockchain and verified through a consensus mechanism. In this way, devices in different clusters can. A trustworthy communication relationship can be established, and the other party's public key can be queried and verified through blockchain. In this way, we have achieved identity verifiability and public key accessibility between devices.

5 Experimental Analysis

This paper proposes a blockchain-based key management scheme. Therefore, this section compares the proposed scheme with [17] and [18], analyzes its advantages and disadvantages, and summarizes it in Table 2.

Table 2. Comparison of key management

	Distributed	Decentralization	Tamper-proof	Recoverability
[17]	No	No	Yes	Depends on the central node
[18]	Yes	Yes	No	Any n nodes
Our	No	Yes	Yes	Depends on block information

After comparing and analyzing the above schemes, it can be seen that the blockchain-based key management scheme proposed in this chapter performs well in terms of security, decentralization, and anti-tampering. Its advantages of lightweight and low communication overhead make it more suitable for resource-constrained IoT systems than other key management schemes.

Simulation experiment: The operating system is Windows 10, the smart contract is written using the Remix IDE that supports the Solidity language, and the MetaMask wallet is used to simulate the blockchain network. Table 3 shows the hardware development environment of this simulation experiment.

Table 3. Hardware environment table

Hardware	CPU	Memory	Hard disk	OS
PC	Intel Core i7-8750H 2.20 Ghz	16 G	500 G	Windows 10

As shown in Table 4, the software development environment for this simulation experiment is displayed.

Table 4. Software environment table

Tool	Version
Remix IDE	Remix IDE v0.31.0
solidity	Solidity IDE 0.6.6

Table 5 shows the smart contracts implemented through experimental simulation.

Table 5. Smart contract cost

function	Smart contract creation	Identity public key generation	Node updates	Node revocation
deplete/Gas	225 864	103 128	46 432	12 583

Comparing the contract operation overhead for different numbers of users with traditional blockchain key management [19], as shown in Fig. 3, it is evident that the proposed scheme significantly reduces costs in terms of cost control. Therefore, this scheme can better reduce expenses, enhancing the system's usability and practicality.

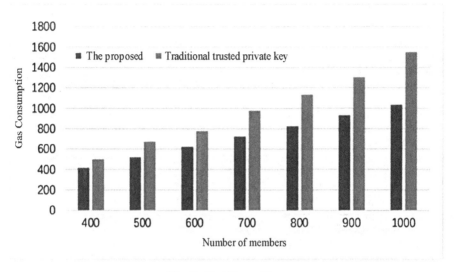

Fig. 3. Cost Expenditure

6 Conclusion

This article proposes a blockchain-based key management scheme, providing a new idea for exploring lightweight key management schemes suitable for IoT systems and improving IoT key management. Based on the analysis and research of existing key management schemes, combined with the routing-driven key management scheme, blockchain technology is added to design a blockchain-based IoT key management scheme. The analysis shows that the blockchain-based key management scheme not only enables key generation, storage, update, and transmission functions, but also has significant characteristics such as lightweight, high security, and adaptability compared to traditional key management schemes. Therefore, the blockchain-based key management scheme is more suitable for resource-constrained, highly dynamic, and diverse IoT systems.

References

1. Moudgil, V., Hewage, K., Hussain, S.A., Sadiq R.: Integration of IoT in building energy infrastructure: a critical review on challenges and solutions. Renew. Sustain. Energy Rev. **174**, 113121 (2023)
2. Sadeghi-Niaraki, A.: Internet of Thing (IoT) review of review: Bibliometric overview since its foundation. Future Gen. Comput. Syst. **143**, 361–377 (2023)
3. Juels, A.: RFID security and privacy: a research survey. IEEE J. Sel. Areas Commun. **24**(2), 381–394 (2006)
4. Suresh, S., Chakaravarthi, G.: RFID technology and its diverse applications: a brief exposition with a proposed machine learning approach. Measurement **195** (2022)
5. Ding, W., Abdel-Basset, M., Mohamed, R.: DeepAK-IoT: an effective deep learning model for cyberattack detection in IoT networks. Inf. Sci. **634**, 157–171 (2023)

6. Zhang, J., Li, B., Zhao, B.: Blockchain-based AI big data platform for agricultural Internet of Things. Internet of Things Technol. **14**(2), 121–122, 126 (2024)
7. Himeur, Y., Elnour, M., Fadli, F., et al.: AI-big data analytics for building automation and management systems: a survey, actual challenges and future perspectives. Artif. Intell. Rev. **56**(6), 4929–5021 (2023)
8. Singh, N., Hamid, Y., Juneja, S., et al.: Load balancing and service discovery using Docker Swarm for microservice-based big data applications. J. Cloud Comput. **12**(1), 4 (2023)
9. Ghosh, A., Edwards, D.J., Hosseini, M.R.: Patterns and trends in Internet of Things (IoT) research: future applications in the construction industry. Eng. Constr. Archit. Manag. **28**(2), 457–481 (2021)
10. Yangui, S.: A panorama of cloud platforms for IoT applications across industries. Sensors **20**(9), 2701 (2020)
11. Xu, J., Zhao, Y., Chen, H., et al.: ABC-GSPBFT: PBFT with grouping score mechanism and optimized consensus process for flight operation data-sharing. Inf. Sci. **624**, 110–127 (2023)
12. Celik, Y., Petri, I., Barati, M.: Blockchain supported BIM data provenance for construction projects. Comput. Ind. **144**, 103768 (2023)
13. Pasdar, A., Lee, Y.C., Dong, Z.: Connect API with blockchain: a survey on blockchain oracle implementation. ACM Comput. Surv. **55**(10), 1–39 (2023)
14. Huynh-The, T., Gadekallu, T.R., Wang, W., et al.: Blockchain for the metaverse: a review. Futur. Gener. Comput. Syst. **143**, 401–419 (2023)
15. Deepa, N., Pham, Q.V., Nguyen, D.C., et al.: A survey on blockchain for big data: approaches, opportunities, and future directions. Futur. Gener. Comput. Syst. **131**, 209–226 (2022)
16. Yaqoob, I., Salah, K., Jayaraman, R., et al.: Blockchain for healthcare data management: opportunities, challenges, and future recommendations. Neural Comput. Appl. 1–16 (2022)
17. Wei, L., Cui, J., Xu, Y., et al.: Secure and lightweight conditional privacy-preserving authentication for securing traffic emergency messages in VANETs. IEEE Trans. Inf. Forensics Secur. **16**, 1681–1695 (2020)
18. Harn, L., Hsu, C.F.: Li B Centralized group key establishment protocol without a mutually trusted third party. Mobile Netw. Appl. **23**, 1132–1140 (2018)
19. Zhou, J., Liu, H., Zhou, Y.: Blockchain-based key management scheme for aerospace self-organizing networks. J. Beijing Univ. Posts Telecommun. **46**(1), 63–68 (2023)

Privacy Optimization of Deep Recommendation Algorithm in Federated Framework

Xiaopeng Zhao$^{(\boxtimes)}$, Xiao Bai, Guohao Sun, and Zhe Yan

School of Computer Science and Technology, Donghua University,
201620 Shanghai, China
zxp@dhu.edu.cn

Abstract. Federated Learning (FL) presents a promising solution to the privacy concerns associated with deep learning-based recommender systems. Our work introduces FedxDeepFM, an advanced recommendation model that integrates deep learning with FL to enhance user privacy. FedxDeepFM operates on the principles of FL, conducting decentralized training on user devices and sharing only model parameters, thereby ensuring that no user data is exposed to the server. The model also incorporates privacy features, such as pseudo-interaction padding, which enhance its resistance to inference attacks. Evaluated on benchmark datasets, FedxDeepFM demonstrates exceptional recommendation quality while maintaining stringent privacy standards, outperforming contemporary models and addressing the common challenges such as sparsity and cold starts in recommendations.

Keywords: Recommender systems · federated learning · privacy-preserving · xDeepFM

1 Introduction

Recommender systems have become essential in mitigating information overload by analyzing past interactions between users and items, thereby significantly enhancing the online user experience [11]. These systems intelligently select items that align with user preferences and generate personalized prediction models. With the massive data generated by Internet of Things (IoT) devices, analyzing this data can significantly enhance the user experience [14]. To enhance the accuracy of recommendations, recommender systems consistently collect a diverse array of user data. These data encompass personal information, including names, phone numbers, and addresses, as well as sensitive information related to item interactions, such as app usage, click history, and purchase history [5]. However, the collection of extensive data raises significant privacy concerns and increases the risk of data breaches, highlighting the necessity for innovative approaches that prioritize user privacy while still leveraging the value of this data. Although

W. Li et al. (Eds.): EISA 2024, CCIS 2266, pp. 219–229, 2025.
https://doi.org/10.1007/978-3-031-80419-9_16

various methods can be applied to tackle these challenges, a distributed framework is particularly effective in achieving the dual objectives of safeguarding user privacy and reducing network traffic. Therefore, it is essential to develop a distributed framework for analyzing IoT data locally to protect data privacy and reduce network traffic [13].

Facing data privacy issues, Google's introduction of the FL framework in 2017 marked a significant advancement in machine learning [10]. This framework aims to protect user privacy during the training of machine learning models. FL trains models using local datasets distributed across IoT devices, changing the traditional training approach by only requiring the transmission of essential model details for updates to a central server for integration [18]. Even with these protections, attackers may still manage to guess user information by analyzing the model updates sent to the server. Furthermore, this approach introduces new challenges, such as efficiently aggregating updates from numerous devices, ensuring that the updated model remains accurate, and stays robust against potential security threats.

Inspired by FL and the challenges it presents in ensuring user privacy, this study explores the privacy-preserving computing techniques integrated with advanced deep learning algorithms within the FL framework to enhance privacy protection while maintaining the quality of recommendations. In summary, our contributions are as follows:

- To protect the privacy of user-item interactions on individual clients, our model training utilizes pseudo-interaction padding. This privacy-preserving method guarantees the security of user-item interaction records, preventing accurate inferences and strengthening the privacy measures of our approach.
- In this study, we introduce an advanced deep learning recommendation system framework called FedxDeepFM, which has been developed within the context of FL. Our model integrates the xDeepFM recommendation technique with a FL architecture by exchanging model parameters, specifically to predict click-through rates (CTR). By strategically avoiding the collection of user data and skillfully learning both explicit and implicit high-order feature interactions, FedxDeepFM enhances predictive accuracy.
- Rigorous experiments conducted on two real-world datasets underscore the superior performance of our FedxDeepFM. The results demonstrate significant advantages over several cutting-edge models, validating the effectiveness of our proposed method for predicting CTR within a FL context.

2   Related Work

Our research is closely associated with recommendation systems and federated learning. In this section, we will review the existing research findings related to these two areas.

2.1   Deep Learning-Based Recommendation Algorithms

Recent advances in deep learning have revolutionized recommendation systems, offering sophisticated models that surpass traditional algorithms in capturing complex interactions and providing personalized suggestions. Notable innovations include: In content recommendation, Hansen et al. [1] proposed a contextual and sequential recurrent neural network (CoSeRNN) model to capture user preferences based on context. The model effectively generates context-sensitive dynamic recommendations. In contextual information, there is often a bias towards popularity. To eliminate biased information, Zhou et al. [19] proposed a novel two-head attention fusion autoencoder (TAFA) model. For CTR prediction, Lian et al. [7] proposed the xDeepFM model, which innovates by capturing both explicit and implicit feature interactions, resulting in accurate predictions in complex scenarios. He et al. [3] employed MLPs to learn second-order feature crosses, integrating dropout and batch normalization to combat overfitting and enhance generalizability. Meanwhile, the combined application of reinforcement learning techniques with online recommendation [17], contextual recommendation [12], and other methods has demonstrated superior recommendation performance.

2.2   Federated Recommender System

Federated learning, originally introduced by McMahan et al. [10] and further elaborated by Kairouz et al. [6], revolutionizes machine learning by enabling collaborative model training across multiple parties without the need to share raw data, thus ensuring the privacy of participants' data. FL allows participants to maintain control over their data while meeting various privacy requirements during training. To tackle the complexity of explicit feedback, Lin et al. [8] developed the federated recommender system FedRec, which enhances privacy through a hybrid estimation method based on user averages. FedRec creates virtual item interaction sets to enhance privacy and reduce vulnerability to attacks.

3   Our Proposed Model

This section introduces FedxDeepFM, our novel federated recommender system model that utilizes federated learning to enable collaborative learning across user devices while ensuring user privacy and security against inference attacks.

3.1   Overview of FedxDeepFM

In the FedxDeepFM framework illustrated in Fig. 1, the training process for CTR prediction is designed to safeguard user privacy through communication between a central server and user devices, such as those belonging to users i and j. The server coordinates the learning process, while the devices contribute to the model by utilizing their private data without disclosing it. Here is a comprehensive explanation of the steps involved in the training process:

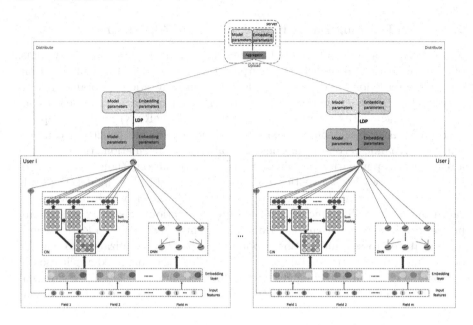

Fig. 1. The framework of our FedxDeepFM approach

Step 1: The server selects a subset of user devices, such as those belonging to user i and user j, based on specific selection criteria to participate in the current training round.

Step 2: The server sends the latest global model parameters, which include both model and embedding parameters, to the selected devices. Each user device (client) receives only the parameters necessary to perform its computations.

Step 3: User devices utilize local data for model training. They apply the parameters to their local DNN and CIN for updating the parameters. The user data never leaves the device, ensuring that each user's privacy is maintained.

Step 4: After the training, the clients (the devices of users i, j, etc.) send only the updated parameters back to the server. Importantly, the devices do not upload raw data, thereby safeguarding users' private information.

Step 5: An aggregator on the server collects all updated parameters from various clients. It then integrates these updates into the global model, effectively enhancing its performance while maintaining user data privacy. This aggregation enables the system to leverage the diverse data from various clients without requiring direct access to that data.

This process is repeated for multiple iterations until the model is fully trained. Each device's contribution enhances the model's predictive accuracy, while the central server maintains the integrity and improves the global model. As illustrated in Fig. 1, the parameter flow guarantees that the training process effectively utilizes the computational power and available data on the client side without compromising sensitive information. This approach maintains rigorous privacy standards while providing precise CTR predictions.

3.2 Integrating Privacy-Preserving

During the model training process, directly uploading all model settings may compromise user privacy for several reasons. Unchanged global model parameters can allow servers to infer features present in actual user data during component updates. Moreover, the parameters of the xDeepFM model and the rating predictors could potentially expose sensitive user information, including historical behaviors and ratings [20]. This is because the parameters of neural network models encapsulate the user's preferences for particular items.

Pseudo-Interaction Padding. To address these challenges, we propose a strategy to protect user privacy during model update processes. The method is pseudo-interaction padding. To obfuscate the real user data and prevent the server from making accurate inferences, a method of synthetic data integration is used. This method involves padding the actual user dataset with a set of artificially generated interactions that mimic possible user behaviors. Considering a scenario where the user u_k has a set of real data D_{real}^k, we employ a strategy where the training data D_{train}^k is combination of the actual data and additional synthetic data generated through a random process. The equation representing this strategy is given by:

$$D_{train}^k = D_{real}^k + random(n_k, \mu, inf(\boldsymbol{x}), \phi) \tag{1}$$

where the function $random(\bullet)$ represents the process of random generation and the value n_k corresponds to the amount of local data for user u_k. The hyperparameter μ, along with n_k, determines the number of pseudo-interactions to be generated. Moreover, $inf(\boldsymbol{x})$ describes the composition of features in the vector $\boldsymbol{x}$. The parameter ϕ controls the variability of the generated pseudo-interactions to make them statistically similar to the real interactions.

To further detail the process of pseudo-interaction generation, the output of the $random(\bullet)$ function can be defined as follows:

$$random(n_k, \mu, inf(\boldsymbol{x}), \phi) = \{\boldsymbol{x}_1, \boldsymbol{x}_2, \ldots, \boldsymbol{x}_{n_k'}\} \tag{2}$$

where $n_k' = \mu \times n_k$ represents the number of pseudo-interactions to be generated. Each $\boldsymbol{x}_i$ is generated from a normal distribution with the mean and standard deviation (ϕ) of the real data.

Although the training data may be reconstructed using the technique described in [20], the server still cannot accurately determine the actual composition of the data, as the training data combines both genuine and fabricated interaction items. By integrating real and synthetic data, the server obtains a dataset that is indistinguishable in terms of actual and simulated interactions, thereby protecting the user's privacy. Figure 2 illustrates the distinction between the actual and synthetic data within the training dataset.

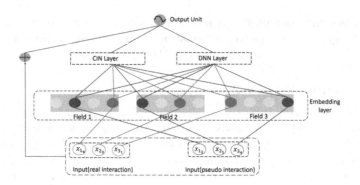

Fig. 2. Training process with pseudo-interaction padding

4   Experiment Evaluation

In this section, we conduct experiments using real-world datasets to compare the effectiveness of our proposed FedxDeepFM method with that of existing state-of-the-art methods.

Table 1. Statistics of the experimental dataset

Dataset	MovieLens1M	MovieLens100K
Interaction	1000209	100000
User	6040	943
Item	3952	1682
Rating Range	$1, 2, \ldots, 5$	$1, 2, \ldots, 5$

4.1   Experimental Setup

Datasets. In our experiments, we utilize two benchmark datasets commonly employed in recommender system research, namely MovieLens1M and Movie-Lens100K [2]. The MovieLens1M dataset comprises approximately one million ratings for 3,952 movies provided by 6,040 users. The MovieLens100K dataset includes 100,000 ratings for 1,682 movies from 943 users. Detailed statistics of the datasets are presented in Table 1. To address the issue of CTR prediction, explicit feedback in the datasets, which ranges from 1 to 5, was converted into implicit feedback, represented as 0 and 1 (see [4]). Following standard procedure, ratings below 3 were normalized to 0, ratings above 3 were normalized to 1, and ratings equal to 3 were excluded to minimize noise. In the experiments, we allocate 80% of the data for the training set, 10% for the test set, and the remaining 10% for the validation set.

Baselines. We compare FedxDeepFM with the following four state-of-the-art baselines:

- AFM [16]. A supervised learning model that distinguishes the importance of various feature interactions using neural network attention mechanisms and performs well on regression tasks.
- NFM [3]. A model that integrates the second-order feature interaction linear model of factorization machines with the higher-order nonlinear interaction capabilities of neural networks.
- FedGNN [15]. A FL framework for implementing graph neural network-based recommender systems while preserving privacy.
- FedGR [9]. A model for social recommender systems that combines graph attention networks and FL.

To evaluate the performance of our proposed FedxDeepFM model, we employ three fundamental metrics: Mean Absolute Error (MAE), Root Mean Squared Error (RMSE), and the total runtime of the model. The first two error metrics are commonly used to assess the effectiveness of recommendation systems. Furthermore, we present the average results obtained from ten distinct experimental runs.

4.2   Performance Evaluation

Table 2. Performance of different models on MAE and RMSE

Dataset	MovieLens1M		MovieLens100K	
Metrics	MAE	RMSE	MAE	RMSE
FedAFM	0.3067	0.5308	0.3664	0.5468
FedNFM	0.3423	0.5521	0.3599	0.5962
FedGNN	0.3353	0.4528	0.3577	0.5742
FedGR	0.3894	0.4954	0.3449	0.5757
FedxDeepFM	0.3307	**0.4321**	0.3502	**0.4490**

Table 2 shows that FedxDeepFM outperforms the other models in terms of accuracy on the MovieLens dataset. Among others, FedAFM and FedNFM utilize the same federation framework described in this paper to implement recommendation algorithms based on various decomposition machines. Specifically, on the MovieLens1M dataset, FedxDeepFM achieves a lower error with an MAE of 0.3307 and an RMSE of 0.4321, outperforming FedGNN with an improvement of nearly 1.82% in RMSE and 0.65% increase in MAE. Additionally, it demonstrates a significant improvement in precision compared to FedAFM. On the smaller MovieLens100K dataset, the advantage of FedxDeepFM is even more noticeable. It achieves an MAE of 0.3502 and an RMSE of 0.4490, which is

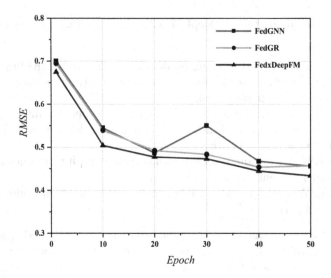

Fig. 3. Comparison of prediction performance of different methods

notably superior to FedGR's RMSE by approximately 22%. The data clearly indicate that FedxDeepFM excels in both precision and predictive power.

Figure 3 illustrates the performance comparison of various joint learning models using the MovieLens dataset. FedxDeepFM consistently demonstrates low RMSE, indicating superior prediction of user preferences. FedGNN initially exhibits a rapid reduction in RMSE, but this improvement eventually levels off. In contrast, FedGR shows a consistent and gradual decrease in RMSE, indicating a more stable learning process. These differences underscore the long-term advantages of FedxDeepFM's architecture regarding prediction accuracy.

4.3   Effect of the Number of Clients

Figure 4 compares the RMSE and MAE performance metrics using the Movie-Lens1M dataset across various numbers of clients. The results show minimal changes in performance when scaling from 10 to 100 clients, with only a slight increase in RMSE of approximately 0.85% and an even smaller change in MAE of about 0.58%. When the number of clients increases from 12 to 18, the RMSE slightly increases by 3.06%. This suggests that reducing the number of clients to which the data is divided may have a minor impact on prediction accuracy, but the overall performance loss is not significant. Overall, this demonstrates that the FedxDeepFM framework can effectively adjust the data allocation strategy as the number of clients increases to sustain stable performance.

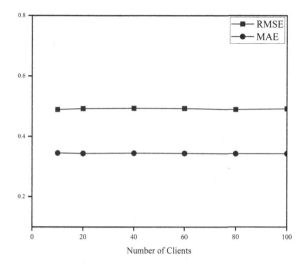

Fig. 4. Effect of the number of clients

5   Conclusion

In this paper, we implement a straightforward yet effective pseudo-interaction padding strategy to safeguard user privacy. In addition, we introduce a privacy-centric federated deep learning framework called FedxDeepFM. Our objective is to locally train the xDeepFM model utilizing distributed user data while simultaneously enhancing privacy protection. Specifically, we utilize local data stored on users' devices to conduct personalized model training for each user on the client side. The local parameters calculated on the client side will be uploaded to the server for aggregation after undergoing privacy protection processing. This approach ensures data privacy while providing personalized recommendations. Extensive experiments conducted on two benchmark datasets demonstrate that our method not only improves recommendation quality by delving deeper into user-item interactions but also effectively safeguards user privacy. In the future, we intend to build upon the algorithm presented in this paper. Our goal is to address the challenges associated with providing recommendations for new users while enhancing the privacy protection of user information. This approach aims to improve the interpretability of the algorithm.

Acknowledgement. We are grateful to the referee for carefully reading our manuscript and for his/her valuable comments. This work was supported in part by the Shanghai Science and Technology Commission 23YF1401000, and in part by the Fundamental Research Funds for the Central Universities under Grant 2232022D-25.

References

1. Hansen, C., et al.: Contextual and sequential user embeddings for large-scale music recommendation. In: Proceedings of the 14th ACM Conference on Recommender Systems, pp. 53–62 (2020)
2. Harper, F.M., Konstan, J.A.: The MovieLens datasets: history and context. ACM Trans. Interact. Intell. Syst. TIIS **5**(4), 1–19 (2015)
3. He, X., Chua, T.S.: Neural factorization machines for sparse predictive analytics. In: Proceedings of the 40th International ACM SIGIR Conference on Research and Development in Information Retrieval, pp. 355–364 (2017)
4. Hu, Y., Koren, Y., Volinsky, C.: Collaborative filtering for implicit feedback datasets. In: 2008 Eighth IEEE International Conference on Data Mining, pp. 263–272 (2008)
5. Jeckmans, A.J., Beye, M., Erkin, Z., Hartel, P., Lagendijk, R.L., Tang, Q.: Privacy in recommender systems. Soc. Media Retrieval, pp. 263–281 (2013)
6. Kairouz, P., et al.: Advances and open problems in federated learning. Found. Trends Mach. Learn. **14**(1–2), 1–210 (2021)
7. Lian, J., Zhou, X., Zhang, F., Chen, Z., Xie, X., Sun, G.: xDeepFM: combining explicit and implicit feature interactions for recommender systems. In: Proceedings of the 24th ACM SIGKDD International Conference on Knowledge Discovery and Data Mining, pp. 1754–1763 (2018)
8. Lin, G., Liang, F., Pan, W., Ming, Z.: FedRec: federated recommendation with explicit feedback. IEEE Intell. Syst. **36**(5), 21–30 (2020)
9. Ma, C., Ren, X., Xu, G., He, B.: FedGr: federated graph neural network for recommendation systems. Axioms **12**(2), 170–184 (2023)
10. McMahan, B., Moore, E., Ramage, D., Hampson, S., Arcas, B.A.y.: Communication-efficient learning of deep networks from decentralized data. In: Proceedings of the 20th International Conference on Artificial Intelligence and Statistics, vol. 54, pp. 1273–1282 (2017)
11. Resnick, P., Varian, H.R.: Recommender systems. Commun. ACM **40**(3), 56–58 (1997)
12. Santana, M.R., et al.: Contextual meta-bandit for recommender systems selection. In: Proceedings of the 14th ACM Conference on Recommender Systems, pp. 444–449 (2020)
13. Shin, H., Kim, S., Shin, J., Xiao, X.: Privacy enhanced matrix factorization for recommendation with local differential privacy. IEEE Trans. Knowl. Data Eng. **30**(9), 1770–1782 (2018)
14. Sun, X., Ansari, N.: EdgeIoT: mobile edge computing for the internet of things. IEEE Commun. Mag. **54**(12), 22–29 (2016)
15. Wu, C., Wu, F., Cao, Y., Huang, Y., Xie, X.: FedGNN: federated graph neural network for privacy-preserving recommendation. arXiv preprint arXiv:2102.04925 (2021)
16. Xiao, J., Ye, H., He, X., Zhang, H., Wu, F., Chua, T.S.: Attentional factorization machines: learning the weight of feature interactions via attention networks. In: Proceedings of the 26th International Joint Conference on Artificial Intelligence, pp. 3119–3125 (2017)
17. Yang, L., Liu, B., Lin, L., Xia, F., Chen, K., Yang, Q.: Exploring clustering of bandits for online recommendation system. In: Proceedings of the 14th ACM Conference on Recommender Systems, pp. 120–129 (2020)

18. Yao, J., Ansari, N.: Enhancing federated learning in fog-aided IOT by CPU frequency and wireless power control. IEEE Internet Things J. **8**(5), 3438–3445 (2020)
19. Zhou, J.P., Cheng, Z., Pérez, F., Volkovs, M.: TAFA: two-headed attention fused autoencoder for context-aware recommendations. In: Proceedings of the 14th ACM Conference on Recommender systems, pp. 338–347 (2020)
20. Zhu, L., Liu, Z., Han, S.: Deep leakage from gradients. Adv. Neural. Inf. Process. Syst. **32**, 17–31 (2019)

Delegated Proof of Stake Consensus Mechanism Based on the Overall Perspective of Voting

Chengtang Cao$^{(\boxtimes)}$ (ID), Shupei Mo, and Zongzheng Huang

Department of Big Data and Information Engineering, Guizhou Industry Polytechnic College, Guiyang 550008, Guizhou, China
caochengtang@163.com, mspdk2000@sina.com

Abstract. Delegated proof of stake (DPoS) involves nodes voting to select newly generated blocks. In existing schemes, voting entails tallying affirmative, abstention, and negative votes for each node. This article introduces a novel approach wherein the votes cast by each node in every ballot are aggregated into a set, including nodes with all affirmative votes. The inclusion relationship of the set is treated as a partial order relation, and a lattice is defined based on this partial order relation. The calculation of the DPoS consensus algorithm based on the lattice is presented. In the existing schemes, voting results are calculated by counting the affirmative votes, abstention votes, and negative votes for a node. In such a voting system, the impact of a voting node on the possible selection of several affirmative votes and multiple voting results for an election vote was not considered. Some voting nodes may tend to cast more affirmative votes, while some voting nodes may prefer to cast fewer affirmative votes. In this paper, the new DPoS consensus mechanism is constructed to solve the impact of voting tendencies at these stages by counting the voting results of a node in a single vote.

Keywords: Blockchain · Delegated Proof of Stake · Fuzzy set · Vague set · Lattice · Consensus mechanism

1 Introduction

The consensus mechanism stands as a pivotal component within blockchain technology. Numerous consensus mechanisms exist [1], including practical Byzantine fault tolerance (PBFT) [2,3], the proof of work mechanism (PoW) [4], the proof-of-stake mechanism (PoS) [5], and delegated proof of stake (DPoS) [6,7]. DPoS [7] was proposed in 2014. In DPoS, token holders vote to elect nodes and generate blocks. The voting power of token holders is proportional to the equity they possess [8], with nodes holding more equity wielding greater influence. Subsequently, after the voting stage, the fixed number of nodes are selected based on the calculation results of the voting model to become committee member generation blocks.

The DPoS voting model is proposed based on the conversion from a vague set to a fuzzy set [9]. In voting model [10], each node has the option to vote in favor, against, or to abstain. The true membership degree is $t_V(u) = \frac{\text{favor votes}}{\text{total votes}}$. The false membership degree is $f_V(u) = \frac{\text{against notes}}{\text{total votes}}$. Due to possible abstention votes, it is clear that $t_V(u) + f_V(u) \leq 1$ is valid. In [11], Liu et al. proposed several voting calculation methods and discussed their advantages and disadvantages. In [12], You et al. constructed an improved model on the Vague Sets-Based DPoS's voting phase in Blockchain. Tan et al. [13] proposed an improved DPoS consensus mechanism based on Borda count for node behavior. Hu et al. [14] proposed an improved DPoS consensus based on reputation by evaluating node behavior and classifying nodes into different trust states. Kim et al. [15] proposed a DPoS model that reduces the influence of nodes with high weights by utilizing a voting coefficient based on secondary delegation.

In existing DPoS that is calculated by counting the affirmative and negative votes a certain node to obtain the overall result. In such a voting system, the impact of a voting node on the possible selection of multiple affirmative votes and multiple voting outcomes for an election is not considered. Consequently, some voting nodes may exhibit a bias towards casting more affirmative votes, while others may tend to cast fewer. This article will construct a new type of DPoS to mitigate the impact of voting bias by counting the voting results of a node on all nodes in a single vote. The voting models of existing DPoS and the DPoS in this article are shown in Fig. 1.

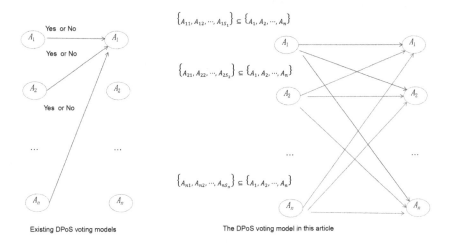

Existing DPoS voting models   The DPoS voting model in this article

Fig. 1. The Voting Models of Existing DPoS and the DPoS in This Article

2 Preliminaries

Definition 1 ([16] fuzzy set). *Suppose $U = \{u_1, u_2, \ldots, u_n\}$ and a fuzzy membership function $\mu_F : U \to [0,1]$, we define the fuzzy set*

$$F = \{(u_1, \mu_F(u_1)), (u_2, \mu_F(u_2)), (u_n, \mu_F(u_n))\}.$$

Definition 2 ([17] vague set). *Suppose $U = \{u_1, u_2, \ldots, u_n\}$ and a generic element of U denoted by u. A vague set A in U is characterized by a truth-membership function $t_A(u) : U \to [0,1]$ and a false-membership function $f_A(u) : U \to [0,1]$, where $t_A(u) + f_A(u) \leq 1$. $V(u) = [t_V(u), 1 - f_V(u)]$ is always indicating the vague value of $u \in U$.*

From [11] we get that the vague set V to fuzzy set is defined by

$$\mu_{F(V)}(u) = t_V(u) + \frac{1}{2}(1 + \frac{t_V(u) - f_V(u)}{t_V(u) + f_V(u) + 2\lambda})(1 - t_V(u) - f_V(u)), \tag{1}$$

where $[t_V(u), 1 - f_V(u)]$ is the vague value of $u \in U$.

A lattice is a partially ordered set ($\preceq$) with a special structure where any two elements have a minimum upper bound and a maximum lower bound.

Definition 3 ([18] fuzzy lattice). *A fuzzy lattice is a pair $(\mathbb{L}, \mu_P(x, y))$, where $\mathbb{L}$ is a conventional lattice and $\mu_P(x, y) : S \to [0,1]$ is a fuzzy membership function on $S = \{(x, y) : x, y \in \mathbb{L}\}$. It is $\mu_P(x, y) = 1$ if and only if $x \preceq y$ in $\mathbb{L}$.*

3 DPoS Based on Lattice

3.1 The Model of DPoS on Lattice

In blockchain systems, DPoS can utilize node voting to select newly generated blocks. In the current Delegated Proof of Stake (DPoS) system, voting is calculated based on the number of affirmative votes, abstentions, and negative votes cast by nodes. However, this voting system fails to consider the impact of voting nodes on the potential multiple affirmative votes and varied voting outcomes in the election. Some voting nodes may cast more affirmative votes, while others may prefer to cast fewer. This project aims to address this issue by constructing a new DPoS consensus mechanism that influences the voting tendency in this phase by calculating the voting results of nodes in a single round of voting.

In Table 1, a_1, a_2, a_3, a_4, a_5 are nodes, ✓ represents a favorable vote, while × indicates an opposing vote.

$$t_V(a_1) = \frac{\text{favor votes}}{\text{total votes}} = \frac{2}{5},$$

$$f_V(a_1) = \frac{\text{against votes}}{\text{total votes}} = \frac{3}{5},$$

$$t_V(a_2) = \frac{\text{favor votes}}{\text{total votes}} = \frac{2}{5},$$

$$f_V(a_2) = \frac{\text{against votes}}{\text{total votes}} = \frac{3}{5}.$$

Table 1. Node Voting Results

Nodes	a_1	a_2	a_3	a_4	a_5
a_1	✓	×	×	✓	×
a_2	×	✓	✓	×	×
a_3	✓	×	✓	✓	×
a_4	×	✓	×	✓	×
a_5	×	×	×	✓	✓

By calculation, it can be obtained that both $V(a_1)$ and $V(a_2)$ are $[0.4, 0.4]$. The fuzzy membership degree of node a_1 and node a_2 are both, then a_1 and a_2 are indistinguishable.

Next, we assume that all subsets of a set are elements and treat the inclusion relationship of the set ($\subseteq$) as a partial order ($\preceq$), which a lattice can be defined.

Example 1. If $U = \{a_1, a_2, a_3\}$, then we can define a lattice on all subsets of U. We can calculate $\{a_1\} \wedge \{a_2\} = \emptyset$ and $\{a_1\} \vee \{a_2\} = \{a_1, a_2\}$.

The model based on lattice of voting is defined as follows:

- Set: U is the collection of all nodes and $U_1, U_2, \ldots, U_{|U|}$ are all voting results.
- Set:

$$t_V(u) = \frac{1}{|U|} \sum_{i=1}^{|U|} |\{u\} \wedge U_j| / |\{u\} \vee U_j|,$$

$$f_V(u) = \frac{1}{|U|} \sum_{i=1}^{|U|} |\{u\} \wedge C_U U_j| / |\{u\} \vee C_U U_j|,$$

where $1 \leq j \leq |U|$.
From Definition 3, we get

$$
\begin{aligned}
t_V(u) &= \frac{1}{|U|} \sum_{i=1}^{|U|} |\{u\} \wedge U_j| / |\{u\} \vee U_j| \\
&= \frac{1}{|U|} \sum_{\{u\} \preceq U_j} \mu_p(\{u\}, U_j) / |U_j|, \\
f_V(u) &= \frac{1}{|U|} \sum_{i=1}^{|U|} |\{u\} \wedge C_U U_j| / |\{u\} \vee C_U U_j| \\
&= \frac{1}{|U|} \sum_{\{u\} \preceq C_U U_j} \mu_p(\{u\}, C_U U_j) / |C_U U_j|.
\end{aligned}
$$

Since $1 \leq j \leq |U|$, $\mu_p(\{u\}, U_j) \in [0, 1]$ and $\mu_p(\{u\}, C_U U_j) \in [0, 1]$, we obtain

$$0 \leq \frac{1}{|U|} \sum_{\{u\} \preceq U_j} \mu_p(\{u\}, U_j) / |U_j| \leq 1,$$

$$0 \leq \frac{1}{|U|} \sum_{\{u\} \preceq C_U U_j} \mu_p(\{u\}, C_U U_j) / |C_U U_j| \leq 1.$$

234   C. Cao et al.

From at most one of $u \in U_j$ and $u \in C_U U_j$ is valid, we can obtain $0 \leq t_V(u) + f_V(u) \leq 1$.

- Set:

$$\mu_{F(V)}(u) = t_V(u) + \frac{1}{2}(1 + \frac{t_V(u) - f_V(u)}{t_V(u) + f_V(u) + 2\lambda})(1 - t_V(u) - f_V(u)).$$

Example 2. Let $\lambda = 1$, from model based on lattice of voting, we get the voting result in Table 1 as

$$\{a_1, a_4\}, \{a_2, a_3\}, \{a_1, a_3, , a_4\}, \{a_2, a_4\}, \{a_4, a_5\}.$$

So

$$
\begin{aligned}
t_V(a_1) &= \frac{1}{5} \times (\frac{1}{2} + \frac{1}{3}) = \frac{1}{6}, \\
f_V(a_1) &= \frac{1}{5} \times (\frac{1}{3} + \frac{1}{3} + \frac{1}{3}) = \frac{1}{5}, \\
\mu_{F(V)}(a_1) &= t_V(a_1) + \frac{1}{2}(1 + \frac{t_V(a_1) - f_V(a_1)}{t_V(a_1) + f_V(a_1) + 2})(1 - t_V(a_1) - f_V(a_1)) \\
&= \frac{114}{330}, \\
t_V(a_2) &= \frac{1}{5} \times (\frac{1}{2} + \frac{1}{2}) = \frac{1}{5}, \\
f_V(a_2) &= \frac{1}{5} \times (\frac{1}{3} + \frac{1}{2} + \frac{1}{3}) = \frac{7}{30}, \\
\mu_{F(V)}(a_2) &= t_V(a_2) + \frac{1}{2}(1 + \frac{t_V(a_2) - f_V(a_2)}{t_V(a_2) + f_V(a_2) + 2})(1 - t_V(a_2) - f_V(a_2)) \\
&= \frac{179}{450},
\end{aligned}
$$

so $\mu_{F(V)}(a_2) > \mu_{F(V)}(a_1)$. We can get $V(a_1) = [1/6, 4/5]$ and $V(a_2) = [1/5, 23/30]$.

3.2 Model Analysis

The number of all nodes is n. Suppose U_1, U_2, U_3 are the voting results and $n = 3$, then the distribution of 3 nodes is shown in Table 2, where $\sum_{k=1}^{3} |\{u\} \wedge U_k| = i$ is the number of sets with affirmative votes and $\sum_{k=1}^{3} |\{u\} \wedge C_U U_k| = j$ is the number of sets with opposing votes.

Suppose U_1, U_2, U_3, U_4 are the voting results and $n = 4$, then the distribution of nodes is shown in Table 3, where $\sum_{k=1}^{4} |\{u\} \wedge U_k| = i$ is the number of sets with affirmative votes and $\sum_{k=1}^{4} |\{u\} \wedge C_U U_k| = j$ is the number of sets with opposing votes.

Let i indicates the number of sets that voted in favor of U_k and j indicates the number of sets that voted against U_k, where $k = 1, 2, \ldots, n$ and U_k is the set of node votes.

Table 2. Distribution of 3 Nodes

$i \backslash j$	0	1	2	3
0				$2^{3-1}C_{2^3-1}^3$
1			$C_{2^3-1}^1 C_{2^3-1}^2$	
2		$C_{2^3-1}^2 C_{2^3-1}^1$		
3	$2^{3-1}C_{2^3-1}^3$			

Table 3. Distribution of 4 Nodes

$i \backslash j$	0	1	2	3	4
0					$2^{4-1}C_{2^4-1}^4$
1				$C_{2^4-1}^1 C_{2^4-1}^3$	
2			$C_{2^4-1}^2 C_{2^4-1}^2$		
3		$C_{2^4-1}^3 C_{2^4-1}^1$			
4	$2^{4-1}C_{2^4-1}^4$				

Since only one of $u \in U_k$ and $u \in C_U U_k$ holds, for $i + j = n$, we get

$$p_{i,j}(u) = (\sum_{k=1}^n |\{u\} \wedge U_k| = i, \sum_{k=1}^n |\{u\} \wedge C_U U_k| = j)$$
$$= \begin{cases} C_{2^n-1}^i C_{2^n-1}^{n-i}/(2^n C_{2^n-1}^n + \Sigma_{k=1}^{k=n-1} C_{2^n-1}^k C_{2^n-1}^{n-k}), & 1 \le i \le n-1 \\ 2^{n-1}C_{2^n-1}^n/(2^n C_{2^n-1}^n + \Sigma_{k=1}^{k=n-1} C_{2^n-1}^k C_{2^n-1}^{n-k}), & i = 0\, \text{or}\, i = n \end{cases}.$$

4   DPoS with Affirmative, Negative, and Abstention Votes from the Overall Perspective

4.1   The Model of DPoS with Affirmative, Negative, and Abstention Votes from the Overall Perspective

Next, we will discuss that the DPoS with affirmative, negative, and abstention votes from the overall perspective.

Using the voting results in Table 4 as an example, analyze voting results. A, B, C, D, E are nodes. ✓ indicates the favor vote. ◯ indicates the abstention vote. × indicates the against vote.

Table 4. Node voting results

Nodes	Votes				
	Node A	Node B	Node C	Node D	Node E
Node A	✓	×	×	✓	○
Node B	×	✓	✓	×	○
Node C	✓	✓	✓	×	×
Node D	✓	×	×	✓	×
Node E	×	×	×	✓	✓

$$t_V(A) = \frac{\text{favor votes}}{\text{total votes}} = \frac{2}{5},$$

$$f_V(A) = \frac{\text{against votes}}{\text{total votes}} = \frac{2}{5},$$

$$t_V(B) = \frac{\text{favor votes}}{\text{total votes}} = \frac{2}{5},$$

$$f_V(B) = \frac{\text{against votes}}{\text{total votes}} = \frac{2}{5}.$$

From Definition 2, we can get $V(A) = [0.4, 0.6]$ and $V(B) = [0.4, 0.6]$. The fuzzy membership degree of node A and node B are both, in this case node A and node B are indistinguishable. But according to intuition, node A and node D voted for node A in this vote. Node A voted in favor of three nodes in this vote, while Node D also voted in favor of three nodes in this vote. In this vote, Node B and Node C voted for Node B. Node B voted in favor of two nodes in this vote, while Node C also voted in favor of two nodes in this vote. Voting node D for node A may be more inclined to cast more affirmative votes, while node C for node B may be more inclined to cast fewer affirmative votes. We can calculate the fuzzy membership degree of nodes A and B separately by model based on the overall perspective of voting.

The model based on the overall perspective of voting is defined as follows:

– Set:
$$T = \{t : U \to 2^U \,|\, t \text{ is a mapping}\}.$$

– Set: $r : u \to (r_1(u), r_2(u), r_3(u))$, where $u \in U$, $r_i(u) \in T$ and $r_1(u)$, $r_2(u)$, $r_3(u)$ is a partition of U.

Let $r_1(u)$ represents a collection of affirmative votes, $r_2(u)$ represents the set of opposing votes and $r_3(u)$ represents the set of abstaining votes.

– Set:

$$t_V(u) = \begin{cases} \frac{1}{|U|} \sum_{u \in r_1(u_j)} 1/|r_1(u_j)|, & \exists j, \, s.t \, u \in r_1(u_j) \\ 0, & others \end{cases},$$

$$f_V(u) = \begin{cases} \frac{1}{|U|} \sum_{u \in r_2(u_j)} 1/|r_2(u_j)|, & \exists j, \, s.t \, u \in r_2(u_j) \\ 0, & others \end{cases},$$

where $1 \leq j \leq |U|$.
Since $1 \leq j \leq |U|$, we obtain

$$0 < \frac{1}{|U|} \sum_{u \in r_1(u_j)} \frac{1}{|r_1(u_j)|} \leq 1,$$

$$0 \leq \frac{1}{|U|} \sum_{u \in r_2(u_j)} \frac{1}{|r_2(u_j)|} \leq 1.$$

From at most one of $u \in r_1(u_j)$ and $u \in r_2(u_j)$ is valid, we can obtain $0 \leq t_V(u) + f_V(u) \leq 1$.
- Set:

$$\mu_{F(V)}(u) = t_V(u) + \frac{1}{2}(1 + \frac{t_V(u) - f_V(u)}{t_V(u) + f_V(u) + 2\lambda})(1 - t_V(u) - f_V(u)).$$

Example 3. Let $\lambda = 1$, from model based on the overall perspective of voting, we get

$$t_V(A) = \frac{1}{5} \times (\frac{1}{2} + \frac{1}{3} + \frac{1}{2}) = \frac{4}{15},$$

$$f_V(A) = \frac{1}{5} \times (\frac{1}{2} + \frac{1}{3}) = \frac{1}{6},$$

$$\mu_{F(V)}(A) = t_V(A) + \frac{1}{2}(1 + \frac{t_V(A) - f_V(A)}{t_V(u) + f_V(A) + 2})(1 - t_V(A) - f_V(A))$$
$$= \frac{41}{73},$$

$$t_V(B) = \frac{1}{5} \times (\frac{1}{2} + \frac{1}{3}) = \frac{1}{6},$$

$$f_V(B) = \frac{1}{5} \times (\frac{1}{2} + \frac{1}{3} + \frac{1}{2}) = \frac{4}{15},$$

$$\mu_{F(V)}(B) = t_V(A) + \frac{1}{2}(1 + \frac{t_V(A) - f_V(A)}{t_V(u) + f_V(A) + 2})(1 - t_V(A) - f_V(A))$$
$$= \frac{119}{2628},$$

so $\mu_{F(V)}(A) > \mu_{F(V)}(B)$, $V(A) = [4/15, 5/6]$ and $V(B) = [1/6, 11/15]$.

4.2 Model Analysis

Suppose n is the number of all nodes. According to the second type of Stirling number, a set of n elements can be divided into 3 sets, and there are $S(n,3) = \frac{1}{2}(3^{n-1} + 1) - 2^{n-1}$ types of partitions. We can obtain that there are a total of $(r_1(u), r_2(u), r_3(u))$ types of $3^n - 3 \cdot 2^n$.

Theorem 1. *Suppose $|U| = n$ and $r_1(u)$, $r_2(u)$, $r_3(u)$ is a partition of U. Then*

$$|\{(r_1(u), r_2(u), r_3(u)) : u \in U\}|$$
$$= A_3^3(S(n,3) - 1) + 3$$
$$= 3^n - 3 \cdot 2^n.$$

Proof. From $|U| = n$ and the second type of Stirling number, we can obtain that a set of n elements can be divided into 3 sets. Then there are $S(n,3) = \frac{1}{2}(3^{n-1}+1) - 2^{n-1}$ types of partitions.

From $(r_1(u), r_2(u), r_3(u))$ is ordered and $\emptyset, \emptyset, U$ is a partition of U, we can get that the number of $(r_1(u), r_2(u), r_3(u))$ is $A_3^3(S(n,3)-1)+3 = 3^n - 3 \cdot 2^n$. So

$$|\{r_1(u), r_2(u), r_3(u) : u \in U\}|$$
$$= A_3^3(S(n,3)-1)+3$$
$$= 3^n - 3 \cdot 2^n.$$

Theorem 2. *Suppose $|U| = n$ and $r_1(u), r_2(u), r_3(u)$ is a partition of U. Then*

$$|\{r_1(u), r_2(u), r_3(u) : u', u \in U, u' \in r_1(u)\}|$$
$$= A_3^3 S(n-1,3)$$
$$= 3^{n-1} - 3 \cdot 2^{n-1} + 3.$$

Proof. From $|U \setminus \{u'\}| = n - 1$ and the second type of Stirling number, we can obtain that a set of $n-1$ elements can be divided into 3 sets. Then there are $S(n-1,3) = \frac{1}{6}(3^{n-1} - 3 \cdot 2^{n-1} + 3)$ types of partitions. If $u' \in r_1(u)$ and $r_1(u), r_2(u), r_3(u)$ is a partition of U, then the number of the partition is $S(n-1,3)$.

From $(r_1(u), r_2(u), r_3(u))$ is ordered and $u' \in r_1(u)$, we can get that the number of $(r_1(u), r_2(u), r_3(u))$ is $A_3^3 S(n-1,3) = 3^n - 3 \cdot 2^n$. So

$$|\{r_1(u), r_2(u), r_3(u) : u \in U\}|$$
$$= A_3^3 S(n-1,3)$$
$$= 3^{n-1} - 3 \cdot 2^{n-1} + 3.$$

Let i indicates the number of $u \in r_1(u_k)$ and j indicates the number of $u \in r_2(u_k)$, where $k = 1, 2, \ldots, n$.

From $r_1(u), r_2(u), r_3(u)$ is a partition of U, u belongs to at most one of r_1 and $r_2(u)$, for $0 \le i + j \le n$, we get

$$p_{i,j} = (\sum_{k=1}^n |\{u\} \wedge r_1(u_k)| = i, \sum_{k=1}^n |\{u\} \wedge r_2(u_k)| = j)$$
$$= \frac{C_{A_3^3 S(n-1,3)}^i C_{A_3^3 S(n-1,3)}^j}{[A_3^3(S(n,3)-1)+3]^n}.$$

5   Conclusion

This article proposed a new model for the DPoS's voting stage in blockchain. In the previous voting model, a node's vote calculation was based solely on affirmative or negative votes. The model constructed in the article calculated the votes of one node while considering whether the voter voted in favor of other nodes. This model limits the weight of certain nodes voting on biased nodes.

Acknowledgement. This research is supported by Doctoral Fund of Guizhou Industry Polytechnic College (No. 2024-rc-01).

References

1. Liu, Y., Liu, J., Zhang, Z.: Overview on blockchain consensus mechanism. J. Cryptologic Res. **6**, 395–432 (2019)
2. Castro, M., Liskov, B.: Practical byzantine fault tolerance and proactive recovery. ACM Trans. Comput. Syst. **4**, 398–461 (2002)
3. Veronese, G.S., Correia, M., Bessani, A.N., Ling, L.C., Verissimo, P.: Efficient byzantine fault-tolerance. IEEE Trans. Comput. **62**, 16–30 (2013)
4. Boyd, C., Carr, C.: PPcoin: Aluable Puzzles for Proofs-of-Work, pp. 130–139. Cryptocurrencies and Blockchain Technology, Data Privacy Management (2018)
5. King, S., Nadal, S.: PPcoin: peer-to-peer crypto-currency with proof-of-stake (2012). https://bitcoin.peryaudo.org/vendor/peercoin-paper
6. Grigg, I.: EOS-An introduction (2017). http://eos.io//documents//EOS-An introduction.pdf
7. Gao, Y., Tan, X.: Improvement of DPoS consensus mechanism. Appl. Res. Comput. **37**, 3086–3090 (2020)
8. Ta, R., Tanrver, M.Z.: A systematic review of challenges and opportunities of blockchain for e-voting. Symmetry **12**, 1328 (2020)
9. Jian, L., Wu, S., Liu, Z., Zhang, Y.: New method for approximating vague sets to fuzzy sets based on voting model. In: 2008 IEEE Conference on Cybernetics and Intelligent Systems, vol. 16, pp. 21–24 (2008)
10. Xu, G., Liu, Y., Khan, P.W.: Improvement of the DPoS consensus mechanism in blockchain based on vague sets. IEEE Trans. Industr. Inf. **16**, 133–144 (2020)
11. Liu, Y., Wang, G., Lin, F.: A general model for transforming vague sets into fuzzy sets. Trans. Comput. Sci. **2**, 133–144 (2008)
12. You, L., Wang, Z., Hu, G., Cao, C., Li, L.: An improved model on the vague sets-based DPoS's voting phase in blockchain. IEEE Trans. Network Sci. Eng. **10**, 4010–4019 (2023)
13. Tan, C., Xiong, L.: DPoSB: delegated proof of stake with node's behavior and borda count. In: 2020 IEEE 5th Information Technology and Mechatronics Engineering Conference, pp. 1429–1434 (2020)
14. Hu, Q., Yan, B., Han, Y., Yu, J.: An improved delegated proof of stake consensus algorithm. In: International Conference on Identification, Information and Knowledge in the internet of Things, pp. 341–346 (2020)
15. Kim, J., Oh, S., Kim, Y., Kim, H.: Improving voting of block producers for delegated proof-of-stake with quadratic delegate. Int. Conf. Platform Technol. Serv. **2023**, 13–17 (2023)
16. Zadeh, L.A.: Fuzzy sets. Inf. Control **3**, 338–353 (1965)
17. Gau, W.L., Buehrer, D.J.: Vague sets. IEEE Trans. Syst. Man Cybern. **23**, 133–144 (1993)
18. Petridis, V., Kaburlasos, V.G.: Fuzzy lattice neural network (FLNN): a hybrid model for learning. IEEE Trans. Neural Networks **9**, 877–890 (1998)

A Distributed Privacy-Preserving Data Aggregation Scheme for MaaS Data Sharing

Lin Zhu, Zhengjun Jing$^{(\boxtimes)}$, Yuanjian Zhou$^{(\boxtimes)}$, and Quanyu Zhao

Jiangsu University of Technology, Changzhou 213001, Jiangsu, China
{jzjing,zhouyuanjian}@jsut.edu.cn

Abstract. Machine-as-a-Service (MaaS) is a service model in the Industrial Internet of Things (IIoT). In general, OEM expects to collect data from multiple machine users for aggregate analysis to improve production efficiency. However, potential security and privacy challenges may also result in the leakage of individual machine user data. Therefore, this paper proposes a distributed privacy-preserving data aggregation scheme for data sharing in MaaS. Specifically, the proposed method realizes data aggregation by designing smart contracts, and generates synthetic data sets that meet the probability distribution of fault data through differential privacy technology to achieve efficient data sharing and privacy protection. Finally, we theoretically analyzed the security of the scheme, and deployed the differential privacy contract on the Hyperledger Fabric platform. The prototype evaluation results show the utility of the proposed scheme in practical applications.

Keywords: Machine as a Service · Date aggregation · Hyperledger Fabric · Differential privacy

1 Introduction

Machine-as-a-Service(MaaS) [1] is a service model for machine rental scenarios. The original equipment manufacturer (OEM) leases the produced machine as a service resource to the machine user(MU). The production data during the operation of the machine is collected through the built-in sensors, such as the parameters of the machine operation, the running state, the number of products produced, the type of products, the cause of failure, etc. Sharing the data can not only help MU understand the machine's production efficiency, but also support OEM to analyze the operation process of the machine, optimize the machine performance. However, the shared data compromise the production privacy of machine users. In MaaS mode, an OEM typically deals with multiple MUs, The urgent issue to be addressed is how to protect the production privacy of individual MU during the sharing process.

Data aggregation [2] is an effective way to protect the privacy of individual data, which provides query services to end users by aggregating different or the same type of data from multiple devices. The common aggregate queries include extremum, sum, count, etc. Othman et al. [3] proposed a data aggregation scheme based on homomorphic encryption, which used symmetric key homomorphic encryption technology to protect data security during the aggregation process. Furthermore, homomorphic signature was employed to verify the integrity of the aggregated results. Heidari et al. [4] proposed a data aggregation method for the IIoT, which combined artificial bee colony algorithm, genetic algorithm and density correlation algorithm to construct the optimal spanning tree, improve the efficiency of data aggregation in the industrial Internet of things. However, the above schemes only focus on the efficiency of data aggregation and data security during the aggregation process, without considering the privacy of aggregation results. For example, OEM collects different types of fault type data, and the aggregated fault data may expose the production efficiency, technical level and other commercial secrets of the factory. Therefore, ensuring the privacy of data aggregation results is a crucial challenge.

Differential privacy [5] (DP) is a privacy protection method based on data perturbation, which can perform meaningful analysis and calculation within a limited error range. Literature [5] divides differential privacy into center differential privacy (CDP) and local differential privacy (LDP). Following literature [5], most of references adopt local differential privacy technology to protect data privacy, that is, data owners add noise to the original data before data sharing. Although this process ensures the data privacy during collection, it is complicated to manage the noise-added data of different machine users, which reduces the accuracy of OEM analysis and aggregation results. On the contrary, central differential privacy technology can collect and process multi-party data aggregation results with a trusted data center, effectively control the perturbation results of the overall data, and ensure the accuracy of OEM in analysis. Subsequently, Zhu et al. [6] proposed a differential privacy solution to the privacy problem of linked data sets, which enhanced the privacy protection of related data sets by defining the correlation sensitivity and the linked data set publishing mechanism designed based on the iterative method. Roy et al. [7] proposed a systematic programming framework to implement differential privacy on two non-colluding servers, ensuring the accuracy of the central model without the need for a trusted data collector. Steinke et al. [8] realized multi-center differential privacy, relaxed the trust requirement of central differential privacy, and avoided the high privacy protection cost of local differential privacy.

In conclusion, the above scheme relies on the honest centers that do not (maliciously) deviate from the predefined protocol. However, this assumption is unrealistic in practical applications, as broken (and unsupervised) servers may return incorrect results due to random failures or profit maximization. To eliminate the reliance on centralized trust, many existing schemes [9–12] use decentralized blockchain instead of a centralized server. Zhao et al. [9] proposed a method based on the Ethereum blockchain to deal with different instances of the same query type by completely or partially reusing noise, so as to save the cumulative differential privacy cost. Hassan et al. [10] discussed the integration of differential privacy in each layer of blockchain, and analyzed the related application scenarios and future challenges. Zhu Jianming et al. [11] addressed the issue of intermediate parameter privacy leakage in centralized parameter servers in federated learning by adding Laplace noise of different degrees using blockchain and differential privacy. Kus et al. [12] innovatively applied differential privacy to transaction amount and user graph in Bitcoin, which improved the anonymity and privacy of Bitcoin.

In order to solve the challenges of secure aggregation of multi-party data, data tamper proofing and single-machine processing bottleneck in MaaS mode, a distributed privacy-preserving data aggregation solution for MaaS data sharing is proposed in this paper. The scheme realizes data collection and automatic processing through smart contracts to avoid the threat of untrusted third parties. Furthermore, the data aggregation contract is deployed on the Hyperledger Fabric platform, enabling secure analysis and sharing of aggregated data using differential privacy techniques. The main contributions are as follows:

1) In response to the traditional MaaS data sharing model, a data sharing framework based on Hyperledger Fabric blockchain is designed. As the framework uses smart contract, no centralized server is required, thereby alleviating the issues of centralized storage and single points of failure in the MaaS model.

2) To address the privacy of multi-party data aggregation results, we design a DPSyn smart contract based on differential privacy. This ensures data privacy for individual machine users without affecting OEM's analysis of data aggregation results.

The remainder of this article is structured as follows: Sect. 2 introduces the concepts and definitions of Hyperledger Fabric and differential privacy. Section 3 describes the design objectives and system model of the proposed scheme. Section 4 constructs the concrete implementation of the scheme. Section 5 analyzes the security of the proposed scheme. Section 6 deploys the experimental environment and analyzes the experimental results of the proposed scheme. Finally, this paper concludes the overall work and provides a perspective on future work.

2   Prerequisites

This section introduces the basic concepts of Hyperledger Fabric and the relevant definitions of differential privacy.

2.1   Hyperledger Fabric

Hyperledger Fabric, introduced by IBM, is an open-source licensed blockchain that only allows authorized entities to access the network. Unlike Bitcoin and Ethereum, Fabric does not use cryptocurrencies and aims to develop modular architecture applications to achieve plug-and-play consensus services. Fabric employs Practical Byzantine Fault Tolerance (PBFT) as a consensus mechanism,

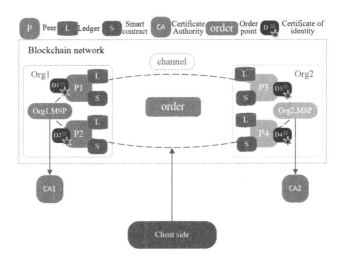

Fig. 1. Hyperledger Fabric Blockchain network

which can meet the requirements of IoT for low power consumption, no mining, no PoW, and fast transactions.

As shown in Fig. 1, there can be multiple organizations in a blockchain network, and each organization contains multiple nodes. Each peer node has the capability to store multiple ledgers and smart contracts. Entities in the organization is identified by X.509 identity certificate issued by a Certificate Authority (CA). These certificates are essential to determine who has access to which network resources. There are three types of nodes in Fabric: clients, peer nodes and order nodes.

The client can be a Web/mobile application, command line interface, or software development kit which interacts with the blockchain network by submitting transaction requests. Peers are divided into endorsement node and submission node. The endorsement node needs to install the chain codes, verify the validity of the transaction, and return endorsement results by executing smart contracts in simulation. The submission node is responsible for verifying the legitimacy of transactions and updating the ledger. Order is responsible for building consensus in the network and ensuring that transactions are executed in order.

2.2 Differential Privacy

Differential privacy [5] is a data privacy protection method proposed by Dwork in 2006. Random noise is added to the query results, so that the attacker cannot infer the addition and modification of a single record based on the changes in the output results. Dwork gives the relevant definition of differential privacy in the paper:

Definition 1. ϵ-*differential privacy [5]. Assuming x and x' are a pair of adjacent data sets (only one data is different in the two data sets). If a random* *function F satisfies Eq. 1 for all possible output results of x and x', F is said to satisfy differential privacy.*

$$\frac{\Pr[F(x) = S]}{\Pr[F(x') = S]} \leq e^{\epsilon} \tag{1}$$

where ϵ is called the privacy budget which is used to specify the amount of privacy provided by differential privacy. The smaller ϵ is, the closer the query results are, and the better the privacy is.

Definition 2. *Laplace mechanism [13]. Suppose that the query function $f(x)$ can output a numerical result, and the noise satisfying the Laplacian mechanism is added to the function $f(x)$, as shown in Eq. 2. If $F(x)$ satisfies the following equation, then $F(x)$ satisfies ϵ-differential privacy.*

$$F(x) = f(x) + Lap(\frac{s}{\epsilon}) \tag{2}$$

where s is the sensitivity of f, which is the change in the output of f when the input data set x changes to the set x'. Lap(s) is sampled from a Laplacian distribution with mean 0 and scaling factor s. For counting queries, the sensitivity is always 1.

Definition 3. *Parallel compositionality [13]. For the data set X, it is divided into n mutually exclusive subsets of $X_1, X_2, ..., X_n$, if the query result $F(x)$ of dataset X satisfies ϵ-differential privacy, then the query results of each part $F(X_1), F(X_1), ..., F(X_n)$ also satisfies ϵ-differential privacy. When multiple query mechanisms are applied on different subsets of the same data set, the total privacy budget is equal to the maximum of each privacy budget.*

Definition 4. *Synthetic data [14]. By using differential privacy to generate synthetic data, a sample distribution roughly equivalent to that of the original dataset can be obtained, that is, the synthetic data set can be used to replace the original data to reply to the query, and the query results satisfy differential privacy.*

3   System Model

This section describes the design goals of the scheme and the functionality of each entity in the system.

3.1   Design Goals

In terms of data security, OEM may develop curiosity about the data of individual machine users during data analysis. Therefore, the design objectives of this paper will consider the following points:

(1) **Decentralization:** Not relying on third-party management institutions, achieving automatic processing in the data-sharing process, and protecting data from malicious tampering.

(2) Privacy: Only the failure statistics data of all machines can be obtained by OEM, and the data of a machine user cannot be analyzed from the statistics, so as to ensure that the production information of the machine user is not leaked.

(3) Resistance to collusion: If OEM has obtained the machine operation statistical data of three machine users A, B and C, it cannot accurately deduce the data of C when OEM conspires with A and B.

3.2 System Architecture

In the context of MaaS, a data sharing scheme based on Hyperledger Fabric blockchain technology and differential privacy techniques is designed in this paper. The scheme model is shown in Fig. 2, including CA, blockchain network, data provider, and data user.

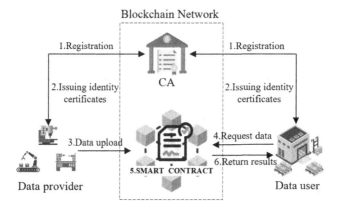

Fig. 2. Blockchain data security sharing scheme model based on differential privacy

(1) CA: Before engaging in transactions on the blockchain network, users are required to register with CA and obtain an identity certificate.

(2) Data provider: The data provider refers to the intelligent machine leased by the OEM, which is responsible for collecting the operating parameters and fault information generated during the work process and uploading the relevant data to the blockchain.

(3) Blockchain network: The blockchain network in the scheme is built using Fabric, and the data user interacts with the blockchain network to request data resources. The blockchain network realizes data aggregation and differential privacy processing through the smart contract DPSyn.

(4) Data user: The data user in the scheme refers to the machine provider OEM. When the data user requests data from the blockchain, the smart contract is called to obtain the request result.

In the scheme model, CA is a part of the blockchain network and is trustworthy. Smart contract is capable of automatically executing established procedures.

However, there may exist malicious machine users among the data consumers who conspire with the OEM to try to obtain the production information of other users. At the same time, external attackers will be curious about the data uploaded by the data owner and try to enter the blockchain network by forging an identity.

4   Scheme Construction

This section describes the construction of the distributed privacy-preserving data aggregation scheme for MaaS data sharing and provides algorithm pseudocode.

4.1   System Initialization

During the system initialization phase, the configuration of the entire Fabric blockchain network and the deployment of contracts are completed. Firstly, the root certificates and key pairs for peer nodes and order nodes are generated using the cryptogen tool of Hyperledger Fabric. Then, the genesis block and channel file are produced utilizing the configtxgen tool. After that, docker-compose files for the remaining nodes are configured with node images. Finally, channels are created, and all peer nodes are added to the channel. Upon the completion of the blockchain network setup, the installation and instantiation of the DPSyn contract are implemented.

4.2   Identity Registration and Data Upload

This phase completes the property registration of the participant client and the upload of the machine data. All participants in the system, register their identity information in Fabric-CA. CA administrator issues them an X.509 identity certificates. After obtaining the legal identity, machine user uploads the machine data through the machine node.

4.3   Data Aggregation

When OEM requests data, differential privacy processing is applied to the aggregated data results by smart contracts. A synthetic dataset based on differential privacy is used to respond to access requests, that can ensure the privacy of data and the accuracy of analysis. In MaaS, OEM usually cares about failure number and failure cause during machine operations. Therefore, the failures and their corresponding frequencies can be aggregated, allowing for the generation of synthetic data on the causes of failures to respond to OEM inquiries. The same statistical results can be obtained using the synthetic data as the original data. The synthetic dataset generation process is shown in Fig. 3, which consists of four stages: generation of two-dimensional cross table, enhancing differential privacy, normalization probability distribution, and generation of tabular data.

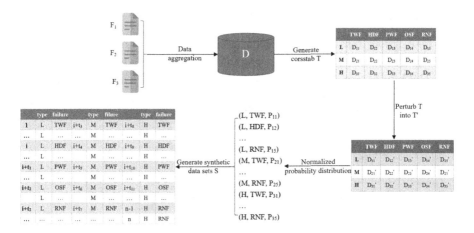

Fig. 3. Synthetic Data with Differential Privacy

(1) Generating the two-dimensional cross table: After obtaining the machine data of different machine users by file ID, the data is aggregated to generate a two-dimensional intersection table T. Row headers represent production types: low intensity (L), medium intensity (M), high intensity (H), while column headers indicate failure causes during machine runs. The failure causes are categorized into five groups: tool wear fault (TWF), heat dissipation fault (HDF), power failure (PWF), over-strain fault (OSF), and random fault (RNF).

(2) Enhancing differential privacy: Traverse the two-dimensional cross table and add Laplace noise to the data to satisfy the same privacy budget. Ensure that the perturbed values are non-negative.

(3) Normalization probability distribution: Normalize the perturbed two-dimensional cross-table, that is, the results of all counts sum to 1. The processed data was transformed into a list, where each element is a tuple of the form (R, C, P), with (R, C) representing the row and column indices and P denoting the probability value associated with the respective element.

(4)Generating the tabular data: To minimize query errors, the fault data is firstly queried by differential privacy to obtain the number n of fault data. Then, generate n records of synthetic data S based on the normalized probability values. Finally, respond to the query based on the statistical results of the generated list data.

The pseudocode of the smart contract DPsyn for synthetic data based on differential privacy is shown in Algorithm 1.

5 Security Analysis

This section provides a correctness analysis of the data processing method proposed in Sect. 4.3, demonstrating that the method satisfies ϵ-differential privacy. Then, we analyze the overall security of the scheme.

5.1   Correctness Analysis

Let the original data set of the scheme be D, the adjacent data set be D', and the data in the two-dimensional intersection table be $\sum_{i=1}^{k} D_i$. Where $D_1 \bigcap D_2 \bigcap ... \bigcap D_k = D$, and $D_i \bigcup D_j = \emptyset$, then $\sum_{i=1}^{k} |D_i \oplus D_i'| = |D \oplus D'| = 1$.

Assuming Algorithm $A(D_1), A(D_2), ..., A(D_k)$ all satisfy ϵ-differential privacy, by the parallel compositionality of differential privacy, we have:

$$Pr(A(D) = t) = \prod_{i=1}^{k} Pr(A(D_i) = t_i)$$

$$\leq \prod_{i=1}^{k} (e^{\epsilon * |D_i \oplus D_i'|} * Pr(A(D_i') = t_i))$$

$$= e^{\epsilon * \sum_{i=1}^{k} |D_i \oplus D_i'|} * \prod_{i=1}^{k} Pr(A(D_i') = t_i)$$

$$= e^{\epsilon} Pr(A(D') = t)$$

Therefore, the synthetic data satisfies ϵ-differential privacy.

Algorithm 1. Differential privacy processing contract

Input: NAR(Original access request)
Output: $Result$(Statistical results for the synthetic dataset)
1: $FID\_set \leftarrow NAR.FileID$
2: **for** each $t \in FID\_set$ **do**
3:      $data \leftarrow file[t]$
4: **end for**
5: $ct \leftarrow crossTab(data.type, data.failure)$
6: **for** each $i \in ct.row$ **do**
7:      **for** each $j \in ct.column$ **do**
8:          $prob \leftarrow laplace(ct[i][j])$
9:          $vals \leftarrow (i, j)$
10:     **end for**
11: **end for**
12: $probs\_norm = probs/probs.sum$
13: $n = laplace(data.failure.length)$
14: $syn\_data \leftarrow Generate(vals, n, probs_norm)$
15: $syn\_count \leftarrow Statistic(syn_data.failure)$
16: **return** syn_counts

5.2   Security Analysis

This scheme can effectively meet the design objectives proposed in 3.1, and the specific analysis is as follows:

(1) Decentralization: Hyperledger Fabric blockchain was used in the scheme. When OEM requests machine operation data, a preset smart contract is triggered to achieve automated data acquisition and processing. Since the client nodes participating in the transaction must register at Fabric-CA before accessing the blockchain network. Therefore, malicious users cannot forge identities to maliciously tamper with data on the chain.

(2) Privacy: In this scheme, when OEM queries data, the smart contract DPsyn for differential privacy processing will be triggered, and the accessed data will be aggregated and processed by differential privacy before returning. It can be inferred from Sect. 4.1 that the processed data satisfies ϵ-differential privacy. Therefore, OEM can only obtain aggregated data processed with differential privacy, ensuring data privacy during the analysis.

(3) Resistance to collusion: In this approach, machine fault data is aggregated based on differential privacy to produce synthetic statistical data corresponding to five fault causes for three production types. Even if the OEM colludes with the machine users A and B, the data of C can only be obtained after the disturbance, and the specific data of C cannot be derived.

6 Experimental Results and Analysis

In this section, we compare the differences in functional characteristics between the proposed scheme and other existing schemes, then analyze the performance of the scheme

6.1 Experimental Environment

The experiment ran on the Hyperledger Fabric 2.3 blockchain platform on R7-7840HS CPU 3.8GHz,16GB, Ubuntu 20.04 system. In this experiment, two organizations, each with two peer nodes and a CA node were set up, along with an order node. Due to the challenge of obtaining actual maintenance data, the experiment utilized the predictive maintenance dataset ai4i2020. The data set consists of 10,000 records, reflecting various parameters of the machine operation, including product number, product type, failure cause and other attributes.

6.2 Functional Comparison

This section compares the functional characteristics of the proposed scheme with those of references [15–17]. As shown in Table 2, references [15] and [17] are based on Ethereum. However, the Ethereum platform is not a permissioned chain and cannot guarantee the legitimate rights of authorized users. On the contrary, our scheme and reference [16] are Hyperledger Fabric based on permissioned chain, which is fast to develop smart contracts and can verify the legitimacy of authorized users. Considering the data sharing scenario, reference [17] only focuses on sharing of single-user data, which is not suitable for MaaS mode. Our solution address multi-party data sharing and employ differential privacy techniques to protect the privacy of aggregated data. In addition, references [17] and our solution can resist collusion attacks to prevent data leakage from machine users. In summary, the proposed scheme is functionally superior to other schemes (Table 1).

Table 1. Functional comparison

Scheme	Permissioned chain	Privacy protection	Tamper proof	Resistance to collusion
reference [15]	×	×	✓	×
reference [16]	✓	✓	✓	×
reference [17]	×	×	✓	✓
our scheme	✓	✓	✓	✓

6.3   Performance Analysis

Analysis of the Error Rate Under Different ϵ. In this paper, synthetic data based on differential privacy is used to reply to queries. Figure 4 shows the query results under various privacy budgets. In order to eliminate the impact of errors, the method is iterated 50 times, and the average values are obtained. The x-axis represents the reasons for malfunctions, the primary y-axis denotes the number of failures, and the secondary y-axis indicates the error rate between perturbed results and actual results.

When $\epsilon = 0.1$, the error rate ranges from 0.01 to 0.08; for ϵ between 0.5 and 1.0, the error rate remains below 0.04; with ϵ ranging from 1.5 to 2.0, the error rate generally stays below 0.02. If ϵ is too small, significant data disparities lead to increased error rates, which can impact data analysis. Conversely, an excessively large ϵ reduces the strength of privacy protection. Therefore, in this experiment $\epsilon = 1.0$.

This approach enables responding to queries based on synthetic data. The experimental results demonstrate that employing differential privacy not only safeguards user privacy but also ensures data availability.

Network Performance. In this section, the system performance is evaluated in terms of transaction throughput and latency, and performs stress tests on contract methods in the blockchain using the tape tool. 1000 query requests are set to OEM according to the query keywords. Figure 5 shows the performance test results of OEM in accessing the blockchain network, TPS represents the number of transactions per second. The throughput increases linearly with the increase of query requests. The average contract execution latency ranges between 0.2 to 0.4 s.

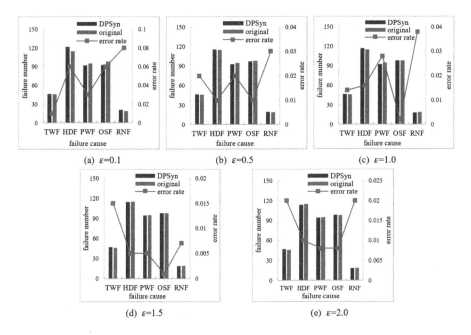

Fig. 4. Privacy Budget on Query Results

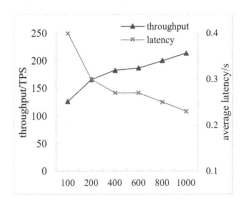

Fig. 5. System transaction throughput and average latency

7   Conclusion

In this work, we focused on the data security and data privacy issues in MaaS and constructed a blockchain-based data aggregation scheme. The proposed scheme combines the advantages of the differential privacy technology and blockchain. With the help of differential privacy technology, the scheme constructs the perturbed synthetic data set to ensure the privacy of data aggregation results in the analysis process. Then, we avoid the need to rely on a central server to manipulate data aggregation jobs by leveraging blockchain. A comparative summary with three other existing solutions demonstrated the potential of the proposed scheme in practice. Future research will focus on dynamic changes in member participation in multi-party data sharing, data sharing revocation, and fault tolerance issues arising from single node failures.

Acknowledgments. This research has been supported by the Technology Development Project of Jiangsu University of Technology (Grant NO. 2024320400000449).

Disclosure of Interests. The authors declare that they have no competing financial interests or personal relationships that could have appeared to influence the work reported in this paper.

References

1. Stojkovski, I., Achleitner, A.-K., Lange, T.: Equipment as a service: the transition towards usage-based business models. Available at SSRN 3763004 (2021)
2. Clark, W.A., Avery, K.L.: The effects of data aggregation in statistical analysis. Geogr. Anal. **8**(4), 428–438 (1976)
3. Othman, S.B., Bahattab, A.A., Trad, A., Youssef, H.: Confidentiality and integrity for data aggregation in WSN using homomorphic encryption. Wireless Pers. Commun. **80**, 867–889 (2015)
4. Heidari, A., Shishehlou, H., Darbandi, M., Navimipour, N.J., Yalcin, S.: A reliable method for data aggregation on the industrial internet of things using a hybrid optimization algorithm and density correlation degree. Cluster Comput. **27**, 7521–7539 (2024)
5. Dwork, C.: Differential privacy. In: International Colloquium on Automata, Languages, and Programming, pp. 1–12. Springer (2006)
6. Zhu, T., Xiong, P., Li, G., Zhou, W.: Correlated differential privacy: hiding information in non-IID data set. IEEE Trans. Inf. Forensics Secur. **10**(2), 229–242 (2014)
7. Roy Chowdhury, A., Wang, C., He, X., Machanavajjhala, A., Jha, S.: Crypt ϵ: crypto-assisted differential privacy on untrusted servers. In: Proceedings of the 2020 ACM SIGMOD International Conference on Management of Data, pp. 603–619 (2020)
8. Steinke, T.: Multi-central differential privacy. arXiv preprint arXiv:2009.05401 (2020)
9. Zhao, Y., et al.: A blockchain-based approach for saving and tracking differential-privacy cost. IEEE Internet Things J. **8**(11), 8865–8882 (2021)
10. Ul Hassan, M., Rehmani, M.H., Chen, J.: Differential privacy in blockchain technology: a futuristic approach. J. Parallel Distrib. Comput. **145**, 50–74 (2020)
11. Zhu, J., Zhang, Q., Gao, S., Ding, Q., Yuan, L.: Privacy-preserving trusted federated learning model based on blockchain. J. Comput. Sci. **44**, 2464–2484 (2021)
12. Kus, M.C., Levi, A.: Investigation and application of differential privacy in bitcoin. IEEE Access **10**, 25534–25554 (2022)
13. Dwork, C.: Differential privacy: a survey of results. In: International Conference on Theory and Applications of Models of Computation, pp. 1–19, Springer (2008)
14. Near, J.P., Abuah, C.: Programming Differential Privacy, vol. 1 (2021)
15. Tran, V.H., et al.: Machine-as-a-service: blockchain-based management and maintenance of industrial appliances. Eng. Rep. **5**(7), e12567 (2023)

16. Chen, C.-L., Yang, J., Tsaur, W.-J., Weng, W., Wu, C.-M., Wei, X.: Enterprise data sharing with privacy-preserved based on hyperledger fabric blockchain in IIOT's application. Sensors **22**(3), 1146 (2022)
17. Yu, K., Tan, L., Aloqaily, M., Yang, H., Jararweh, Y.: Blockchain-enhanced data sharing with traceable and direct revocation in IIOT. IEEE Trans. Industr. Inf. **17**(11), 7669–7678 (2021)

Author Index

A
Amandi, Ogbebisi Chukwuebuka 72

B
Bai, Xiao 219
Bingbing, Li 192

C
Cao, Chengtang 99, 230
Chen, Bing 178
Chen, Hao 86
Chen, Jingxue 118
Cheng, Hongyuan 208
Chunsheng, Gu 192

D
Deng, Liangjun 118
Duan, Junyi 1

G
Gu, Chunsheng 54
Guo, Mengya 178

H
Huang, Zongzheng 99, 230

J
Jing, Zhengjun 20, 37, 54, 240

L
Lei, Hang 118
Li, Bingbing 72
Li, Jiaxun 86
Liu, Jiewen 178
Liu, Xiaoqian 137

M
Ma, Zhuo 107
Mo, Shupei 99, 230

P
Peizhong, Shi 192

Q
Qian, Hanwei 86
Qin, Yi 165
Qiu, Yao 118
Quanyu, Zhao 192

S
Shi, Peizhong 54
Shi, Weiyu 137
Song, Bo 107, 165
Song, Jingcheng 208
Song, Yu-Rong 165
Sun, Guohao 219

T
Tan, Chenkai 1
Tang, Yongwei 208

W
Wang, Qun 107
Wang, Xu 165
Wang, Zihan 208

X
Xia, Ling-Ling 107
Xin, Zexi 20
Xu, Ershuai 153
Xu, Mingxin 86
Xue, Baolu 178

Y
Yan, Zhang 192
Yan, Zhe 219
Yang, Hua 1
Yuan, Hao 153
Yuan, Qi 153

© The Editor(s) (if applicable) and The Author(s), under exclusive license
to Springer Nature Switzerland AG 2025
W. Li et al. (Eds.): EISA 2024, CCIS 2266, pp. 255–256, 2025.
https://doi.org/10.1007/978-3-031-80419-9

Z
Zhai, Zhengyong 54
Zhang, Jiqun 208
Zhang, Mingwu 72
Zhang, Yan 54
Zhang, Yuan 20
Zhao, Quanyu 20, 37, 54, 240
Zhao, Shuo 153

Zhao, Tianci 1, 37
Zhao, Xiaopeng 219
Zhengjun, Jing 192
Zhong, Qi 118
Zhou, Gaoyuan 86
Zhou, Yuanjian 20, 37, 240
Zhu, Lin 240
Zhu, Yongkang 37

Printed in the United States
by Baker & Taylor Publisher Services